Lecture Notes in Computer Science 4600

Commenced Publication in 1973
Founding and Former Series Editors:
Gerhard Goos, Juris Hartmanis, and Jan van Leeuwen

Hubert Comon-Lundh   Claude Kirchner
Hélène Kirchner (Eds.)

Rewriting
Computation and Proof

Essays Dedicated to Jean-Pierre Jouannaud
on the Occasion of His 60th Birthday

 Springer

Volume Editors

Hubert Comon-Lundh
Ecole Normale Supérieure de Cachan
Laboratoire Spécification et Vérification
CNRS UMR 8643, 61, avenue du Président Wilson, 94235 Cachan Cedex, France
E-mail: comon@lsv.ens-cachan.fr

Claude Kirchner
INRIA & LORIA
615, rue du Jardin Botanique, 54602 Villers-lès-Nancy Cedex, France
E-mail: Claude.Kirchner@inria.fr

Hélène Kirchner
CNRS & INRIA, LORIA
Campus Scientifique, BP 239, 54506 Vandœuvre-lès-Nancy, France
E-mail: Helene.Kirchner@loria.fr

Library of Congress Control Number: 2007928575

CR Subject Classification (1998): F.3.1-2, F.4, D.1.6, D.3, I.1, I.2.2-3

LNCS Sublibrary: SL 1 – Theoretical Computer Science and General Issues

ISSN   0302-9743
ISBN-10   3-540-73146-6 Springer Berlin Heidelberg New York
ISBN-13   978-3-540-73146-7 Springer Berlin Heidelberg New York

Springer is a part of Springer Science+Business Media

springer.com

© Springer-Verlag Berlin Heidelberg 2007
Printed in Germany

Typesetting: Camera-ready by author, data conversion by Scientific Publishing Services, Chennai, India
Printed on acid-free paper   SPIN: 12078622   06/3180   5 4 3 2 1 0

Preface

This volume is dedicated to Jean-Pierre Jouannaud on his 60th birthday. It contains refereed contributions by leading researchers in the different areas spanned by Jean-Pierre Jouannaud's work. These papers were presented at the symposium held in Cachan near Paris, on June 21–22, 2007, in Jean-Pierre Jouannaud's honor.

Jean-Pierre has deeply influenced, and is still influencing, research in Informatics, through the many important results he has produced in various research fields, through the generations of scholars he has educated, and through the role he has played in helping the Informatics discipline to reach maturity and its place among the other disciplines.

Jean-Pierre's Origins and Contributions

Jean-Pierre defended his first thesis in 1972 on "Filtres digitaux autoadaptifs : algorithmes de calcul et simulation". Together with the emergence of Informatics, he then moved to more symbolic topics and, as assistant professor at the university of Paris 6 in Jussieu, he defended his "thése d'état" in 1977 entitled "Sur l'inférence et la synthèse automatiques de fonctions LISP à partir d'exemples". This led him to investigate the foundational concepts emerging at that time: lambda-calculus and rewriting.

Jean-Pierre then played a leading role in rewriting and its technology: he introduced this field in Nancy, when he took up an Associate Professor position in 1979, and founded there, together with Pierre Lescanne, the *Eureca* team that got the CNRS silver medal in 1986. He was also at the origin of the RTA (Rewriting Techniques and Applications) conference series in 1985. In this domain Jean-Pierre's major contributions spanned to unification, rewriting and completion modulo, conditional rewriting, termination proofs, modular properties, and automated proofs by induction in rewrite theories.

During his one year sabbatical at SRI International in 1984–85, Jean-Pierre Jouannaud developed further his strong interest for algebraic specification languages and their efficient implementation. He contributed with Kokichi Futatsugi, Joseph Goguen and José Meseguer to the design, semantics and implementation of OBJ2. Further important contributions of Jean-Pierre Jouannaud concern order-sorted algebras and more recently membership equational logic, an essential feature of the Maude system.

In 1985, Jean-Pierre moved to the university of Paris Sud in Orsay, where he became full professor in 1986. There he founded the *Demons* team, which focused on automated deduction and constraint solving. Then, with interactions in particular with Gérard Huet, his interests widened to higher-order rewriting and the calculus of constructions. He contributed to strong results on the integration of rewriting and deduction leading to the design of proof assistants with rewriting as a first-class concept. His results on termination of higher-order rewriting are also leading the way.

In recognition of these outstanding scientific achievements, he was awarded the "Prix Montpetit" from the French Academy of Sciences in 2000.

Jean-Pierre started several international collaborations and forged scientific links and friendships, which continue over the years, in particular in the USA, Canada, Argentina, Spain, Japan and Taiwan. The outcomes were formal joint research projects (especially through NSF grants and European working groups), general collaboration agreements, such as the French-Taiwanese collaboration, which has been awarded a "Grand Prix" from the French Academy of Science, or simply intensive visits both ways.

To promote and animate the theoretical computer science community has been and remains one of his concerns. He was a member of the CNU (National University Council), a member of the CNRS national committee, and he is heading with great success the computer science laboratory at Ecole Polytechnique.

Jean-Pierre has exceptional qualities as a research team manager and as a supervisor of students. His work with his students has always involved a close, friendly relationship, a daily meeting, weekly encouragements, monthly entertainment and a close care of the future of the students. One of the keys of Jean-Pierre Jouannaud as a research team manager is his motto: "enjoy!". Enjoy everything that is good, which includes working together on research problems, and also drinking good wine, eating good food, skiing, climbing, windsurfing,... The best being to combine several of these activities. Having fun working together, it is easy to spend hours on a problem, to launch new projects, to arouse enthusiasm among students.

Jean-Pierre Jouannaud's Doctoral Descendants

Jean-Pierre is an excellent teacher. He not only knows how to motivate work on difficult and rich concepts, but he has also a profound understanding of their deep properties and relationships. He loves to communicate his knowledge, know-how and real enthusiasm. He has lectured generations of students and liked to be involved in doctoral teaching. His ideas and practice have strongly influenced many PhD students.

The following table summarizes his doctoral descendants. We have tried to be as exhaustive as possible, and we did not take into account the many students that will defend after 2007. A few persons appear several time, as they have been supervised by two people.

1. Jean-Pierre Treuil, 1978: *LQAS : Un systéme question-réponse qui acquiert ses connaissances par apprentissage*;
2. Fernand Reining, 1981: *L'Ordre de Décomposition : un Outil Incrémental pour Prouver la Terminaison Finie des Systémes de Réécriture équationnels*;

3. Jean-Luc Rémy, 1982: *Etude des systèmes de Réécriture Conditionnels et Applications aux Types Abstraits Algébriques*;

   (a) Hantao Zhang, 1984: *REVEUR4 : Etude et mise en œuvre de la réécriture conditionnelle*;

   (b) Wadoud Bousdira, 1990: *Etude des Propriétés des Systèmes de Réécriture Conditionnelle. Mise en Oeuvre d'un Algorithme de Complétion*;

4. Claude Kirchner, 1982: *Résolution d'équations dans les algèbres libres et les variétés équationnelles d'algèbres*;

   (a) Jalel Mzali, 1986: *Méthodes de filtrage équationnel et de preuve automatique de théorèmes*;

   (b) Pierre Réty, 1988: *Méthodes d'unification par surréduction*;

      i. Jacques Chabin, 1994: *Unification générale par surréduction ordonnée contrainte et surréduction dirigée*;

      ii. Sébastien Limet, 1996: *Unification dans la programmation logico-équationnelle*;

         A. Pierre Pillot, 2007: *Utilisation des langages d'arbres pour la modélisation et la vérification de systèmes à états infinis*;

      iii. Julie Vuotto, 2004: *Langages d'arbres réguliers et algébriques pour la réécriture et la vérification*;

   (c) Aristide Mégrelis, 1990: *Algèbre galactique — Un procédé de calcul formel*;

   (d) Éric Domenjoud, 1991: *Outils pour la déduction automatique dans les théories associatives-commutatives*;

   (e) Mohamed Adi, 1991: *Calculs associatif et commutatifs. Etude et réalisation du système UNIF$_{AC}$*;

   (f) Patrick Viry, 1992: *La réécriture concurrente*;

   (g) Francis Klay, 1992: *Unification dans les Théories Syntaxiques*;

      i. Karim Berkanu, 2003: *Un cadre méthodologique pour l'intégration de services par évitement des interactions*;

      ii. Stéphanie Delaune, 2006: *Vérification des protocoles cryptographiques et propriétés algébriques*;

   (h) Marian Vittek, 1994: ELAN *: Un cadre logique pour le prototypage de langages de programmation avec contraintes*;

   (i) Pauline Strogova, 1996: *Techniques de Réécriture pour le Traitement de Problème de Routage dans des Graphes de Cayley*;

   (j) Iliès Alouini, : *Étude et mise en oeuvre de la réécriture conditionnelle concurrente sur des machines parallèles à mémoire distribuée*;

   (k) Farid Ajili, 1998: *Contraintes Diophantiennes Linéaires : résolution et coopération inter-résolveurs*;

   (l) Carlos Castro, 1998: *Une approche déductive de la résolution de problèmes de satisfaction de contraintes*;

   (m) Christelle Scharff, 1999: *Déduction avec contraintes et simplification dans les théories équationnelles*;

   (n) Horatiu Cirstea, 2000: *Calcul de réécriture : fondements et applications*;

(b) Ponsini Olivier, 2005: *Des programmes impératifs vers la logique équationnelle pour la vérification*;

7. Michael Rusinowitch, 1987; partial: *Démonstration automatique par des techniques de réécriture (thése d'état)*;

   (a) Adel Bouhoula, 1994: *Preuves automatiques par récurrence dans les théories conditionnelles*;

   (b) Laurent Vigneron, 1994: *Déduction automatique avec contraintes symboliques dans les théories équationnelles*;

   (c) Eric Monfroy, 1996: *Collaboration de solveurs pour la programmation par contraintes*;

      i. Lucas Bordeaux, 2003: *Résolution de problémes combinatoires modélisés par des contraintes quantifiées*;

      ii. Brice Pajot, 2006: *Modèles et architectures pour la résolution coopérative par solveurs de contraintes*;

      iii. Tony Lambert, 2006: *Hybridation de méthodes complètes et incomplètes pour la résolution de CSP*;

   (d) Narjes Berregeb, 1997: *Preuves par induction implicite : cas des théories associatives-commutatives et observationnelles*;

   (e) Sorin Stratulat, 2000: *Preuves par récurrence avec ensembles couvrants contextuels. Application à la vérification de logiciels de télécommunications*;

   (f) Silvio Ranise, 2002: *On the Integration of Decision Procedures in Automated Deduction*;

   (g) Matthieu Turuani, 2003: *Sécurité des Protocoles Cryptographiques: Décidabilité et Complexité*;

   (h) Julien Musset, 2003: *Approximation of transition relations. Application to infinite states systems verification*;

   (i) Yannick Chevalier, 2003: *Résolution de problèmes d'accessibilité pour la compilation et la validation de protocoles cryptographiques*;

   (j) Tarek Abbes, 2004: *Classification du trafic et optimisation des règles de filtrage pour la détection d'intrusions*;

   (k) Abdessamad Imine, 2006: *Conception Formelle d'Algorithmes de Réplication Optimiste. Vers l'Edition Collaborative dans les Réseaux Pair-à-Pair*;

   (l) Eugen Zalinescu, 2007: *Sécurité des protocoles cryptographiques: décidabilité et résultats de transfert*;

8. Hubert Comon, 1988; unofficial: *Unification et disunification. Théories et applications*;

   (a) Marianne Haberstrau, 1993: *ECOLOG : un Environnement pour la programmation en LOGique COntrainte*;

   (b) Florent Jacquemard, 1996: *automates d'arbres et réécriture de termes*;

   (c) Yan Jurski, 1999: *Expression de la relation binaire d'accessibilité pour les automates à compteurs plats et les automates temporisés*;

We feel privileged to edit this volume, as a way to thank Jean-Pierre Jouannaud for all his scientific contributions and for communicating to us his enthusiasm for research. We are most grateful to all the authors who enthusiastically contributed to this special issue and participated in the symposium. We are also thankful to all those who helped us in the refereeing process and to

Alfred Hofmann at Springer who supported our initiative. CNRS, Ecole Normale Supérieure de Cachan, INRIA and LSV are gratefully acknowledged for their organizational and financial support.

April 2007

Hubert Comon-Lundh
Claude Kirchner
Héléne Kirchner

Organization

Referees

Frédéric Blanqui
Olivier Bournez
Paul Brauner
Yannick Chevalier
Nachum Dershowitz
Gilles Dowek
Bernhard Gramlich

Emmanuel Hainry
Claude Marché
Stephan Merz
François Lamarche
Yohishito Toyama
Femke van Raamsdonk

Table of Contents

The Hydra Battle Revisited*

Nachum Dershowitz[1,2] and Georg Moser[3]

[1] School of Computer Science, Tel Aviv University,
69978 Ramat Aviv, Israel
nachum.dershowitz@cs.tau.ac.il
[2] Microsoft Research, Redmond, WA 98052
[3] Institute of Computer Science, University of Innsbruck,
Technikerstrasse 21a, A-6020 Innsbruck, Austria
georg.moser@uibk.ac.at

To Jean-Pierre on this momentous occasion.

Abstract. Showing termination of the Battle of Hercules and Hydra is
a challenge. We present the battle both as a rewrite system and as an
arithmetic while program, provide proofs of their termination, and recall
why their termination cannot be proved within Peano arithmetic.

> As a second labour he ordered him to kill the Lernaean hydra.
> That creature, bred in the swamp of Lerna,
> used to go forth into the plain
> and ravage both the cattle and the country.
> Now the hydra had a huge body, with nine heads,
> eight mortal, but the middle one immortal. . . .
> By pelting it with fiery shafts he forced it to come out,
> and in the act of doing so he seized and held it fast.
> But the hydra wound itself about one of his feet and clung to him.
> Nor could he effect anything by smashing its heads with his club,
> for as fast as one head was smashed there grew up two.
>
> – Pausanias, *Description of Greece*, 2.37.4

1   Introduction

The Battle of Hydra and Hercules, as described in the above-quoted myth, and
depicted on the Etruscan hydra (water jar) in Fig. 1, inspired Laurie Kirby and
Jeff Paris [24] to formulate a process, the termination of which cannot be proved
by ordinary induction on the natural numbers. Instead, recourse must be made
to induction on the ordinals less than the ordinal number "epsilon naught", in
the ordinal hierarchy created by Georg Cantor.

---

* The first author's research was supported in part by the Israel Science Foundation
(grant no. 250/05).

H. Comon-Lundh et al. (Eds.): Jouannaud Festschrift, LNCS 4600, pp. 1–27, 2007.
© Springer-Verlag Berlin Heidelberg 2007

Fig. 1. Caeretan hydra, attributed to Eagle Painter, c. 525 B.C.E. See [19]. (Courtesy of the J. Paul Getty Museum, Villa Collection, Malibu, CA).

The alternating steps of Hercules and Hydra in the formal battle are quite easy to understand (and are more appealing than the similar but older Goodstein sequence [17], also treated in [24]). The battle itself is described in Sect. 2. Yet the fact that Hercules is always the declared winner, as shown in Sect. 4, is far from obvious. As such, it is arguably the simplest example of a terminating process that is not amenable to argument by means of Peano's famous axioms of arithmetic. Termination is a conceptually clear notion. Thus, it is fair to claim that the Hydra Battle is more intuitive, as an independence result, than employing Ramsey-like theorems, for instance; cf. [30].

In the popular survey on rewriting [10][2] by Jean-Pierre Jouannaud and the first author (and in several later publications, [11, Prob. 23], [7]), a rewrite system for the battle was presented, but it was unfortunately fraught with *lapsus calami*. Nevertheless, proving its termination has been a challenge for contestants in termination competitions [28]. A repaired version was promulgated years later [26].

In the sections that follow, we describe the vicissitudes of this formalization of the battle in rewrite systems (Sect. 5), prove their termination (Sect. 8), and also encode the battle as a **while** program (Sect. 9). This paper concentrates on the interpretation of successive hydræ as decreasing ordinal numbers. But there are alternative, less "highbrow" arguments (in Alan Turing's words [35]); see Martin Gardner's column [15]. Some properties of ordinals and orders are briefly reviewed in Sects. 3, 6 and 7.

For more on the problem and its extensions, see [13]. See also [27,21,34]. We conclude with one such extension.

2   The Hydra Battle

In a landmark paper [24], Kirby and Paris showed that – for their version of the battle – more than ordinary induction on the natural numbers is needed to show that Hercules prevails.

2.1   The Formal Battle

In the mathematical battle, hydræ are represented as (unordered, rooted, finite) trees, with each leaf corresponding to one head of the monster. Whereas Hercules decapitates Hydra, one head at a time, Hydra regenerates according to the following rule: If the severed head has a grandparent node, then the branch issuing from that node together with the mutilated subtree is multiplied by a certain factor; otherwise, Hydra suffers the loss without any regrowth. Hercules wins when (not if!) the beast is reduced to the empty tree.

(In the original formulation of this game, the multiplication factor is one more than the stage of the game. We modify the definition slightly and set the multiplication factor equal to the stage of the game, as otherwise the system $\mathcal{D}$ below fails to encode the Hydra Battle. The results in [24] are unaffected by this change.)

We write (H, n) to describe a single *configuration* in the game, where H denotes Hydra and n the current stage of the game.

---

[2] This survey is the most cited document for its year of publication (1990) in the CiteSeer database [31], and has always been high in the overall list.

Example 1.

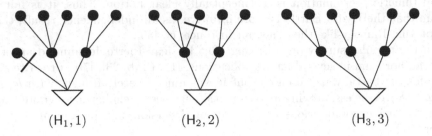

$$(H_1, 1) \qquad\qquad (H_2, 2) \qquad\qquad (H_3, 3)$$

In the first stage, Hercules chops off the leftmost head. As this head has no grandparent, Hydra shrinks. However, in Stage 2, Hercules chops off a head with a grandparent (the triangular root). Consequently, Hydra grows two replacement branches, as indicated.   ☐

More examples can be found in [24,34].

2.2   Functional Hydra

It is easy to express the Hydra Battle in a functional language with list operations, like Lisp. However, so as not to complicate matters unnecessarily, we do not follow the original definition of Kirby and Paris, but rather restrict attention to ordered trees (with immediate subtrees ordered sequentially from left to right). Let $\mathtt{nil}$ denote an empty list and $\mathtt{cons}(x, y)$ be the list obtained by prepending an element x (the right-most subtree) to a list y (the remaining tree). Thus, the first hydra in Example 1 would be represented as follows:

$$\mathtt{cons}(\ell, \mathtt{cons}(\mathtt{cons}(\mathtt{cons}(\ell, \mathtt{cons}(\ell, \mathtt{nil})), \mathtt{nil}), \mathtt{cons}(\ell, \mathtt{cons}(\ell, \mathtt{cons}(\ell, \mathtt{nil}))))) \,,$$

where $\ell = \mathtt{cons}(\mathtt{nil}, \mathtt{nil})$ stands for a leaf of a Hydra and we have reordered the immediate subtrees of the root of H_1 such that the number of nodes is non-increasing. In the rewrite system to be introduced below, a "cons-cell" is grafted together by the function symbol g.

Let $\mathtt{car}(\mathtt{cons}(x, y)) = x$ and $\mathtt{cdr}(\mathtt{cons}(x, y)) = y$ extract the first item in a nonempty list $\mathtt{cons}(x, y)$ and the remainder of the list, respectively. The battle can be encoded by the following program, $\mathcal{L}$:

$$h_0(x)$$
$$\text{where}$$

$$h_n(x) \quad := \begin{cases} \mathtt{nil} & x = \mathtt{nil} \\ h_{n+1}(d_n(x)) & \text{otherwise} \end{cases}$$

$$d_n(x) \quad := \begin{cases} \mathtt{cdr}(x) & \mathtt{car}(x) = \mathtt{nil} \\ f_n(\mathtt{cdr}(\mathtt{car}(x)), \mathtt{cdr}(x)) & \mathtt{car}(\mathtt{car}(x)) = \mathtt{nil} \\ \mathtt{cons}(d_n(\mathtt{car}(x)), \mathtt{cdr}(x)) & \text{otherwise} \end{cases}$$

$$f_n(y, x) := \begin{cases} x & n = 0 \\ \mathtt{cons}(y, f_{n-1}(y, x)) & \text{otherwise} \end{cases}$$

Here, $h_n(x)$ plays the game with initial hydra x, starting at stage n, $d_n(x)$ plays one round of the battle, by travelling along a leftmost branch until encountering a branch z such that $\mathtt{car}(\mathtt{car}(z))$ is empty, and then using $f_n(y, x)$ to prepend k copies of $y = \mathtt{cdr}(\mathtt{car}(z))$ to x.

Better yet, if we let ε symbolize $\mathtt{nil}$ and use a colon : for $\mathtt{cons}$, then the following pattern-directed program plays the battle $h_0(x)$ until its inevitable end:

$$
\begin{aligned}
h_n(\varepsilon) &:= \varepsilon \\
h_n(x : y) &:= h_{n+1}(d_n(x : y)) \\
d_n(\varepsilon : y) &:= y \\
d_n((\varepsilon : x) : y) &:= f_n(x, y) \\
d_n(((u : v) : x) : y) &:= d_n((u : v) : x) : y \\
f_0(y, x) &:= x \\
f_{n+1}(y, x) &:= y : f_n(y, x)
\end{aligned}
$$

3 Orders and Ordinals

Termination proofs are often based on well-founded orderings. Our proofs are no exception.

3.1 Well-Founded Orders

A *partial order* $\succ$ is an irreflexive and transitive binary relation. Its converse is written with a reflected symbol $\prec$. A *quasi-order* $\succeq$ is a reflexive and transitive relation. A quasi-order $\succeq$ induces a (strict) partial order $\succ$, such that $a \succ b$ if $a \succeq b \not\succeq a$. A partial order $\succ$ on a set A is *well-founded* (on A) if there exists no infinite descending sequence $a_1 \succ a_2 \succ \cdots$ of elements of A. A partial order is *linear* (or *total*) on A if for all $a, b \in A$, a different from b, a and b are comparable by $\succ$. A linear well-founded order is called a *well-order*.

Let $\mathcal{F}$ be a signature. An $\mathcal{F}$-*algebra* $\mathcal{A}$ is a set A, its *domain*, together with operations $f_{\mathcal{A}} \colon A^n \to A$ for each function symbol $f \in \mathcal{F}$ of arity n. An $\mathcal{F}$-algebra $(\mathcal{A}, \prec)$ is called *monotone* if $\mathcal{A}$ is associated with a partial order $\succ$ and every algebra operation $f_{\mathcal{A}}$ is strictly monotone in all its arguments. A monotone $\mathcal{F}$-algebra $(\mathcal{A}, \succ)$ is called *well-founded* if $\succ$ is well-founded.

Let $(\mathcal{A}, \succ)$ denote an $\mathcal{F}$-algebra and let $\mathbf{a} \colon \mathcal{V} \to A$ denote an *assignment*. We write $[\mathbf{a}]_{\mathcal{A}}$ to denote the homeomorphic extension of the assignment $\mathbf{a}$ and define an ordering $\succ_{\mathcal{A}}$ on terms $\mathcal{T}(\mathcal{F}, \mathcal{V})$ in the usual way: $s \succ_{\mathcal{A}} t$ if $[\mathbf{a}]_{\mathcal{A}}(s) \succ [\mathbf{a}]_{\mathcal{A}}(t)$ for every assignment $\mathbf{a}$.

3.2 Order Types

We assume some very basic knowledge of set theory and in particular of ordinals, as in, for example, [22]. We write $>$ to denote the well-order on ordinals. This order can, of course, be employed for inductive arguments.

The ordinal ϵ_0 ("epsilon naught") is the smallest solution to $\omega^x = x$. Recall that any ordinal $\alpha < \epsilon_0$, $\alpha \neq 0$, can be uniquely represented in Cantor Normal Form (CNF) as a sum

$$\omega^{\alpha_1} + \cdots + \omega^{\alpha_n},$$

where $\alpha_1 \geqslant \cdots \geqslant \alpha_n$. The set of ordinals below ϵ_0 in CNF will also be denoted CNF. For $\alpha = \omega^{\alpha_1} + \cdots + \omega^{\alpha_n}$ and $\beta = \omega^{\alpha_{n+1}} + \cdots + \omega^{\alpha_{n+m}}$, the *natural sum* $\alpha \oplus \beta$ is defined as $\omega^{\alpha_{\pi(1)}} + \cdots + \omega^{\alpha_{\pi(n+m)}}$, where π denotes a permutation of the indices $[1, n+m]$ ($= \{1, \ldots, n+m\}$) such that $\alpha_{\pi(1)} \geqslant \alpha_{\pi(2)} \geqslant \cdots \geqslant \alpha_{\pi(n+m)}$ is guaranteed. We write $\alpha \cdot n$ as an abbreviation for $\alpha + \cdots + \alpha$ (n times α), and we identify the natural numbers ($\mathbf{N}$) with the ordinals below ω. We denote the set of limit ordinals by Lim.

To each well-founded order $\succ$ on a set A, one can associate a (set-theoretic) ordinal, its *order type*. First, we associate an ordinal to each element a of A by setting

$$\mathrm{otype}_\succ(a) := \sup\{\mathrm{otype}_\succ(b) + 1 \mid b \in A \text{ and } a \succ b\}.$$

Then the *order type* of $\succ$, denoted $\mathrm{otype}(\succ)$, is defined as $\sup\{\mathrm{otype}_\succ(a) + 1 \mid a \in A\}$. For two partial orders $\succ$ and $\succ'$ on A and A', respectively, a mapping $o \colon A \to A'$ *embeds* $\succ$ into $\succ'$ if, for all $x, y \in A$, we have that $x \succ y$ implies $o(x) \succ' o(y)$.

Lemma 1. *If both $\succ$ and $\succ'$ are well founded and if $\succ$ can be embedded into $\succ'$, then $\mathrm{otype}(\succ) \leqslant \mathrm{otype}(\succ')$.*

Two linear partial orders $(A, \succ)$ and $(B, \succ')$ are *order-isomorphic* (or *equivalent*) if there exists a surjective mapping $o \colon A \to B$ such that $(x \succ y \iff o(x) \succ' o(y))$ for all $x, y \in A$.

4   Herculean Strength

The natural game-theoretic question is whether Hercules has a winning strategy. A *strategy* is a mapping determining which head Hercules should chop off at each stage.

4.1   Hercules Prevails

It turns out that whatever strategy Hercules fights by he eventually wins. It's only a question of time. In our proof, we follow Kirby and Paris [24] and associate with each hydra an ordinal below ϵ_0:

1. Assign 0 to each leaf.
2. Assign $\omega^{\alpha_1} \oplus \cdots \oplus \omega^{\alpha_n}$ to each internal node, where α_i are the ordinals assigned to the children of the node.

The ordinal representing Hydra is the ordinal assigned to her root node.

Example 2. Consider hydræ H_1–H_3, above. These have the representations $\omega^3 \oplus \omega^2 \oplus 1$, $\omega^3 \oplus \omega^2$, and $\omega^2 \cdot 3$, respectively.   □

In the sequel, we confound the representation of a hydra as finite tree and as ordinal. Let (H, n) denote a configuration of the game. Then $(H)_n^S$ denotes the resulting Hydra if strategy S is applied to H at stage n. That is, the next configuration is $((H)_n^S, n+1)$.

Lemma 2 (Kirby & Paris [24]). *For any strategy S, Hydra H and natural number n, we obtain $H > (H)_n^S$.*

Theorem 1 (Kirby & Paris [24]). *Every strategy is a winning strategy.*

Proof. The theorem follows from the lemma together with the fact that $>$ is well-founded.   □

One can readily see from the proof that Hercules also wins a seemingly more challenging battle, wherein Hydra generates an arbitrary number of replacement branches at any level of the tree, but the resulting Hydra is smaller (as an ordinal) than the original. Again, any strategy is a winning strategy. Such a reformulation of the Hydra Battle is depicted in Fig. 2, taken from a survey lecture on proofs and computation by Jouannaud [23].[3] Similar extensions of the Hydra Battle have recently been considered by Rudolf Fleischer in [13].

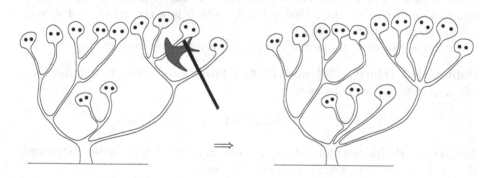

Fig. 2. Evelyne Contejean's rendition of the battle (from Jouannaud's survey [23])

Now we formally define a specific strategy for the Hydra Battle that has been called *standard* in [34]. For $n \in \mathbf{N}$, we associate an ordinal $\alpha_n \in \mathrm{CNF}$ with every $\alpha \in \mathrm{CNF}$:

$$
\alpha_n = \begin{cases}
0 & \text{if } \alpha = 0 \\
\beta & \text{if } \alpha = \beta + 1 \\
\beta + \omega^\gamma \cdot n & \text{if } \alpha = \beta + \omega^{\gamma+1} \\
\beta + \omega^{\gamma_n} & \text{if } \alpha = \beta + \omega^\gamma \text{ and } \gamma \in \mathrm{Lim}
\end{cases}
$$

---

[3] "This is one of Nachum Dershowitz's favorite examples" [23].

Then we can define the *standard Hydra Battle* as follows:

Definition 1 (Hydra Battle). *A* hydra *is an ordinal in CNF. The* Hydra Battle *is a sequence of configurations. A* configuration *is a pair* (α, n)*, where* α *denotes a hydra and* $n \geqslant 1$*, the current* step*. Let* (α, n) *be a configuration, such that* $\alpha > 0$*. Then the next configuration in the standard strategy is* $(\alpha_n, n + 1)$*.*

This definition implies that we force a one-to-one correspondence between finite trees and ordinals. Hence, we again restrict ourselves to ordered trees.

This strategy conforms with the prior description of the battle, provided Hydra's immediate subtrees in the functional battle are arranged (at all levels) from the largest on the left to the smallest on the right. Here, largeness or smallness of subtrees is measured by the corresponding ordinal.

Remark 1. The sequence $(\alpha_n)_{n \in \mathbb{N}}$ is usually referred to as a *fundamental sequence* of α. A fundamental sequence fulfills the property that for limit ordinal $\lambda \in \text{Lim}$, the sequence $(\lambda_n)_n$ is strictly increasing and its limit is λ. For the connection between rewriting and fundamental sequences, see, for example, [29].

4.2 Beyond Peano

In the remainder of this section, we show that Peano Arithmetic cannot prove termination of the standard Hydra Battle, which is a special case of a more general theorem stated in [24,13].

We define two ordinal-indexed hierarchies of number-theoretic functions.

Definition 2 (Hardy [36] and Hydra Functions). *The* Hardy functions $(\mathsf{H}_\alpha)_{\alpha < \epsilon_0}$ *are defined as follows:*

$$\mathsf{H}_0(n) := n, \quad and \quad \mathsf{H}_\alpha(n) := \mathsf{H}_{\alpha_n}(n + 1) \quad (if \ \alpha > 0) .$$

The related Hydra functions $(\mathsf{L}_\alpha)_{\alpha < \epsilon_0}$*, counting the length of the (standard) Hydra Battle, starting stage* n *with hydra* α*, are:*

$$\mathsf{L}_0(n) := 0, \quad and \quad \mathsf{L}_\alpha(n) := \mathsf{L}_{\alpha_n}(n + 1) + 1 \quad (if \ \alpha > 0) .$$

The following lemma is an easy consequence of the definitions:

Lemma 3. *The hierarchies* $(\mathsf{H}_\alpha)_{\alpha < \epsilon_0}$ *and* $(\mathsf{L}_\alpha)_{\alpha < \epsilon_0}$ *form a majorization hierarchy on* ϵ_0*, in the sense that the functions are strictly increasing and each function at level* α *eventually dominates the functions at level* β *for all* $\beta < \alpha$*.*

Next, we relate the functions H_α and L_α.

Lemma 4. *For any* $\alpha < \epsilon_0$ *and any* $n \in \mathbb{N}$ *we have*

$$\mathsf{H}_\alpha(n) = \mathsf{H}_{\mathsf{L}_\alpha(n)}(n) = n + \mathsf{L}_\alpha(n) .$$

Proof. The second equation is easily established by noting that, for finite m, we have $H_m(n) = m + n$. The first equation is proved by induction on α. The case $\alpha = 0$ follows from $L_0(n) = 0$. For $\alpha > 0$, put $\gamma := \alpha_n$ and note that

$$H_\alpha(n) = H_\gamma(n+1) = H_{L_\gamma(n+1)}(n+1) = H_{L_\gamma(n+1)+1}(n) = H_{L_\alpha(n)}(n) .$$

In the second equality, we employ the induction hypothesis. For the third let $m = L_\gamma(n+1)$ and observe $H_{m+1}(n) = H_m(n+1)$. □

A function f is *provably recursive* in Peano Arithmetic (PA) if there exists a primitive recursive predicate P and a primitive recursive function g such that $PA \vdash \forall y_1 \cdots \forall y_k \exists x P(y_1, \ldots, y_k, x)$ and f satisfies

$$f(n_1, \ldots, n_k) = g(\mu_x P(n_1, \ldots, n_k, x)) ,$$

where μ_x denotes the least number operator.

Let the *Hardy class* $\mathcal{H}$ be defined as the smallest class of functions (1) containing 0, S (successor), all H_α, for $\alpha < \epsilon_0$, and all projection functions $I_{n,i}(a_1, \ldots, a_n) := a_i$, and (2) closed under primitive recursion and composition.

Theorem 2. *The Hardy class $\mathcal{H}$ is the class of all provably recursive functions in PA.*

For a proof see [32].

Theorem 3. *PA cannot prove termination of the standard Hydra Battle.*

Proof. Suppose termination of the standard Hydra Battle would be PA-provable. This is equivalent to the fact that

$$PA \vdash \ulcorner \forall \, \alpha, n \, \exists m \, L_\alpha(n) = m \urcorner ,$$

for a suitable arithmetization $\ulcorner \cdot \urcorner$. Hence, for all $\alpha < \epsilon_0$ and all $n \in \mathbf{N}$: $L_\alpha(n)$ is a provably recursive function in PA. In particular, $L_{(\epsilon_0)_n}(n+1) + 1$ is provably recursive, and thus by definition $L_{\epsilon_0}(n)$ is provably recursive. (The same holds for $L_{\epsilon_0}(n) + n$.) By Lemma 4, we conclude $L_{\epsilon_0}(n) + n = H_{\epsilon_0}(n)$, which would imply that $H_{\epsilon_0}(n)$ is provably recursive, contradicting Theorem 2. □

Remark 2. It bears mentioning that if Hydra is constrained to a bounded initial height, or if there is a fixed bound on her growth factor [27], then termination is provable in PA.

5   Rewriting Hydra

A *(term-) rewriting system* is a (finite) set of rewrite rules, each of which is an ordered pair of terms. Let $\mathcal{F}$ denote a signature and $\mathcal{V}$, a (countably infinite) set of variables. The terms over $\mathcal{F}$ and $\mathcal{V}$ are denoted $\mathcal{T}(\mathcal{F}, \mathcal{V})$. A binary relation on $\mathcal{T}(\mathcal{F}, \mathcal{V})$ is a *rewrite relation* if it is compatible with $\mathcal{F}$-operations and closed under substitutions. The smallest rewrite relation that contains $\mathcal{R}$ is denoted $\to_{\mathcal{R}}$. The reflexive-transitive closure of rewrite steps $\to_{\mathcal{R}}$ is denoted $\to_{\mathcal{R}}^*$; the transitive closure, $\to_{\mathcal{R}}^+$. For further details about rewriting, see the survey by the first author and Jouannaud [10] or one of the books [2,33].

In [10], the following rewrite system $\mathcal{H}$ was introduced as an encoding of the Hydra Battle:[4]

$$h(e(x), y) \to h(d(x, y), S(y)) \tag{1}$$
$$d(g(0, 0), y) \to e(0) \tag{2}$$
$$d(g(x, y), z) \to g(e(x), d(y, z)) \tag{3}$$
$$d(g(g(x, y), 0), S(z)) \to g(d(g(x, y), S(z)), d(g(x, y), z)) \tag{4}$$
$$g(e(x), e(y)) \to e(g(x, y)) \tag{5}$$

(To clarify the connection to the standard Hydra Battle, as presented in Sect. 2, we have swapped the original arguments of the symbols d and h and make use of the unary function symbol S instead of the original c.)

The idea was for $h(x, n)$ to represent the nth stage of the battle, with Hydra current being x, and with g serving as cons and 0 as nil. Then, $d(n, x)$ marks the position of Hercules' search for a head to chop off (n is the replication factor); d was also meant to perform the duplication (which is the rôle of f in the functional program described in Section 2.2). The d in the first argument of g on the right side of rule (4) forces that branch to get smaller, via rules (3) and (2), assuming that branch has a head dangling at its right edge. The symbol e is used to signal completion of the operation on a branch, and settles towards the root after replication. The system was designed to allow various sterile derivations, as well as the primary, battle one.

Unfortunately, rule (4) does not perform as advertised; the system does not simulate the standard Hydra Battle, as defined in Sect. 2.[5] To rectify this, the first author proposed (on Pierre Lescanne's rewriting list [26]) the following System $\mathcal{D}$, comprising six rules:

$$h(e(x), y) \to h(d(x, y), S(y)) \tag{6}$$
$$d(g(0, x), y) \to e(x) \tag{7}$$
$$d(g(x, y), z) \to g(d(x, z), e(y)) \tag{8}$$
$$d(g(g(0, x), y), 0) \to e(y) \tag{9}$$
$$d(g(g(0, x), y), S(z)) \to g(e(x), d(g(g(0, x), y), z)) \tag{10}$$
$$g(e(x), e(y)) \to e(g(x, y)) \tag{11}$$

---

[4] Some (lost) version of this rewrite system had been presented by the first author at the Interdisciplinary Conference on Axiomatic Systems, in Columbus, OH, on December 16, 1988.

[5] The originally intended system probably had $g(d(g(x, y), S(z)), d(g(g(x, y), 0), z))$ as the right-hand side of rule (4). Some additional changes are needed for it to be able to simulate the standard Hydra Battle. We do not discuss this version any further.

We will see below that the underlying semantics of the symbol g changed in the transition from $\mathcal{H}$ to $\mathcal{D}$. (Here again we have swapped the arguments of the symbols d and h and make use of the unary function symbol S instead of the original c.)

5.1   Faithfulness

It is not hard to see that, indeed, $\mathcal{D}$ faithfully represents the standard Hydra Battle. We define a mapping $\mathcal{O}\colon CNF \to T(\mathcal{F}, \emptyset)$, where $\mathcal{F}$ is the set of function symbols in $\mathcal{D}$:

$$\mathcal{O}(\alpha) := \begin{cases} 0 & \text{if } \alpha = 0 \\ \mathsf{g}(\mathcal{O}(\gamma), 0) & \text{if } \alpha = \omega^\gamma \\ \mathsf{g}(\mathcal{O}(\gamma), \mathcal{O}(\beta)) & \text{if } \alpha = \beta + \omega^\gamma \end{cases}$$

Each configuration (α, n) of the game is encoded by a term $\mathsf{h}(\mathsf{e}(\mathcal{O}(\alpha)), \mathsf{S}^n(0))$.

Lemma 5. *Let* $\alpha \in CNF$, $\alpha > 0$, $n \in \mathbf{N} \setminus \{0\}$. *Then* $\mathsf{h}(\mathsf{e}(\mathcal{O}(\alpha)), \mathsf{S}^n(0)) \to_\mathcal{D}^+ \mathsf{h}(\mathsf{e}(\mathcal{O}(\alpha_n)), \mathsf{S}^{n+1}(0))$.

Proof. Due to the presence of the rule $\mathsf{h}(\mathsf{e}(x), y) \to \mathsf{h}(\mathsf{d}(x, y), \mathsf{S}(y))$ in $\mathcal{D}$, it suffices to verify that $\mathsf{d}(\mathcal{O}(\alpha), \mathsf{S}^n(0)) \to_\mathcal{D}^+ \mathsf{e}(\mathcal{O}(\alpha_n))$. We proceed by induction on α.

1. CASE $\alpha = \beta + 1$: By definition, $\alpha_n = \beta$ and $\mathcal{O}(\alpha) = \mathsf{g}(0, \mathcal{O}(\beta))$. Let $t = \mathcal{O}(\alpha)$ and $s = \mathcal{O}(\beta)$. To establish $\mathsf{d}(\mathcal{O}(\alpha), \mathsf{S}^n(0)) \to_\mathcal{D}^+ \mathsf{e}(\mathcal{O}(\alpha_n))$, we only need one rewrite step by rule (7):

$$\mathsf{d}(\mathsf{g}(0, s), \mathsf{S}^n(0)) \to_\mathcal{D} \mathsf{e}(s) \, .$$

2. CASE $\alpha = \beta + \omega^{\gamma+1}$: By definition, $\alpha_n = \beta + \omega^\gamma \cdot n$ and $t = \mathcal{O}(\alpha) = \mathsf{g}(\mathsf{g}(0, \mathcal{O}(\gamma)), \mathcal{O}(\beta))$. Let $s = \mathcal{O}(\beta)$, $r = \mathcal{O}(\gamma)$. Then

$$\mathcal{O}(\alpha_n) = \underbrace{\mathsf{g}(r, \mathsf{g}(r, \cdots \mathsf{g}(r, s) \cdots))}_{n \text{ occurrences of } r} \, ,$$

and the following rewrite sequence suffices:

$$\begin{aligned} \mathsf{d}(\mathsf{g}(\mathsf{g}(0, r), s), \mathsf{S}^n(0)) &\to_\mathcal{D}^+ \mathsf{g}(\mathsf{e}(r), \mathsf{g}(\mathsf{e}(r), \cdots \mathsf{d}(\mathsf{g}(\mathsf{g}(0, r), s), 0) \cdots)) && (10)^n \\ &\to_\mathcal{D} \mathsf{g}(\mathsf{e}(r), \mathsf{g}(\mathsf{e}(r), \cdots \mathsf{g}(\mathsf{e}(r), \mathsf{e}(s)) \cdots)) && (9) \\ &\to_\mathcal{D}^+ \mathsf{e}(\mathsf{g}(r, \mathsf{g}(r, \cdots \mathsf{g}(r, s) \cdots))) \, . && (11)^n \end{aligned}$$

3. CASE $\alpha = \beta + \omega^\gamma$, $\gamma \in \mathrm{Lim}$: By definition, $\alpha_n = \beta + \omega^{\gamma_n}$ and $\mathcal{O}(\alpha) = \mathsf{g}(\mathcal{O}(\gamma), \mathcal{O}(\beta))$. Let $t = \mathcal{O}(\alpha)$, $s = \mathcal{O}(\beta)$, $r = \mathcal{O}(\gamma)$, and $u = \mathcal{O}(\gamma_n)$. By the induction hypotheses (IH), $\mathsf{d}(r, \mathsf{S}^n(0)) \to_\mathcal{D}^+ \mathsf{e}(u)$ holds. Hence, the following rewrite sequence suffices:

$$\begin{aligned} \mathsf{d}(\mathsf{g}(r, s), \mathsf{S}^n(0)) &\to_\mathcal{D} \mathsf{g}(\mathsf{d}(r, \mathsf{S}^n(0)), \mathsf{e}(s)) && (8) \\ &\to_\mathcal{D}^+ \mathsf{g}(\mathsf{e}(u), \mathsf{e}(s)) && (\text{IH}) \\ &\to_\mathcal{D} \mathsf{e}(\mathsf{g}(u, s)) \, . && (11) \end{aligned}$$

$\square$

6   Termination

We will employ "reduction orders" to prove termination of the Hydra systems.

6.1   Reduction Orders

A rewrite system $\mathcal{R}$ and a partial order $\succ$ are *compatible* if $\mathcal{R} \subseteq \succ$. A rewrite relation that is also a well-founded partial order is called a *reduction order*. It is easy to see that an interpretation-based term order $\succ_{\mathcal{A}}$ is a reduction order if the algebra $(\mathcal{A}, \succ)$ is well-founded and monotone. We say that $(\mathcal{A}, \succ)$ is compatible with a rewrite system $\mathcal{R}$ if $\succ_{\mathcal{A}}$ is compatible with $\mathcal{R}$.

A system $\mathcal{R}$ is *terminating* if no infinite sequence of rewrite steps exists. Thus, $\mathcal{R}$ is terminating iff it is compatible with a reduction order $\succ$.

6.2   Termination Properties

The rules of System $\mathcal{D}$ are similar to the original proposed formalization of the Hydra battle. While the rules of System $\mathcal{H}$ defining h and g have been kept, the three rules defining d have been replaced by four rules.

As given, all but the first rule of $\mathcal{H}$ and $\mathcal{D}$ decrease in a simple recursive path order [5], with precedence d > g > e. The difficulty is in arranging for the first argument of h to show a decrease, as well.

A terminating rewrite system is *simply terminating* if its termination can be proved by a reduction order, like the recursive path order, that enjoys the subterm property (namely, that subterms are smaller in the order).

Theorem 4. *System $\mathcal{H}$ is terminating, but not simply terminating.*

Proof. For now, we only prove the easy fact that $\mathcal{H}$ is not simply terminating, the termination proof is postponed to Sect. 8. To show that $\mathcal{H}$ is not simply terminating, note that the rewrite step

$$h(e(x), e(x)) \rightarrow_{\mathcal{H}} h(d(x, e(x)), S(e(x)))$$

leads to a term that has the initial term embedded (homeomorphically) within it.   □

By the same token, $\mathcal{D}$ is not simply terminating.

Theorem 5. *System $\mathcal{D}$ is terminating, but not simply terminating.*

Again the proof of termination is deferred until Sect. 8.

6.3   Previous Problems

While termination of $\mathcal{H}$, and implicitly of $\mathcal{D}$, has been claimed a number of times in the literature, to our best knowledge no (full, correct) termination proof has been provided.

For example, consider the proof sketch in [7, p. 8]. The idea of the proof is to use a general path order [9] that employs the following interpretations of the function symbols in $\mathcal{H}$ into the ordinals:

$$[\![g(x,y)]\!] := \omega^{[\![x]\!]} + [\![y]\!] \qquad\qquad [\![h(x,z)]\!] := [\![x]\!] + [\![z]\!]$$
$$[\![d(x,z)]\!] := \mathsf{pred}_{[\![z]\!]}([\![x]\!]) \qquad\qquad [\![e(x)]\!] := [\![x]\!]$$
$$[\![S(x)]\!] := [\![x]\!] + 1 \qquad\qquad [\![0]\!] := 1 \; .$$

The operator pred_ζ is conceived as a suitable extension of the operator α_ζ for $\zeta < \omega$; that is, we can assume $\mathsf{pred}_n(\alpha) = \alpha_n$.

One prerequisite to employ a general path order successfully is that, for all ground instances $l\sigma \to r\sigma$ of rules in $\mathcal{H}$, $[\![l\sigma]\!] \geqslant [\![r\sigma]\!]$ holds. However, by definition, we have

$$[\![d(0,0)]\!] = [\![d]\!](1,1) = 1_1 = 0 \; ,$$

and therefore

$$[\![d(g(d(0,0),d(0,0)),0)]\!] = [\![d]\!]([\![g]\!]([\![d(0,0)]\!], [\![d(0,0)]\!]), 1)$$
$$= [\![d]\!](1,1)$$
$$= 0 < 1 = [\![g(e(d(0,0)),d(d(0,0),0))]\!] \; .$$

Unfortunately, $d(g(d(0,0),d(0,0)),0) \to g(e(d(0,0)),d(d(0,0),0))$ is an instance of rule (3).

Although this problem can be relatively easily rectified, there is a more serious problem with the proposed interpretation $[\![\cdot]\!]$. This interpretation is employed as one of the component functions of the general path order; to infer termination, these component functions (and hence the interpretation $[\![\cdot]\!]$) should be weakly monotone.

However, the interpretation function $[\![d]\!]$ is not weakly monotone in its first argument: Consider two hydræ $a = g(0,d(0,0))$ and $b = g(d(0,0),g(d(0,0), g(d(0,0),0)))$ with ordinal values $[\![a]\!] = \omega$ and $[\![b]\!] = 4$, respectively. Clearly $\omega > 4$ in the usual comparison of (set-theoretic) ordinals. But,

$$[\![d(a,0)]\!] = [\![d]\!](\omega,1) = \mathsf{pred}_1(\omega) = 1 < 3 = \mathsf{pred}_1(4) = [\![d]\!](4,1) = [\![d(b,0)]\!] \; .$$

Strictly speaking, one only needs monotonicity for terms that can rewrite to each other, that is, $f_\mathcal{A}(\ldots x \ldots) > f_\mathcal{A}(\ldots y \ldots)$ when $x > y$ and $x \to_\mathcal{R} y$; cf. [9, Thm. 2]. (Here $\mathcal{A}$ denotes an $\mathcal{F}$-algebra.) But consider rule (4) instantiated as follows:

$$x = d(g(g(0,d(0,0)),0),S(b)) \to g(d(g(0,d(0,0)),S(b)),d(g(0,d(0,0)),b)) = y \; ,$$

where b is defined as above. Then $[\![g(g(0,d(0,0)),0)]\!] = [\![g]\!](\omega,1) = \omega^\omega + 1$ with $[\![g(0,d(0,0))]\!] = \omega$. Hence $[\![x]\!] = [\![d]\!](\omega^\omega + 1, 5) = \omega^\omega > \omega^5 + 4 = [\![g]\!](\mathsf{pred}_5(\omega), \mathsf{pred}_4(\omega)) = [\![y]\!]$ and thus *both* assumptions are fulfilled with respect to x and y; unfortunately $\mathsf{pred}_1(\omega^\omega) = \omega < \omega^5 + 3 = \mathsf{pred}_1(\omega^5 + 4)$. Proceeding in the same way as above, we again derive a counterexample.

To overcome this problem, we introduce (in the next section) a notation system for ordinals and use it, instead, as the domain of our interpretation functions.

7   In Preparation

Following an approach taken by Gaisi Takeuti [32], we introduce an alternate notation for ordinals below ϵ_0. This notation will enjoy the desired weak monotonicity property. We define a subset OT of terms over the signature $\{\omega, +\}$. (The
function symbol ω is unary; the symbol $+$ is varyadic.) We write ω^α for $\omega(\alpha)$.
In the definition of OT, we make use of an auxiliary subset P $\subset$ OT.

Definition 3. *The definition of* OT *and* P *proceeds by mutual induction:*

1. $0 \in$ OT
2. If $\alpha_1, \ldots, \alpha_m \in$ P, then $\alpha_1 + \cdots + \alpha_m \in$ OT.
3. If $\alpha \in$ OT, then $\omega^\alpha \in$ P, and $\omega^\alpha \in$ OT.

The elements of OT *are called* ordinal terms *and are denoted by lower-case Greek
letters. If no confusion can arise, we simply speak of* ordinals.

To simplify reading, we abbreviate the term ω^0 by 1. For the remainder of this
section, the expression "ordinal" will always refer to an element of OT, unless
stated otherwise.

It follows from the definition of the set OT that any object in OT different
from 0 can be written in the following form:

$$\omega^{\alpha_1} + \omega^{\alpha_2} + \cdots + \omega^{\alpha_n} , \tag{12}$$

where each of the $\alpha_1, \ldots, \alpha_n$ has the same property.[6] However, due to the above
definition, $\alpha + 0$ is *not* an ordinal, as $0 \notin$ P. To cure this, we introduce a binary
operation $+$ on OT: Let $\alpha, \beta \in$ OT be of form $\omega^{\alpha_1} + \cdots + \omega^{\alpha_n}$, $\beta = \omega^{\beta_1} + \cdots + \omega^{\beta_m}$.
Then $\alpha + \beta$ is defined as $\omega^{\alpha_1} + \cdots + \omega^{\alpha_n} + \omega^{\beta_1} + \cdots + \omega^{\beta_m}$. Otherwise, we
define $\alpha + 0 = 0 + \alpha = \alpha$. We will not distinguish between the binary operation
$+$ and its varyadic rendering.

Definition 4 (Takeuti [32]). *We inductively define an equivalence $\sim$ and a
partial order $\succ$ so that they satisfy the following clauses:*

1. 0 is the minimal element of $\succ$.
*2. For $\alpha \in$ OT of form (12), assume α contains two consecutive terms ω^{α_i} and
$\omega^{\alpha_{i+1}}$ with $\alpha_{i+1} \succ \alpha_i$. So, α has the form*

$$\cdots + \omega^{\alpha_i} + \omega^{\alpha_{i+1}} + \ldots .$$

*Let β be obtained by removing the expression "$\omega^{\alpha_i} + $" from α, so that β is
of the form*

$$\cdots + \omega^{\alpha_{i+1}} + \ldots .$$

Then $\alpha \sim \beta$.

---

[6] This would not hold had we defined OT to be the set of terms over the signature
$\{\omega, +\}$.

3. *Suppose $\alpha = \omega^{\alpha_1} + \cdots + \omega^{\alpha_m}$, $\beta = \omega^{\beta_1} + \cdots + \omega^{\beta_n}$, $\alpha_1 \succcurlyeq \alpha_2 \succcurlyeq \cdots \succcurlyeq \alpha_m$, and $\beta_1 \succcurlyeq \beta_2 \succcurlyeq \cdots \succcurlyeq \beta_n$, hold. ($\alpha \succcurlyeq \beta$ means $\alpha \succ \beta$ or $\alpha \sim \beta$.) Then, $\alpha \succ \beta$ if either $\alpha_i \succ \beta_i$ for some $i \in [1, m]$ and $\alpha_j \sim \beta_j$ for all $j \in [1, i-1]$, or $m > n$ and $\alpha_i \sim \beta_i$ holds for all $i \in [1, n]$.*

Remark 3. Note that ordinal addition $+$ is not commutative, not even up to the equivalence $\sim$, as we have $1 + \omega \sim \omega \not\sim \omega + 1$.   □

We can identify the natural numbers $\mathbf{N}$ with the ordinals less than ω, as the usual comparison of natural numbers coincides with the above partial order $\succ$ on ordinal terms less than ω. So, we freely write $1 + 1$ as 2, $1 + 1 + 1$ as 3, and so on. By definition, for any $\alpha > 0$ in OT, there exists a unique $\beta \in$ OT with $\alpha \sim \beta$ so that β can be written as

$$\omega^{\beta_1} + \omega^{\beta_2} + \cdots + \omega^{\beta_n} \qquad \text{with } \beta_1 \succcurlyeq \cdots \succcurlyeq \beta_n , \tag{13}$$

where $\beta_1 \succcurlyeq \cdots \succcurlyeq \beta_n$. If β is written in this way, we say that it is in *normal-form*. The set of all ordinal terms in normal-form together with 0 is denoted NF. The unique normal-form of a given ordinal term α is denoted NF(α).

Remark 4. Note that our definition of the ordinal notation system OT is non-standard. Usually one identifies $\alpha \in$ OT and its normal-form NF(α) and instead of $\sim$ simply the equality $=$ is written.

Any $\alpha \in$ NF uniquely represents a set-theoretic ordinals in CNF. The following lemma is immediate:

Lemma 6

1. *The relation $\succ$ is a linear partial order on* NF.
2. *The relation $\succ$ is well-founded and* otype($\succ$) $= \epsilon_0$.

We extend the well-founded, linear order $\succ$ on NF to a well-founded, partial order $\succ$ on OT. To simplify notation we denote the extended relation with the same symbol, no confusion will arise from this. For $\alpha, \beta \in$ OT define: $\alpha \succ \beta$, if NF(α) $\succ$ NF(β). It follows that $\succ$ is a partial order and that $\alpha \succcurlyeq \beta \succ \gamma$ and $\alpha \succ \beta \succcurlyeq \gamma$ each imply $\alpha \succ \gamma$. The next lemma is a direct consequence of the definitions; we essentially employ the fact that NF($\alpha + \beta$) = NF(NF(α) + NF(β)).

Lemma 7. *Let $\alpha, \beta, \gamma \in$ OT.*

1. $\alpha + \beta \succcurlyeq \alpha, \beta$.
2. $\omega^\alpha \succ \alpha$.
3. *If $\alpha \succ \beta$, then $\omega^\alpha \succ \omega^\beta$.*
4. *If $\alpha \succ \beta$, then $\gamma + \alpha \succ \gamma + \beta$ and $\alpha + \gamma \succcurlyeq \beta + \gamma$.*
5. *If $\alpha \in$ P and $\alpha \succ \beta, \gamma$, then $\alpha \succ \beta + \gamma$.*

The central idea of the above notation system is the separation of the identity of ordinal terms (denoted by $=$) and the identity of their set-theoretic counterparts (denoted by $\sim$). We will see in the next section that this pedantry is essential for a successful definition of the interpretation functions.

Based on $\succ$ and $\sim$, we define a partial order $\sqsupset$ and an equivalence relation $\equiv$ on OT. We write $N(\alpha)$ to denote the number of occurrences of ω in α. Note that $N(n) = n$ for any natural number n, since $1 = \omega^0$.

Definition 5. *Let* $\alpha, \beta \in$ OT. *We set:*

1. $\alpha \sqsupset \beta$ *if* $\alpha \succ \beta$, $N(\alpha) \geqslant N(\beta)$ *or* $\alpha \sim \beta$, $N(\alpha) > N(\beta)$ *and*
2. $\alpha \equiv \beta$ *if* $\alpha \sim \beta$, $N(\alpha) = N(\beta)$.

Define the quasi-order $\sqsupset^\equiv$: $\alpha \sqsupset^\equiv \beta$, *if* $\alpha \ (\sqsupset \cup \equiv) \ \beta$.

Example 3. Consider $\omega + \omega^2$ and $\omega + 3$. Then $\omega + \omega^2 \sqsupset \omega + 3$, as $\mathsf{NF}(\omega + \omega^2) = \omega^2 \succ \omega + 3 = \mathsf{NF}(\omega + 3)$ and $N(\omega + \omega^2) = 5 = N(\omega + 3)$. On the other hand, $\omega^2 \not\sqsupset \omega + 3$ as $N(\omega + 3) = 5 > 3 = N(\omega^2)$. □

This example shows that the relation $\sim$ is not compatible with the strict order $\sqsupset$.

Lemma 8. *The binary relation* $\sqsupset$ *is a well-founded order and* $\mathrm{otype}(\sqsupset) \leq \epsilon_0$. *Furthermore, for all* $n, m \in \mathbf{N}$, $n \sqsupset m$ *iff* $n > m$.

Proof. That $\sqsupset$ is a partial order is immediate from the definition. To verify that $\sqsupset$ is well-founded with $\mathrm{otype}(\sqsupset) \leq \epsilon_0$, it suffices to define an embedding $o\colon$ OT $\rightarrow$ CNF: $o(\alpha) := \omega^{\mathsf{NF}(\alpha)} + N(\alpha)$. By case analysis on the definition of $\sqsupset$, one verifies that for all $\alpha, \beta \in$ OT, $\alpha \sqsupset \beta$ implies $o(\alpha) > o(\beta)$. Assume first that $\alpha \succ \beta$ and $N(\alpha) \geqslant N(\beta)$. Then, $\omega^{\mathsf{NF}(\alpha)} + N(\alpha) > \omega^{\mathsf{NF}(\beta)} + N(\beta)$ is immediate from the definition of the comparison $>$ of set-theoretic ordinals. Now assume $\alpha \sim \beta$ and $N(\alpha) > N(\beta)$. Then, $\omega^{\mathsf{NF}(\alpha)} + N(\alpha) > \omega^{\mathsf{NF}(\beta)} + N(\beta)$ follows similarly.

The second half of the lemma is a direct result of the definition of $\sqsupset$ and the definition of N. □

The following is again a direct consequence of the definitions:

Lemma 9. *Let* $\alpha, \beta, \gamma \in$ OT.

1. *If* $\alpha \sqsupset \beta$, *then* $\omega^\alpha \sqsupset \omega^\beta$.
2. *If* $\alpha \sqsupset \beta$, *then* $\gamma + \alpha \sqsupset \gamma + \beta$ *and* $\alpha + \gamma \sqsupset^\equiv \beta + \gamma$.
3. $\alpha + \beta \sqsupset^\equiv \alpha, \gamma$.
4. $\omega^\alpha \sqsupset \alpha$.

Let $p\colon \mathbf{N} \times \mathbf{N} \rightarrow \mathbf{N}$ denote a fixed polynomial, strictly monotone in each argument.

Definition 6 (Predecessor). *We define the set of n-predecessors of α induced by p. Let $\alpha \in$ OT. Then*

$$\alpha[n] := \{\beta \mid \alpha \succ \beta \text{ and } p(\mathsf{N}(\alpha), n) \geqslant \mathsf{N}(\beta)\} \ .$$

The notion of an n-predecessor stems from [12]. However, we follow the idea of norm-based fundamental sequences; cf. [4].

Lemma 10. *Let $\alpha \in$ OT and let δ denote a $\sqsupset$-maximal element of $\alpha[n]$.*

1. *The set $\alpha[n]$ is finite.*
2. *For each $\beta \in \alpha[n]$: $\delta \sqsupset^{\equiv} \beta$.*

Proof. The first assertion is trivial. For the second, observe that it follows from the definition of δ that for all $\beta \in \alpha[n]$, either $\delta \sqsupset \beta$, $\beta \equiv \delta$, or β and δ are incomparable with respect to $\sqsupset$. We prove that the last case can never happen. We assume $\alpha > 0$, as otherwise the assertion follows trivially. Let $\beta \in \alpha[n]$ be arbitrary but fixed, so that β, δ are incomparable.

The ordinals β and δ can only be incomparable if either of the following cases holds: (i) $\delta \prec \beta$ and $\mathsf{N}(\beta) < \mathsf{N}(\delta)$, or (ii) $\delta \succ \beta$ and $\mathsf{N}(\beta) > \mathsf{N}(\delta)$. As the cases are dual, it suffices to consider the first one. Assume $\beta \in \mathbf{N}$, then $\delta \in \mathbf{N}$ and $\mathsf{N}(\beta) = \beta \succ \delta = \mathsf{N}(\delta)$, which contradicts the assumption $\mathsf{N}(\delta) > \mathsf{N}(\beta)$. Hence, we can assume $\beta \not\succcurlyeq \omega$.

We define an ordinal term β^* as follows: $\beta^* := (\mathsf{N}(\delta) - \mathsf{N}(\beta)) + \beta$. As $\beta \not\succcurlyeq \omega$, $\beta^* \sim \beta$ holds. Furthermore, $\mathsf{N}(\beta^*) = \mathsf{N}(\delta) > \mathsf{N}(\beta)$, as $\mathsf{N}(\beta^*) = (\mathsf{N}(\delta) - \mathsf{N}(\beta)) + \mathsf{N}(\beta) = \mathsf{N}(\delta)$. So, $\beta^* \sqsupset \beta$. We show that $\beta^* \in \alpha[n]$: $\alpha \succ \beta \sim \beta^*$ implies $\alpha \succ \beta^*$. And $p(\mathsf{N}(\alpha), n) \geqslant \mathsf{N}(\delta) = \mathsf{N}(\beta^*)$ implies $p(\mathsf{N}(\alpha), n) \geqslant \mathsf{N}(\beta^*)$. We derive a contradiction to the assumption that δ is $\sqsupset$-maximal. $\square$

By the above lemma a $\sqsupset$-maximal element of $\alpha[n]$ is, up to the equivalence $\equiv$, unique. In the following, for each $\alpha \in$ OT and each $n \in \mathbf{N}$, we fix an arbitrary $\sqsupset$-maximal element and denote it with $P_n(\alpha)$.

Lemma 11. *Let $\alpha \in$ OT and suppose $\alpha \succcurlyeq \omega$. Then $\mathsf{N}(P_n(\alpha)) = p(\mathsf{N}(\alpha), n)$.*

Proof. The proof follows the pattern of the proof of the previous lemma. $\square$

The following lemma explains why the pedantry in the definition of the set of ordinal terms OT and the given definition of the partial order $\sqsupset$ is necessary:

Lemma 12. *Let $\alpha, \beta \in$ OT, $n \in \mathbf{N}$.*

1. *If $\alpha, \beta > 0$ and $\alpha \sqsupset \beta$, then $P_n(\alpha) \sqsupset P_n(\beta)$.*
2. *If $\alpha \equiv \beta$, then $P_n(\alpha) \equiv P_n(\beta)$.*
3. *Suppose $m > n$. Then $P_m(\alpha) \sqsupset^{\equiv} P_n(\alpha)$.*

We want to emphasize that the first property fails for the specific fundamental sequence $(\alpha_n)_{n \in \mathbf{N}}$ employed in the definition of the standard Hydra Battle; cf. Definition 1: We have $\omega > m$, but $\omega_n = n \not\succ m - 1 = (m)_n$ for any $m > n$.

Proof (of the lemma). We only show the first point; the arguments for the other points are similar, but simpler. Assume $\alpha \sqsupseteq \beta$. First, we show the lemma for the special-case, where $\alpha \in \mathbf{N}$. This assumption implies $\beta \in \mathbf{N}$. Hence, $P_n(\alpha) = \alpha - 1 \sqsupseteq \beta - 1 = P_n(\beta)$. Consider the case $\alpha \succcurlyeq \omega$. We proceed by cases, according to the definition of $\sqsupseteq$:

1. SUBCASE $\alpha \succ \beta$ and $\mathsf{N}(\alpha) \geqslant \mathsf{N}(\beta)$: Then monotonicity of p implies that $p(\mathsf{N}(\alpha), n) \geqslant \mathsf{N}(\beta)$ holds. Thus, $\beta \in \alpha[n]$. By Lemma 10(2), we conclude $P_n(\alpha) \succcurlyeq \beta \succ P_n(\beta)$, which implies $P_n(\alpha) \succ P_n(\beta)$. By Lemma 11, we get: $\mathsf{N}(P_n(\alpha)) = p(\mathsf{N}(\alpha), n) \geqslant p(\mathsf{N}(\beta), n) \geqslant \mathsf{N}(P_n(\beta))$. In summary, we see $P_n(\alpha) \sqsupseteq P_n(\beta)$.

2. SUBCASE $\alpha \sim \beta$ and $\mathsf{N}(\alpha) > \mathsf{N}(\beta)$: From the assumptions we conclude $P_n(\beta) \in \alpha[n]$, as $\alpha \sim \beta \succ P_n(\beta)$ and $p(\mathsf{N}(\alpha), n) > p(\mathsf{N}(\beta), n) \geqslant \mathsf{N}(P_n(\beta))$. Hence, Lemma 10 implies $P_n(\alpha) \sqsupseteq P_n(\beta)$ or $P_n(\alpha) \equiv P_n(\beta)$. If the former case holds, the lemma is established. Assume the latter. By definition of $\equiv$, we see that $\mathsf{N}(P_n(\alpha)) = \mathsf{N}(P_n(\beta))$. On the other hand, we obtain: $\mathsf{N}(P_n(\alpha)) = p(\mathsf{N}(\alpha), n) > p(\mathsf{N}(\beta), n) \geqslant \mathsf{N}(P_n(\beta))$. We have derived a contradiction. □

8   Termination

The purpose of this section is to prove Theorem 5. Based on the construction given below, it is easy to see how to also prove Theorem 4; hence, we leave that one to the reader.

8.1   Interpretation

Using the ordinal notation of the previous section, the termination proof is relatively simple. Let $\mathcal{F}$ denote the signature of System $\mathcal{D}$. We define the $\mathcal{F}$-algebra $(\mathcal{A}, \rhd)$ and provide a proof that $\mathcal{A}$ is well-founded, which is easy, but – more significantly – $\mathcal{A}$ is weakly monotone. The domain of $\mathcal{A}$ is the set

$$\{(\alpha, 1) \mid \alpha \in \mathsf{OT}\} \cup \{(0, 0)\} \, .$$

We define the quasi-order $\unrhd$ on the pairs as follows:

$$(\alpha, a) \unrhd (\beta, b) \quad \text{iff} \quad (\alpha \sqsupseteq^{\equiv} \beta \wedge a = b = 1) \text{ or } (\alpha \sqsupseteq^{\equiv} \beta \wedge a > b) \, .$$

The following operations interpret the elements of $\mathcal{F}$:

$$\mathsf{d}_{\mathcal{A}} : \qquad (\alpha, a), (\beta, b) \mapsto (P_{\mathsf{N}(\beta)}(\alpha), 1) \qquad\qquad \alpha \neq 0$$
$$(0, a), (\beta, b) \mapsto (0, 0)$$

$$\mathsf{h}_{\mathcal{A}} : \qquad (\alpha, a), (\beta, b) \mapsto (0, 0)$$

$$g_{\mathcal{A}} : \qquad (\alpha, 1), (\beta, b) \mapsto (\beta + \omega^{\alpha}, 1)$$
$$(0, 0), (\beta, b) \mapsto (0, 0)$$

$$e_{\mathcal{A}} : \qquad (\alpha, a) \mapsto (\alpha, 1)$$

$$S_{\mathcal{A}} : \qquad (\alpha, a) \mapsto (\alpha + 1, 1)$$

$$0_{\mathcal{A}} : \qquad (0, 1)$$

Define the strict order $\blacktriangleright$ by replacing $\sqsupseteq^{=}$ by $\succ$ in the above definition. The orders $\trianglerighteq$ and $\blacktriangleright$ naturally extend to terms, denoted $\trianglerighteq_{\mathcal{A}}$ and $\blacktriangleright_{\mathcal{A}}$, respectively. Fix the parameter in the definition of n-predecessors:

$$p(m, n) := (m + 1) \cdot (n + 1) .$$

Let $\triangleright$ denote the partial order induced by the quasi-order $\trianglerighteq$. With the help of Lemma 12, the following is not difficult to prove.

Lemma 13. *The $\mathcal{F}$-algebra $(\mathcal{A}, \triangleright)$ is weakly monotone and well-founded.*

Lemma 14. *For each rule $l \rightarrow r$ in $\mathcal{D}$, we have $l \trianglerighteq_{\mathcal{A}} r$, that is, $\mathcal{A}$ is a quasi-model of $\mathcal{D}$.*

Proof. We consider only the rules (8) and (10), as it is easy to check the properties for the other rules.

1. CASE $d(g(x, y), z) \rightarrow g(d(x, z), e(y))$: We have to show

$$d_{\mathcal{A}}(g_{\mathcal{A}}((\alpha, a), (\beta, b)), (\gamma, c)) \trianglerighteq g_{\mathcal{A}}(d_{\mathcal{A}}((\alpha, a), (\gamma, c)), e_{\mathcal{A}}((\beta, b))) .$$

One of the following subcases holds (i) $\alpha > 0$ (ii) $\alpha = 0$. We may assume subcase (i) holds. Assume otherwise; then it is not hard to see that the right-hand side of the above equation rewrites to $(0, 0)$. From this the claim follows easily.
Accordingly, we obtain

$$d_{\mathcal{A}}(g_{\mathcal{A}}((\alpha, 1), (\beta, b)), (\gamma, c)) = (P_n(\beta + \omega^{\alpha}), 1) \trianglerighteq$$
$$\trianglerighteq (\beta + \omega^{P_n(\alpha)}, 1) = g_{\mathcal{A}}(d_{\mathcal{A}}((\alpha, 1), (\gamma, c)), e_{\mathcal{A}}((\beta, b))) ,$$

for $n = N(\gamma)$. We have to show that $P_n(\beta + \omega^{\alpha}) \sqsupseteq^{=} \beta + \omega^{P_n(\alpha)}$. By Lemma 7, we obtain $\beta + \omega^{\alpha} \succ \beta + \omega^{P_n(\alpha)}$. By definition of the polynomial p and the norm-function N, and Lemma 12 it suffices to observe:

$$(N(\beta + \omega^{\alpha}) + 1)(n + 1) = (N(\beta) + N(\alpha) + 2)(n + 1) \geqslant$$
$$\geqslant N(\beta) + 1 + (N(\alpha) + 1)(n + 1) \geqslant N(\beta + \omega^{P_n(\alpha)}) .$$

2. CASE $d(g(g(0,x),y),S(z)) \to g(e(x),d(g(g(0,x),y),z))$: We show

$$d_{\mathcal{A}}(g_{\mathcal{A}}(g_{\mathcal{A}}(0_{\mathcal{A}},(\alpha,a)),(\beta,b)),S_{\mathcal{A}}((\gamma,c))) \trianglerighteq$$
$$\trianglerighteq g_{\mathcal{A}}(e_{\mathcal{A}}((\alpha,a)),d_{\mathcal{A}}(g_{\mathcal{A}}(g_{\mathcal{A}}(0_{\mathcal{A}},(\alpha,a)),(\beta,b)),(\gamma,c))) ,$$

for all $(\alpha,a),(\beta,b),(\gamma,c) \in \mathcal{A}$. By definition, the left-hand side rewrites to

$$(P_{\mathsf{N}(\gamma+1)}(\beta+\omega^{\alpha+1}),1) ,$$

while the right side becomes

$$(P_{\mathsf{N}(\gamma)}(\beta+\omega^{\alpha+1})+\omega^{\alpha},1) ,$$

and we have to show $P_{\mathsf{N}(\gamma)+1}(\beta+\omega^{\alpha+1}) \sqsupseteq^{\equiv} P_{\mathsf{N}(\gamma)}(\beta+\omega^{\alpha+1})+\omega^{\alpha}$. By Definition 6 and Lemma 7(5) we obtain:

$$\beta+\omega^{\alpha+1} \succ P_{\mathsf{N}(\gamma)}(\beta+\omega^{\alpha+1})+\omega^{\alpha} .$$

Therefore, it suffices to show

$$(\mathsf{N}(\beta+\omega^{\alpha+1})+1)(\mathsf{N}(\gamma)+2) \geqslant \mathsf{N}(P_{\mathsf{N}(\gamma)}(\beta+\omega^{\alpha+1})+\omega^{\alpha}) ,$$

which follows by a simply calculation:

$$(\mathsf{N}(\beta+\omega^{\alpha+1})+1)(n+2) \geqslant (\mathsf{N}(\beta+\omega^{\alpha+1})+1)(n+1)+\mathsf{N}(\omega^{\alpha+1}) \geqslant$$
$$\geqslant \mathsf{N}(P_n(\beta+\omega^{\alpha+1})+\omega^{\alpha}) ,$$

with $n = \mathsf{N}(\gamma)$. $\qquad\square$

8.2   Dependencies

Finally, we are in position to prove Theorem 5, and employ a specific variant of the dependency-pair method of [1]. (This choice of method is not critical; equivalently, a proof by induction upto ϵ_0 could be given, or some other method employed.)

To keep this paper more-or-less self-contained, we first recall some basic definitions and lemmas. We write $\lhd$ to denote the proper subterm relation and $\unrhd$ for (not necessarily proper) superterm. Let $\mathcal{R}$ be some rewrite system and denote the set of all minimal non-terminating terms by $\mathcal{T}_\infty$ (minimal in the sense of the subterm relation).

Lemma 15. *For every term $t \in \mathcal{T}_\infty$ there exist a rewrite rule $l \to r \in \mathcal{R}$, a substitution σ, and a non-variable subterm u of r, such that $t \xrightarrow[\mathcal{R}]{\text{not top} \,*} l\sigma \xrightarrow[\mathcal{R}]{\text{top}} r\sigma \unrhd u\sigma$ and $u\sigma \in \mathcal{T}_\infty$.*

By the lemma, it is not difficult to see that any term in $\mathcal{T}_\infty$ has a defined root symbol. This, we exploit in the next definition.

Let $\mathcal{R}$ be a rewriting system over a signature $\mathcal{F}$. Let $\hat{f}$ denote a fresh function symbol with the same arity as $f \in \mathcal{F}$ and let $\hat{t}$ denote $\hat{f}(t_1, \ldots, t_n)$, for term $t = f(t_1, \ldots, t_n)$. The set $\mathsf{DP}(\mathcal{R})$ of *dependency pairs* is defined as follows:

$$\mathsf{DP}(\mathcal{R}) := \{\hat{l} \to \hat{u} \mid l \to r \in \mathcal{R}, r \trianglerighteq u \ntriangleleft l, \text{root of } u \text{ defined}\} \ .$$

The nodes of the *dependency graph* $\mathsf{DG}(\mathcal{R})$, for rewrite system $\mathcal{R}$, are the dependency pairs of $\mathcal{R}$ and there is an arrow from $s \to t$ to $u \to v$ if and only if there exist substitutions σ and ρ such that $t\sigma \to_{\mathcal{R}} u\rho$. A *dp-cycle* is a nonempty subset $\mathcal{C}$ of dependency pairs of $\mathsf{DP}(\mathcal{R})$ if for every two (not necessarily distinct) pairs $s \to t$ and $u \to v$ in $\mathcal{C}$ there exists a nonempty path in $\mathcal{C}$ between them. By the above lemma and employing the notion of dependency graph, nontermination of $\mathcal{R}$ implies the existence of an infinite sequence of the following form:

$$t_1 \to_{\mathcal{R}}^* t_2 \to_{\mathcal{C}} t_3 \to_{\mathcal{R}}^* t_4 \to_{\mathcal{C}} t_5 \cdots ,$$

where $t_i \in \{\hat{t} \mid t \in \mathcal{T}_\infty\}$, $\mathcal{C} \subseteq \mathsf{DG}(\mathcal{R})$ and the rules in $\mathcal{C}$ are applied infinitely often. Such a sequence is called $\mathcal{C}$-*minimal*. Thus, to prove termination it suffices to verify that no such sequences can exist.

Theorem 6 (Arts & Giesl [1]). *A finite term-rewriting system $\mathcal{R}$ is terminating if no $\mathcal{C}$-minimal sequence exists for any dp-cycle in $\mathsf{DG}(\mathcal{R})$.*

An *argument filtering* is a mapping ρ that associates with every function symbol either an argument position or a list of argument positions. The signature $\mathcal{F}_\rho$ contains m-ary function symbols f^ρ for any $f \in \mathcal{F}$ with $\rho(f) = [i_1, \ldots, i_m]$. The mapping ρ naturally gives rise to a function $\rho \colon \mathcal{T}(\mathcal{F}, \mathcal{V}) \to \mathcal{T}(\mathcal{F}_\rho, \mathcal{V})$.

Theorem 7 (Arts, Giesl & Ohlebusch [16]). *Let $\mathcal{R}$ be a term-rewriting system and $\mathcal{C}$ be a dp-cycle in $\mathsf{DG}(\mathcal{R})$. If there exists an argument filtering and a reduction pair $(\gtrsim, >)$ such that $\rho(\mathcal{R}) \subseteq \gtrsim$, $\rho(\mathcal{C}) \subseteq \gtrsim \cup >$, and $\rho(\mathcal{C}) \cap > \neq \emptyset$, then there are no $\mathcal{C}$-minimal rewrite sequences.*

8.3 Reduction

The proof depends on the following:

Lemma 16. *The pair $(\trianglerighteq_\mathcal{A}, \blacktriangleright_\mathcal{A})$ forms a reduction pair.*

Proof. One has to show that $\trianglerighteq_\mathcal{A}$ is a quasi-order that is closed under $\mathcal{F}$-operations and substitutions, that $\blacktriangleright_\mathcal{A}$ is well-founded and closed under substitutions, and – finally – that $\trianglerighteq_\mathcal{A} \circ \blacktriangleright_\mathcal{A} \subseteq \blacktriangleright_\mathcal{A}$. The first two items follow directly from the definitions. Therefore, we only have to verify that, for all $(\alpha, a), (\beta, b), (\gamma, c) \in \mathcal{A}$, if $(\alpha, a) \trianglerighteq (\beta, b) \blacktriangleright (\gamma, c)$, then also $(\alpha, a) \blacktriangleright (\gamma, c)$.

Without loss of generality, assume $a = b = c = 1$: Assume otherwise, then $a = b = c = 0$ is impossible, as $(\beta, 0) \blacktriangleright (\gamma, 0)$ cannot hold. Hence, the only possibility is $a = b = 1$ and $c = 0$. But, by definition of $\mathcal{A}$, this implies $\gamma = 0$ and clearly $(\alpha, 1) \blacktriangleright (0, 0)$.

Given that $a = b = c = 1$ holds, the assumption specializes to $\alpha \sqsupset^= \beta \succ \gamma$. We proceed by case analysis on $\alpha \sqsupset^= \beta$. Either $\alpha \succ \beta$ and $\mathsf{N}(\alpha) \geqslant \mathsf{N}(\beta)$ or $\alpha \sim \beta$ and $\mathsf{N}(\alpha) \geqslant \mathsf{N}(\beta)$. In both cases, $\alpha \succcurlyeq \beta$ holds. Hence, by transitivity of $\succ$, $\alpha \succ \gamma$ follows. □

Proof (of Theorem 5). Consider the dependency pairs of $\mathcal{D}$:

$$\widehat{\mathsf{h}}(\mathsf{e}(x), y) \to \widehat{\mathsf{h}}(\mathsf{d}(x, y), \mathsf{S}(y)) \tag{14}$$

$$\widehat{\mathsf{h}}(\mathsf{e}(x), y) \to \widehat{\mathsf{d}}(x, y) \tag{15}$$

$$\widehat{\mathsf{d}}(\mathsf{g}(\mathsf{g}(0, x), y), \mathsf{S}(z)) \to \widehat{\mathsf{g}}(\mathsf{e}(x), \mathsf{d}(\mathsf{g}(\mathsf{g}(0, x), y), z)) \tag{16}$$

$$\widehat{\mathsf{d}}(\mathsf{g}(\mathsf{g}(0, x), y), \mathsf{S}(z)) \to \widehat{\mathsf{d}}(\mathsf{g}(\mathsf{g}(0, x), y), z) \tag{17}$$

$$\widehat{\mathsf{d}}(\mathsf{g}(x, y), z) \to \widehat{\mathsf{g}}(\mathsf{d}(x, z), \mathsf{e}(y)) \tag{18}$$

$$\widehat{\mathsf{d}}(\mathsf{g}(x, y), z) \to \widehat{\mathsf{d}}(x, z) \tag{19}$$

$$\widehat{\mathsf{g}}(\mathsf{e}(x), \mathsf{e}(y)) \to \widehat{\mathsf{g}}(x, y) \tag{20}$$

We construct the dependency graph $\mathsf{DG}(\mathcal{D})$:

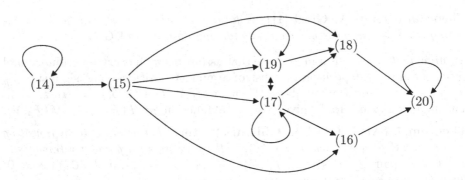

The above interpretation extends to the extra dependency-pair functions $\widehat{f}$ as follows: We set $\widehat{f}_{\mathcal{A}}$ equal to $f_{\mathcal{A}}$, with the exception of $\widehat{\mathsf{h}}$, which we define via

$$\widehat{\mathsf{h}}_{\mathcal{A}}((\alpha, a), (\beta, b)) = (\alpha, a) .$$

Due to Theorems 6 and 7, it suffices to define suitable combinations of argument filterings and reduction pairs for cycles in $\mathsf{DP}(\mathcal{D})$. First, we consider the cycle $\{14\}$ and reduction pair $(\unrhd_{\mathcal{A}}, \blacktriangleright_{\mathcal{A}})$. Due to Lemma 14, it remains to show that

$$\widehat{\mathsf{h}}(\mathsf{e}(x), y) \blacktriangleright \widehat{\mathsf{h}}(\mathsf{d}(x, y), \mathsf{S}(y)) . \tag{21}$$

Let $\mathbf{a} \colon \mathcal{V} \to A$ denote an arbitrary assignment with $[\mathbf{a}]_{\mathcal{A}}(x) = (\alpha, a)$, $[\mathbf{a}]_{\mathcal{A}}(y) = (\beta, b)$. If $\alpha > 0$, then (21) becomes $(\alpha, 1) \blacktriangleright (P_n(\alpha), 1)$, where $n = \mathsf{N}(\beta)$ and we have to show $\alpha \succ P_n(\alpha)$, which is a consequence of Definition 6. Assume otherwise $\alpha = 0$. Then (21) becomes $(0, 1) \rhd (0, 0)$, which follows from the definition of the relation $\blacktriangleright$.

With respect to the remaining dp-cycles, it is easy to see how a suitable combination of argument filterings and reduction pairs should be defined. In particular, note that these cycles can also be handled by applying the subterm criterion iteratively; cf. [20]. $\qquad\square$

9   While Hydra Do

In this section, we convert the functional Hydra program $\mathcal{L}$ into an imperative, **while** program in stages. First, we replace each function with a similarly named procedure call, and the tail-recursive calls with iteration:

procedure $H(x)$:
$n := 0$
while $x \neq \mathtt{nil}$ **do**
$\quad n := n + 1$
$\quad D(n, x)$

procedure $F(n, y, x)$:
for $i := 1$ **to** n **do**
$\quad x := \mathsf{cons}(y, x)$

procedure $D(n, x)$:
$u := \mathsf{car}(x)$
if $u = \mathtt{nil}$
then $x := \mathsf{cdr}(x)$
else if $\mathsf{car}(u) = \mathtt{nil}$
$\quad\quad$ **then** $F(n, \mathsf{cdr}(u), \mathsf{cdr}(x))$
$\quad\quad$ **else** $D(n, u)$
$\quad\quad\quad x := \mathsf{cons}(u, \mathsf{cdr}(x))$

Using a stack s, implemented as a list (pushing via cons, popping via car), for the recursive calls to G, and combining all the procedures (x is the input hydra), we get:

$n := 0$
while $x \neq \mathtt{nil}$ **do**
$\quad n := n + 1$
$\quad u := \mathsf{car}(x)$
$\quad$ **if** $u = \mathtt{nil}$
$\quad$ **then** $x := \mathsf{cdr}(x)$
$\quad$ **else** $s := \mathtt{nil}$
$\quad\quad$ **while** $\mathsf{car}(u) \neq \mathtt{nil}$ **do**
$\quad\quad\quad s := \mathsf{cons}(s, \mathsf{cdr}(x))$
$\quad\quad\quad x := u$
$\quad\quad\quad u := \mathsf{car}(x)$
$\quad\quad$ **for** $i := 1$ **to** n **do**
$\quad\quad\quad x := \mathsf{cons}(\mathsf{cdr}(u), x)$
$\quad\quad$ **while** $s \neq \mathtt{nil}$ **do**
$\quad\quad\quad x := \mathsf{cons}(x, \mathsf{cdr}(s))$
$\quad\quad\quad s := \mathsf{car}(s)$

It is easy to see that the inner loops all terminate. To show that the outer one does, one would need to show that x, qua ordinal, decreases with each outer iteration.

The list operations can be arithmetized by using a pairing function, such as $\mathtt{cons}(x, y) := (x+y+1)^2 + x$. Then $\mathtt{nil} := 0$, $\mathtt{car}(z) := z - \lfloor \sqrt{z} \rfloor^2$, and $\mathtt{cdr}(z) := \lfloor \sqrt{z} \rfloor^2 + \lfloor \sqrt{z} \rfloor - z - 1$. (Any other set of pairing and projection functions would do just as well.) With this in mind, and with a tiny bit of algebraic manipulation, our final, wholly arithmetic, hard-to-prove-terminating **while** program is as follows:

$$n := 0$$
while $x > 0$ **do**
$\quad n := n + 1$
$\quad u := x - \lfloor \sqrt{x} \rfloor^2$
$\quad$ **if** $u = 0$
$\quad$ **then** $x := \lfloor \sqrt{x} \rfloor - 1$
$\quad$ **else** $s := 0$
$\qquad$ **while** $u > \lfloor \sqrt{u} \rfloor^2$ **do**
$\qquad\quad s := s + (s + \lfloor \sqrt{x} \rfloor^2 + \lfloor \sqrt{x} \rfloor - x)^2$
$\qquad\quad x := u$
$\qquad\quad u := x - \lfloor \sqrt{x} \rfloor^2$
$\qquad$ **for** $i := 1$ **to** n **do**
$\qquad\quad x := (\lfloor \sqrt{u} \rfloor + x)^2 + \lfloor \sqrt{u} \rfloor - 1$
$\qquad$ **while** $s > 0$ **do**
$\qquad\quad x := x + (x + \lfloor \sqrt{s} \rfloor^2 + \lfloor \sqrt{s} \rfloor - s)^2$
$\qquad\quad s := s - \lfloor \sqrt{s} \rfloor^2$

Finally, the (integer-valued) truncated square-root $\lfloor \sqrt{z} \rfloor$ can be computed each time by a simple loop, searching for the largest integer whose square is no more than z:

$$n := 0$$
while $x > 0$ **do**
$\quad n := n + 1$
$\quad y := 0;$ **while** $y^2 + 2y \le x$ **do** $y := y + 1$
$\quad$ **if** $x = y^2$
$\quad$ **then** $x := y - 1$
$\quad$ **else** $s := 0$
$\qquad r := 0;$ **while** $r^2 + 2r \le x - y^2$ **do** $r := r + 1$
$\qquad$ **while** $x > y^2 + r^2$ **do**
$\qquad\quad y := 0;$ **while** $y^2 + 2y \le x$ **do** $y := y + 1$
$\qquad\quad s := s + (s + y^2 + y - x)^2$
$\qquad\quad x := x - y^2$
$\qquad\quad r := 0;$ **while** $r^2 + 2r \le x - y^2$ **do** $r := r + 1$
$\qquad$ **for** $i := 1$ **to** n **do** $x := r^2 + r - 1$
$\qquad$ **while** $s > 0$ **do**
$\qquad\quad r := 0;$ **while** $r^2 + 2r \le s$ **do** $r := r + 1$
$\qquad\quad x := x + (x + r^2 + r - s)^2$
$\qquad\quad s := s - r^2$

Further simplifications are possible.

10   The Sky's the Limit

David Gries [18] has averred that for deterministic (or bounded nondeterministic) programs, since the number of steps of any terminating program is just some integer-valued function $t(\bar{x})$ that depends only on the program inputs $\bar{x}$, it is preferable to prove termination by showing "that each execution of the loop body decreases t by at least 1", than to use complicated well-founded orderings. This begs the issue, however, since the proof such a t exists for a program like Hydra requires transfinite induction up to ϵ_0, as we have seen above.

It is not hard to conjure up bigger battles, for example ones in which trees also grow in height. The following one – meant to require Γ_0 – is from [6]:

$$G_n(\bar{x}) \to G_{n+1}(p_n x)$$
$$p_n \langle x, y, z \rangle \to \langle x, \bar{y}, p_n z \rangle$$
$$p_{n+1} \langle A, y, z \rangle \to \langle A, p_{n+1} y, r_n \langle B, \langle A, y, z \rangle, z \rangle \rangle$$
$$p_n \langle x, y, z \rangle \to \bar{y}$$
$$p_n \langle B, y, z \rangle \to r_n \langle B, y, z \rangle$$
$$r_{n+1} \langle B, y, z \rangle \to \langle B, p_{n+1} y, r_n \langle B, y, z \rangle \rangle$$
$$r_n \langle x, y, z \rangle \to \bar{z}$$
$$\langle x, \bar{y}, \bar{z} \rangle \to \overline{\langle x, y, z \rangle}$$

The A nodes are meant to act lexicographically; the B nodes, more like multisets. The bar acts like e of the Hydra system. Regarding the relevance to computer science of the (least) impredicative ordinal Γ_0, see [14].

Moreover, Γ_0 is by no means the end of the games. See [25] for rewrite systems that formalize the Hydra Battle up to the small Veblen ordinal, the maximal order type of the lexicographic path order [8]. Even larger hydras (so called Buchholz Hydræ) have been considered by Wilfried Buchholz [3].

References

1. Arts, T., Giesl, J.: Termination of term rewriting using dependency pairs. Theor. Comput. Sci. 236, 133–178 (2000)
2. Baader, F., Nipkow, T.: Term Rewriting and All That. Cambridge University Press, Cambridge (1998)
3. Buchholz, W.: An independence result for $(\Pi_1^1 - CA) + BI$. Ann. Pure Appl. Logic 33, 131–155 (1987)
4. Buchholz, W., Cichon, E.A., Weiermann, A.: A uniform approach to fundamental sequences and hierarchies. MLQ Math. Log. Q. 40, 273–286 (1994)
5. Dershowitz, N.: Orderings for term-rewriting systems. Theor. Comput. Sci. 17(3), 279–301 (1982)
6. Dershowitz, N.: Trees, ordinals, and termination. In: Gaudel, M.-C., Jouannaud, J.-P. (eds.) CAAP 1993, FASE 1993, and TAPSOFT 1993. LNCS, vol. 668, pp. 243–250. Springer, Heidelberg (1993)

7. Dershowitz, N.: 33 examples of termination. French Spring School of Theoretical Computer Science. In: Comon, H., Jouannaud, J.-P. (eds.) Advanced Course on Term Rewriting. LNCS, vol. 909, pp. 16–26. Springer, Heidelberg (1995)
8. Dershowitz, N., Okada, M.: Proof-theoretic techniques for term rewriting theory. Proceedings of the 3rd Annual Symposium on Logic in Computer Science, pp. 104–111. IEEE (1988)
9. Dershowitz, N., Hoot, C.: Natural termination. Theor. Comput. Sci. 142(2), 179–207 (1995)
10. Dershowitz, N., Jouannaud, J.P.: Rewrite systems. In: van Leeuwen, J. (ed.) Formal Methods and Semantics. Handbook of Theoretical Computer Science, Chap. 6, vol. B, pp. 245–319. Elsevier Science, North-Holland, Amsterdam (1990)
11. Dershowitz, N., Jouannaud, J.-P., Klop, J.W.: Open problems in rewriting. In: Book, R.V. (ed.) Rewriting Techniques and Applications. LNCS, vol. 488, pp. 445–456. Springer, Heidelberg (1991)
12. Fairtlough, M.V.H., Wainer, S.S.: Hierarchies of provably recursive functions. In: Buss, S.R. (ed.) Handbook of Proof Theory, pp. 149–207. Elsevier Science, North-Holland, Amsterdam (1998)
13. Fleischer, R.: Die another day. Proceedings of the 4th International Conference FUN with Algorithms. LNCS, vol. 4475, pp. 146–155. Springer Verlag, Heidelberg (2007), http://www.cs.ust.hk/~rudolf/Paper/hydra_fun07.pdf
14. Gallier, J. H.: What's so special about Kruskal's Theorem and the ordinal Γ_0? A survey of some results in proof theory. Ann. Pure Appl. Logic, 53(3), 199–260 (1991); Erratum, Ann. Pure Appl. Logic 89(2–3), 275 (1997). http://handle.dtic.mil/100.2/ADA290387.
15. Gardner, M.: Mathematical games: Tasks you cannot help finishing no matter how hard you try to block finishing them, Scientific American 24(2),12–21 (Reprinted in Martin Gardner, The Last Recreations) pp. 27–43, Springer Verlag, Heidelberg (1998)
16. Giesl, J., Arts, T., Ohlebusch, E.: Modular termination proofs for rewriting using dependency pairs. J. of Symbolic Computation 34, 21–58 (2002)
17. Goodstein, R.L.: On the restricted ordinal theorem. J. Symbolic Logic 9, 33–41 (1944)
18. Gries, D.: Is sometimes ever better than alway? ACM Transactions on Programming Languages and Systems 0, 258–265 (1979), http://doi.acm.org/10.1145/357073.357080
19. Hemelrijk, J.M., Hydriae, C.: American Journal of Archaeology 89(4), 701–703 (1985)
20. Hirokawa, N., Middeldorp, A.: Dependency pair revisted. In: van Oostrom, V. (ed.) RTA 2004. LNCS, vol. 3091, pp. 249–268. Springer, Heidelberg (2004)
21. Hodgson, B. R.: Herculean or Sisyphean tasks. Newsletter of the European Mathematical Society, vol. 51 (2004)
22. Jech, T.J.: Set Theory. Springer Verlag, Heidelberg (2002)
23. Jouannaud, J.-P.: Proof and computation. In: Schwichtenberg, H. (ed.) NATO series F: Computer and Systems Sciences, vol. 139, pp. 173–218. Springer Verlag, Heidelberg (1995), http://rewriting.loria.fr/documents/rpac.ps.gz
24. Kirby, L., Paris, J.: Accessible independence results for Peano arithmetic. Bull. London Mathematical Society 4, 285–293 (1982)
25. Lepper, I.: Simply terminating rewrite systems with long derivations. Arch. Math. Logic 43, 1–18 (2004)
26. Lescanne, P.(ed.) Rewriting mailing list. (February 19 2004) https://listes.ens-lyon.fr/wws/arc/rewriting,

27. Luccio, F., Pagli, L.: Death of a monster. SIGACT News. 31(4), 130–133 (2000),
    http://doi.acm.org/10.1145/369836.369904
28. Marché, C., Zantema, H.: The termination competition. In: Baader, F. (ed.) RTA
    2007. LNCS, vol. 4553, Springer, Heidelberg (to appear 2007)
29. Moser, G., Weiermann, A.: Relating derivation lengths with the slow-growing hier-
    archy directly. In: Nieuwenhuis, R. (ed.) RTA 2003. LNCS, vol. 2706, pp. 296–310.
    Springer, Heidelberg (2003)
30. Paris, J., Harrington, L.: A mathematical incompleteness in Peano arithmetic. In:
    Barwise, J. (ed.) Handbook for Mathematical Logic, North-Holland, Amsterdam
    (1977)
31. Penn State College of Information Sciences and Technology. CiteSeer Scientific
    Literature Digital Library. http://citeseer.ist.psu.edu.
32. Takeuti, G.: Proof Theory. 2nd edition. North-Holland, Amsterdam (1987)
33. Terese, Bezem, M., Klop, J.W., de Vrijer, R.: Term Rewriting Systems. In: Cam-
    bridge Tracks in Theoretical Computer Science, vol. 55, Cambridge University
    Press, Cambridge (2003)
34. Touzet, H.: Encoding the Hydra battle as a rewrite system. In: Brim, L., Gruska, J.,
    Zlatuška, J. (eds.) MFCS 1998. LNCS, vol. 1450, pp. 267–276. Springer, Heidelberg
    (1998)
35. A. M. Turing.: Checking a large routine. In: Report of a Conference on High Speed
    Automatic Calculating Machines, Univ. Math. Lab. Cambridge, pp. 67-69 (1949).
    Reprinted in Morris, F. L., Jones, C. B.: An early program proof by Alan Turing.
    Annals of the History of Computing, vol. 6, pp. 139–143, (1984)
    http://www.turingarchive.org/browse.php/B/8.
36. Wainer, S.S.: Ordinal recursion, and a refinement of the extended Grzegorezyk
    hierarchy. J. Symbolic Logic 37, 281–292 (1972)

Orderings and Constraints: Theory and Practice of Proving Termination

Cristina Borralleras[1] and Albert Rubio[2],*

[1] Universitat de Vic, Spain
`cristina.borralleras@uvic.es`
[2] Universitat Politècnica de Catalunya, Barcelona, Spain
`rubio@lsi.upc.es`

Abstract. In contrast to the current general way of developing tools for proving termination automatically, this paper intends to show an alternative program based on using on the one hand the theory of term orderings to develop powerful and widely applicable methods and on the other hand constraint based techniques to put them in practice.

In order to show that this program is realizable a constraint-based framework is presented where ordering based methods for term rewriting, including extensions like Associative-Commutative rewriting, Context-Sensitive rewriting or Higher-Order rewriting, as well as the use of rewriting strategies, can be put in practice in a natural way.

1 Introduction

In this paper we show how to translate into a constraint solving problem any termination proof using the *Monotonic Semantic Path Ordering* (MSPO) [BFR00] and its variants for Associative-Commutative (AC) rewriting [BR03], Higher-Order (HO) rewriting [BR01] and Context-Sensitive (CS) rewriting [Bor03]. By using the definition of MSPO a disjunction of constraints is obtained, such that, if any of these constraints can be solved, then the TRS is proved to be terminating.

Our constraints have the same semantics as the ones obtained in the dependency pair method (DP) [AG00], and, in particular, one of the constraints obtained from the definition of the MSPO coincides with the one given by DP method (and it is unclear whether this one is always the best to be solved). Moreover, since both kind of constraints share the same semantics, we can reuse all techniques developed to solve DP constraints like the DP graph or many other further developments [AG00, GTSK04, HM05, GTSKF06].

The framework we propose was first described in [Bor03]. A similar framework for the DP-method was independently proposed in [GTSK04]. These results show that MSPO can be seen as an ordering-based way to understand the DP-method, and that the key point for the success of this method is the use, in

---

* Supported by spanish project LOGICTOOLS, ref. TIN2004-07925.

H. Comon-Lundh et al. (Eds.): Jouannaud Festschrift, LNCS 4600, pp. 28–43, 2007.
© Springer-Verlag Berlin Heidelberg 2007

practice, of ordering constraints, for which a wide variety of sound solvers have been developed.

Additionally, we study the application of our techniques to prove termination of innermost rewriting. In order to reuse our framework, the TRS is modified by adding constraints to the rules, which approximate the restrictions imposed by the strategy. A constrained rule can be applied if the substitution satisfies the constraint. Hence, a TRS is innermost terminating if its constrained version is terminating.

A constrained TRS is terminating if all instances of each constrained rule (i.e. the instances satisfying the constraint) are included in a reduction ordering. Therefore, we can apply MSPO but taking the constraints of the rules into account. This is done by inheriting the constraints when applying MSPO. As a result, we obtain a disjunction of constrained constraints, which, to avoid confusion, will be called *decorated constraints* (note that the constraints coming from the rules are applied to the ordering constraints coming from MSPO). Using these decorated constraints we can cover all techniques applied in the DP method for innermost rewriting. Furthermore, these decorated constraints can be used to store other information which can be relevant for the termination proof. The same ideas applied to the innermost strategy can be applied, as well, to other strategies that can be approximated by means of constrained rules, like, for instance, rewriting with priorities [vdP98].

Finally, we show, as an example, how our framework also extends to the higher-order version of the MSPO, which can also be done for the AC-version and the CS-version.

These results should be seen as a proof of the thesis that developing results at the ordering level and implementing and applying them at the constraint level is an appropriate program to obtain a general purpose tool for proving termination.

Our method has been implemented in a system called *Termptation* which automatically proves termination of rewriting and innermost rewriting. The implementation does not cover any of the extensions of MSPO to associativity-commutativity, higher-order or context-sensitive rewriting, which is planed for future development.

Basic notions and definitions are given in section 2. In sections 3 and 4 we revise the dependency pair method and the monotonic semantic path ordering respectively. Section 5 is devoted to present and apply our constraint framework. In section 6 we adapt our framework to deal with innermost rewriting and in section 7 we consider higher-order rewriting. Some conclusions are given in section 8. An extended version of these results and all proofs can be found in [Bor03].

2   Preliminaries

In the following we consider that $\mathcal{F}$ is a set of function symbols, $\mathcal{X}$ a set of variables and $\mathcal{T}(\mathcal{F}, \mathcal{X})$ is the set of terms built from $\mathcal{F}$ and $\mathcal{X}$. Let s and t be arbitrary terms in $\mathcal{T}(\mathcal{F}, \mathcal{X})$, let f be a function symbol in $\mathcal{F}$ and let σ be a substitution. A (strict partial) ordering $\succ$ is a transitive irreflexive relation. It is *monotonic* if $s \succ t$ implies $f(\ldots s \ldots) \succ f(\ldots t \ldots)$, and *stable under substitution* if $s \succ t$ implies $s\sigma \succ t\sigma$. Monotonic orderings that are stable under substitutions are called *rewrite orderings*. A *reduction ordering* is a rewrite ordering that is *well-founded*: there are no infinite sequences $t_1 \succ t_2 \succ \ldots$

A term rewrite system (TRS) is a (possibly infinite) set of rules $l \to r$ where l and r are terms. Given a TRS R, s rewrites to t with R, denoted by $s \to_R t$, if there is some rule $l \to r$ in R, $s|_p = l\sigma$ for some position p and substitution σ and $t = s[r\sigma]_p$. The defined symbols D are the root symbols of left-hand sides of rules. All other function symbols are called constructors.

A TRS R is terminating if there exists no infinite sequence $t_1 \to_R t_2 \to_R \cdots$ Thus, the transitive closure $\overset{+}{\to}_R$ of any terminating TRS is a reduction ordering. Furthermore, reduction orderings characterize termination of TRSs, i.e. a rewrite system R is terminating if and only if all rules are contained in a reduction ordering $\succ$, i.e., $l \succ r$ for every $l \to r \in R$.

Given a relation $\succ$, the multiset extension of $\succ$ on finite multisets, denoted by $\succ\!\succ$, is defined as the smallest transitive relation containing $X \cup \{s\} \succ\!\succ X \cup \{t_1, \ldots, t_n\}$ if $s \succ t_i$ for all $i \in \{1 \ldots n\}$. If $\succ$ is a well-founded ordering on terms then $\succ\!\succ$ is a well-founded ordering on finite multisets of terms.

A *quasi-ordering* $\succeq$ is a transitive and reflexive binary relation. Its inverse is denoted by $\preceq$. Its *strict part* $\succ$ is the strict ordering $\succeq \setminus \preceq$ (i.e, $s \succ t$ iff $s \succeq t$ and $s \not\preceq t$). Its *equivalence* $\sim$ is $\succeq \cap \preceq$. Note that $\succeq$ is the disjoint union of $\succ$ and $\sim$, and that if $=$ denotes syntactic equality then $\succ \cup =$ is a quasi-ordering whose strict part is $\succ$. $\succeq$ is *monotonic* if $f(\ldots, s, \ldots) \succeq f(\ldots, t, \ldots)$ whenever $s \succeq t$. An ordering $\succ_2$ is compatible with a quasi-ordering $\succeq_1$ if $\succeq_1 \cdot \succ_2 \subseteq \succ_2$.

Let $\succeq_1$ be a quasi-ordering and let $\succ_2$ be an ordering. Then $\langle \succeq_1, \succ_2 \rangle$ is a *compatible ordering pair* if $\succ_2$ and $\succeq_1$ are stable under substitutions, $\succ_2$ is compatible with $\succeq_1$ and $\succ_2$ is well-founded.

A *precedence* $\succeq_{\mathcal{F}}$ is a well-founded quasi-ordering on $\mathcal{F}$. It is extended to a quasi-ordering on terms as $s \succeq_{\mathcal{F}} t$ iff $top(s) \succeq_{\mathcal{F}} top(t)$.

3   The Dependency Pair Method

For every defined symbol $f \in D$, we introduce a fresh tuple symbol $f^\#$ (sometimes written as F for simplicity) with the same arity. If $t = f(\,\bar{t}\,)$ then $t^\#$ denotes the term $f^\#(\,\bar{t}\,)$. If $l \to r \in R$ and t is a subterm of r with a defined root symbol, then $\langle l^\#, t^\# \rangle$ is a dependency pair of R. The set of all dependency pairs of R is denoted $DP(R)$. An R-chain is a sequence $\langle s_1, t_1 \rangle, \langle s_2, t_2 \rangle, \ldots$ of pairs in $DP(R)$ such that there is a substitution σ where $t_i\sigma \to_R^* s_{i+1}\sigma$.

Theorem 1 (Termination Criterion [AG00]). *A TRS R is terminating if and only if no infinite R-chain exists.*

Definition 1. *A pair $\langle \succeq_I, \succ_q \rangle$ is called a DP-reduction pair if $\succeq_I$ is monotonic, and $\langle \succeq_I, \succ_q \rangle$ is a compatible ordering pair.*

Then a TRS R is terminating if there is a DP-reduction pair $\langle \succeq_I, \succ_q \rangle$ such that $l \succeq_I r$ for every rule in R and $s \succ_q t$ for every dependency pair $\langle s, t \rangle$ in $DP(R)$.

Many refinements and improvements for solving the obtained constraints have been described. See [GTSK04] for a general framework for solving DP-constraints.

4   The Monotonic Semantic Path Order

Let us now recall the definition of the *semantic path ordering* (SPO) [KL80], with a slight modification, since we use a compatible ordering pair instead of a quasi-ordering as underlying (or base) ordering:

Definition 2. *Given a compatible ordering pair* $\langle \succeq_Q, \succ_q \rangle$, *the SPO, denoted as* $\succ_{spo}$, *is defined as* $s = f(s_1, \ldots, s_m) \succ_{spo} t$ *iff*

1. $s_i \succeq_{spo} t$, *for some* $i = 1, \ldots, m$, *or*
2. $s \succ_q t = g(t_1, \ldots, t_n)$ *and* $s \succ_{spo} t_i$ *for all* $i = 1, \ldots, n$, *or*
3. $s \succeq_Q t = g(t_1, \ldots, t_n)$ *and* $\{s_1, \ldots, s_m\} \twoheadrightarrow_{spo} \{t_1, \ldots, t_n\}$,

where $\succeq_{spo}$ *is defined as* $\succ_{spo} \cup =$.

The semantic path ordering is well-defined, but, in general, it is not monotonic, even when $\succeq_Q$ is monotonic (in fact, the same problem appears if $\succ_Q$ is monotonic).

Definition 3. *We say that* $\succeq_I$ *is monotonic on* $\succeq_Q$ *(or* $\succeq_Q$ *is monotonic wrt.* $\succeq_I$*) if* $s \succeq_I t$ *implies* $f(\ldots s \ldots) \succeq_Q f(\ldots t \ldots)$ *for all terms* s *and* t *and function symbols* f.

A pair $\langle \succeq_I, \succeq_Q \rangle$ *is called a* reduction pair *if* $\succeq_I$ *is monotonic,* $\succ_Q$ *is well-founded,* $\succeq_I$, $\succeq_Q$ *and* $\succ_Q$ *are stable under substitutions and* $\succeq_I$ *is monotonic on* $\succeq_Q$.

A triplet $\langle \succeq_I, \succeq_Q, \succ_q \rangle$ *is called a* reduction triplet *if* $\succeq_I$ *is monotonic,* $\succeq_I$ *is stable under substitutions,* $\langle \succeq_Q, \succ_q \rangle$ *is a compatible ordering pair and* $\succeq_I$ *is monotonic on* $\succeq_Q$.

Note that in particular, if $\langle \succeq_I, \succeq_Q \rangle$ is a reduction pair then $\langle \succeq_I, \succeq_Q, \succ_Q \rangle$ is a reduction triplet.

Now we define the *monotonic semantic path ordering* (MSPO) [BFR00]:

Definition 4. *Let* $\langle \succeq_I, \succeq_Q, \succ_q \rangle$ *be a reduction triplet. The corresponding monotonic semantic path ordering, denoted by* $\succ_{mspo}$, *is defined as:*

$$s \succ_{mspo} t \quad \text{if and only if} \quad s \succeq_I t \text{ and } s \succ_{spo} t$$

Theorem 2. $\succ_{mspo}$ *is a reduction ordering. Furthermore, MSPO characterizes termination.*

5   Reduction Constraints

In this section we present the constraint framework where our termination problems are translated to. We will first present the syntax and semantics of our constraints. Then, we show how the termination problems are translated into constraint problem through the definition of the MSPO. Then, we present some transformation techniques in order to solve the obtained constraints and show how the DP method is included in ours. Finally, we show how all other transformation techniques applied in the DP framework apply to ours.

5.1   Syntax and Semantics

Definition 5. *A reduction constraint is a pair $\langle C_1, C_2 \rangle$, where C_1 is a conjunction of positive literals over the relation $\sqsupseteq_1$ and C_2 is conjunction of positive literals over $\sqsupset_2$ and $\sqsupseteq_2$.*

Now we provide the notion of satisfiability for reduction constraints, which is based on reduction triplets. Hence, it is easy to show that these kind of constraints are the ones obtained by applying MSPO.

Definition 6. *A reduction constraint $\langle C_1, C_2 \rangle$ is satisfiable iff there exists a reduction triplet $\langle \geq_1, \geq_2, >_2 \rangle$ such that $\geq_1$ satisfies C_1 and $\langle \geq_2, >_2 \rangle$ satisfies C_2, i.e. $\geq_2$ satisfies all literals $s \sqsupseteq_2 t$ in C_2 and $>_2$ satisfies all literals $s \sqsupset_2 t$ in C_2.*

The following definition and theorem allow us to connect the reduction triplet semantics given above for reduction constraints with the R-chain semantics given for the constraints obtained by the dependency pair method.

In what follows, we will speak about the relation $\sqsupseteq_1$ in C_1, or simply $\sqsupseteq_1$, as the relation defined by all instances of all $s \sqsupseteq_1 t$ in C_1. We have not used a new relation symbol to ease the reading. The same will be done for the relation $\sqsupseteq_2$ in C_2 (or simply $\sqsupseteq_2$) and the relation $\sqsupset_2$ in C_2 (or simply $\sqsupset_2$).

Then, we use $\xrightarrow{\chi}{}^*_{\sqsupseteq_1}$ for the reflexive and transitive closure of the monotonic with non-empty contexts (and stable under substitution) closure of $\sqsupseteq_1$ in C_1.

Definition 7. *Let $\langle C_1, C_2 \rangle$ be a reduction constraint. A pair $\langle s, t \rangle_O$, with O being either $\sqsupseteq_2$ or $\sqsupset_2$, is said to be in C_2 iff $s \ O \ t$ occur in C_2 (up to renaming of variables). It is said to be strict if O is $\sqsupset_2$.*

A sequence of pairs of terms $\langle s_1, t_1 \rangle_{O_1}, \langle s_2, t_2 \rangle_{O_2}, \ldots$ is a chain in $\langle C_1, C_2 \rangle$ if every $\langle s_i, t_i \rangle_{O_i}$ is in C_2 and there exists a substitution σ such that $t_i \sigma \xrightarrow{\chi}{}^*_{\sqsupseteq_1} s_{i+1} \sigma$ holds for all consecutive pairs $\langle s_i, t_i \rangle_{O_i}$ and $\langle s_{i+1}, t_{i+1} \rangle_{O_{i+1}}$ in the sequence.

Lemma 1. *If $C_1 = \{ l \sqsupseteq_1 r \mid \forall l \to r \in R \}$ the notion of R-chain using dependency pairs coincides with the notion of chain using our pairs $\langle s, t \rangle_O$.*

Theorem 3. *A reduction constraint $\langle C_1, C_2 \rangle$ is satisfiable iff there is no chain in $\langle C_1, C_2 \rangle$ with infinitely many strict pairs.*

From this theorem it follows that the constraints obtained by the dependency pair method are reduction constraints, as we will show in detail in section 5.4.

5.2 Translating MSPO-Termination of Rewriting into Reduction Constraint Solving

Using MSPO, we can translate our termination problem into a reduction constraint solving problem. This translation is simply based on applying the definition of MSPO, and SPO, to the rules of the TRS.

Let R be a set of rules $\{l_i \rightarrow r_i \mid 1 \leq i \leq n\}$. We consider the following initial MSPO-constraint:

$$l_1 \succ_{mspo} r_1 \wedge \ldots \wedge l_n \succ_{mspo} r_n$$

Which is transformed by applying the definition of MSPO into a conjunction of two constraints, C_I and C_{SPO}

$$C_I : \quad l_1 \succeq_I r_1 \wedge \ldots \wedge l_n \succeq_I r_n$$
$$C_{SPO} : l_1 \succ_{spo} r_1 \wedge \ldots \wedge l_n \succ_{spo} r_n$$

Now the definition of SPO given in Section 4 is applied to the second part of the constraint. This is formalized by means of correct constraint transformation rules:

$$\begin{aligned}
s \succeq_{spo} t &\Longrightarrow \top & &\text{if } s \equiv t \\
s \succeq_{spo} t &\Longrightarrow s \succ_{spo} t & &\text{if } s \not\equiv t \\
x \succ_{spo} t &\Longrightarrow \bot & & \\
s \succ_{spo} x &\Longrightarrow \top & &\text{if } s \not\equiv x \in Vars(s) \\
s = f(s_1, \ldots, s_m) \succ_{spo} g(t_1, \ldots, t_n) &= t \Longrightarrow & & \\
& \multicolumn{3}{l}{s_1 \succeq_{spo} t \vee \ldots \vee s_m \succeq_{spo} t \vee} \\
& \multicolumn{3}{l}{(s \succ_q t \wedge s \succ_{spo} t_1 \wedge \ldots \wedge s \succ_{spo} t_n) \vee} \\
& \multicolumn{3}{l}{(s \succeq_Q t \wedge \{s_1, \ldots, s_m\} \succ\!\!\succ_{spo} \{t_1, \ldots, t_n\})}
\end{aligned}$$

where $\{s_1, \ldots, s_m\} \succ\!\!\succ_{spo} \{t_1, \ldots, t_n\}$ is translated into a constraint over $\succ_{spo}$ and $\succeq_{spo}$.

It is easy to see that these transformation rules are correct, terminating and confluent. Moreover, the resulting normal form is an ordering constraint over $\succ_q$ and $\succeq_Q$ which represents the conditions on $\succ_q$ and $\succeq_Q$ that are necessary to show that C_{SPO} is true. Then after computing the disjunctive normal form, the initial constraint C_{SPO} has been translated into a disjunction of constraints over $\succ_q$ and $\succeq_Q$ each one of the form

$$C_Q : \quad s_1 \succ_q t_1 \wedge \ldots \wedge s_p \succ_q t_p \wedge s'_1 \succeq_Q t'_1 \wedge \ldots \wedge s'_q \succeq_Q t'_q$$

where none of the terms are variables.

Now we have to find a reduction triplet $\langle \succeq_I, \succeq_Q, \succ_q \rangle$ satisfying C_I and one of these constraints C_Q, which means that this is a reduction constraint satisfaction problem as the following theorem states.

Theorem 4. *Let R be a TRS and let C_I be the constraint over $\succeq_I$ and let $C_Q^1 \vee \ldots \vee C_Q^k$ be the disjunction of constraints over $\succ_q$ and $\succeq_Q$ obtained by applying the MSPO method. Then R is terminating iff some reduction constraint $\langle C_I, C_Q^i \rangle$ is satisfiable.*

From the previous theorem, in order to prove termination, we have to show that some reduction constraint $\langle C_I, C_Q^i \rangle$ is satisfiable. To this end, we have to provide some correct (wrt. satisfiability) constraint transformation techniques which allow us to simplify the constraints until they can directly be shown to be satisfiable by building an actual reduction triplet (or pair).

From now on, we will assume that we have a reduction constraint $\langle C_1, C_2 \rangle$, which is transformed step by step, preserving satisfiability, into one or several simpler reduction constraints of the form $\langle S_1, S_2 \rangle$. After this simplification process, each resulting reduction constraint $\langle S_1, S_2 \rangle$ is proved satisfiable separately by building an appropriate reduction quasi-ordering $\succeq$ (or a compatible ordering pair $\langle \succeq, \succ \rangle$ where $\succeq$ is monotonic), which includes all literals in S_1 and S_2. Note that, if $\succeq$ is a reduction quasi-ordering and $\succ$ is the strict part of it, then $\langle \succeq, \succeq, \succ \rangle$ is a reduction triplet.

5.3 Constraint Transformations

In this section we propose some basic techniques for simplifying the reduction constraint $\langle C_1, C_2 \rangle$.

A first simple example of such a simplification, is obtained by using a well-founded precedence on the set of symbols. Thus every literal $s \sqsupset_2 t$ or $s \sqsupseteq_2 t$ can be removed if the top symbol of s is strictly greater than the top symbol of t in the precedence. Moreover, the remaining literals $s \sqsupset_2 t$ or $s \sqsupseteq_2 t$ in C_2 have to fulfil that the top symbol of s is greater than or equal to the top symbol of t in the precedence.

Being precise, if $\succeq_{\mathcal{F}}$ is a precedence, such that $top(s) \succeq_{\mathcal{F}} top(t)$ for every $s \sqsupset_2 t$ or $s \sqsupseteq_2 t$ in C_2, then we can simplify the constraint C_2 by using the following rules:

Precedence simplification rules

$$s \sqsupset_2 t \Longrightarrow \top \quad \text{if } top(s) \succ_{\mathcal{F}} top(t)$$
$$s \sqsupseteq_2 t \Longrightarrow \top \quad \text{if } top(s) \succ_{\mathcal{F}} top(t)$$

By building appropriate reduction triplets, we can easily show the correctness of this transformation.

Transformation 1. *Let $\langle C_1, C_2 \rangle$ be a reduction constraint and let $\langle C_1, C_2' \rangle$ be a reduction constraint obtained by applying the precedence simplification rules wrt. some precedence $\succeq_{\mathcal{F}}$ such that $top(s) \succeq_{\mathcal{F}} top(t)$ for every $s \sqsupset_2 t$ or $s \sqsupseteq_2 t$ in C_2. Then $\langle C_1, C_2 \rangle$ is satisfiable if and only if $\langle C_1, C_2' \rangle$ is satisfiable.*

Moreover, if we choose adequately the precedence we can apply an optimal simplification with respect to this precedence-based transformation.

Now we present a transformation technique, based on renamings of top function symbols (as already done in the dependency pair method). This transformation is not a simplification in the sense that no literal is removed, but it allows us to apply, in the future, a different treatment to the symbols when they occur on top of a term in C_2 (which will ease the proof of satisfiability of the final reduction constraint obtained after all the simplification process).

Transformation 2. *(Renaming) Let $\langle C_1, C_2 \rangle$ be a reduction constraint and let C_2' the result of renaming all function symbols f heading a term in C_2 by a new symbol $f^\#$. Then $\langle C_1, C_2 \rangle$ is satisfiable iff $\langle C_1, C_2' \rangle$ is satisfiable.*

5.4   Reduction Constraints and the DP Method

In this section we show that the constraints obtained in our method have the same semantics as the ones produced by the dependency pair method. In particular, we show that one of the constraints obtained in the disjunction when using the MSPO constraint method coincides, after applying the precedence and the renaming transformations, with the one given by the DP method.

The following results states that the constraint obtained by the dependency pair method is a reduction constraint.

Theorem 5. *Let R be a TRS and let C_1 be the constraint containing $l_i \sqsupseteq_1 r_i$ for every rule $l_i \to r_i$ in R and let C_2 be the constraint containing $s \sqsupset_2 t$ for every dependency pair $\langle s, t \rangle$ in $DP(R)$. Then R is terminating iff the reduction constraint $\langle C_1, C_2 \rangle$ is satisfiable.*

Now, using always case 2 of the definition of SPO, except when the term on the right is a variable (where we apply case 1), and applying precedence transformation (with defined symbols greater than constructors) and finally the renaming transformation we get the constraint given by the DP method. Moreover, it is not difficult to prove that there is a reduction triplet $\langle \succeq_I, \succeq_Q, \succ_q \rangle$ if and only if there is a DP-reduction pair $\langle \succeq_I, \succ_q \rangle$ solving the resulting reduction constraint.

Theorem 6. *The dependency pair method is included in the MSPO constraint method.*

The following example shows a case in which the constraint obtained by DP-method is, in principle, not the easiest one to be solved among all constraints generated by MSPO.

Example 1. The following system is an automatic translation of a prolog program that computes the Ackermann function.

$$ack\_in(0, x) \to ack\_out(s(x))$$
$$ack\_in(s(y), 0) \to u11(ack\_in(y, s(0)))$$
$$u11(ack\_out(x)) \to ack\_out(x)$$
$$ack\_in(s(y), s(x)) \to u21(ack\_in(s(y), x), y)$$
$$u21(ack\_out(x), y) \to u22(ack\_in(y, x))$$
$$u22(ack\_out(x)) \to ack\_out(x)$$

This system has been proved included in the MSPO with a constraint which for the rule

$$u21(ack\_out(x), y) \rightarrow u22(ack\_in(y, x))$$

contains the following literals which correspond to the application of case 2 first and then case 3 of the SPO:

$$u21(ack\_out(x), y) \succ_q u22(ack\_in(y, x))$$
$$u21(ack\_out(x), y) \succeq_Q ack\_in(y, x)$$

Note that with the DP-method both, at least initially, would be strict.

Similarly, the constraint framework defined in [GTSK04] is basically the same as the one described in this paper, except on the fact that, since we extract our constraints from the definition of MSPO, our constraint C_2 may include non-strict inequalities from the beginning.

Due to this equivalence between both frameworks all sound transformation techniques described in [GTSK04] (called there *processors*), including , for instance, the DP graph or many other ideas developed in [AG00, HM05, GTSKF06] can be used in our framework and vice versa.

6   Innermost Rewriting: Constrained Rules

In innermost rewriting, a subterm is a redex only if all arguments are in normal form. Therefore, we can impose this condition on the left-hand sides of the rules. In this section we show a way to keep this condition aside of the rules and then use this information to prove innermost termination with the reduction constraint framework.

Definition 8. *Let R be a TRS. Then $s \xrightarrow{i}_R t$ is an innermost rewriting step if $s = u[l\sigma]$, $t = u[r\sigma]$, $l \rightarrow r \in R$, and all the proper subterms of $l\sigma$ are in normal form, that is, $l\sigma$ is irreducible in non-top positions.*

As a first consequence of the above definition, when using innermost rewriting, all the rules in a TRS which has a proper subterm $l|_p$ such that for any normal substitution σ, $l|_p\sigma$ is a redex, can be eliminated.

Note that we can still have rules which have a proper subterm $l|_p$ such that $l|_p\sigma$ is a redex for some normal substitution σ, but not in general.

To prove innermost termination of a TRS, we have to show that any innermost reduction is finite, which can be proved by showing that any innermost reduction is included in a well-founded ordering.

Theorem 7. *A rewrite system R over a set of terms $T(F, X)$ is innermost terminating if and only if there is a well-founded, monotonic ordering over $T(F, X)$ such that for every $l \rightarrow r \in R$ and for all substitutions σ such that $l\sigma$ is irreducible in non-top positions, $l\sigma \succ r\sigma$.*

Note that if a term t is irreducible then any subterm of t is also irreducible. Thus, the condition "$l\sigma$ is irreducible in non-top positions" in the above theorem can also be written as "$l_i\sigma$ is irreducible for all l_i argument of l".

This condition of irreducibility can be expressed by adding a constraint to the rules. For instance, given the rules

$$f(x, g(x)) \rightarrow f(1, g(x))$$
$$g(1) \rightarrow g(0)$$

the innermost condition can be expressed by the constrained rules

$$f(x, g(x)) \rightarrow f(1, g(x)) \mid \{irred(x), irred(g(x))\}$$
$$g(1) \rightarrow g(0) \qquad \mid \{irred(1)\}$$

Let us formalize the notion of constrained rule and its use in innermost rewriting.

Definition 9. *Given a rule $l \rightarrow r$ and a conjunction K of literals build on a given set of predicates, we say that $l \rightarrow r \mid K$ is a constrained rule.*

A rewrite step using a constrained rule $l \rightarrow r \mid K$ is a rewrite step using $l \rightarrow r$ which is only applicable for those substitutions σ satisfying K, i.e., $s \rightarrow t$ using the constrained rule $l \rightarrow r \mid K$ iff $s = u[l\sigma] \rightarrow u[r\sigma] = t$ for some context u and substitution σ solution of K.

Now we show that by using constrained rewriting with *irreducibility constraints* we can characterize the innermost rewriting strategy.

Definition 10. *Let R be a set of rules. The set R^i of constrained rules for innermost rewriting contains for each rule $l \rightarrow r \in R$ a constrained rule $l \rightarrow r \mid K^i(l)$ where $K^i(f(t_1, \ldots, t_n)) = \{irred_R(t_i) \mid \forall i \in \{1, \ldots, n\}\}$ and $irred_R(t)$ means that t is irreducible with respect to R.*

Irreducibility constraints are used in the CARIBOO system [FGK02], by means of *abstraction constraints*. However, our aim when using these constraints is to be able to apply the same constraint solving techniques as in the innermost version of the DP method, like, for instance, when building the approximated *innermost DP graph*.

Lemma 2. *Let R be a set of rules. Then, $s \xrightarrow{i} t$ using $l \rightarrow r \in R$ if and only if $s \rightarrow t$ using the constrained rewrite rule $l \rightarrow r \mid K^i(l) \in R^i$*

This notion of constrained rewriting can be generalized other relations like orderings.

Definition 11. *Given two terms s and t and a set of literals K, $s \succeq t \mid K$ denotes that $s\sigma \succeq t\sigma$ for all solutions σ of K; and $s \succ t \mid K$ denotes that $s\sigma \succ t\sigma$ for all solutions σ of K.*

The following theorem for innermost termination follows from Theorem 7 using Lemma 2 and Definition 11.

Theorem 8. *Let $\succ$ be a reduction ordering. A TRS $\mathcal{R}$ is innermost terminating iff $l \succ r \mid K^i(l)$ holds for every rule $l \to r \in R$.*

Corollary 1. *A TRS $\mathcal{R}$ is innermost terminating iff there exists a reduction triplet $\langle \succeq_I, \succeq_Q, \succ_q \rangle$ s.t. $l \succ_{mspo} r \mid K^i(l)$, for every $l \to r \in R$.*

In order to be able to use constrained rules in our method, first we have to adapt the notion of reduction constraints.

6.1   Decorated Reduction Constraints

We will now increase the expressive power of our reduction constraints $\langle C_1, C_2 \rangle$ by attaching conditions to the pairs in C_1 and C_2. These conditions will contain all or part of the information coming from the constraints of the rules.

Definition 12. *A decorated literal (or pair) $l \mid D$ is a literal (pair) l with an attached condition D.*

A decorated reduction constraint is a tuple $\langle C_1, C_2 \rangle$, where C_1 is a conjunction of decorated positive literals over the relation $\sqsupseteq_1$ and C_2 is a conjunction of decorated positive literals over $\sqsupset_2$ and $\sqsupseteq_2$.

Definition 13. *A decorated reduction constraint $\langle C_1, C_2 \rangle$ is satisfiable iff there exists a reduction triplet $\langle \geq_1, \geq_2, >_2 \rangle$ such that $\geq_1$ satisfies C_1 and $\langle \geq_2, >_2 \rangle$ satisfies C_2, i.e., $\geq_2$ satisfies all decorated literals $s \sqsupseteq_2 t \mid D$ in C_2 and $>_2$ satisfies all decorated literals $s \sqsupset_2 t \mid D$ in C_2.*

From this, all definitions and results given for reduction constraints can be extended in a natural way to decorated reduction constraint (see [Bor03] for details).

6.2   Proving Termination of Constrained Rules by MSPO Using Decorated Reduction Constraints

We can translate the termination problem of a set of constrained rules into an *ordering constraint solving problem* using decorated reduction constraints. This translation is simply based on applying the definition of MSPO, and SPO, to a set of constrained rules.

Let R be a set of constrained rules $\{(l_i \to r_i \mid K_i) \mid 1 \leq i \leq n\}$. We consider the following initial MSPO-constraint:

$$l_1 \succ_{mspo} r_1 \mid K_1 \wedge \ldots \wedge l_n \succ_{mspo} r_n \mid K_n$$

This decorated ordering constraint is transformed by applying the definition of MSPO into the conjunction of two decorated ordering constraints, C_I and C_{SPO}

$$C_I : \quad l_1 \succeq_I r_1 \mid K_1 \wedge \ldots \wedge l_n \succeq_I r_n \mid K_n$$
$$C_{SPO} : l_1 \succ_{spo} r_1 \mid K_1 \wedge \ldots \wedge l_n \succ_{spo} r_n \mid K_n$$

Now the definition of SPO given in Section 4 is applied to the second part of the constraint. This is formalized by means of correct constraint transformation rules:

$$s \succeq_{spo} t \mid K \Longrightarrow \bot \qquad\qquad\qquad\qquad\qquad \text{if } K \text{ is false}$$
$$s \succeq_{spo} t \mid K \Longrightarrow \top \qquad\qquad\qquad\qquad\qquad \text{if } s \equiv t$$
$$s \succeq_{spo} t \mid K \Longrightarrow s \succ_{spo} t \mid K \qquad\qquad\qquad \text{if } s \not\equiv t$$
$$s \succ_{spo} t \mid K \Longrightarrow \bot \qquad\qquad\qquad\qquad\qquad \text{if } K \text{ is false}$$
$$x \succ_{spo} t \mid K \Longrightarrow \bot$$
$$s \succ_{spo} x \mid K \Longrightarrow \top \qquad\qquad\qquad\qquad\qquad \text{if } s \not\equiv x \in Vars(s)$$
$$s = f(s_1, \ldots, s_m) \succ_{spo} g(t_1, \ldots, t_n) = t \mid K \Longrightarrow$$
$$s_1 \succeq_{spo} t \mid K \vee \ldots \vee s_m \succeq_{spo} t \mid K \; \vee$$
$$(s \succ_q t \mid K \wedge s \succ_{spo} t_1 \mid K \wedge \ldots \wedge s \succ_{spo} t_n \mid K) \; \vee$$
$$(s \succeq_Q t \mid K \wedge \{s_1, \ldots, s_m\} \ggcurly_{spo} \{t_1, \ldots, t_n\} \mid K)$$

where $\{s_1, \ldots, s_m\} \ggcurly_{spo} \{t_1, \ldots, t_n\} \mid K$ is translated into a decorated ordering constraint over $\succ_{spo}$ and $\succeq_{spo}$.

As for the case of (non-constrained) rewriting, it is easy to see that these transformation rules are correct, terminating and confluent. Moreover, the resulting normal form is a decorated ordering constraint over $\succ_q$ and $\succeq_Q$. Then after computing the disjunctive normal form, the initial constraint C_{SPO} has been translated into a disjunction of constraints over $\succ_q$ and $\succeq_Q$ each one of the form

$$C_Q : \quad s_1 \succ_q t_1 \mid K_1' \wedge \ldots \wedge s_p \succ_q t_p \mid K_p' \wedge s_1' \succeq_Q t_1' \mid K_{p+1}' \wedge \ldots \wedge s_q' \succeq_Q t_q' \mid K_q'$$

where none of the terms are variables.

Note that all K_j' coincides with some of the K_i coming from the rules R (i.e., no new constraints are generated).

Now, as for the non-decorated case, we have to find a reduction triplet satisfying C_I and one of these decorated constraints C_Q.

Theorem 9. *Let R be a set of constrained rules and let C_I be the constraint containing $l_i \succeq_I r_i \mid K_i$ for every constrained rule $l_i \to r_i \mid K_i \in R$, and let $C_Q^1 \cup \ldots \cup C_Q^k$ be the disjunction of decorated ordering constraints over $\succ_q$ and $\succeq_Q$ obtained by applying the MSPO constraint method for constrained termination. Then the set of constrained rules R is terminating iff some decorated reduction constraint $\langle C_I, C_Q^i \rangle$ is satisfiable.*

In particular, for innermost termination, we have the following corollary.

Corollary 2. *Let R be a TRS and let R^i be the set of constrained rules $l \succ r \mid K^i(l)$ for every $l \to r \in R$. Then $\mathcal{R}$ is innermost terminating iff $\langle C_I, C_Q^i \rangle$ is satisfiable for some decorated reduction constraint $\langle C_I, C_Q^i \rangle$ obtained by applying the MSPO method to R^i.*

Now, as seen for (non-constrained) rewriting, in order to prove termination we have to show that some decorated reduction constraint $\langle C_I, C_Q^i \rangle$ is satisfiable. All transformations known for non-decorated constraints can also be used for transforming decorated reduction constraints, although, in some cases, the transformation can be improved by using the additional information of the decorated pairs (see [Bor03] for details).

7   Higher-Order Rewriting

In this section we extend the results on first-order rewriting to the higher-order case. The aim of this section is to show the generality of our approach and how simple is to extend it to other kind of rewriting. Due to the lack of room we will present a very simple form of the monotonic higher-order semantic path ordering. Moreover, we will consider a very simple type system, which is enough to present our ideas. See [JR07, BR01] for more powerful versions.

7.1   Types, Signatures and Terms

We consider terms of a simply typed lambda-calculus generated by a signature of higher-order function symbols.

The set of types $\mathbb{T}$ is generated from the set $V_\mathbb{T}$ of *type variables* (considered as sorts) by the constructor $\to$ for *functional types* in the usual way. As usual, $\to$ associates to the right. In the following, we use α, β for type variables and $\sigma, \tau, \rho, \theta$ for arbitrary types.

A signature $\mathcal{F}$ is a set of function symbols which are meant to be algebraic operators, equipped with a fixed number n of arguments (called the *arity*) of respective types $\sigma_1 \in \mathbb{T}, \ldots, \sigma_n \in \mathbb{T}$, and an output type $\sigma \in \mathbb{T}$. A *type declaration* for a function symbol f will be written as $f : \sigma_1 \times \ldots \times \sigma_n \to \sigma$. Type declarations are not types, although they are used for typing purposes.

The set $\mathcal{T}(\mathcal{F}, \mathcal{X})$ of *raw algebraic λ-terms* is generated from the signature $\mathcal{F}$ and a denumerable set $\mathcal{X}$ of variables according to the grammar rules
$$\mathcal{T} := \mathcal{X} \mid (\lambda \mathcal{X} : \mathbb{T}.\mathcal{T}) \mid @(\mathcal{T}, \mathcal{T}) \mid \mathcal{F}(\mathcal{T}, \ldots, \mathcal{T}).$$
Terms of the form $\lambda x : \sigma.u$ are called *abstractions*, while the other terms are said to be *neutral*. For sake of brevity, we will often omit types. $@(u, v)$ denotes the application of u to v. The application operator is allowed to have a variable arity. As a matter of convenience, we may write $@(u, v_1, \ldots, v_n)$ for $@(@(\ldots @(u, v_1) \ldots), v_n)$, assuming $n \geq 1$.

7.2   Typing Rules

Typing rules restrict the set of terms by constraining them to follow a precise discipline. Environments are sets of pairs written $x : \sigma$, where x is a variable and σ is a type. Our typing judgments are written as $\Gamma \vdash M : \sigma$ if the term M can be proved to have the type σ in the environment Γ with the following type system

Variables:

$$\frac{x : \sigma \in \Gamma}{\Gamma \vdash x : \sigma}$$

Functions:

$$\frac{f : \sigma_1 \times \ldots \times \sigma_n \to \sigma \in \mathcal{F} \quad \Gamma \vdash t_1 : \sigma_1 \ \ldots \ \Gamma \vdash t_n : \sigma_n}{\Gamma \vdash f(t_1, \ldots, t_n) : \sigma}$$

Abstraction:
$$\frac{\Gamma \cup \{x : \sigma\} \vdash t : \tau}{\Gamma \vdash (\lambda x : \sigma.t) : \sigma \to \tau}$$

Application:
$$\frac{\Gamma \vdash s : \sigma \to \tau \quad \Gamma \vdash t : \sigma}{\Gamma \vdash @(s,t) : \tau}$$

7.3 Higher-Order Rewriting and Termination

The rewrite relation considered in this paper is the union of the one induced by a set of higher-order rewrite rules and the β-reduction rule $@(\lambda x.v, u) \longrightarrow_\beta v\{x \mapsto u\}$, both working modulo α-conversion. For simplicity reasons, in this work we do not consider η-reduction, although all results can be extended to include it.

A higher-order *term rewrite system* is a set of rewrite rules $R = \{\Gamma \vdash l_i \to r_i\}_i$, where l_i and r_i are higher-order terms such that l_i and r_i have the same type σ_i in the environment Γ.

Given a term rewriting system R, a term s rewrites to a term t at position p with the rule $\Gamma \vdash l \to r$ and the substitution γ, written $s \xrightarrow[l \to r]{p} t$, or simply $s \to_R t$, if $s|_p = l\gamma$ and $t = s[r\gamma]_p$ (modulo α-conversion).

Higher-order reduction orderings are basically reduction orderings (monotonic, stable under substitutions and well-founded) operating on typed higher-order terms and including β-reduction. A higher-order rewrite system R is terminating if there is a higher-order reduction ordering $\succ$ such that $l \succ r$ for all rules $l \to r$ in R.

7.4 The Higher-Order Semantic Path Ordering (HOSPO)

From now on, to ease the reading, we will omit the environments in judgments.

Definition 14. *Given a compatible ordering pair on higher-order typed terms $\langle \succeq_Q, \succ_q \rangle$ (where none of $\succeq_Q$ and $\succ_q$ needs to include β-reduction), the HOSPO, denoted as $\succ_{hspo}$, is defined as* $\quad s : \tau \succ_{hspo} t : \tau \quad$ *iff*

1. *$f \in \mathcal{F}$, $s = f(s_1, \ldots, s_m)$ and $s_i \succeq_{hspo} t$, for some $i = 1, \ldots, m$, or*
2. *$f, g \in \mathcal{F}, s = f(s_1, \ldots, s_m) \succ_q t = g(t_1, \ldots, t_n)$ and for all $i = 1, \ldots, n$, either $s \succ_{hspo} t_i$ or $s_j \succeq_{hspo} t$ for some $j = 1, \ldots, m$, or*
3. *$f, g \in \mathcal{F}$, $s = f(s_1, \ldots, s_m) \succeq_Q t = g(t_1, \ldots, t_n)$ and $\{s_1, \ldots, s_m\} \gg\!\!\succ_{hspo} \{t_1, \ldots, t_n\}$, or*
4. *$f \in \mathcal{F}$, $s = f(s_1, \ldots, s_m)$, $t = @(t_1, \ldots, t_n)$, and for all $i = 1, \ldots, n$, either $s \succ_{hspo} t_i$ or $s_j \succeq_{hspo} t$ for some $j = 1, \ldots, m$, or*
5. *$s = @(s_1, s_2)$, $t = @(t_1, t_2)$, $\{s_1, s_2\} \gg\!\!\succ_{hspo} \{t_1, t_2\}$, or*
6. *$s = \lambda x.u$, $t = \lambda x.v$, $u \succ_{hspo} v$, or*
7. *$s = @(\lambda x.u, v)$ and $u\{x \mapsto v\} \succeq_{hspo} t$*

where $\succeq_{hspo}$ is defined as $\succ_{hspo} \cup \alpha$-conversion.

Definition 15. *Let $\langle \succeq_I, \succeq_Q, \succ_q \rangle$ be a reduction triplet on higher-order typed terms. The monotonic higher-order semantic path ordering (MHOSPO), denoted by $\succ_{mhspo}$, is defined as*

$$s \succ_{mhspo} t \quad \text{if and only if} \quad s \succeq_I t \text{ and } s \succ_{hspo} t$$

Theorem 10. $\succ_{mhspo}$ *is a higher-order reduction ordering.*

Finally we show how to translate a MHOSPO termination proof into a (higher-order) reduction constraint problem $\langle C_1, C_2 \rangle$. The constraint C_1 is obtained as before from $\succeq_I$. To obtain C_2 we use the definition of HOSPO.

This is formalized by means of correct constraint transformation rules like (we only outline the ones that are different from those in 5.2):

$$s = f(s_1,\ldots,s_m) \succ_{hspo} g(t_1,\ldots,t_n) = t \Longrightarrow$$
$$\bigvee_{s_i:\tau} s_i \succeq_{hspo} t \;\vee$$
$$(s \succ_q t \wedge_{t_i:\tau'} (s \succ_{hspo} t_i \vee \bigvee_{s_j:\tau} s_j \succeq_{hspo} t_i)) \;\vee$$
$$(s \succeq_Q t \wedge \{s_1,\ldots,s_m\} \gg_{hspo} \{t_1,\ldots,t_n\})$$
$$s = f(s_1,\ldots,s_m) \succ_{hspo} @(t_1,\ldots,t_n) = t \Longrightarrow$$
$$\bigwedge_{t_i:\tau'} (s \succ_{hspo} t_i \vee \bigvee_{s_j:\tau} s_j \succeq_{hspo} t_i)$$

$$\vdots$$

But, note that, due to the type conditions, the transformation rule
$$s \succ_{hspo} x \Longrightarrow \top \text{ if } s \not\equiv x \in Vars(s)$$
does not hold in general, and hence there might be terms on the right hand side of literals in C_2 being a variable.

Example 2. Filter. To make it simpler we only consider a type variable α.
Let $V_{\mathbb{T}} = \{\alpha\}$, $\mathcal{X} = \{\, x, xs : \alpha, \; P : \alpha \to \alpha \,\}$ and
$\mathcal{F} = \{[] : \alpha, \; cons : \alpha \times \alpha \to \alpha, \; True, False : \alpha, \; filter : (\alpha \to \alpha) \times \alpha \to \alpha,$
$iffil : \alpha \times (\alpha \to \alpha) \times \alpha \times \alpha \to \alpha\}$

$$filter(P, []) \to []$$
$$filter(P, cons(x, xs)) \to iffil(@(P, x), P, x, xs)$$
$$iffil(True, P, x, xs) \to cons(x, filter(P, xs))$$
$$iffil(False, P, x, xs) \to filter(P, xs)$$

The constraint C_1 is obtained as before:
$filter(P, []) \succeq_I [] \;\wedge\; filter(P, cons(x, xs)) \succeq_I iffil(@(P, x), P, x, xs) \;\wedge$
$iffil(True, P, x, xs) \succeq_I cons(x, filter(P, xs)) \;\wedge$
$iffil(False, P, x, xs) \succeq_I filter(P, xs)$
and as one of the constraints for C_2 we have:
$filter(P, cons(x, xs)) \succ_q iffil(@(P, x), P, x, xs) \;\wedge$
$iffil(True, P, x, xs) \succ_q cons(x, filter(P, xs)) \;\wedge$
$iffil(True, P, x, xs) \succeq_Q filter(P, xs) \;\wedge\; iffil(False, P, x, xs) \succeq_Q filter(P, xs)$
    Now using the precedence transformation and then the renaming transformation we obtain
$Filter(P, cons(x, xs)) \succ_q Iffil(@(P, x), P, x, xs) \;\wedge$
$Iffil(True, P, x, xs) \succeq_Q Filter(P, xs) \;\wedge\; Iffil(False, P, x, xs) \succeq_Q Filter(P, xs)$
    Finally, the reduction constraint is solved by taking $\succeq_I = \succeq_Q$ and $\succ_q$ as the strict part of $\succeq_Q$, which is defined by a simple polynomial interpretation like
$|nil| = 0; |cons(x_1, x_2)| = x_2 + 1; |filter(x_1, x_2, x_3)| = x_3;$
$|iffil(x_1, x_2, x_3, x_4)| = x_4 + 1; |Filter(x_1, x_2, x_3)| = x_3; |Iffil(x_1, x_2, x_3, x_4)| = x_4.$

8   Conclusions and Future Work

Termptation (available at `http://www.lsi.upc.es/~albert`) is a fully automated system for proving termination of first-order term rewrite systems which follows the termination proof techniques described in this paper.

The current implementation of the system has to be improved in several ways. On the one hand, by incorporating the state of the art techniques for solving reduction constraints. On the other hand, by extending the system to handle other reduction strategies, as well as AC-rewriting, CS-rewriting and HO-rewriting.

We are especially interested in the HO-case, since we consider that it is a difficult case were our working program of developing theory at the level of orderings and practice at the level of constraints may be the right one to build a powerful termination tool.

References

[AG00]   Arts, T., Giesl, J.: Termination of term rewriting using dependency pairs. Theoretical Computer Science 236(1-2), 133–178 (2000)

[BFR00]   Borralleras, C., Ferreira, M., Rubio, A.: Complete monotonic semantic path orderings. In: McAllester, D. (ed.) Automated Deduction - CADE-17. LNCS, vol. 1831, pp. 346–364. Springer, Heidelberg (2000)

[Bor03]   Borralleras, C.: Ordering-based methods for proving termination automatically. PhD thesis, Dpto. LSI, Universitat Politècnica de Catalunya (2003)

[BR01]   Borralleras, C., Rubio, A.: A monotonic higher-order semantic path ordering. In: Nieuwenhuis, R., Voronkov, A. (eds.) LPAR 2001. LNCS (LNAI), vol. 2250, pp. 531–547. Springer, Heidelberg (2001)

[BR03]   Borralleras, C., Rubio, A.: Monotonic AC-compatible semantic path orderings. In: Nieuwenhuis, R. (ed.) RTA 2003. LNCS, vol. 2706, pp. 279–295. Springer, Heidelberg (2003)

[FGK02]   Fissore, O., Gnaedig, I., Kirchner, H.: CARIBOO: An Induction Based Proof Tool for Termination with Strategies. In: Proc. 4th Int. Conf. on Principles and Practice of Declarative Programming, pp. 62–73. ACM Press, New York (2002)

[GTSK04]   Giesl, J., Thiemann, R., Schneider-Kamp, P.: The dependency pair framework: Combining techniques for automated termination proofs. In: Baader, F., Voronkov, A. (eds.) LPAR 2004. LNCS (LNAI), vol. 3452, pp. 301–331. Springer, Heidelberg (2005)

[GTSKF06]   Giesl, J., Thiemann, R., Schneider-Kamp, P., Falke, S.: Mechanizing and improving dependency pairs. J. Autom. Reasoning 37(3), 155–203 (2006)

[HM05]   Hirokawa, N., Middeldorp, A.: Automating the dependency pair method. Information and Computation 199(1-2), 172–199 (2005)

[JR07]   Jouannaud, J.-P., Rubio, A.: Polymorphic higher-order recursive path orderings. Journal of the ACM, 54(1) (2007)

[KL80]   Kamin, S., Levy, J.J.: Two generalizations of the recursive path ordering. Dept. of Computer Science, Univ. of Illinois, Urbana, IL (1980)

[vdP98]   van de Pol, J.: Operational semantics of rewriting with priorities. Theoretical Computer Science 200(1-2), 289–312 (1998)

Narrowing, Abstraction and Constraints for Proving Properties of Reduction Relations

Isabelle Gnaedig[1] and Hélène Kirchner[2]

[1] INRIA & LORIA*
[2] CNRS & LORIA

Abstract. We describe in this paper an inductive proof method for properties of reduction relations. The reduction trees are simulated with proof trees generated by narrowing and an abstraction mechanism. While narrowing simulates reduction, abstraction relies on the induction principle to replace subterms by variables representing specific reduced forms that trivially satisfy the property to be proved. The induction ordering is not given a priori, but defined with ordering constraints, incrementally set during the proof. Abstraction constraints are used to control the narrowing mechanism, well-known to easily diverge. The proof method is briefly illustrated on various examples of properties.

1 Introduction

When working with infinite sets in verification or theorem proving, several concepts have been proved quite useful: induction, constraints, abstraction, narrowing. Equation solving, inductive theorem proving, deduction with constraints, model checking, abstract interpretations, reachability analysis are a few domains in which they have been introduced as essential features. In particular, they are often used in the context of reduction relations, and especially rewriting relations, that can model many kinds of deduction or computation processes, thanks to the power of rewriting logic [49] and rewriting calculus [9]. We propose in this paper a method that combines these different ingredients to prove properties often required for reduction relations.

The main idea of the proof principle is to proceed by induction on a well-founded set with a noetherian ordering $\succ$, assuming that for any t' such that $t \succ t'$, the proposition P holds for t', and then deducing that P holds for t. Unlike classical induction proofs, where the ordering is given, we do not need to define it *a priori*. We only have to check its existence by ensuring the satisfiability of ordering constraints incrementally set along the proof.

The class of properties expressed by propositions P that may be handled will be made more precise later on, but in order to support intuition, we can already mention some of them:

---

* UMR 7503 CNRS-INPL-INRIA-Nancy2-UHP. Campus Scientifique, BP 239, 54506 Vandoeuvre-ls-Nancy Cedex, France.

H. Comon-Lundh et al. (Eds.): Jouannaud Festschrift, LNCS 4600, pp. 44–67, 2007.

- termination under a strategy: the proposition P for a given term t is "all S-derivations issued from t terminate", where a S-derivation is a sequence of rewriting under a strategy S,
- weak termination proofs: P is "there is a terminating S-derivation issued from t",
- definition completeness and existence of constructor forms: P is "there is a derivation issued from t, leading to a constructor form".

Such properties will serve as examples all along this paper to illustrate the different notions in our general approach. We rely on our previous works on termination under the innermost [18], outermost [19], and local strategies [17], weak termination under the innermost strategy [20] and existence of constructor forms [26]. Further examples are being explored and may give an idea of other ways to apply the proof method for different properties:

- (weak-)reducibility of requests to specific answers: for any given ground term t headed by a defined symbol, "t has a derivation leading to a constant in a given set",
- termination of probabilistic rewriting: for a given t, "the average length of probabilistic derivations issued from t is finite",
- termination of a transition system: for a given initial state s, "all transition sequences starting from s terminate".

Some of these properties may be or have been proved with alternative methods, which are based for instance on automata techniques for reachability problems, or on reduction orderings or dependency pairs for termination. For properties like termination under the outermost strategy, weak termination, or reducibility to a constructor form when the reduction relation does not terminate, to our knowledge, our approach is the first one to provide a proof technique.

The paper is organized as follows: after introducing the background in Section 2, we present in Section 3 the inductive proof principle of our approach. Section 4 develops the basic concepts of the inductive proof mechanism based on abstraction and narrowing, and the involved constraints. Section 5 presents the proof procedure and states the general theorem with its conditions of application. Section 6 shows how the proof of a weak property with this method also provides a way to constructively select interesting derivations. Applicability of the approach and related work are addressed in Section 7 and 8 respectively.

2   The Background

We assume the reader familiar with the basic definitions and notations of algebras and term rewriting given for instance in [2,15,14,4]. For simpler notations, we only consider here unsorted terms, but the framework could be generalized to order-sorted signatures as defined for instance in [29,50].

Abstract Reduction Systems. An abstract reduction system $(\mathcal{M}, \rightarrow)$ is given by a set and a reduction relation $\rightarrow \subseteq \mathcal{M} \times \mathcal{M}$. A derivation is a chain of elements $a_1 \rightarrow a_2 \rightarrow \ldots a_n$; a_1 and a_n are respectively called the source and the target of the derivation. The element a is irreducible iff there exist no b such that $a \rightarrow b$.

Terms, Substitutions, Instantiations. $\mathcal{T}(\mathcal{F}, \mathcal{X})$ is the set of terms built from a finite set $\mathcal{F}$ of function symbols f with arity $n \in \mathbb{N}$ (denoted $f : n$), and a set $\mathcal{X}$ of variables denoted $x, y \ldots$. $Var(t)$ is the set of variables of the term t. $\mathcal{T}(\mathcal{F})$ is the set of ground terms (without variables). Symbols of arity 0 are called *constants*. Positions in a term are represented as sequences of integers. The empty sequence ϵ denotes the top position. Let p and p' be two positions. The position p is a (strict) prefix of p' (and p' suffix of p) if $p' = p\lambda$, where λ is a (non-empty) sequence of integers. If p is a position in t, then $t[t']_p$ denotes the term obtained from t by replacing the subterm at position p by the term t'.

A substitution is an assignment from $\mathcal{X}$ to $\mathcal{T}(\mathcal{F}, \mathcal{X})$, written $\sigma = (x \mapsto t) \ldots (y \mapsto u)$. It uniquely extends to an endomorphism of $\mathcal{T}(\mathcal{F}, \mathcal{X})$. The result of applying σ to a term $t \in \mathcal{T}(\mathcal{F}, \mathcal{X})$ is written $\sigma(t)$ or σt. The domain of σ, denoted $Dom(\sigma)$ is the finite subset of $\mathcal{X}$ such that $\sigma x \neq x$. Id denotes the identity substitution. The composition of substitutions σ_1 followed by σ_2 is denoted $\sigma_2 \circ \sigma_1$ or simply $\sigma_2 \sigma_1$.

An $(\mathcal{A}\text{-})$instantiation is an assignment θ from $\mathcal{X}$ to an $\mathcal{F}$-algebra $\mathcal{A}$, which extends to terms by setting $\theta(f(t_1, \ldots, t_n)) = f_\mathcal{A}(\theta(t_1), \ldots, \theta(t_n))$, where $f_\mathcal{A}$ denotes the interpretation of f in $\mathcal{A}$.

An $\mathcal{F}$-equality is an unoriented pair of terms of $\mathcal{T}(\mathcal{F}, \mathcal{X})$. A set E of $\mathcal{F}$-equalities defines a congruence relation on terms denoted $=_E$. The E-subsumption ordering on terms is defined as follows: $t \leq_E t'$ if there exists a substitution σ such that $t' =_E \sigma(t)$. The relations $=_E$ and $\leq_E$ are extended to substitutions. An E-unifier of two terms t and t' is a substitution σ such that $\sigma(t) =_E \sigma(t')$. A complete set of E-unifiers of t and t' is denoted $CSU_E(t, t')$. When E is empty, the $CSU_E(t, t')$ has at most one element, called most general unifier (mgu) when it exists.

Orderings. An ordering $\succ$ on $\mathcal{T}(\mathcal{F}, \mathcal{X})$ (and more generally on a set $\mathcal{M}$) is noetherian iff there is no infinite decreasing chain for this ordering. It is monotone iff for any pair of terms t, t' of $\mathcal{T}(\mathcal{F}, \mathcal{X})$, for any context $f(\ldots \ldots)$, $t \succ t'$ implies $f(\ldots t \ldots) \succ f(\ldots t' \ldots)$. It has the subterm property iff for any t of $\mathcal{T}(\mathcal{F}, \mathcal{X})$, $f(\ldots t \ldots) \succ t$. It is stable by substitution iff for every substitution σ, $t \succ t'$ implies $\sigma t \succ \sigma t'$. For $\mathcal{F}$ and $\mathcal{X}$ finite, if $\succ$ is monotone and has the subterm property, then it is noetherian [43].

Rewriting. A set $\mathcal{R}$ of rewrite rules is a set of pairs of terms of $\mathcal{T}(\mathcal{F}, \mathcal{X})$, denoted $l \rightarrow r$, such that $l \notin \mathcal{X}$ and $Var(r) \subseteq Var(l)$. In this paper, we only consider finite sets of rewrite rules.

The rewriting relation induced by $\mathcal{R}$ is denoted by $\rightarrow_\mathcal{R}$ ($\rightarrow$ if there is no ambiguity on $\mathcal{R}$), and defined by $s \rightarrow t$ iff there is a substitution σ and a position p in s such that $s|_p = \sigma l$ for some rule $l \to r$ of $\mathcal{R}$, and $t = s[\sigma r]_p$. This is written $s \to_{\mathcal{R}}^{p, l \to r, \sigma} t$ where either p, $l \to r$, σ or $\mathcal{R}$ may be omitted; $s|_p$ is called a redex. The reflexive transitive closure of the rewriting relation induced by $\mathcal{R}$ is denoted by $\xrightarrow{*}_{\mathcal{R}}$.

In the rewriting context, the set of function symbols is often split into a set $\mathcal{C}$ of constructors and a set $\mathcal{D}$ of defined functions. $\mathcal{C}$ and $\mathcal{D}$ are either arbitrarily given, or defined w.r.t. the rewrite system $\mathcal{R}$: a function symbol is a *constructor* iff it does not occur in $\mathcal{R}$ at the top position of a left-hand side of rule, and a *defined function symbol* otherwise. A *constructor term* is a term built only with constructors.

The notion of strategy is fundamental for rewriting and can be defined in a general way, slightly different from the one used in [4]: a *rewrite strategy S* for the rewrite system $\mathcal{R}$ is a subset of the set of all derivations of $\mathcal{R}$. The *application of a strategy S* on a term t is denoted $S(t)$ and defined as the set of the targets t' of all derivations of source t in S. When a rewrite step belongs to a derivation of the strategy S, it is denoted by $\to^S$.

A strategy could be described extensively or more suitably by a *strategy language* like in ELAN [40] Stratego [57], Tom [52,3] or more recently Maude [11] The semantics of such a language is naturally described in the rewriting calculus [9,10]. A strategy language involves rules as basic elements and offers strategy combinators and iterators to build more complex strategy expressions. Well-known rewriting strategies allow controlling the application of rules over subterms, performing term traversal and normalizing terms: in this paper, we consider in particular the innermost, outermost and local strategies on operators whose definitions can be found in [27] and in [52].

For any term of a term algebra, t terminates (under the strategy S) iff every rewriting derivation (under the strategy S) starting from t is finite. If $t \xrightarrow{*} t'$ and t' is irreducible (under the strategy S), then t' is called a normal form of t (under the strategy S). Remark that given t, its normal form (under the strategy S) may be not unique.

A rewrite theory on $\mathcal{T}(\mathcal{F}, \mathcal{X})$ is a triple $(\mathcal{F}, E, \mathcal{R})$ where E is a finite set of equalities and $\mathcal{R}$ a finite set of rewrite rules. The relation $\to_{\mathcal{R}/E}$ on $\mathcal{T}(\mathcal{F}, \mathcal{X})$ is the sequential composition of relations $=_E; \to_{\mathcal{R}}; =_E$. It induces a relation $\to_{\mathcal{R}/E}$ on the quotient algebra $\mathcal{T}(\mathcal{F})/ =_E$ by $[t]_E \to_{\mathcal{R}/E} [t']_E$ iff $t \to_{\mathcal{R}/E} t'$. The relation $\to_{\mathcal{R},E}$ on $\mathcal{T}(\mathcal{F}, \mathcal{X})$ is defined by $s \to_{\mathcal{R},E} t$ iff there is a substitution σ and a position p in s such that $s|_p =_E \sigma l$ for some rule $l \to r$ of $\mathcal{R}$, and $t = s[\sigma r]_p$.

Narrowing. Let $\mathcal{R}$ be a rewrite system on $\mathcal{T}(\mathcal{F}, \mathcal{X})$. A term t is *narrowed* into t', at the non-variable position p, using the rewrite rule $l \to r$ of $\mathcal{R}$ and the substitution σ, when σ is a most general unifier of $t|_p$ and l, and $t' = \sigma(t[r]_p)$. This is denoted $t \leadsto_{\mathcal{R}}^{p, l \to r, \sigma} t'$ where either p, $l \to r$, σ or $\mathcal{R}$ may be omitted. It is always assumed that there is no variable in common between the rule and the term, i.e. that $Var(l) \cap Var(t) = \emptyset$. Assuming that E has a finitary complete unification algorithm, the narrowing relation $\leadsto_{R,E}$ on $\mathcal{T}(\mathcal{F}, \mathcal{X})$ is defined by

$t \leadsto_{R,E}^{p,l\to r,\sigma} t'$ iff there exist a non-variable position p, a rewrite rule $l \to r$ of $\mathcal{R}$ and a substitution $\sigma \in CSU_E(t|_p, l)$, and $t' = \sigma(t[r]_p)$.

In this paper, the sets $\mathcal{M}$ of interest are $\mathcal{F}$-algebras $\mathcal{A}$, and in particular the terms algebras $\mathcal{T}(\mathcal{F})$, $\mathcal{T}(\mathcal{F})/ =_E$ and $\mathcal{T}(\mathcal{F}, \mathcal{X})$. The reduction relations $\to$ are the rewriting relations $\to_{\mathcal{R}}$, $\to_{\mathcal{R}/E}$, $\to_{\mathcal{R},E}$, rewriting relations according to strategies (innermost, outermost, local), or the narrowing relations $\leadsto_{\mathcal{R}}$, $\leadsto_{\mathcal{R},E}$.

3   The Inductive Proof Process

From now on, we assume that the set $\mathcal{M}$ is non empty and that there is a noetherian ordering $\succ$ defined on elements of $\mathcal{M}$. For proving the proposition P for any element t of $\mathcal{M}$, we proceed by induction on $\mathcal{M}$ with the ordering $\succ$ as noetherian induction relation, assuming that for any t' such that $t \succ t'$, the proposition P holds for t'.

3.1   *P*-Canonical Forms

All properties addressed in this paper can be expressed by propositions P involving the reduction relation $\to$ and specific elements of $\mathcal{M}$ characterized by a decidable property: for termination proofs, this is the property of irreducibility w.r.t the reduction relation, for completeness proofs, this is the syntactic property to be built only with constructors. We distinguish those particular elements of $\mathcal{M}$ by calling them *P-canonical elements*. Then a strong proposition is stated on any given element t of $\mathcal{M}$ as: on every derivation of source t, there is a P-canonical element, while a weak proposition is: there is a derivation of source t having a P-canonical element. This leads to the definition of P-canonical form of an element.

Definition 1. *Let $(\mathcal{M}, \to)$ be an abstract reduction system, P a proposition to be proved on $\mathcal{M}$ and $T \subseteq \mathcal{M}$ a decidable set of P-canonical elements. A P-canonical form $t\Downarrow$ of a term t is an element of T belonging to a derivation of source t.*

3.2   Covering Patterns and Simulation

Our goal is to inductively prove a proposition P on $\mathcal{M}$. For that, we simulate $(\mathcal{M}, \to)$ with another abstract system $(\mathcal{N}, \leadsto)$, by establishing a correspondence between the elements of $\mathcal{M}$ and $\mathcal{N}$ and between the reduction relations $\to$ and $\leadsto$.

In the following, we choose for $\mathcal{N}$ the set of terms with variables $\mathcal{T}(\mathcal{F}, \mathcal{X})$. Let us first define a set of patterns which are flat terms, i.e. terms of the form $f(x_1, \ldots, x_n)$ with $f \in \mathcal{F}$. We relate patterns to elements of $\mathcal{M}$ by considering all their possible instantiations $\theta(f(x_1, \ldots, x_n))$. More generally, for a term u with variables, we denote by $\langle u \rangle$ the set $\{\theta(u) \mid \theta \in \Phi\}$ where Φ is the set of all instantiations of $\mathcal{T}(\mathcal{F}, \mathcal{X})$ into $\mathcal{M}$. This definition extends to set of terms $U = \{u_1, \ldots, u_k\}$ in the following way: $\langle U \rangle = \{\langle u_1 \rangle, \ldots, \langle u_k \rangle\}$.

Then the correspondence between the reduction relations $\rightarrow$ and $\rightsquigarrow$ is expressed with a simulation. According to the property to be proved, from a given term, only relevant reduction steps have to be considered. For example, for strong proposition statements, the set of P-relevant reduction steps from a term is the set of all reduction steps from this term. For weak proposition statements, the set of P-relevant reduction steps from a term is reduced to any reduction step from the term.

Definition 2 (P-simulation). *Let $(\mathcal{M}, \rightarrow)$ and $(\mathcal{N}, \rightsquigarrow)$ be two abstract reduction systems. $(\mathcal{N}, \rightsquigarrow)$ is a P-simulation of $(\mathcal{M}, \rightarrow)$ iff there is a relation $L \subseteq \mathcal{N} \times \mathcal{M}$, such that for every P-relevant reduction step $a_1 \rightarrow a_2$, with $a_1, a_2 \in \mathcal{M}$, there is a corresponding reduction step $b_1 \rightsquigarrow b_2$, with $b_1, b_2 \in \mathcal{N}$, and $b_1 L a_1, b_2 L a_2$.*

3.3   Lifting Rewriting Trees into Proof Trees

Let us now observe the derivation tree of $\rightarrow$ starting from an element $t \in \mathcal{M}$ which is any instance of a term $f(x_1, \ldots, x_m)$ for some function symbol $f \in \mathcal{F}$, and variables $x_1, \ldots, x_m$.

This derivation tree is simulated, using a lifting mechanism, by a proof tree, developed from $f(x_1, \ldots, x_m)$ on $\mathcal{T}(\mathcal{F}, \mathcal{X})$, by alternatively using two main operations, namely narrowing and abstraction, adapted to the property to be proved and to the considered reduction relation. Narrowing simulates the reduction possibilities of elements of $\mathcal{M}$, according to the instances of the narrowed terms. The abstraction process simulates sequences of reductions steps in the derivations, which are valid under the induction hypothesis. More precisely, it consists of replacing subterms by special variables, denoting any of their P-canonical forms, without computing them. It is performed on subterms whose instances can be assumed to satisfy the proposition P by induction hypothesis.

The schematization of derivation trees is achieved through constraints. Each node of the developed proof trees is composed of a current term of $\mathcal{T}(\mathcal{F}, \mathcal{X})$ and a constraint progressively built along the successive abstraction and narrowing steps. A node schematizes the set of elements of $\mathcal{M}$ given by the instantiations of the current term, that are solutions of the constraint.

The constraint is in fact composed of two kinds of formulas: ordering constraints, set to warrant the validity of the inductive steps, and abstraction constraints combined to narrowing substitutions, which effectively characterize sets of elements of $\mathcal{M}$. The latter are actually useful for controlling the narrowing process, well known to easily diverge.

3.4   The Overall Mechanism

Let us now consider a proof tree whose root is the pattern $f(x_1, \ldots, x_m)$ and see how we can schematize the reduction relation on instances of $f(x_1, \ldots, x_m)$, with abstraction and narrowing applied on a current term t of the proof tree:

- first, some subterms t_j of the current term t of the proof tree are selected: if $\theta f(x_1, \ldots, x_m) \succ \theta t_j$ for the induction ordering $\succ$ and for every θ solution of the constraint associated to t, we may suppose, by induction hypothesis, that the θt_j satisfy the proposition P. The t_j are then replaced in t by *abstraction variables* X_j representing respectively any of their P-canonical forms $t_j \Downarrow$. Reasoning by induction allows us to suppose the existence of the $t_j \Downarrow$ *without explicitly computing them;*
- second, narrowing the resulting term $u = t[X_j]_{j \in \{i_1, \ldots, i_p\}}$ (where $i_1, \ldots, i_p$ are the positions of the abstracted subterm t_j in t) into terms v, according to the possible instances of the X_j. In general, the narrowing step of u is not unique, but we consider a set of narrowing steps simulating the relevant reductions of the instantiations of u (characterized by the constraint associated to u).

Then the problem of proving P on the instantiations of t is reduced to the problem of proving P on the instantiations of v. If $\theta f(x_1, \ldots, x_m) \succ \theta v$ for every instantiation θ solution of the constraint associated to v, by induction hypothesis, θv is supposed to satisfy P. Otherwise, the process is iterated on v, until getting a term t' such that either $\theta f(x_1, \ldots, x_m) \succ \theta t'$, or $\theta t'$ satisfies P.

The proof procedure given in this paper is described by deduction rules applied with a special control *Strat−Rules*, that depends on the studied reduction relation, and on the proposition to be proved. Applying the deduction rules, according to the strategy, to the initial term $f(x_1, \ldots, x_m)$ builds a proof tree. Branching is produced by the different possible narrowing steps. The proposition P is established when the procedure terminates because the deduction rules do not apply anymore and all terminal nodes of all proof trees represent terms satisfying P.

4   Abstraction, Narrowing, and the Involved Constraints

Let us now formalize the concepts required for our technique, and illustrate them with some particular cases.

4.1   Ordering Constraints

The induction ordering is constrained along the proof by imposing constraints between terms that must be comparable, each time the induction hypothesis is used in the abstraction mechanism. So inequalities of the form $t > u_1, \ldots, u_m$ are accumulated and are called *ordering constraints*.

Definition 3 (ordering constraint). An ordering constraint *is a pair of terms of* $\mathcal{T}(\mathcal{F}, \mathcal{X})$ *denoted by* $(t > t')$. *It is* satisfiable *if there is an ordering* $\succ$, *such that for every instantiation* θ *whose domain contains* $\mathcal{V}ar(t) \cup \mathcal{V}ar(t')$, *we have* $\theta t \succ \theta t'$. *Then we say that* $\succ$ satisfies $(t > t')$. *A conjunction* C *of ordering constraints is satisfiable if there is an ordering satisfying all conjuncts. The empty conjunction, always satisfied, is denoted by* $\top$.

As we are working with a lifting mechanism on the proof trees with terms of $T(\mathcal{F}, \mathcal{X})$, we directly work with an ordering $\succ_{\mathcal{N}}$ on $T(\mathcal{F}, \mathcal{X})$ such that $t \succ_{\mathcal{N}} u$ implies on $\mathcal{M}$ that $\theta t \succ \theta u$, for every θ solution of the constraint associated to u. Any ordering $\succ_{\mathcal{N}}$ on $T(\mathcal{F}, \mathcal{X})$ satisfying the above constraints and which is stable by instantiation fulfills the previous requirements on $\mathcal{M}$. For convenience, the ordering $\succ_{\mathcal{N}}$ is also written $\succ$.

Satisfiability of a constraint conjunction C of the above form is undecidable in general. But a sufficient condition is to find an ordering $\succ$ on $T(\mathcal{F}, \mathcal{X})$ which is stable by instantiation and such that $t \succ t'$ for any constraint $t > t'$ of C.

When $\mathcal{M}$ is $T(\mathcal{F})$, we often try to solve the constraints of C by finding simplification orderings. This is a well-known problem in rewriting. The simplest and most automatable way to proceed is to test simple existing orderings like the subterm ordering, the Recursive Path Ordering, or the Lexicographic Path Ordering. This is often sufficient for the constraints considered here: thanks to the power of induction, they are often simpler than for termination methods directly using orderings for orienting rewrite rules. If these simple orderings are not powerful enough, automatic solvers like Cime [1] can provide adequate polynomial orderings.

4.2   Abstraction

To abstract a term t at positions $j \in \{i_1, \ldots, i_p\}$, we assume that the $t|_j$ are such that every instantiation $\theta t|_j$ verifies the proposition P. It then reduces to a P-canonical form $\theta t|_j\Downarrow$, and we replace the $t|_j$ by abstraction variables X_j representing respectively any of these possible P-canonical forms. Let us define these special variables more formally.

Definition 4. *Let $\mathcal{X}_A$ be a set of variables disjoint from $\mathcal{X}$. Symbols of $\mathcal{X}_A$ are called abstraction variables. Instantiations are extended to $T(\mathcal{F}, \mathcal{X} \cup \mathcal{X}_A)$ in the following way: for any instantiation θ such that $Dom(\theta)$ contains a variable $X \in \mathcal{X}_A$, θX is a P-canonical form.*

Definition 5 (term abstraction). *The term $t[t|_j]_{j \in \{i_1, \ldots, i_p\}}$ is abstracted into the term u (called abstraction of t) at positions $\{i_1, \ldots, i_p\}$ iff $u = t[X_j]_{j \in \{i_1, \ldots, i_p\}}$, where the $X_j, j \in \{i_1, \ldots, i_p\}$ are fresh distinct abstraction variables.*

Term abstraction may involve restrictions related to the choice of abstraction positions according to the proposition P and the reduction relation $\rightarrow$. This is the case for instance for termination proofs under the outermost strategy, where i is an abstraction position only if there is no redex at prefix positions of i.

The proposition P is proved by reasoning on terms with abstraction variables, i.e. in fact on terms of $T(\mathcal{F}, \mathcal{X} \cup \mathcal{X}_A)$. Ordering constraints are extended to pairs of terms of $T(\mathcal{F}, \mathcal{X} \cup \mathcal{X}_A)$. When subterms $t|_j$ are abstracted by X_j, we state constraints on abstraction variables, called *abstraction constraints*, to express

---

[1] Available at http://cime.lri.fr/

that their instantiations can only be P-canonical forms of the corresponding instantiations of $t|_j$. Initially, they are of the form $t\Downarrow = X$ where $t \in \mathcal{T}(\mathcal{F}, \mathcal{X} \cup \mathcal{X}_A)$, and $X \in \mathcal{X}_A$, but we will see later how they are combined with the substitutions used for the narrowing process.

4.3 Narrowing

After abstraction of the current term t into $t[X_j]_{j \in \{i_1, \ldots, i_p\}}$, we check whether the possible instantiations of $t[X_j]_{j \in \{i_1, \ldots, i_p\}}$ are reducible, according to the possible values assigned to the X_j. This is achieved by narrowing $t[X_j]_{j \in \{i_1, \ldots, i_p\}}$.

To simulate the reduction relation on $\mathcal{M}$, a specific narrowing relation $\rightsquigarrow$ is chosen in such a way that $(\mathcal{T}(\mathcal{F}, \mathcal{X} \cup \mathcal{X}_A), \rightsquigarrow)$ is a P-simulation of $(\mathcal{M}, \rightarrow)$.

Let us give examples of such simulations. In these examples, the relation L used in Definition 2 is the $(E\text{-})$subsumption ordering $\leq$, possibly with restrictions expressed via the constraints.

The Case of Rewriting Under Strategies. Let $(\mathcal{M}, \rightarrow)$ be $(\mathcal{T}(\mathcal{F}), \rightarrow^S)$. The narrowing relation depends on the considered strategy S and the usual definition needs to be refined.

First, in the innermost and outermost cases, to ensure P-simulation, an S-narrowing redex in t must correspond to an S-rewriting redex in a ground instance of t. This is the case only if, in the rewriting chain of the ground instance of t, there is no rewriting redex anymore in the part of the term brought by the instantiation. In the innermost case, this condition is fulfilled thanks to normalized instances of abstraction variables. In the outermost case, the condition is ensured by a variable renaming performed before narrowing [27].

Then, among the ground instances of t, there may be innermost (resp. outermost) rewriting positions p for some instances, and p' for some other instances, such that p' is a suffix (resp. a prefix) of p. So, when narrowing at some position p, the set of corresponding ground instances of t is defined by excluding the ground instances that would be narrowable at some suffix (resp. prefix) position p' of p. These positions p' are said S-better than p.

The narrowing steps of a given term t are thus computed in the following way. After applying the variable renaming to t, we look at every non-variable position p of t such that $t|_p$ unifies with the left-hand side of a rule using a substitution σ. The position p is a narrowing position of t, iff there is no S-better position p' of t such that $\sigma t|_{p'}$ unifies with a left-hand side of rule. Then we look for every S-better position p' than p in t such that $\sigma t|_{p'}$ narrows with some substitution σ' and some rule $l' \rightarrow r'$, and we set a constraint to exclude these substitutions. So the substitutions used to narrow a term have in general to satisfy a set of disequalities coming from the negation of previous substitutions. To formalize this point, we need the following notations and definitions.

In the following, we identify a substitution $\sigma = (x_1 \mapsto t_1) \ldots (x_n \mapsto t_n)$ on $\mathcal{T}(\mathcal{F}, \mathcal{X} \cup \mathcal{X}_A)$ with the finite set of solved equations $(x_1 = t_1) \wedge \ldots \wedge (x_n = t_n)$, also denoted by the equality formula $\bigwedge_i(x_i = t_i)$, with $x_i \in \mathcal{X} \cup \mathcal{X}_A$, $t_i \in$

$T(\mathcal{F}, \mathcal{X} \cup \mathcal{X}_A)$, where $=$ is the syntactic equality. Similarly, we call *negation* $\overline{\sigma}$ of the substitution σ the formula $\bigvee_i (x_i \neq t_i)$.

Definition 6 (constrained substitution). *[27] A* constrained substitution σ *is a formula* $\sigma_0 \wedge \bigwedge_j \bigvee_{i_j} (x_{i_j} \neq t_{i_j})$, *where* σ_0 *is a substitution.*

This leads to an adapted definition of narrowing.

Definition 7 (S-narrowing). *[27] A term* $t \in T(\mathcal{F}, \mathcal{X} \cup \mathcal{X}_A)$ S-narrows *into a term* $t' \in T(\mathcal{F}, \mathcal{X} \cup \mathcal{X}_A)$ *at the non-variable position* p *of* t, *using the rule* $l \to r \in \mathcal{R}$ *with the constrained substitution* $\sigma = \sigma_0 \wedge \bigwedge_{j \in [1..k]} \overline{\sigma_j}$, *which is written* $t \leadsto^S_{p, l \to r, \sigma} t'$ *iff*

$$\sigma_0(l) = \sigma_0(t|_p) \text{ and } t' = \sigma_0(t[r]_p)$$

where σ_0 *is the most general unifier of* $t|_p$ *and* l *and* $\sigma_j, j \in [1..k]$ *are all most general unifiers of* $\sigma_0 t|_{p'}$ *and a left-hand side* l' *of a rule of* $\mathcal{R}$, *for all positions* p' *which are* S-better *than* p *in* t.

The following lifting lemma generalizes [51] and states that $(T(\mathcal{F}, \mathcal{X}), \leadsto)$ P-simulates $(T(\mathcal{F}), \to^S)$.

Lemma 1 (S-lifting Lemma). *[27] Let* $\mathcal{R}$ *be a rewrite system. Let* $s \in T(\mathcal{F}, \mathcal{X})$, α *a ground substitution such that* αs *is* S-reducible *at a non variable position* p *of* s, *and* $\mathcal{Y} \subseteq \mathcal{X}$ *a set of variables such that* $Var(s) \cup Dom(\alpha) \subseteq \mathcal{Y}$. *If* $\alpha s \to^S_{p, l \to r} t'$, *then there exist a term* $s' \in T(\mathcal{F}, \mathcal{X})$ *and substitutions* $\beta, \sigma = \sigma_0 \wedge \bigwedge_{j \in [1..k]} \overline{\sigma_j}$ *such that:*

1. $s \leadsto^S_{p, l \to r, \sigma} s'$,
2. $\beta s' = t'$,
3. $\beta \sigma_0 = \alpha[\mathcal{Y}]$
4. β *satisfies* $\bigwedge_{j \in [1..k]} \overline{\sigma_j}$

where σ_0 *is the most general unifier of* $s|_p$ *and* l, *for* $j \in [1..k]$ *the* σ_j *are the most general unifiers of* $\sigma_0 s|_{p'}$ *with a left-hand side* l' *of a rule of* $\mathcal{R}$, *for all positions* p' *which are* S-better *than* p *in* s.

The Case of C-Reducibility. Let $(\mathcal{M}, \to)$ be $(T(\mathcal{F}), \to_{\mathcal{R}})$. There we need a covering property of the narrowed term by narrowing substitutions (see [26]), and the following lemma.

Lemma 2. *[26] Let* $\mathcal{R}$ *be a rewrite system,* u *a term of* $T(\mathcal{F}, \mathcal{X}_A)$, *and* Σ *the set of narrowing substitutions of* u *for* $\mathcal{R}$. *If* Σ *is covering* u, *then every ground instance* αu *of* u *is such that* $\alpha u \to^{p, l \to r, \beta \sigma}_{\mathcal{R}} t'$, *for some ground substitution* β, *and we have* $u \leadsto^{p, l \to r, \sigma}_{\mathcal{R}} v$ *for some* v *of* $T(\mathcal{F}, \mathcal{X}_A)$, $\beta \sigma = \alpha$ *on any variable set* $\mathcal{Y} \supseteq Var(u) \cup Dom(\alpha)$, *and* $t' = \beta v$.

The Case of Transition Systems. In rewriting logic, a concurrent system is axiomatized as a rewrite theory modulo some equational axioms with system transitions described by rewrite rules. As defined in [50], a topmost rewrite theory is such that E-equivalence classes of ground terms are made of terms of a given sort and rewrite rules $l \rightarrow r$ are such that l and r are of the same sort. Such rewrite theories specify concurrent systems in Maude. They enjoy a specific lifting lemma, thanks to the fact that the relations $\rightarrow_{R/E}$ and $\rightarrow_{R,E}$ coincide in this context.

Lemma 3. *[50] For a topmost theory $(\mathcal{F}, E, \mathcal{R})$, let t in $\mathcal{T}(\mathcal{F}, \mathcal{X})$ be a non variable term and V a set of variables containing $\mathcal{V}ar(t)$. For some substitution ρ, let $\rho(t) \rightarrow_{R/E} t'$ using the rule $l \rightarrow r$ in $\mathcal{R}$. Then there are σ, θ, t'' such that $t \rightsquigarrow_{\mathcal{R},E}^{\sigma} t''$ using the same rule $l \rightarrow r$, t'' is not a variable, $\rho =_E (\theta \circ \sigma)$ on V and $\theta(t'') =_E t'$.*

4.4 Cumulating Constraints

Abstraction constraints have to be combined with the narrowing substitutions to characterize the set of elements of $\mathcal{M}$ schematized in the proof trees. A narrowing step effectively corresponds to a rewriting step of instantiations of u if the narrowing substitution σ is *compatible* with the abstraction constraints associated to u. Otherwise, the narrowing step is meaningless. So the narrowing constraint attached to the narrowing step is added to abstraction constraints, to get an *abstraction constraint formula* (ACF for short).

In the case of termination under strategies, the ACF may be a complex formula of the form $\bigwedge_i (t_i \Downarrow = t_i') \wedge \bigwedge_j (x_j = t_j) \wedge \bigwedge_k \bigvee_{l_k} (u_{l_k} \neq v_{l_k})$, where $t_i, t_i', t_j, u_{l_k}, v_{l_k} \in \mathcal{T}(\mathcal{F}, \mathcal{X} \cup \mathcal{X}_A)$, $x_j \in \mathcal{X} \cup \mathcal{X}_A$. For specific definitions of an ACF and its solutions, see [27,20,26].

An ACF A is attached to each term u in the proof trees; its solutions characterize the interesting instantiations of u, i.e. the θu such that θ is a solution of A. When A has no solution, the current node of the proof tree represents no element of $\mathcal{M}$. Such nodes are then useless for the proof. Detecting and suppressing them when applying a narrowing step allows controlling the narrowing mechanism. So we have the choice between generating only the useful nodes of the proof tree, by testing the satisfiability of A at each step, or stopping the proof on a branch on an useless node, by testing the unsatisfiability of A. These are both facets of the same question, but in practice, they are handled in different ways. Checking the satisfiability of A is in general undecidable, but sufficient conditions can be given, relying on a characterization of P-canonical forms. The unsatisfiability of A is also undecidable in general, but simple automatable sufficient conditions can be used, very often applicable in practice. They rely on reducibility, unifiability, narrowing and constructor tests [27].

4.5 Relaxing the Induction Hypothesis

It is important to point out the flexibility of the proof method that allows the combination with auxiliary proofs of P using different techniques: when the induction hypothesis cannot be applied on a term u, i.e. when it is not possible to decide whether the ordering constraints are satisfiable, it may be possible to prove P for any instantiation of u (which is denoted by $P(\langle u \rangle)$) by another way.

When termination properties are addressed, the notion of usable rules [1], adapted to the case of strategies [27,19,17], can be very useful to prove P.

Moreover, $P(\langle u \rangle)$ is true when, in particular, every instantiation of u is a P-canonical form. For termination, this is the case when u is not narrowable, and all variables of u are abstraction variables in $\mathcal{X}_A$. Indeed, by Definition 4 and Lemma 1 for weak innermost or S-termination of rewriting, every instantiation of u is a P-canonical form. This includes the cases where u itself is an abstraction variable, and where u is a non narrowable ground term. P is also true on a narrowable u whose variables are all in $\mathcal{X}_A$, and whose narrowing substitutions are not compatible with A. As said in Section 4.4, these narrowing possibilities do not represent any reduction step for the instantiations of u, which are then P-canonical forms. For C-reducibility, terms of $\mathcal{T}(\mathcal{C}, \mathcal{X}_A)$ are P-canonical forms.

5   The Proof Procedure

5.1   Inference Rules

We are now ready to describe the different steps of the proof mechanism presented in Section 3.

The proof steps generate proof trees in transforming 3-tuples (T, A, C) where

- T is either a singleton containing the current term u of $\mathcal{T}(\mathcal{F}, \mathcal{X} \cup \mathcal{X}_A)$ or the empty set,
- A is a conjunction of abstraction constraints. At each abstraction step, constraints of the form $u{\Downarrow} = X, u \in \mathcal{T}(\mathcal{F}, \mathcal{X} \cup \mathcal{X}_A), X \in \mathcal{X}_A$ are added to A for each subterm u abstracted into a new abstraction variable X. At each narrowing step with narrowing substitution σ, σ is added to A,
- C is a conjunction of ordering constraints stated by the abstraction steps.

Starting from initial nodes $(T = \{f(x_1, \ldots, x_m)\}, A = \top, C = \top)$, with $f \in \mathcal{F}$, the proof process consists in applying the inference rules described in Table 1.

In these rules, the satisfiability of A is checked before each narrowing step only. For the abstraction and stop steps, arguments on variables and the application order of the rules allow deducing that the satisfiability of A is preserved. For details and variants on the conditions of the inference rules, especially with unsatisfiability test of A, see [27].

5.2   How to Combine the Inference Rules

The previous inference rules, applied to every pattern $p = f(x_1, \ldots, x_m)$, where $x_1, \ldots, x_m \in \mathcal{X}$ and $f \in \mathcal{F}$, are combined with the following control:

$$Strat-Rules = repeat^*(try(abstract),\ try-dk(narrow),\ try(stop)).$$

Table 1. Inference rules applied on the pattern $p = f(x_1, \ldots, x_m)$

Abstract: $\dfrac{\{t\}, \quad A, \quad C}{\{u\}, \quad A \wedge \bigwedge\limits_{j \in \{i_1, \ldots, i_p\}} t|_j \!\Downarrow\, = X_j, \quad C \wedge \bigwedge\limits_{j \in \{i_1, \ldots, i_p\}} H_C(t|_j)}$

where t is abstracted into u at positions $i_1, \ldots, i_p \neq \epsilon$

if $C \wedge H_C(t|_{i_1}) \ldots \wedge H_C(|t_{i_p})$ is satisfiable

Narrow: $\dfrac{\{t\}, \quad A, \quad C}{\{u\}, \quad A \wedge \sigma, \quad C}$

if $t \rightsquigarrow_\sigma u$ and $A \wedge \sigma$ is satisfiable

Stop: $\dfrac{\{t\}, \quad A, \quad C}{\emptyset, \quad A \wedge H_A(t), \quad C \wedge H_C(t)}$

if $(C \wedge H_C(t))$ is satisfiable.

and $H_A(t) = \begin{cases} \top & \text{if all instantiations of } t \text{ are P−canonical forms} \\ t\!\Downarrow\, = X & \text{otherwise.} \end{cases}$

$H_C(t) = \begin{cases} \top & \text{if } P(\langle t \rangle) \\ p > t & \text{otherwise.} \end{cases}$

The control strategy $"repeat^*(T_1, \ldots, T_n)"$ repeats the control strategies of the list $(T_1, \ldots, T_n)$ until it is not possible anymore. The operator $"try"$ is a generic operator that can be instantiated, following the given reduction relation, by $try-skip(T)$, expressing that the strategy or rule T is tried and skipped when it cannot be applied, or by $try-stop(T)$, stopping the strategy if T cannot be applied. The operator $"try-dk"$ is defined like $"try"$, but the strategy T has to be applied in all possible ways (which generates branching nodes in the proof trees). This is required to generate all narrowing steps simulating the relevant reductions.

5.3   The General Theorem

Let us assume that the rule **Narrow** is applied with a narrowing relation such that $(\mathcal{T}(\mathcal{F}, \mathcal{X} \cup \mathcal{X}_A), \rightsquigarrow)$ is a simulation of $(\mathcal{M}, \rightarrow)$. We write $SUCCESS(f, \rightsquigarrow, \succ)$ if the application of $Strat-Rules$ on $(\{f(x_1, \ldots, x_m)\}, \top, \top)$, gives a finite proof tree, whose sets C of ordering constraints are satisfied by a same ordering $\succ$, and whose leaves are nodes of the form $(\emptyset, A, C)$.

The following theorem is stated provided an emptiness lemma, an abstraction lemma, a narrowing lemma and a stopping lemma hold (see below). These lemmas depend on the proposition P, on the set $\mathcal{M}$ and on the relations $\rightarrow$ and $\rightsquigarrow$, and are established for each case.

Theorem 1. *Let $(\mathcal{M}, \rightarrow)$ be an abstract reduction system, where $\mathcal{M}$ is an $\mathcal{F}$-algebra, P be a proposition to be proved on $(\mathcal{M}, \rightarrow)$, and $(\mathcal{T}(\mathcal{F}, \mathcal{X} \cup \mathcal{X}_A), \rightsquigarrow)$ a*

P-simulation of $(\mathcal{M}, \rightarrow)$. *Let* $\mathcal{I}$ *be the subset of constants of* $\mathcal{F}$ *such that the elements of* $\langle \mathcal{I} \rangle$ *are irreducible for* $\rightarrow$. $\mathcal{I}$ *is assumed to be non-empty. If*

- *there is a noetherian ordering* $\succ$ *such that for each* $f \in \mathcal{F} \setminus \mathcal{I}$, *we have* $SUCCESS(f, \leadsto, \succ)$,
- P *is true on* $\langle \mathcal{I} \rangle$,

then P *is true on* $\mathcal{M}$.

Proof. By hypothesis, on $\langle \mathcal{I} \rangle$, P is true. We may thus restrict our attention to the elements of $\mathcal{M} \setminus \langle \mathcal{I} \rangle$, simulated by the patterns $f(x_1, ..., x_n)$.

Let us prove that $\theta f(x_1, ..., x_m)$ satisfies P for any θ satisfying $A = \top$ if we have $SUCCESS(f, \leadsto, \succ)$ for every defined symbol $f \in \mathcal{F} \setminus \mathcal{I}$.

To each node N of the proof tree of f, characterized by a current term t and the set of constraints A, we associate the set of elements $G = \{\alpha t \mid \alpha \text{ satisfies } A\}$, that is the set of elements of $\mathcal{M}$ represented by N.

Inference rule **Abstract** (resp. **Narrow**) transforms $(\{t\}, A)$ into $(\{t'\}, A')$ to which is associated $G' = \{\beta t' \mid \beta \text{ satisfies } A'\}$ (resp. into $(\{t'_i\}, A'_i), i \in [1..l]$ to which are associated $G' = \{\beta_i t'_i \mid \beta_i \text{ satisfies } A'_i\}$).

By Abstraction (resp. narrowing) Lemma, applying **Abstract** (resp. **Narrow**), for each αt in G, there is a $\beta t'$ (resp. $\beta_i t'_i$) in G' and such that P is true for $\beta t'$ (resp. for the $\beta_i t'_i$) implies P is true for αt.

When the inference rule **Stop** applies on $(\{t\}, A, C)$, A is satisfiable, and then, by Stopping Lemma, every element of $G = \{\alpha t \mid \alpha \text{ satisfies } A\}$ satisfies P.

Therefore, the proposition P is true for all terms in all sets G.

As the process is initialized with $\{f(x_1, ..., x_m)\}$ and a constraint problem satisfiable by any instantiation, we get that $\theta f(x_1, ..., x_m)$ satisfies P, for any $f(x_1, ..., x_m)$ and any instantiation θ. □

The following lemmas are necessary for the proof of Theorem 1 and have to be proved for each instance of P and $\rightarrow$.

Lemma 4 (Abstraction Lemma). *Let* $(\{t\}, A, C)$ *be a node of any proof tree, giving the node* $(\{t' = t[X_j]_{j \in \{i_1, ..., i_p\}}\}, A', C')$ *by application of* **Abstract**.

For any instantiation α *satisfying* A, *if* αt *is reducible, there is* β *such that* P *is true for* $\beta t'$ *implies* P *is true on* αt. *Moreover,* β *satisfies* A'.

The narrowing lemma has two versions, according to the strong (resp. weak) character of the proposition P to be proved.

Lemma 5 (Narrowing Lemma). *Let the narrowing relation used in* **Narrow** *be such that* $(\mathcal{T}(\mathcal{F}, \mathcal{X} \cup \mathcal{X}_A), \leadsto)$ *is a P-simulation of* $(\mathcal{M}, \rightarrow)$. *Let* $(\{t\}, A, C)$ *be a node of any proof tree, giving the nodes* $(\{v_i\}, A'_i, C'_i), i \in [1..l]$, *by application of* **Narrow**.

For any instantiation α *satisfying* A, *if* αt *is reducible, then, for each* $i \in [1..l]$, *there exist* β_i *such that* P *is true for all (resp. one of) the* $\beta_i v_i, i \in [1..l]$, *implies* P *is true for* αt. *Moreover,* β_i *satisfies* A'_i *for each* $i \in [1..l]$.

Lemma 6 (Stopping Lemma). *Let* $(\{t\}, A, C)$ *be a node of any proof tree with* A *satisfiable, and giving the node* $(\emptyset, A', C')$ *by application of an inference rule. Then for any instantiation* α *satisfying* A, αt *satisfies* P.

5.4 An Example

Consider the following rewrite system $\mathcal{R}$, taken from [20], which is not terminating, nor even, because of the rule (2), innermost terminating.

$$f(g(x), s(0)) \rightarrow f(g(x), g(x)) \tag{1}$$
$$f(g(x), s(y)) \rightarrow f(h(x, y), s(0)) \tag{2}$$
$$g(s(x)) \rightarrow s(g(x)) \tag{3}$$
$$g(0) \rightarrow 0 \tag{4}$$
$$h(x, y) \rightarrow g(x). \tag{5}$$

Let us prove weak innermost termination of $\mathcal{R}$ on $\mathcal{T}(\mathcal{F})$, with $\mathcal{F} = \{f : 2, h : 2, g : 1, s : 1, 0 : 0\}$. Since the defined symbols of $\mathcal{R}$ are f, g, and h, we have to apply the inference rules to $f(x_1, x_2)$, $g(x_1)$ and $h(x_1, x_2)$. The proof trees, given in Figure 1 show how the inference rules are applied. When **Narrow** applies, we specify the narrowing substitution, and in parentheses, the rewrite rule number used to narrow.

For weak propositions, when narrowing produces several steps simulating reduction steps for the same set of ground instances, we develop all branches in parallel to increase the chances to get success, i.e. to get branches ending with an application of **Stop**. As soon as one is successful, the other ones are cut.

On the example, the subtree marked by $\odot$ in the proof tree of f is cut as soon as the subtree generated on the left from $f(\mathbf{X_6}, \mathbf{s(0)})$ with the same substitution (up to a renaming) $\sigma = (X_6 = g(X_7)) \wedge (X_7 \neq s(X_8) \wedge X_7 \neq 0)$ is successful. The final proof trees are **bold**.

6   Finding P-Canonical Forms for Weak Properties

When P is a weak proposition, computing a P-canonical form with the reduction relation $\rightarrow$ in general requires to develop the reduction trees with a breadth-first strategy to capture the branch leading to the good elements. But such a strategy is often very costly, and it is much better to have hints about the good derivations to compute them directly with a depth-first mechanism.

Our proof process, as it simulates the reduction mechanism, gives complete information on the interesting reduction branches. It allows extracting the exact application of reduction that yields an interesting form, like a normal form or a constructor form. The breadth-first strategy is used once, for generating the proof trees. Then, to reduce an element, it is enough to follow the reduction scheme simulated by abstraction and narrowing in the proof trees.

When $\mathcal{M}$ is $\mathcal{T}(\mathcal{F})$ and $\rightarrow$ a rewriting relation, a P-canonical form for any element of $\mathcal{M}$ is computed with a reduction strategy ST that is built according to the proof trees establishing the proposition P.

Definition 8. *Let P be a proposition on $(\mathcal{T}(\mathcal{F}), \rightarrow)$ proved using Theorem 1. The strategy tree ST_f associated to $f \in \mathcal{F}$ is the proof tree obtained from the initial node $(\{f(x_1, \ldots, x_m)\}, \top, \top)$.*

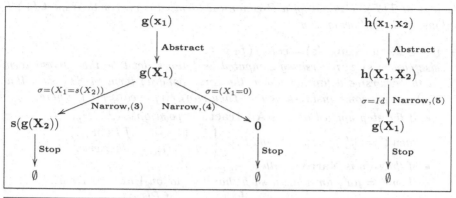

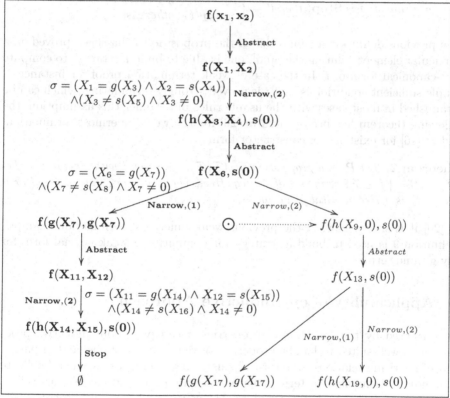

Fig. 1. Example. Proof trees for symbols g, h and f.

The computation of a P-canonical form of any element of $\mathcal{T}(\mathcal{F})$ follows the strategy trees.

Definition 9. *Let P be a proposition on $(\mathcal{T}(\mathcal{F}), \to)$ proved using Theorem 1. Let $ST = \{ST_f \mid f \in \mathcal{F}\}$ be the set of strategy trees, and $s = f(t_1, \ldots, t_n)$ be an* *element of $\mathcal{T}(\mathcal{F})$. Computing a P-canonical form $can_{ST}(s)$ with respect to ST is done in the following way:*

- *if $f \in \mathcal{I}$, then $can_{ST}(s) = can_{ST}(f) = f$,*
- *else $can_{ST}(s)$ is recursively computed as follows: let t be the current term in the recursive definition and u the corresponding term in ST_f such that $\theta(u) = t$ for some instantiation θ. Then $can_{ST}(t) = can_{ST}(t')$, where*
  - *if the step applied on u is **Abstract**, at positions $i_1, \ldots, i_p$,*
    then $t' = t[t'_1]_{i_1} \ldots [t'_p]_{i_p}$, and $t'_j = \begin{cases} t|_{i_j} \Downarrow & \text{if } P(\langle u|_{i_j} \rangle) \\ can_{ST}(t|_{i_j}) & \text{otherwise,} \end{cases}$
  - *if the step is **Narrow** with $u \leadsto_{p,l \to r,\sigma} u'$,*
    then $t' = \mu u'$, for some μ such that $\theta = \mu\sigma$ on $Var(u) \cup \mathcal{D}om(\theta)$,
  - *if the step is **Stop**, then $t' = \begin{cases} t\Downarrow & \text{if } P(\langle u \rangle) \\ can_{ST}(t) & \text{otherwise.} \end{cases}$*

The previous definition assumes that if the proposition P has been proved on a particular element t during the proof, one is able to build a strategy to compute a P-canonical form of t. In the case of weak termination proof for instance, a simple sufficient condition is that t is proved strongly terminating, which can be established in most cases with the usable rules of t. Under this assumption, the following theorem has been proved in [20] for the weak innermost termination, and in [26] for existence of constructor forms.

Theorem 2. *Let P be a proposition on $(\mathcal{T}(\mathcal{F}), \to)$ proved with Theorem 1. Let $ST = \{ST_f \mid f \in \mathcal{F}\}$ be the set of strategy trees. Then for every element $t \in \mathcal{T}(\mathcal{F})$, $can_{ST}(t)$ is a P-canonical form for $\to$.*

In [20] it is shown how, in the previous weak innermost termination example, Definition 9 is used to build a strategy for computing a weak normal form for any ground term.

7   Applicability of our Inductive Approach

As witnessed by the spectrum of properties it can prove, our inductive proof method is well-suited to handle properties of reduction relations, and in particular of rewriting relations. In return, the used ingredients are in general delicate to handle: satisfiability of term ordering constraints is undecidable, as well as satisfiability of abstraction constraints. Moreover the narrowing process easily diverges.

However, in the context where these notions are used, we can deal with them in a reasonable efficient way. Cariboo [18,21], an implementation of our method for termination under the innermost, outermost and local strategies, allowed us to observe how these notions behave in an operational and practical way.

Ordering Constraints. Satisfiability of term ordering constraints can be handled with sufficient conditions based on existing orderings. For instance, testing simple orderings as the subterm ordering or a lexicographic path ordering is sufficient for more than 80% of the innermost examples treated by Cariboo (most than 200 tested), thanks to the power of induction, and to the help of usable rules. For the other ones, a constraint solver providing polynomial interpretations gives a solution. The failure cases are due to generated ordering constraints whose resolution requires to compare abstraction variables with standard variables, or which cannot be satisfied by simplification orderings, because of constraints incompatible with term embedding. In the first case, additional knowledge on normal forms can solve the problem. For the second case, other orderings must be tried.

For C-reducibility, ordering constraints are easier to solve. Indeed, it can be assumed that the constructor terms are minimal for the induction ordering, which allows us to compare abstraction variables with standard variables, and avoids the first above failure case.

Abstraction Constraints. As said before, simple and easily implementable sufficient conditions exist for proving unsatisfiability of A. Meaningless nodes in proof trees are then automatically detected and the process stops with success on the current branch.

Sufficient conditions for satisfiability can also be given, relying on a characterization of P-canonical forms. An obvious solution for an abstraction constraint of the form $t{\Downarrow} = X$ is t itself if t is a P-canonical form.

Narrowing. Narrowing substitutions, in the same way as abstraction constraints, restrict the considered sets of instantiations in the nodes of the proof trees. As the abstraction formula A, collecting both kinds of restrictions, is proved to be (un)satisfiable at each step of the proofs, useless narrowing steps are detected and discarded.

Moreover, for weak properties, as said before, redundant branches generated by narrowing i.e. branches representing the same sets of ground instances can be detected and cut.

8 Related Work

Several properties considered in our approach are also provable with other methods. A number of works address the termination property for the innermost, context sensitive and lazy rewriting strategies. Sufficient completeness has also been investigated for conditional and typed specifications, in the confluent (every derivation chain from a given element leads to the same form) and terminating case. Let us see more in detail how these works relate to our approach.

Innermost Termination. The termination proof for the innermost strategy has also be tackled with the dependency pair method, designed from 1996 by T. Arts and J. Giesl for universal termination of rewriting [1,24,23]. The comparison between this method and our approach is not easy to do. Indeed, several basic ingredients are shared: narrowing, ordering constraints, usable rules are present in both contexts. But while the dependency pairs method is initially based on an analysis of the rules syntax to detect forward closures, our approach was guided by the idea to schematize derivation trees, which allows us to abstract the reduction relation. Except for the innermost case, handling specific rewriting strategies seems more difficult with the dependency pair approach.

Simulation by narrowing has been used as the basis of our method, since 1999 [28], to schematize rewriting steps of terms, following their possible ground instances. In the dependency pair approach instead [1], narrowing has been introduced to provide a sufficient condition to detect the dependencies between pairs.

Usable rules have been introduced in the dependency pair approach [1] for innermost termination. We then have adapted the notion to local strategies [17], and to the outermost strategy [19], to enrich our inductive proof principle.

Let us mention another work establishing that orderings suitable for proving innermost termination have to be at least monotonic after each maximal parallel innermost rewriting step [16]. A similar structural requirement is expressed on the induction ordering needed for our inductive approach, through constraints $f(x_1, ..., x_n) > x_i$ for function symbols f in patterns.

Termination under Local Strategies. Many results have recently be given for termination of the context-sensitive rewriting [45,22,48], which involves particular kinds of local strategies [46,47].

Local strategies, giving ordered lists of positions to be rewritten in a term, are more specific than context sensitive strategies, where the order of reduced positions is not specified. They can enable termination while the context sensitive strategy diverges [17].

Outermost Termination. Outermost computations are of interest in particular for functional languages, where interpreters or compilers generally involve a strategy for call by name. Often, lazy evaluation is used instead: operators are labeled in terms as lazy or eager, and the strategy consists of reducing the eager subterms only when their reduction allows a reduction step higher in the term [53]. Termination of lazy evaluation has been studied for functional languages (see for example [55] and [25] for Haskell).

A double motivation for studying the outermost computation is that it is simpler to implement and that lazy evaluation may diverge while the outermost computation terminates [19]. Up to our knowledge, there is still no other termination proof method for specifically proving outermost termination of rewriting.

Weak Termination. The weak termination property has been studied from several perspectives. For instance, B. Gramlich proved that weak termination can imply strong termination [31,32] under some syntactic restrictions. He also established conditions on rewrite systems for the property to be preserved by the union operation [33]. J. Goubault-Larrecq proposed a proof of weak termination of typed Lambda-Sigma calculi in [30]. Beyond these works and our's, we are not aware of other techniques for establishing weak termination of rewriting. Our method even proves weak termination of systems that are not innermost strongly terminating.

C-reducibility. Sufficient completeness has already been widely studied, for example in [35,54,41,37,12,36,44,6,5,34,7], but most of the time, the proposed approaches for proving the property need restrictions like termination and confluence. Under the last two assumptions, sufficient completeness can also be tackled through ground reducibility (expressing that every ground instance of a term is reducible) [56,38,36,42,8,13], provided the normal form of a constructor term is again a constructor term [36].

Our approach for proving C-reducibility goes beyond the previous usual restrictions, proposing for the first time a technique for proving the reachability of constructor forms for programs or rewrite systems that can be neither confluent, nor terminating. No restriction on the domain is required, such as the constructor preserving property, or the absence of relation between constructors. Although our method differs from previous approaches, we naturally encounter basic notions already used for proving sufficient completeness, as unification, used in [44], or covering properties used in many works in the domain, for example in [41,44]. In [5], pattern trees are also developed, but under the assumption that the rewrite system is terminating and ground confluent.

9 Conclusion

In this paper, we have presented an inductive proof method for properties of reduction relations on an abstract reduction system $(\mathcal{M}, \rightarrow)$ where $\mathcal{M}$ is an $\mathcal{F}$-algebra. Let us summarize its main characteristics.

We handle proofs of a proposition P stating a property by observing the possible derivation trees of the relation $\rightarrow$, schematizing them with a narrowing relation on terms. Several examples have been given where $\mathcal{M}$ is $\mathcal{T}(\mathcal{F})$ and $\rightarrow$ various rewrite relations. Other applications are suggested and need further study.

Induction with a noetherian ordering on $\mathcal{M}$ is used to modelize subderivations leading to a P-canonical form, and to stop derivations as soon as P can be supposed true by induction. The inference process is expressed with three inference steps: an abstraction and a stop step, expressing respectively the above induction mechanisms, and a narrowing step, simulating the reductions on a given term. Constraints are heavily used on one hand to gather conditions that the induction ordering must satisfy, on the other hand to represent the set of instantiations of terms. The power of deduction with constraints [39] is once more illustrated in this proof process.

Despite the proof method is strongly based on derivation trees, the induction relation is not the reduction relation, which is then not required to be terminating. Our approach for proving the property of reduction to a constructor form [26] nicely illustrates this fact.

An interesting aspect of this technique is that it allows, for weak properties, the identification of interesting branches leading to P-canonical forms, like normal forms or constructor forms. Their computation is guided by the proof trees of the weak property. How this can be exploited for certifying compilers of rewrite programs needs to be further explored.

References

1. Arts, T., Giesl, J.: Proving innermost normalisation automatically. In: Comon, H. (ed.) Rewriting Techniques and Applications. LNCS, vol. 1232, pp. 157–171. Springer, Heidelberg (1997)
2. Baader, F., Nipkow, T.: Term Rewriting and all That. Cambridge University Press, New York, NY, USA (1998)
3. Balland, E., Brauner, P., Kopetz, R., Moreau, P.-E., Reilles, A.: Tom Manual LORIA, Nancy (France) (version 2.4 edition) (2006)
4. Bezem, M., Klop, J.W., de Vrijer, R.: Term Rewriting Systems. In: Cambridge Tracts in Theoretical Computer Science. Cambridge University Press, Cambridge (2003)
5. Bouhoula, A., Jaquemard, F.: Automatic verification of. sufficient completeness for. specifications of complex data structures. Technical Report RR-LSV-05-17, INRIA (2005)
6. Bouhoula, A.: Using induction and rewriting to verify and complete parameterized specifications. Theoretical Computer Science 170(1-2), 245–276 (1996)
7. Bouhoula, A., Jacquemard, F.: Automating sufficient completeness check for conditional and constrained TRS. In: Levy, J (ed): Proceedings of the 20th International Workshop on Unification (UNIF'06), Seattle, Washington, USA (August 2006)
8. Caron, A-C., Coquide, J-L., Dauchet, M.: Encompassment properties and automata with constraints. In: Kirchner, C. (ed.) Rewriting Techniques and Applications. LNCS, vol. 690, pp. 328–342. Springer, Heidelberg (1993)
9. Cirstea, H., Kirchner, C.: The rewriting calculus — Part I and II. Logic Journal of the Interest Group in Pure and Applied Logics 9, 427–498 (2001)
10. Cirstea, H., Kirchner, C., Liquori, L., Wack, B.: Rewrite strategies in the rewriting calculus. In: Gramlich, B., Lucas, S. (eds.) Electronic Notes in Theoretical Computer Science, vol. 86, Elsevier, North-Holland, Amsterdam (2003)
11. Clavel, M., Durán, F., Eker, S., Lincoln, P., Martí-Oliet, N., Meseguer, J., Quesada, J.F.: Maude: specification and programming in rewriting logic. Theoretical Computer Science 285(2), 187–243 (2002)
12. Comon, H.: Sufficient completeness, term rewriting system and anti-unification. In: Siekmann, J.H. (ed.) CADE 1986. LNCS, vol. 230, pp. 128–140. Springer, Heidelberg (1986)
13. Comon, H., Jacquemard, F.: Ground reducibility is EXPTIME-complete. In: Proc. 12th IEEE Symp. Logic in Computer Science, pp. 26–34. IEEE Comp. Soc. Press, Washington, DC, USA (1997)
14. Dershowitz, N., Jouannaud, J.-P.: Handbook of Theoretical Computer Science In: Rewrite Systems, ch. 6, vol. B, pp. 244–320. Elsevier Science Publishers B. V., North-Holland, Amsterdam (Also as: Research report 478, LRI). (1990)
15. Dershowitz, N., Plaisted, D.A.: Rewriting. In: Robinson, A., Voronkov, A. (eds.) Handbook of Automated Reasoning, vol. I, ch.9, pp. 535–610. Elsevier Science Publisher B.V., North-Holland, Amsterdam (2001)
16. Fernández, M.-L., Godoy, G., Rubio, A.: Orderings for innermost termination. In: Giesl, J. (ed.) RTA 2005. LNCS, vol. 3467, pp. 17–31. Springer, Heidelberg (2005)

17. Fissore, O., Gnaedig, I., Kirchner, H.: Termination of rewriting with local strategies. In: Bonacina, M.P., Gramlich, B. (eds.) Selected papers of the 4th International Workshop on Strategies in Automated Deduction. Electronic Notes in Theoretical Computer Science, vol. 58, Elsevier Science Publishers B. V., North-Holland, Amsterdam (2001)

18. Fissore, O., Gnaedig, I., Kirchner, H.: Cariboo: An induction based proof tool for termination with strategies. Proceedings of the 4th International Conference on Principles and Practice of Declarative Programming, Pittsburgh (USA). ACM Press, New York (2002)

19. Fissore, O., Gnaedig, I., Kirchner, H.: Outermost ground termination. In: Proceedings of the 4th International Workshop on Rewriting Logic and Its Applications, Pisa, Italy, September 2002. Electronic Notes in Theoretical Computer Science, vol. 71. Elsevier Science Publishers B. V., North-Holland, Amsterdam (2002)

20. Fissore, O., Gnaedig, I., Kirchner, H.: A proof of weak termination providing the right way to terminate. In: Liu, Z., Araki, K. (eds.) ICTAC 2004. LNCS, vol. 3407, pp. 356–371. Springer, Heidelberg (2004)

21. Fissore, O., Gnaedig, I., Kirchner, H., Moussa, L.: Cariboo, a termination proof tool for rewriting-based programming languages with strategies, Version 1.1. Free GPL Licence, APP registration IDDN.FR.001.170013.001.S.P.2005.000.10600 (December 2005) Available at http://protheo.loria.fr/softwares/cariboo/

22. Giesl, J., Middeldorp, A.: Transforming Context-Sensitive Rewrite Systems. In: Narendran, P., Rusinowitch, M. (eds.) RTA 1999. LNCS, vol. 1631, pp. 271–285. Springer, Heidelberg (1999)

23. Giesl, J., Middeldorp, A.: Innermost termination of context-sensitive rewriting. In: Ito, M., Toyama, M. (eds.) DLT 2002. LNCS, vol. 2450, pp. 231–244. Springer, Heidelberg (2003)

24. Giesl, J., Thiemann, R., Schneider-Kamp, P., Falke, S.: Improving dependency pairs. In: Vardi, M.Y., Voronkov, A. (eds.) LPAR 2003. LNCS(LNAI), vol. 2850, pp. 165–179. Springer, Heidelberg (2003)

25. Giesl, J., Swiderski, S., Schneider-Kamp, P., Thiemann, R.: Automated Termination Analysis for Haskell: From term rewriting to programming languages. In: Pfenning, F. (ed.) RTA 2006. LNCS, vol. 4098, pp. 297–312. Springer, Heidelberg (2006)

26. Gnaedig, I., Kirchner, H.: Computing constructor forms with non terminating rewrite programs. In: Maher, M. (ed.) Proceedings of the Eighth ACM SIGPLAN Symposium on Principles and Practice of Declarative Programming, Venice, Italy, pp. 121–132. ACM Press, New York (July 2006)

27. Gnaedig, I., Kirchner, H.: Termination of rewriting under strategies: a generic approach, Submitted. Also as HAL-INRIA Open Archive Number inria-00113156 (2006)

28. Gnaedig, I., Kirchner, H., Genet, T.: Induction for Termination. Technical Report 99.R.338, LORIA, Nancy (France) (December 1999)

29. Goguen, J.A., Jouannaud, J.-P., Meseguer, J.: Operational semantics for order-sorted algebra. In: Brauer, W. (ed.) ICALP 1985. LNCS, vol. 194, pp. 221–231. Springer, Heidelberg (1985)

30. Goubault- Larrecq, J.: A proof of weak termination of typed lambda-sigma-calculi. In: Giménez, E. (ed.) TYPES 1996. LNCS, vol. 1512, Springer, Heidelberg (1998)

31. Gramlich, B.: Relating innermost, weak, uniform and modular termination of term rewriting systems. In: Voronkov, A. (ed.) LPAR 1992. LNCS(LNAI) vol. 624, pp. 285–296. Springer, Heidelberg (1992)

32. Gramlich, B.: On proving termination by innermost termination. In: Ganzinger, H. (ed.) Rewriting Techniques and Applications. LNCS, vol. 1103, pp. 93–107. Springer, Heidelberg (1996)
33. Gramlich, B.: On termination and confluence properties of disjoint and constructor-sharing conditional rewrite systems. Theoretical Computer Science 165(1), 97–131 (September 1996)
34. Hendrix, J., Clavel, M., Meseguer, J.: A sufficient completeness reasoning tool for partial specifications. In: Giesl, J. (ed.) RTA 2005. LNCS, vol. 3467, pp. 165–174. Springer, Heidelberg (2005)
35. Huet, G., Hullot, J.-M.: Proofs by induction in equational theories with constructors. Journal of Computer and System Sciences, vol. 25(2) , pp. 239–266, 1982 In: Preliminary version Proceedings 21st Symposium on Foundations of Computer Science, October 1982, IEEE (1980)
36. Jouannaud, J.-P., Kounalis, E.: Automatic proofs by induction in theories without constructors. Information and Computation 82, 1–33 (1989)
37. Kapur, D., Narendran, P., Zhang, H.: Proof by induction using test sets. In: Siekmann, J.H. (ed.) CADE 1986, LNCS, vol. 230, pp. 99–117. Springer, Heidelberg (1986)
38. Kapur, D., Narendran, P., Zhang, H.: On sufficient completeness and related properties of term rewriting systems. Acta Informatica 24, 395–415 (1987)
39. Kirchner, C., Kirchner, H., Rusinowitch, M.: Deduction with symbolic constraints. Revue d'Intelligence Artificielle. (Special issue on Automatic Deduction) 4(3), 9–52 (1990)
40. Kirchner, C., Kirchner, H., Vittek, M.: Designing constraint logic programming languages using computational systems. In: Van Hentenryck, P., Saraswat, V. (eds.) Principles and Practice of Constraint Programming. The Newport Papers, ch. 8, pp. 131–158. The MIT press, Cambridge, MA (1995)
41. Kounalis, E.: Completeness in data type specifications. In: Caviness, B.F. (ed.) ISSAC 1985 and EUROCAL 1985. LNCS, vol. 204, pp. 348–362. Springer, Heidelberg (1985)
42. Kounalis, E.: Testing for the ground (co-)reducibility property in term-rewriting systems. Theoretical Computer Science 106, 87–117 (1992)
43. Kruskal, J.B.: Well-quasi ordering, the tree theorem and Vazsonyi's conjecture. Trans. Amer. Math. Soc. 95, 210–225 (1960)
44. Lazrek, A., Lescanne, P., Thiel, J.-J.: Tools for proving inductive equalities, relative completeness and ω-completeness. Information and Computation 84(1), 47–70 (1990)
45. Lucas, S.: Termination of context-sensitive rewriting by rewriting. In: Meyer auf der Heide, F., Monien, B. (eds.) ICALP 1996. LNCS, vol. 1099, pp. 122–133. Springer, Heidelberg (1996)
46. Lucas, S.: Termination of on-demand rewriting and termination of OBJ programs. In: Sondergaard, H. (ed.) PPDP'01. Proc. of 3rd International ACM SIGPLAN Conference on Principles and Practice of Declarative Programming, Firenze, Italy, pp. 82–93. ACM Press, New York (September 2001)
47. Lucas, S.: Termination of rewriting with strategy annotations. In: Voronkov, A., Nieuwenhuis, R. (eds.) LPAR 2001. LNCS (LNAI), vol. 2250, pp. 669–684. Springer, Heidelberg (2001)
48. Lucas, S.: Context-sensitive rewriting strategies. Information and Computation 178(1), 294–343 (2002)
49. Martí-Oliet, N., Meseguer, J.: Rewriting logic and its applications: Preface. Theoretical Computer Science 285(2), 119–120 (2002)

50. Meseguer, J., Thati, P.: Symbolic reachability analysis using narrowing and its application to the verification of cryptographic protocols. In: Marti-Oliet, N., Thati, P., Martí-Oliet, N. (eds.) WRLA 2004. Proceedings of the Fifth International Workshop on Rewriting Logic and Its Applications. Electronic Notes in Theoretical Computer Science, vol. 117, pp. 153–182. (2004)
51. Middeldorp, A., Hamoen, E.: Completeness results for basic narrowing. Applicable Algebra in Engineering, Communication and Computation 5(3 & 4), 213–253 (1994)
52. Moreau, P.-E., Ringeissen, C., Vittek, M.: A pattern matching compiler for multiple target languages. In: Hedin, G. (ed.) CC 2003 and ETAPS 2003. LNCS, vol. 2622, pp. 61–76. Springer, Heidelberg (2003)
53. Nguyen, Q-H.: Compact normalisation trace via lazy rewriting. In: Lucas, S., Gramlich, B. (eds.) WRS 2001. Proc. 1st International Workshop on Reduction Strategies in Rewriting and Programming, vol. 57, Elsevier Science Publishers B. V., North-Holland, Amsterdam (2001)
54. Nipkow, T., Weikum, G.: A decidability result about sufficient completeness of axiomatically specified abstract data types. In: Cremers, A.B., Kriegel, H.-P. (eds.) Theoretical Computer Science. LNCS, vol. 145, pp. 257–268. Springer, Heidelberg (1983)
55. Panitz, S.E., Schmidt-Schauss, M.: TEA: Automatically proving termination of programs in a non-strict higher-order functional language. In: Van Hentenryck, P. (ed.) SAS 1997. LNCS, vol. 1302, pp. 345–360. Springer, Heidelberg (1997)
56. Plaisted, D.: Semantic confluence tests and completion methods. Information and Control 65, 182–215 (1985)
57. Visser, E.: Stratego: A language for program transformation based on rewriting strategies. System description of Stratego 0.5 (LP:0). In: Middeldorp, A. (ed.) Rewriting Techniques and Applications 2001. LNCS, vol. 2051, pp. 357–361. Springer, Heidelberg (2001)

Computability Closure: Ten Years Later

Frédéric Blanqui

INRIA
LORIA*, Campus Scientifique, BP 239
54506 Vandoeuvre-lès-Nancy Cedex, France

Abstract. The notion of computability closure has been introduced for proving the termination of higher-order rewriting with first-order matching by Jean-Pierre Jouannaud and Mitsuhiro Okada in a 1997 draft which later served as a basis for the author's PhD. In this paper, we show how this notion can also be used for dealing with β-normalized rewriting with matching modulo βη (on patterns *à la* Miller), rewriting with matching modulo some equational theory, and higher-order data types (types with constructors having functional recursive arguments). Finally, we show how the computability closure can easily be turned into a reduction ordering which, in the higher-order case, contains Jean-Pierre Jouannaud and Albert Rubio's higher-order recursive path ordering and, in the first-order case, is equal to the usual first-order recursive path ordering.

1 Introduction

After Jan Willem Klop's PhD thesis on Combinatory Reduction Systems (CRS) [28,29], the interest in higher-order rewriting, or the combination of λ-calculus and rewriting, was relaunched by Dale Miller and Gopalan Nadathur's work on λ-Prolog [38] and Val Breazu-Tannen's paper on the modularity of confluence for the combination of simply-typed λ-calculus and first-order rewriting [10,13]. A year later, Dale Miller proved the decidability of unification modulo βη for "higher-order patterns" [36,37], and the modularity of termination for simply-typed λ-calculus and first-order rewriting was independently proved by Jean Gallier and Val Breazu-Tannen [11,12] and Mitsuhiro Okada [40], both using Jean-Yves Girard's technique of reducibility predicates [18,19,20]. A little bit later, Daniel Dougherty showed, by purely syntactic means (without using reducibility predicates), that these results could be extended to any "stable" set of untyped λ-terms [16,17], the set of simply-typed λ-terms being stable. We must also mention Zhurab Khasidashvili's new approach to higher-order rewriting with his Expression Reduction Systems (ERS) [27].

Then, in 1991, two important papers were published on this subject, both introducing a new approach to higher-order rewriting: Tobias Nipkow's Higher-order Rewrite Systems (HRS) [39,33], and Jean-Pierre Jouannaud and Mitsuhiro Okada's Executable Higher-Order Algebraic Specification Languages [22,23].

---

* UMR 7503 CNRS-INPL-INRIA-Nancy2-UHP.

H. Comon-Lundh et al. (Eds.): Jouannaud Festschrift, LNCS 4600, pp. 68–88, 2007.

Tobias Nipkow's approach is based on Dale Miller's result: the simply-typed λ-calculus, which is confluent and terminating, is used as a framework for encoding higher-order rewriting. He extends to this framework the Critical Pair Lemma. Jean-Pierre Jouannaud and Mitsuhiro Okada's approach can be seen as a typed version of CRS's (restricted to first-order matching). They proved that termination is modular for the combination of simply-typed λ-calculus, a non-duplicating[1] terminating first-order rewrite system, and an higher-order rewrite system which definition follows a "general schema" extending primitive recursion. Later, Vincent van Oostrom and Femke van Raamsdonk compared CRS's and HRS's [46] and developed an axiomatized framework subsuming them [47,49].

The combination of β-reduction and rewriting is naturally used in dependent type systems and proof assistants implementing the proposition-as-type and proof-as-object paradigm [6]. In these systems, two propositions equivalent modulo β-reduction and rewriting are considered as equivalent (*e.g.* $P(2+2)$ and $P(4)$). This is essential for enabling users to formalize large proofs with many computations, as recently shown by Georges Gonthier and Benjamin Werner's proof of the Four Color Theorem in the Coq proof assistant. However, checking the correctness of user proofs requires to check the equivalence of two terms. Hence, the necessity to have termination criteria for the combination of β-reduction and a set R of higher-order rewrite rules.

For proving the correctness of the general schema, Jean-Pierre Jouannaud and Mitsuhiro Okada used Jean-Yves Girard's technique of reducibility predicates. Roughly speaking, since proving the (strong) β-normalization by induction on the structure of terms does not work directly, one needs to prove a stronger predicate. In 1967, William Tait introduced a "convertibility predicate" for proving the weak normalization of some extension of Kurt Gödel's system T [43]. Later, in 1971, Jean-Yves Girard introduced "reducibility predicates" (called *computability predicates* in the following) for proving the weak and strong normalization of the polymorphic λ-calculus [18,19]. This technique can be applied to (higher-order) rewriting by proving that every function symbol is computable, that is, that every function call is computable whenever its arguments so are.

This naturally leads to the following question: which operations preserve computability? Indeed, from a set of such operations, one can define the *computability closure* of a term t, written $CC(t)$, as the set of terms that are computable whenever t so is. Then, to get normalization, it suffices to check that, for every rule $fl \rightarrow r \in R$, r belongs to the computability closure of l. Examples of computability-preserving operations are: application, function calls on arguments smaller than l in some well-founded ordering $>$, etc. Jean-Pierre Jouannaud and Mitsuhiro Okada introduced this notion in a 1997 draft which served as a basis for [8,9]. In this paper, we show how this notion can be extended for dealing with β-normalized rewriting with matching modulo $\beta\eta$ on patterns *à la* Miller and matching modulo some equational theory.

Another way to prove the termination of R is to find a decidable well-founded rewrite relation containing R. A well known such relation in the first-order case

---

[1] $l \rightarrow r$ is non-duplicating if no variable has more occurrences in r than it has in l.

is the recursive path ordering [41,14] which well-foundedness was initially based on Kruskal theorem [30]. The first attempts made for generalizing this ordering to the higher-order case were not able to orient system T [31,32,26]. Finally, in 1999, Jean-Pierre Jouannaud and Albert Rubio succeeded in finding such an ordering [25] by using computability-based techniques again, hence providing the first well-foundedness proof of RPO not based on Kruskal theorem. This ordering was later extended to the calculus of constructions by Daria Walukiewicz [50,51].

Although the computability closure on one hand, and the recursive path ordering on the other hand, share the same computability-based techniques, there has been no precise comparison between these two termination criteria. In [51], one can find examples of rules that are accepted by one criterion but not the other. And Jean-Pierre Jouannaud and Albert Rubio themselves use the notion of computability closure for strengthening HORPO.

In this paper, we explore the relations between both criteria. We start from the trivial remark that the computability closure itself provides us with an ordering: let t CR$(>)$ u if $t = ft$ and $u \in \mathrm{CC}_>(t)$, where $\mathrm{CC}_>$ is the computability closure built by using a well-founded relation $>$ for comparing the arguments between function calls. Proving the well-foundedness of this ordering simply consists in proving that the computability closure is correct, which can be done by induction on $>$. Then, we remark that the function mapping $>$ to CR$(>)$ is monotone wrt inclusion. Thus, it admits a least fixpoint which is a well-founded ordering. We prove that this fixpoint contains HORPO and is equal to RPO in the first-order case.

2   Terms and Types

We consider simply-typed λ-terms with curried constants. See [2] for details about typed λ-calculus. For rewriting, we follow the notations of Nachum Dershowitz and Jean-Pierre Jouannaud's survey [15].

Let $\mathcal{B}$ be a set of *base types*. The set $\mathbb{T}$ of *simple types* is inductively defined as usual: $T \in \mathbb{T} = B \in \mathcal{B} \mid T \Rightarrow T$.

Let $\mathcal{X}$ be a set of *variables* and $\mathcal{F}$ be a set of *function symbols* disjoint from $\mathcal{X}$. We assume that every $a \in \mathcal{X} \cup \mathcal{F}$ is equipped with a type $\tau_a \in \mathbb{T}$. The sets $\mathcal{T}^T$ of *terms of type T* are inductively defined as follows:

- If $a \in \mathcal{X} \cup \mathcal{F}$, then $a \in \mathcal{T}^{\tau_a}$.
- If $x \in \mathcal{X}$ and $t \in \mathcal{T}^U$, then $\lambda x t \in \mathcal{T}^{\tau_x \Rightarrow U}$.
- If $v \in \mathcal{T}^{T \Rightarrow U}$ and $t \in \mathcal{T}^T$, then $vt \in \mathcal{T}^U$.

As usual, we assume that, for all type T, the set of variables of type T is infinite and consider terms up to α-conversion (type-preserving renaming of bound variables). Let FV(t) be the set of variables *free* in t. Let t denote a sequence of terms $t_1, \ldots, t_n$ of length $n = |t| \geq 0$.

Let $\tau(t)$ denote the type of a term t. In the following, writing $t : T$ or t^T means that $\tau(t) = T$.

The set $\mathrm{Pos}(t)$ of positions in a term t is defined as usual as words on $\{1,2\}$. Let $t|_p$ be the subterm of t at position $p \in \mathrm{Pos}(t)$, and $t[u]_p$ be the term obtained by replacing in t its subterm at position $p \in \mathrm{Pos}(t)$ by u.

A term is *algebraic* if it contains no abstraction and no subterm of the form xt. A term t is *linear* if no variable free in t occurs more than once in t.

The β-reduction is the closure by context of the relation $(\lambda x t)u \to_\beta t_x^u$ where t_x^u denotes the higher-order substitution of x by u in t.

A *rewrite rule* is a pair of terms $l \to r$ such that l is of the form fl, $\mathrm{FV}(r) \subseteq \mathrm{FV}(l)$ and $\tau(l) = \tau(r)$. Given a set R of rewrite rules, let $\to_R$ be the closure by context and substitution of R. Hence, matching is modulo α-conversion (but α-conversion is needed only for left-hand sides having abstractions). A rule $l \to r$ is linear (resp. algebraic) if both l and r are linear (resp. algebraic).

Given a relation $\to$ on terms, let $\leftarrow$, $\to^=$ and $\to^*$ be its inverse, its reflexive closure and its reflexive and transitive closure respectively. Let also $\to (t) = \{t' \in \mathcal{T} \mid t \to t'\}$ be the set of reducts of t, and $\mathrm{SN}(\to)$ (resp. $\mathrm{SN}^T(\to)$) be the set of terms (resp. of type T) that are strongly normalizable wrt $\to$. Our aim is to prove the termination (strong normalization, well-foundedness) of $\to = \to_\beta \cup \to_R$.

Given a relation $>$, let $>_{\mathrm{lex}}$, $>_{\mathrm{mul}}$ and $>_{\mathrm{prod}}$ respectively denote the lexicographic, multiset and product extensions of $>$. Note that all these extensions are well-founded whenever $>$ is well-founded.

3 Computability

In this section, we remind the notion of computability predicate introduced by William Tait [43,44] and extended by Jean-Yves Girard with the notion of *neutral*[2] term [19,20]. Every type is interpreted by a set of *computable* terms of that type. Since computability is defined so as to imply strong normalization, the latter is obtained by proving that every term is computable.

In the following, we assume given a set R of rewrite rules.

Definition 1 (Reducibility candidates). *A term is* neutral *if it is of the form xv or of the form $(\lambda x t)uv$. Let $\to = \to_\beta \cup \to_R$. A reducibility candidate for the type T is a set P of terms such that:*

(1) $P \subseteq \mathrm{SN}^T(\to)$.

(2) P is stable by $\to$: $\to(P) \subseteq P$.

(3) If $t : T$ is neutral and $\to(t) \subseteq P$, then $t \in P$.

Let $\mathcal{Q}_R^T$ be the set of all reducibility candidates for the type T, and $\mathcal{I}_R$ be the set of functions I from $\mathcal{B}$ to 2^T such that, for all $\mathsf{B} \in \mathcal{B}$, $I(\mathsf{B}) \in \mathcal{Q}_R^\mathsf{B}$. Given an interpretation of base types $I \in \mathcal{I}_R$, we define an interpretation $[\![T]\!]_R^I \in \mathcal{Q}_R^T$ for every type T as follows:

– $[\![\mathsf{B}]\!]_R^I = I(\mathsf{B})$,

– $[\![T \Rightarrow U]\!]_R^I = \{v \in \mathrm{SN}^{T \Rightarrow U} \mid \forall t \in [\![T]\!]_R^I, vt \in [\![U]\!]_R^I\}$.

---

[2] simple in [19].

One can check that SN^T is a reducibility candidate for T.

We now check that the interpretation of a type is a reducibility candidate.

Lemma 1. *If $I \in \mathcal{I}_R$ then, for all type T, $[\![T]\!]_R^I \in \mathcal{Q}_R^T$.*

Proof. We proceed by induction on T. The lemma is immediate for $T \in \mathcal{B}$. Assume now that $[\![T]\!]_R^I \in \mathcal{Q}_R^T$ and $[\![U]\!]_R^I \in \mathcal{Q}_R^U$. We prove that $[\![T \Rightarrow U]\!]_R^I \in \mathcal{Q}_R^{T \Rightarrow U}$.

(1) $[\![T \Rightarrow U]\!]_R^I \subseteq \mathrm{SN}^{T \Rightarrow U}$ by definition.
(2) Let $v \in [\![T \Rightarrow U]\!]_R^I$, $v' \in \rightarrow(v)$ and $t \in [\![T]\!]_R^I$. We must prove that $v't \in [\![U]\!]_R^I$. This follows from the facts that $[\![U]\!]_R^I \in \mathcal{Q}_R^U$, $vt \in [\![U]\!]_R^I$ and $v't \in \rightarrow(vt)$.
(3) Let $v^{T \Rightarrow U}$ be a neutral term such that $\rightarrow(v) \subseteq [\![T \Rightarrow U]\!]_R^I$ and $t \in [\![T]\!]_R^I$. We must prove that $vt \in [\![U]\!]_R^I$. Since v is neutral, vt is neutral too. Since $[\![U]\!]_R^I \in \mathcal{Q}_R^U$, it suffices to prove that $\rightarrow(vt) \subseteq [\![U]\!]_R^I$. Since $[\![T]\!]_R^I \in \mathcal{Q}_R^T$, $t \in \mathrm{SN}$ and we can proceed by induction on t with $\rightarrow$ as well-founded ordering. Let $w \in \rightarrow(vt)$. Since v is neutral, either $w = v't$ with $v' \in \rightarrow(v)$, or $w = vt'$ with $t' \in \rightarrow(t)$. In the former case, $w \in [\![U]\!]_R^I$ since $v' \in [\![T \Rightarrow U]\!]_R^I$. In the latter case, we conclude by induction hypothesis on t'. □

Finally, we come to the definition of computability.

Definition 2 (Computability). *Let I be the base type interpretation such that $I(\mathsf{B}) = \mathrm{SN}^\mathsf{B}$. A term $t : T$ is computable if $t \in [\![T]\!]_R^I$.*

In the following, we drop the superscript I in $[\![T]\!]_R^I$.

We do not know how to prove that computability is stable by subterm before proving that every term is computable. However, since, on base types, computability is equivalent to strong normalization, the subterms of base type of a computable term are computable. This is in particular the case for the arguments of base type of a function symbol:

Definition 3 (Accessibility). *For all $f : \boldsymbol{T} \Rightarrow \mathsf{B}$, let $\mathrm{Acc}(f) = \{i \mid T_i \in \mathcal{B}\}$ be the set of accessible arguments of f.*

We now prove some properties of computable terms.

Lemma 2 (Computability properties).

(C1) If t, u and t_x^u are computable, then $(\lambda x t) u$ is computable.

(C2) If every symbol is computable, then every term is computable.

(C3) If ft is computable and $i \in \mathrm{Acc}(f)$, then t_i is computable.

(C4) A term $ft : \mathsf{B}$ is computable whenever $\boldsymbol{t}$ are computable and every head-reduct of ft is computable.

(C5) A symbol $f : \boldsymbol{T} \Rightarrow \mathsf{B}$ is computable if every head-reduct of ft is computable whenever $\boldsymbol{t} : \boldsymbol{T}$ are computable.

(C6) A symbol f is computable if, for every rule $fl \rightarrow r \in R$ and substitution σ, $r\sigma$ is computable whenever $l\sigma$ are computable.

Proof. (C1) Since $(\lambda xt)u$ is neutral, it suffices to prove that every reduct is computable. We proceed by induction on (t, u) with $\to_{\mathrm{prod}}$ as well-founded ordering (t and u are computable). Assume that $(\lambda xt)u \to v$. If $v = t_x^u$, then t' is computable by assumption. Otherwise, $v = (\lambda xt')u$ with $t \to t'$, or $v = (\lambda xt)u'$ with $u \to u'$. In both cases, we can conclude by induction hypothesis.

(C2) First note that the identity substitution is computable since variables are computable (they are neutral and irreducible). We then prove that, for every term t and computable substitution θ, $t\theta$ is computable, by induction on t.

- Assume that $t = f \in \mathcal{F}$. Then, $t\theta = f$ is computable by assumption.
- Assume that $t = x \in \mathcal{X}$. Then, $t\theta = x\theta$ is computable by assumption.
- Assume that $t = \lambda xu$. Then, $t\theta = \lambda xu\theta$. Let $v : V$ computable. We must prove that $t\theta v$ is computable. By induction hypothesis, $u\theta_x^v$ is computable. Since $u\theta$ and v are computable too, by (C1), $t\theta$ is computable.
- Assume that $t = u^{V \Rightarrow T}v$. Then, $t\theta = u\theta v\theta$. By induction hypothesis, $u\theta$ and $v\theta$ are computable. Thus, $t\theta$ is computable.

(C3) By definition of the interpretation of base types.

(C4) By definition of the interpretation of base types, it suffices to prove that every reduct of $f\boldsymbol{t}$ is computable. We prove it by induction on $\boldsymbol{t}$ with $\to_{\mathrm{prod}}$ as well-founded ordering ($\boldsymbol{t}$ are computable). Head-reducts are computable by assumption. For non-head-reducts, this follows by induction hypothesis.

(C5) By definition of the interpretation of arrow types and (C4).

(C6) After (C5), it suffices to prove that every head-reduct of $f\boldsymbol{t}$ is computable whenever $\boldsymbol{t}$ are computable. Let t' be a head-reduct of $f\boldsymbol{t}$. Then, there is $l \to r \in R$ and σ such that $\boldsymbol{t} = \boldsymbol{l}\sigma$ and $t' = r\sigma$. Thus, t' is computable. $\square$

4   Computability Closure

After the properties (C2) and (C6), we are left to prove that, for every rule $f\boldsymbol{l} \to r \in R$, $r\sigma$ is computable whenever $\boldsymbol{l}\sigma$ are computable. This naturally leads us to find a set $\mathrm{CC}^f(\boldsymbol{l})$ of terms t such that $t\sigma$ is computable whenever $\boldsymbol{l}\sigma$ are computable: the computability closure of $\boldsymbol{l}$ wrt f.

We can include $\boldsymbol{l}$ and close this set with computability-preserving operations like applying a term to another or taking the accessible argument of a function call.

We can also include variables distinct from $\mathrm{FV}(\boldsymbol{l})$ and allow abstraction on them by strengthening the property to prove as follows: for all $t \in \mathrm{CC}^f(\boldsymbol{l})$, $t\sigma$ is computable whenever $\boldsymbol{l}\sigma$ are computable and σ is computable on $\mathrm{FV}(t) \setminus \mathrm{FV}(\boldsymbol{l})$.

Now, to allow function calls, the idea is to introduce a precedence on function symbols and a well-founded ordering $>$ on function arguments.

So, we assume given a quasi-ordering $\geq_{\mathcal{F}}$ on $\mathcal{F}$ which strict part $>_{\mathcal{F}} = \geq_{\mathcal{F}} \setminus \leq_{\mathcal{F}}$ is well-founded. Let $\simeq_{\mathcal{F}} = \geq_{\mathcal{F}} \cap \leq_{\mathcal{F}}$ be its associated equivalence relation.

We also assume that every symbol f is equipped with a *status* $\mathrm{stat}_f \in \{\mathrm{lex}, \mathrm{mul}\}$, such that $\mathrm{stat}_f = \mathrm{stat}_g$ whenever $f \simeq_{\mathcal{F}} g$, defining how the arguments of f must be compared: lexicographically (from left to right, or from right to left) or by multiset.

Definition 4 (Status relation). *The* status relation *associated to a relation $>$ is the relation $(f, t) >_{\mathrm{stat}} (g, u)$ such that $f >_{\mathcal{F}} g$ or $f \simeq_{\mathcal{F}} g$ and $t >_{\mathrm{stat}_f} u$.*

Note that the status relation $>_{\mathrm{stat}}$ is well-founded whenever $>$ so is.
We now formalize the notion of computability closure.

Definition 5. *A function* CC *mapping every $f^{T \Rightarrow B}$ and l^T to a set of terms $\mathrm{CC}^f(l)$ is a* computability closure *if, for all $f^{T \Rightarrow B}$, l^T, $r \in \mathrm{CC}^f(l)$ and θ, $r\theta$ is computable whenever $l\theta$ are computable and θ is computable on $\mathcal{X} \setminus \mathrm{FV}(l)$.*

We now check that the computability of symbols, hence the termination of $\rightarrow_\beta \cup \rightarrow_R$ by (C2), can be obtained by using a computability closure.

Lemma 3. *If* CC *is a computability closure and, for all rule $fl \rightarrow r \in R$, $r \in \mathrm{CC}^f(l)$, then every symbol is computable.*

Proof. It follows from (C6) and the fact that $\mathrm{FV}(r) \subseteq \mathrm{FV}(l)$.   □

We now present a computability closure similar to the one introduced in [8,9] except that the relation $>$ used for comparing arguments in recursive calls is

$$(\text{arg}) \quad l_i \in \mathrm{CC}_>^f(l)$$

$$(\text{decomp-symb}) \quad \frac{gu \in \mathrm{CC}_>^f(l) \quad i \in \mathrm{Acc}(g)}{u_i \in \mathrm{CC}_>^f(l)}$$

$$(\text{prec}) \quad \frac{f >_{\mathcal{F}} g}{g \in \mathrm{CC}_>^f(l)}$$

$$(\text{call}) \quad \frac{f \simeq_{\mathcal{F}} g^{U \Rightarrow U} \quad u^U \in \mathrm{CC}_>^f(l) \quad l >_{\mathrm{stat}_f}^{fl} u}{gu \in \mathrm{CC}_>^f(l)}$$

$$(\text{app}) \quad \frac{u^{V \Rightarrow T} \in \mathrm{CC}_>^f(l) \quad v^V \in \mathrm{CC}_>^f(l)}{uv \in \mathrm{CC}_>^f(l)}$$

$$(\text{var}) \quad \frac{x \notin \mathrm{FV}(l)}{x \in \mathrm{CC}_>^f(l)}$$

$$(\text{lam}) \quad \frac{u \in \mathrm{CC}_>^f(l) \quad x \notin \mathrm{FV}(l)}{\lambda x u \in \mathrm{CC}_>^f(l)}$$

Fig. 1. Higher-order computability closure

replaced by an abstract family of relations $(>^l)_{l \in \mathcal{T}}$. We then prove the correctness of this abstract computability closure under some condition.

Definition 6 (Closure-compatibility). *A relation $\succ$ is closure-compatible with a family of relations $(>^l)_{l \in \mathcal{T}}$ if, for all l and θ, $t\theta \succ u\theta$ whenever $t >^l u$, $t\theta$ and $u\theta$ are computable, and θ is computable on $\mathcal{X} \setminus \mathrm{FV}(l)$.*

Note that any relation stable by substitution $>$ is closure-compatible with itself (the constant family equal to $>$). This is in particular the case of the restriction of the subterm ordering $>$ defined by $t > u$ if u is a subterm of t and $\mathrm{FV}(u) \subseteq \mathrm{FV}(t)$.

Lemma 4. *Let $> = (>^l)_{l \in \mathcal{T}}$ be a family of relations. The function $\mathrm{CC}_>$ defined in Figure 1 is a computability closure whenever there exists a well-founded relation on computable terms $\succ$ that is closure-compatible with $>$.*

Proof. We proceed by induction, first on $(f, l\theta)$ with $\succ_{\mathrm{stat}}$ as well-founded ordering (H1), and second, by induction on $\mathrm{CC}^f_>(l)$ (H2).

(arg) $l_i\theta$ is computable by assumption.

(decomp-symb) By (H2), $gu\theta$ is computable. Thus, after (C3), $u_i\theta$ is computable.

(prec) By (H1), g is computable.

(call) By (H2), $u\theta$ are computable. Since $l >^{fl}_{\mathrm{stat}_f} u$, $\succ$ is closure-compatible with $>$, $l\theta$ and $u\theta$ are computable, and θ is computable on $\mathcal{X} \setminus \mathrm{FV}(l)$, we have $l\theta \succ_{\mathrm{stat}_f} u\theta$. Therefore, by (H1), $gu\theta$ is computable.

(app) By (H2), $u\theta$ and $v\theta$ are computable. Thus, $u\theta v\theta$ is computable.

(var) Since $x \in \mathcal{X} \setminus \mathrm{FV}(l)$, $x\theta$ is computable by assumption.

(lam) Wlog we can assume that $x \notin \mathrm{codom}(\theta)$. Thus, $(\lambda x u)\theta = \lambda x u\theta$. Let $v : \tau_x$ computable. After (C1), $(\lambda x u\theta)v$ is computable if $u\theta$, v and $u\theta^v_x$ are computable. We have v computable by assumption and $u\theta$ and $u\theta^v_x$ computable by (H2). $\square$

5 β-Normalized Rewriting with Matching Modulo $\beta\eta$

In this section, we show how the notion of computability closure can be extended to deal with HRS's [39]. This extends our previous results on CRS's and HRS's [5]. This computability closure approach seems simpler than the technique of "neutralization" introduced by Jean-Pierre Jouannaud and Albert Rubio in [24]. However, the comparison between both approaches remains to be done.

In HRS's, rewrite rules are of base type, rule left-hand sides are patterns à la Miller [37], and rewriting is defined on terms in β-normal η-long form as follows: $t \Rightarrow_R u$ if there are $p \in \mathrm{Pos}(t)$, $l \to r \in R$ and σ in β-normal η-long form such that $t|_p = l\sigma \downarrow_\beta \uparrow_\eta$ and $u = t[r\sigma \downarrow_\beta \uparrow_\eta]_p$.

We are going to consider a slightly more general notion of rewriting: β-normalized rewriting with matching modulo $\beta\eta$, defined as follows: $t \to_{R,\beta\eta} u$ if there are $p \in \mathrm{Pos}(t)$, $l \to r \in R$ and σ in β-normal form such that $t|_p$ is in

β-normal form, $t|_p =_{\beta\eta} l\sigma$ and $u = t[r\sigma]_p$. Furthermore, we do not assume that rules are of base type. However, in this case, one can check that, on terms in β-normal η-long form, $\Rightarrow_R \subseteq \to_{R,\beta\eta} \to_\beta^*$.

Matching modulo $\beta\eta$ is necessary when a rule left-hand side contains abstractions. Consider for instance the left-hand side $l = D\lambda x(\sin(Fx))$. With matching modulo α-conversion only, the term $t = D\lambda x(\sin u)$ matches p only if u is of the form vx. In particular, $D\lambda x(\sin x)$ does not match p. Yet, if one substitutes F by λxu in l, then one gets $D(\lambda x(\sin((\lambda xu)x)))$ which β-reduces to t.

Take now $l = D\lambda x(Fx)$. With matching modulo α-conversion only, the term $t = Du$ matches l only if u is of the form λxv. In particular, $(D\sin)$ does not match l. Yet, if one substitutes F by u in l, then one gets $D\lambda x(ux)$ which η-reduces to t since $x \notin \mathrm{FV}(u)$ (by definition of higher-order substitution).

Higher-order patterns are terms in β-normal η-long form which free variables are applied to terms η-equivalent to distinct bound variables. Hence, if l is a pattern, t and σ are in β-normal form and $l\sigma =_{\beta\eta} t$, then $l\sigma \to_{\beta_0}^* =_\eta t$, where $\to_{\beta_0}$ is the restriction of $\to_\beta$ to redexes of the form $(\lambda xt)x$, that is, $(\lambda xt)x \to_{\beta_0} t$ [37].

Now, for proving the termination of $\to_\beta \cup \to_{R,\beta\eta}$ (hence the termination of the HRS rewrite relation $\Rightarrow_R$), it suffices to adapt the notion of computability by replacing $\to_R$ by $\to_{R,\beta\eta}$. One can check that all the proofs of the computability properties are still valid except the one for (C6) for which we give a new proof:

Lemma 5 (C6). *A symbol f is computable if, for every rule $fl \to r \in R$ and substitution σ, $r\sigma$ is computable whenever $l\sigma$ are computable.*

Proof. After (C5), for proving that $f : \boldsymbol{T} \Rightarrow \mathsf{B}$ is computable, it suffices to prove that every head-reduct of $f\boldsymbol{t}$ is computable whenever $\boldsymbol{t} : \boldsymbol{T}$ are computable. Let t' be a head-reduct of $f\boldsymbol{t}$. Then, $f\boldsymbol{t}$ is in β-normal form and there are $fl \to r \in R$ and σ such that $fl\sigma \leftarrow_{\beta_0}^* =_\eta f\boldsymbol{t}$ and $t' = r\sigma$. To conclude, it suffices to check that $l\sigma$ are computable.

To this end, we prove that computability is preserved by η-reduction, η-expansion and β_0-expansion. Let t be a computable term and let u be a term obtained from t by η-reduction, η-expansion or β_0-expansion. We prove that u is computable when u is of base type. If u is not of base type then, by applying it to computable terms of appropriate types, we get a term of base type. On base types, computability is equivalent to strong normalization. Thus, it suffices to prove that every reduct of u is strongly normalizable. In each case, we proceed by induction on t with $\to$ as well-founded ordering (t is computable).

- β_0-expansion: $t \leftarrow_{\beta_0} u$. If $u \to_\beta u'$ then either $u' = t$ is computable or, by confluence of β and since β_0 makes no duplication, there is t' such that $t \to_\beta t' \leftarrow_{\beta_0}^* u'$. Now, if $u \to_R u'$ then, since R-redexes are in β-normal form, the β_0-redex is either above the R-redex or at a disjoint position. Thus, there is u' such that $t \to_R t' \leftarrow_{\beta_0} u'$. In both cases, we can conclude by induction hypothesis.

- η-reduction: $t \to_\eta u$. If $u \to_\beta u'$ then, by postponement of η wrt β ($\to_\eta \to_\beta \subseteq \to_\beta^+ \to_\eta^*$), there is t' such that $t \to_\beta^+ t' \to_\eta^* u'$. Now, if $u \to_R u'$ then, since

R-redexes are in β-normal form, either the η-redex is a β-redex and $t \to_\beta$ $u \to_R t' = u'$, or there is t' such that $t \to_R t' \to_\eta^* u'$. In both cases, we can conclude by induction hypothesis.

– η-expansion: $t \leftarrow_\eta u$. If $u \to_\beta u'$ then either $u' = t$ is computable or, by confluence of $\beta\eta$, there is t' such that $t \to_\beta t' \leftarrow_\eta^* u'$. Now, if $u \to_R u'$ then, since R-redexes are in β-normal form, there is t' such that $t \to_R t' \leftarrow_\eta^* u'$. In both cases, we can conclude by induction hypothesis. $\square$

By property (C2) and Lemma 4, it follows that $\to = \to_\beta \cup \to_{R,\beta\eta}$ is well-founded if, for all rule $fl \to r \in R$, $r \in \mathrm{CC}_>^f(l)$.

(decomp-lam) $\dfrac{\lambda y u \in \mathrm{CC}_>^f(l) \quad y \notin \mathrm{FV}(l)}{u \in \mathrm{CC}_>^f(l)}$

(decomp-app-left) $\dfrac{uy \in \mathrm{CC}_>^f(l) \quad y \notin \mathrm{FV}(l) \cup \mathrm{FV}(u)}{u \in \mathrm{CC}_>^f(l)}$

Fig. 2. Decomposition rules for higher-order patterns

Now, for dealing with patterns à la Miller, we also need to add new decomposition rules in the computability closure.

Lemma 6. *The function* $\mathrm{CC}_>$ *defined by the rules of Figure 1 and 2 is a computability closure whenever there exists a well-founded relation on computable terms that is closure-compatible with* $>$.

Proof. We extend the proof of Lemma 4 with the new decomposition rules.

(decomp-lam) Let θ' be the restriction of θ to $\mathrm{dom}(\theta)\backslash\{y\}$. Wlog, we can assume that $y \notin \mathrm{codom}(\theta)$. Hence, $(\lambda yu)\theta' = \lambda y u\theta'$. Now, since $\mathrm{dom}(\theta) \subseteq \mathrm{FV}(u)\ \backslash$ $\mathrm{FV}(l)$, $\mathrm{dom}(\theta') \subseteq \mathrm{FV}(\lambda yu)\ \backslash\ \mathrm{FV}(l)$. Thus, by (H2), $\lambda yu\theta'$ is computable. Since $y\theta$ is computable, $(\lambda yu\theta')y\theta$ is computable. Thus, by β-reduction, $u\theta'^{y\theta}_y$ is computable too. Finally, since $y \notin \mathrm{dom}(\theta') \cup \mathrm{codom}(\theta')$, $u\theta'^{y\theta}_y = u\theta$.

(decomp-app-left) Let $v : \tau_y$ computable. Since $\mathrm{dom}(\theta) \subseteq \mathrm{FV}(u)\backslash\mathrm{FV}(l)$ and $y \notin$ $\mathrm{FV}(l)$, $\mathrm{dom}(\theta_y^v) = \mathrm{dom}(\theta) \cup \{y\} \subseteq \mathrm{FV}(uy) \setminus \mathrm{FV}(l)$. Thus, by (H2), $(uy)\theta_y^v =$ $u\theta_y^v v$ is computable. Since $y \notin \mathrm{FV}(u)$, $u\theta_y^v = u\theta$. Thus, $u\theta$ is computable. $\square$

6   Matching Modulo Some Equational Theory

In this section, we show how the notion of computability closure can be used for proving the termination of the combination of β-reduction and rewriting with matching modulo some equational theory E [48,21].

To this end, we assume that E is a symmetric set of *rules*, that is, $l \to r \in E$ iff $r \to l$ in E. By definition of rewrite rules (see Section 2), this implies that, for all $l \to r \in E$, r is of the form gr and $\mathrm{FV}(l) = \mathrm{FV}(r)$. This includes associativity and commutativity but excludes collapsing rules like $x+0 \to x$ and erasing rules like $x \times 0 \to 0$.

Then, rewriting with matching modulo can be defined as follow: $t \to_{R,E} u$ if there are $p \in \mathrm{Pos}(t)$, $l \to r \in R$ and σ such that $t|_p \to_E^* l\sigma$ and $u = t[r\sigma]_p$.

Rewriting with matching modulo E is different from rewriting modulo E which is $\to_E^* \to_R$. The point is that, with matching modulo E, no E-step takes place above $t|_p$ when one rewrites a term t at some position $p \in \mathrm{Pos}(t)$.

Hence, we correct an error in [4] (Theorem 6) where it is claimed that $\to_\beta \cup \to_E^* \to_R$ is terminating. What is in fact proved in [4] is the termination of $\to_\beta \cup \to_{E_1}^* \to_{R_1} \cup \to_{R_\omega,E_\omega}$ where E_1 and R_1 (resp. E_ω and R_ω) are the first-order (resp. higher-order) parts of E and R respectively.

For proving the termination of $\to_\beta \cup \to_{R,E}$, it suffices to adapt computability by replacing $\to_R$ by $\to_{R,E}$. One can check that all the proofs of computability properties are still valid except the one for (C6) for which we give a new proof:

Lemma 7 (C6). *Let E be a symmetric set of* rules. *Assume that $\succ$ is a well-founded relation on computable terms closure-compatible with $>$ and that, for all rule $fl \to gr \in E$, $r \in \mathrm{CC}_\succ^f(l)$. Then, f is computable if, for every rule $fl \to r \in R$ and substitution σ, $r\sigma$ is computable whenever $l\sigma$ are computable.*

Proof. By Lemma 4, $\mathrm{CC}_>$ is a computability closure. After (C5), for proving that $f : \boldsymbol{T} \Rightarrow \mathsf{B}$ is computable, it suffices to prove that every head-reduct of ft is computable whenever $t : \boldsymbol{T}$ are computable. Let t' be a head-reduct of ft. Then, there is $gl \to r \in R$ and σ such that $ft \to_E^* gl\sigma$ and $t' = r\sigma$. By definition of computability closure, $l\sigma$ are computable since t are computable (induction on the number of E-steps). Therefore, $r\sigma$ is computable. $\qquad\square$

By property (C2) and Lemma 4, it follows that $\to \; = \; \to_\beta \cup \to_{R,E}$ is well-founded if moreover, for all rule $fl \to r \in R$, $r \in \mathrm{CC}_>^f(l)$.

7   Higher-Order Data Types

Until now, we used the subterm ordering in (call). But this ordering is not strong enough to handle recursive definitions on higher-order data types, *i.e.* data types with constructors having functional recursive arguments. Consider for instance a type P representing processes with a sequence operator $;: \mathsf{P} \Rightarrow \mathsf{P} \Rightarrow \mathsf{P}$ and a data-dependent choice operator $\Sigma : (\mathsf{D} \Rightarrow \mathsf{P}) \Rightarrow \mathsf{P}$. Then, in the following simplification rule [45]:

$$(\Sigma P); x \to \Sigma \lambda y (Py; x)$$

the term Py is not a subterm of ΣP.

In this section, we describe an extension of the computability closure to handle such definitions. It is based on the interpretation of "positive" higher-order data types introduced by Nax Paul Mendler in 1987 [34,35].

As usual, the set $\text{Pos}(T)$ of *positions in a type* T is defined as words on $\{1, 2\}$. The sets $\text{Pos}^+(T)$ and $\text{Pos}^-(T)$ of *positive and negative positions* respectively are inductively defined as follows:

- $\text{Pos}^\delta(\mathsf{B}) = \{\varepsilon\}$.
- $\text{Pos}^\delta(T \Rightarrow U) = 1 \cdot \text{Pos}^{-\delta}(T) \cup 2 \cdot \text{Pos}^\delta(U)$.

Let $\text{Pos}(\mathsf{B}, T)$ be the positions of the occurrences of B in T. A base type B *occurs only positively* (resp. *negatively*) in a type T if $\text{Pos}(\mathsf{B}, T) \subseteq \text{Pos}^+(T)$ (resp. $\text{Pos}(\mathsf{B}, T) \subseteq \text{Pos}^-(T)$).

Nax Paul Mendler showed that the combination of β-reduction and reduction rules for a "case" or "match" construction does not terminate if a data type B has a constructor having an argument in the type of which B occurs negatively (we say that B is not positive). Take for instance $c : (\mathsf{B} \Rightarrow \mathsf{N}) \Rightarrow \mathsf{B}$, $f : \mathsf{B} \Rightarrow (\mathsf{B} \Rightarrow \mathsf{N})$ together with the rule $f(cx) \to_R x$. Then, by taking $\omega = \lambda x f x x : \mathsf{B} \Rightarrow \mathsf{N}$, we have $\omega(c\omega) \to_\beta f(c\omega)(c\omega) \to_R \omega(c\omega) \to_\beta \cdots$

He also showed that the set of all reducibility candidates is a complete lattice for inclusion and that, if B is positive, then one can build an interpretation of B as the fixpoint of a monotone functional on reducibility candidates, in which the reduction rules for the case construction are safe. In this case, we can say that every argument of a constructor is accessible. We extend this notion of accessibility to every (defined or undefined) function symbol as follows.

Definition 7 (Accessible arguments). *For every* $f^{T \Rightarrow \mathsf{B}} \in \mathcal{F}$, *let* $\text{Acc}(f) = \{i \leq |T| \mid \text{Pos}(\mathsf{B}, T_i) \subseteq \text{Pos}^+(T_i)\}$.

In our example, we have $\text{Pos}(\mathsf{P}, \mathsf{D} \Rightarrow \mathsf{P}) = \{2\} = \text{Pos}^+(\mathsf{D} \Rightarrow \mathsf{P})$ and $\text{Pos}(\mathsf{P}, \mathsf{P}) = \{\varepsilon\} = \text{Pos}^+(\mathsf{P})$. Thus, $\text{Acc}(\Sigma) = \{1\}$ and $\text{Acc}(;) = \{1, 2\}$.

We now define the functional the least fixpoint of which will provide the interpretation of base types.

Lemma 8. *The function* $F_R^I(\mathsf{B}) = \{t \in \text{SN}^\mathsf{B} \mid \forall f^{T \Rightarrow \mathsf{B}} t, t \to^* ft \Rightarrow \forall i \in \text{Acc}(f), t_i \in [\![T_i]\!]_R^I\}$ *is a monotone function on* $\mathcal{I}_R$.

Proof. We first prove that $P = F_R^I(\mathsf{B}) \in \mathcal{Q}_R^\mathsf{B}$.

(1) $P \subseteq \text{SN}^\mathsf{B}$ by definition.
(2) Let $t \in P$, $t' \in \to(t)$, $f : T \Rightarrow \mathsf{B}$ and t such that $t' \to^* ft$. We must prove that $t \in [\![T]\!]_R$. It follows from the facts that $t \in P$ and $t \to^* ft$.
(3) Let t^B neutral such that $\to(t) \subseteq P$. Let $f^{T \Rightarrow \mathsf{B}}$, t such that $t \to^* ft$ and $i \in \text{Acc}(f)$. We must prove that $t_i \in [\![T_i]\!]_R$. Since t is neutral, $t \neq ft$. Thus, there is $t' \in \to(t)$ such that $t' \to^* ft$. Since $t' \in P$, $t_i \in [\![T_i]\!]_R$.

For the monotony, let $\leq^+ = \leq$ and $\leq^- = \geq$. Let $I \leq J$ iff, for all B, $I(\mathsf{B}) \subseteq J(\mathsf{B})$. We first prove that $[\![T]\!]_R^I \subseteq^\delta [\![T]\!]_R^J$ whenever $I \leq J$ and $\text{Pos}(\mathsf{B}, T) \subseteq \text{Pos}^\delta(T)$, by induction on T.

- Assume that $T = C \in \mathcal{B}$. Then, $\delta = +$, $[\![T]\!]_R^I = I(C)$ and $[\![T]\!]_R^J = J(C)$. Since $I(C) \subseteq J(C)$, $[\![T]\!]_R^I \subseteq [\![T]\!]_R^J$.
- Assume that $T = U \Rightarrow V$. Then, $\mathrm{Pos}(\mathsf{B}, U) \subseteq \mathrm{Pos}^{-\delta}(U)$ and $\mathrm{Pos}(\mathsf{B}, V) \subseteq \mathrm{Pos}^\delta(V)$. Thus, by induction hypothesis, $[\![U]\!]_R^I \subseteq^{-\delta} [\![U]\!]_R^J$ and $[\![V]\!]_R^I \subseteq^\delta [\![V]\!]_R^J$. Assume that $\delta = +$. Let $t \in [\![T]\!]_R^I$ and $u \in [\![U]\!]_R^J$. We must prove that $tu \in [\![V]\!]_R^J$. Since $[\![U]\!]_R^I \supseteq [\![U]\!]_R^J$, $tu \in [\![V]\!]_R^I$. Since $[\![V]\!]_R^I \subseteq [\![V]\!]_R^J$, $tu \in [\![V]\!]_R^J$. It works similarly for $\delta = -$.

Assume now that $I \leq J$. We must prove that, for all B, $F_R^I(\mathsf{B}) \subseteq F_R^J(\mathsf{B})$. Let $\mathsf{B} \in \mathcal{B}$ and $t \in F_R^I(\mathsf{B})$. We must prove that $t \in F_R^J(\mathsf{B})$. First, we have $t \in \mathrm{SN}^{\mathsf{B}}$ since $t \in F_R^I(\mathsf{B})$. Assume now that $t \to^* f^{T \Rightarrow \mathsf{B}} t$ and let $i \in \mathrm{Acc}(f)$. We must prove that $t_i \in [\![T_i]\!]_R^J$. Since $t \in F_R^I(\mathsf{B})$, $t_i \in [\![T_i]\!]_R^I$. Since $i \in \mathrm{Acc}(f)$, $\mathrm{Pos}(\mathsf{B}, T_i) \subseteq \mathrm{Pos}^+(T_i)$ and $[\![T_i]\!]_R^I \subseteq [\![T_i]\!]_R^J$. □

Definition 8 (Computability). *Let I_R be the least fixpoint of F_R. A term $t : T$ is computable if $t \in [\![T]\!]_R^{I_R}$.*

In the following, we drop the superscript I_R in $[\![T]\!]_R^{I_R}$.

One can check that all the proofs of computability properties are still valid except the one for (C4) for which we give a new proof:

Lemma 9 (C4). *A term $ft : \mathsf{B}$ is computable whenever $\boldsymbol{t}$ are computable and every head-reduct of ft is computable.*

Proof. We first need to prove that ft is SN. This follows from the previous proof of (C4). Assume now that $ft \to^* g\boldsymbol{u}$ and $i \in \mathrm{Acc}(g)$. We prove that u_i is computable by induction on $\boldsymbol{t}$ with $\to_{\mathrm{prod}}$ as well-founded ordering ($\boldsymbol{t}$ are computable). If $ft = g\boldsymbol{u}$, then $u_i = t_i$ is computable by assumption. Otherwise, $ft \to v \to^* g\boldsymbol{u}$. If v is a head-reduct of ft, then v and u_i are computable. Otherwise, we conclude by induction hypothesis. □

The least fixpoint of F_R is reachable by transfinite iteration from the smallest element of $\mathcal{I}_R$. This provides us with an ordering that can handle definitions on higher-order data types.

Definition 9 (Size ordering). *For all $\mathsf{B} \in \mathcal{B}$ and $t \in [\![\mathsf{B}]\!]_R$, let the size of t be the smallest ordinal $o_R^{\mathsf{B}}(t) = \mathfrak{a}$ such that $t \in F_R^{\mathfrak{a}}(\emptyset)(\mathsf{B})$, where $F_R^{\mathfrak{a}}$ is the transfinite $\mathfrak{a}$-iteration of F_R. Let $\succeq_R$ be the union of all the relations $\succeq_R^T$ inductively defined on $[\![T]\!]_R$ as follows:*

- *$t \succeq_R^{\mathsf{B}} u$ if $o_R^{\mathsf{B}}(t) \geq o_R^{\mathsf{B}}(u)$.*
- *$t \succeq_R^{T \Rightarrow U} u$ if, for all $v \in [\![T]\!]_R$, $tv \succeq_R^U uv$.*

In our example, we have $[\![\mathsf{P}]\!]_R = \{t \in \mathrm{SN}^P \mid \forall f^{T \Rightarrow P} t, t \to^* ft \Rightarrow \forall i \in \mathrm{Acc}(f), t_i \in [\![T_i]\!]_R\}$. Since $\mathrm{Acc}(\Sigma) = \{1\}$, if $\Sigma P \in [\![\mathsf{P}]\!]_R$ then, for all $d \in [\![\mathsf{D}]\!]_R$, $Pd \in [\![\mathsf{P}]\!]_R$ and $o_R^P(Pd) < o_R^P(\Sigma P)$.

We immediately check that the size ordering is well-founded.

Lemma 10. $\succeq_R$ *is a well-founded quasi-ordering containing* $\rightarrow$.

Proof. The relation $\succeq_R$ is the union of pairwise disjoint relations. Hence, it suffices to prove that each one is transitive and well-founded. We proceed by induction on T. For $T \in \mathcal{B}$, this is immediate. Assume now that $(t_i)_{i\in\mathbb{N}}$ is an increasing sequence for $\succ_R^{T\Rightarrow U}$. Since variables are computable, let $x \in [\![T]\!]_R$. By definition of $\succ_R^{T\Rightarrow U}$, $(t_i x)_{i\in\mathbb{N}}$ is an increasing sequence for $\succ_R^U$. $\square$

$\quad$(>base)$\qquad \dfrac{i \in \mathrm{Acc}(g) \quad \boldsymbol{b} \in \mathcal{X} \setminus \mathrm{FV}(l)}{g^{A\Rightarrow B}\boldsymbol{a}^A >^l a_i^{B\Rightarrow B}\boldsymbol{b}^B}$

$\quad$(>lam)$\qquad \dfrac{a >^l bx \quad x \in \mathcal{X} \setminus (\mathrm{FV}(b) \cup \mathrm{FV}(l))}{\lambda x a > b}$

$\qquad\qquad$(>red)$\quad \dfrac{a >^l b \quad b \rightarrow_\beta c}{a >^l c}$

$\qquad\qquad$(>trans)$\quad \dfrac{a >^l b \quad b >^l c}{a >^l c}$

Fig. 3. Accessibility ordering

We now define some relation strong enough for capturing definitions on higher-order data types and with which $\succ_R$ is closure-compatible.

Lemma 11. $\succ_R$ *is closure-compatible with the family* $(>^l)_{l\in T}$ *defined Figure 3.*

Proof. We prove that $a\theta \succ_R b\theta$ whenever $a >^l b$, $a\theta$ and $b\theta$ are computable, and θ is computable on $\mathcal{X} \setminus \mathrm{FV}(l)$.

(>base) By definition of I_R, $o_R(ga\theta) = \mathfrak{a} + 1$ and $a_i\theta \in [\![B \Rightarrow B]\!]_R^{I_R^{\mathfrak{a}}}$. Since $\boldsymbol{b} \in \mathcal{X}\setminus\mathrm{FV}(l)$ and θ is computable on $\mathcal{X}\setminus\mathrm{FV}(l)$, $\boldsymbol{b}\theta$ are computable. Therefore, $a_i\theta b\theta \in I_R^{\mathfrak{a}}(B)$ and $a_R(ga\theta) > \mathfrak{a} \geq o_R(a_i\theta b\theta)$.

(>lam) Let $w : \tau_x$ computable. Wlog we can assume that $x \notin \mathrm{dom}(\theta) \cup \mathrm{codom}(\theta)$. Hence, $(\lambda x a)\theta = \lambda x a\theta$. We must prove that $(\lambda x a\theta)w \succ_R b\theta w$. By β-reduction, $(\lambda x a\theta)w \succeq_R a\theta_x^w$. By induction hypothesis, $a\theta_x^w \succ_R (bx)\theta_x^w$. Since $x \notin \mathrm{FV}(b) \cup \mathrm{dom}(\theta) \cup \mathrm{codom}(\theta)$, $(bx)\theta_x^w = b\theta w$.

(>red) By induction hypothesis and since $\rightarrow_\beta \subseteq \succeq_R$.

(>trans) By induction hypothesis and transitivity of $\succ_R$. $\square$

By property (C2) and Lemma 4, it follows that $\rightarrow = \rightarrow_\beta \cup \rightarrow_R$ is well-founded if, for all rule $fl \rightarrow r \in R$, $r \in \mathrm{CC}_{>}^f(l)$.

Note that we could strengthen the definition of $(>^l)_{l\in T}$ by taking in (>base), when $l = fl$, $\boldsymbol{b} \in \mathrm{CC}_{>}^f(l)$ instead of $\boldsymbol{b} \in \mathcal{X} \setminus \mathrm{FV}(l)$, making the definitions of $>$ and $\mathrm{CC}_>$ mutually dependent. See [7] for details.

8   The Recursive Computability Ordering

We now show how the computability closure can be turned into a well-founded ordering containing the monomorphic version of Jean-Pierre Jouannaud and Albert Rubio's higher-order recursive path ordering [25].

Indeed, consider the relation $\mathrm{CR}(>) = \{(fl, r) \mid r \in \mathrm{CC}^f_\geq(l), \mathrm{FV}(r) \subseteq \mathrm{FV}(l), \tau(fl) = \tau(r)\}$ made of all the rules which right-hand side is in the computability closure of its left-hand side. After (C2) and Lemma 3, $\to_\beta \cup \to_{\mathrm{CR}(>)}$ is well-founded whenever $>$ is well-founded and stable by substitution. Hence, $\mathrm{CR}(>)$ is itself well-founded and stable by substitution whenever $>$ is well-founded and stable by substitution.

We now observe that the function mapping $>$ to $\mathrm{CR}(>)$ is monotone wrt inclusion. It has therefore a least fixpoint that is stable by substitution and which closure by context is well-founded when combined with $\to_\beta$.

Lemma 12. *The function mapping $>$ to the relation $\mathrm{CR}(>) = \{(fl, r) \mid r \in \mathrm{CC}^f_\geq(l), \mathrm{FV}(r) \subseteq \mathrm{FV}(l), \tau(fl) = \tau(r)\}$ is monotone wrt inclusion on the set of well-founded relations stable by substitution.*

Proof. Assume that $>_1 \subseteq >_2$. One can prove by induction on $(fl, r) \in \mathrm{CR}(>_1)$ that $(fl, r) \in \mathrm{CR}(>_2)$. In the (call) case, we use the fact that the function mapping $>$ to $>_{\mathrm{stat}}$ is monotone wrt inclusion.

Now, assume that $>$ is well-founded and stable by substitution. After (C2) and Lemma 3, $\to_\beta \cup \to_{\mathrm{CR}(>)}$ is well-founded. Thus, $\mathrm{CR}(>)$ is well-founded. Now, one can check that $\mathrm{CR}(>)$ is stable by substitution whenever $>$ is stable by substitution. $\square$

Definition 10. *Let the* weak higher-order recursive computability (quasi-) ordering $>_{\mathrm{whorco}}$ *be the least fixpoint of* CR, *and the* higher-order recursive computability (quasi-) ordering $>_{\mathrm{horco}}$ *be the closure by context of* $>_{\mathrm{whorco}}$.

In Figure 4, we give an inductive presentation of $>_{\mathrm{horco}}$ obtained by replacing $u \in \mathrm{CC}^f_\geq(l)$ by $fl > u$ in Figure 1, and adding a rule (cont) for the closure by context and a rule (rule) for the conditions on rules.

Strictly speaking, $>_{\mathrm{horco}}$, like $>_{\mathrm{horpo}}$, is not a quasi-ordering. One needs to take its transitive closure to get a quasi-ordering. On the other hand, one can check that $>_{\mathrm{whorco}}$ is transitive, hence is a true quasi-ordering (note that, if $t >_{\mathrm{whorco}} u$, then t is of the form ft).

Moreover, since $>_{\mathrm{whorco}}$ is not closed by context, it is better suited for proving the termination of rewrite systems by using the dependency pair method [1,42,3].

We now would like to compare this ordering with the monomorphic version of $>_{\mathrm{horpo}}$ which definition is reminded in Figure 5. To this end, we need to slightly strengthen the definition of computability closure by replacing $>$ by its closure by context $\to_>$, and by adding the following deduction rule:

$$(\text{red}) \quad \frac{u \in \mathrm{CC}^f_\geq(l) \quad u > v}{v \in \mathrm{CC}^f_\geq(l)}$$

$$(\text{cont}) \quad \frac{t >_{\text{whorco}} u \quad p \in \text{Pos}(C)}{C[t]_p >_{\text{horco}} C[u]_p}$$

$$(\text{rule}) \quad \frac{t^T > u^U \quad \text{FV}(u) \subseteq \text{FV}(t) \quad T = U}{t >_{\text{whorco}} u}$$

$$(\text{arg}) \quad fl > l_i$$

$$(\text{decomp-symb}) \quad \frac{fl > gu \quad i \in \text{Acc}(g)}{fl > u_i}$$

$$(\text{prec}) \quad \frac{f >_{\mathcal{F}} g}{fl > g}$$

$$(\text{call}) \quad \frac{f \simeq_{\mathcal{F}} g^{U \Rightarrow U} \quad fl > u^U \quad l \,(>_{\text{whorco}})\text{stat}_f \, u}{fl > gu}$$

$$(\text{app}) \quad \frac{fl > u^{V \Rightarrow T} \quad fl > v^V}{fl > uv}$$

$$(\text{var}) \quad \frac{x \notin \text{FV}(l)}{fl > x}$$

$$(\text{lam}) \quad \frac{fl > u \quad x \notin \text{FV}(l)}{fl > \lambda x u}$$

Fig. 4. Higher-order computability ordering

One can check that all the properties are preserved. More details can be found in [7]. Hence, we get the following additional deduction rules for $>_{\text{whorco}}$:

$$(\text{call}) \quad \frac{f \simeq_{\mathcal{F}} g^{U \Rightarrow U} \quad fl > u^U \quad l \,(>_{\text{horco}})\text{stat}_f \, u}{fl > gu}$$

$$(\text{red}) \quad \frac{fl > u \quad u >_{\text{horco}} v}{fl > v}$$

We now prove that $>_{\text{horpo}}$ is included in the transitive closure of $>_{\text{horco}}$.

Lemma 13. $>_{\text{horpo}} \subseteq >_{\text{horco}}^{+}$.

Proof. Note that $\text{FV}(u) \subseteq \text{FV}(t)$ and $T = U$ whenever $t^T >_{\text{horpo}} u^U$ ($>_{\text{horpo}}$ is a set of rules).

We first prove the property (*): $ft > v$ whenever $t_j >_{\text{horco}}^{*} v$ or $ft >_{\text{horco}}^{+} v$. Assume that $t_j >_{\text{horco}}^{*} v$. By (arg), $ft > t_j$. Thus, by (red), $ft > v$. Assume now that $ft >_{\text{horco}} u >_{\text{horco}}^{*} v$. By (red), it suffices to prove that $ft > u$. There are two cases:

- $ft = fat_k b$, $u = fat'_k b$ and $t_k >_{\text{horco}} t'_k$. We conclude by (call).
- $ft = flb$, $u = rb$ and $fl >_{\text{whorco}} r$. One can check that $flt > rt$ whenever $fl > r$.

$$P(f, t, u) = ft >_{\text{horpo}} u \vee (\exists j)\ t_j \geq_{\text{horpo}} u$$

$$(1) \quad \frac{t_i \geq_{\text{horpo}} u}{f^T \Rightarrow^T t^T >_{\text{horpo}} u^T}$$

$$(2) \quad \frac{f >_{\mathcal{F}} g \quad P(f, t, u)}{f^T \Rightarrow^T t^T >_{\text{horpo}} g^U \Rightarrow^T u^U}$$

$$(3) \quad \frac{f \simeq_{\mathcal{F}} g \quad \text{stat}_f = \text{mul} \quad t\ (>_{\text{horpo}})_{\text{stat}_f}\ u}{f^T \Rightarrow^T t^T >_{\text{horpo}} g^U \Rightarrow^T u^U}$$

$$(4) \quad \frac{f \simeq_{\mathcal{F}} g \quad \text{stat}_f = \text{lex} \quad t\ (>_{\text{horpo}})_{\text{stat}_f}\ u \quad P(f, t, u)}{f^T \Rightarrow^T t^T >_{\text{horpo}} g^U \Rightarrow^T u^U}$$

$$(5) \quad \frac{P(f, t, u)}{f^T \Rightarrow^T t >_{\text{horpo}} u^T}$$

$$(6) \quad \frac{\{t_1, t_2\}\ (>_{\text{horpo}})_{\text{mul}}\ \{u_1, u_2\}}{t_1^U \Rightarrow^T t_2^U >_{\text{horpo}} u_1^V \Rightarrow^T u_2^V}$$

$$(7) \quad \frac{t >_{\text{horpo}} u}{\lambda x t >_{\text{horpo}} \lambda x u}$$

Fig. 5. HORPO [25]

We now prove the theorem by induction on $>_{\text{horpo}}$.

(1) By induction hypothesis, $t_i >^*_{\text{horco}} u$. By (arg), $ft > t_i$. Since $t_i >_{\text{horpo}} u$ and $ft >_{\text{horpo}} u$, $ft \to t_i$ is a rule. Thus, $ft >_{\text{whorco}} t_i$ and, by (red), $ft >_{\text{whorco}} u$.

(2) By induction hypothesis, for all i, $ft >^+_{\text{horco}} u_i$ or $t_j >^*_{\text{horco}} u_i$. Hence, by (*), $ft > u$. By (prec), $ft > g$. Thus, by (app), $ft > gu$. Since $ft \to gu$ is a rule, $ft >_{\text{whorco}} gu$.

(3) By induction hypothesis, $t\ (>^+_{\text{horco}})_{\text{mul}}\ u$. Hence, by (*), $ft > u$. Thus, by (call), $ft > gu$. Since $ft \to gu$ is a rule, $ft >_{\text{whorco}} gu$.

(4) By induction hypothesis, $t\ (>^+_{\text{horco}})_{\text{stat}_f}\ u$ and, for all i, $ft >^+_{\text{horco}} u_i$ or $t_j >^*_{\text{horco}} u_i$. Hence, by (*), $ft > u$. Thus, by (call), $ft > gu$. Since $ft \to gu$ is a rule, $ft >_{\text{whorco}} gu$.

(5) By induction hypothesis, for all i, $ft >^+_{\text{horco}} u_i$ or $t_j >^*_{\text{horco}} u_i$. Hence, by (*), $ft > u_i$ for all i. Thus, by (app), $ft > u$. Since (ft, u) is a rule, $ft >_{\text{whorco}} u$.

(6) For typing reasons, $(t_1, u1)\ (>_{\text{horpo}})_{\text{prod}}\ (t_2, u_2)$. Thus, by induction hypothesis, $(t_1, u_1)\ (>^+_{\text{horco}})_{\text{prod}}\ (t_2, u_2)$. Hence, by (cont) and transitivity, $t_1 t_2 >^+_{\text{horco}} u_1 u_2$.

(7) By induction hypothesis, $t >^+_{\text{horco}} u$. Thus, by (cont), $\lambda x t >^+_{\text{horco}} \lambda x u$. $\qquad \square$

We observe that, if (6) were restricted to $(t_1 >_{horpo} u_1 \wedge t_2 = u_2) \vee (t_1 = u_1 \wedge t_2 >_{horpo} u_2)$, then we would get $>_{horpo} \subseteq >_{horco}$, since this is the only case requiring transitivity.

Note that $>_{horco}$ can be extended with the accessibility ordering defined in Figure 3. The details can be found in [7].

Finally, we remark that, when restricted to first-order terms, the recursive computability ordering is equal to the usual first-order recursive path ordering [41,14], the subterm rule being simulated by (arg) and (red).

Lemma 14. *The relation defined in Figure 4 by the rules (arg), (decomp-symb), (call) and the rule:*

$$(\text{prec-app}) \quad \frac{f >_{\mathcal{F}} g^{U \Rightarrow U} \quad fl > u^U}{fl > gu}$$

is equal to the usual first-order recursive path ordering.

9   Conclusion

We show through various extensions how powerful is the notion of computability closure introduced by Jean-Pierre Jouannaud and Mitsuhiro Okada. In particular, we show how it can easily be turned into a well-founded ordering containing Jean-Pierre Jouannaud and Albert Rubio's higher-order recursive path ordering. This provides a simple way to extend this ordering to richer type disciplines. However, its definition as the closure by context of another relation is not completely satisfactory, all the more so since one wants to combine it with the accessibility ordering. We should therefore try to find a new definition of HORPO that nicely integrates the notions of computability closure and accessibility ordering in order to capture definitions on higher-order data types (data types with constructors having functional recursive arguments).

References

1. Arts, T., Giesl, J.: Termination of term rewriting using dependency pairs. Theoretical Computer Science 236, 133–178 (2000)
2. Barendregt, H.: Lambda calculi with types. In: Abramsky, S., Gabbay, D., Maibaum, T. (eds.) Handbook of logic in computer science, vol. 2, Oxford University Press, Oxford, UK (1992)
3. Blanqui, F.: Higher-order dependency pairs. In: Proceedings of the 8th International Workshop on Termination (2006)
4. Blanqui, F.: Rewriting modulo in Deduction modulo. In: Nieuwenhuis, R. (ed.) RTA 2003. LNCS, vol. 2706, Springer, Heidelberg (2003)
5. Blanqui, F.: Termination and confluence of higher-order rewrite systems. In: Bachmair, L. (ed.) RTA 2000. LNCS, vol. 1833, Springer, Heidelberg (2000)
6. Blanqui, F.: Definitions by rewriting in the Calculus of Constructions. Mathematical Structures in Computer Science 15(1), 37–92 (2005)

7. Blanqui, F.: (HO) RPO revisited. Research Report 5972, INRIA (2006)
8. Blanqui, F., Jouannaud, J.-P., Okada, M.: The Calculus of Algebraic Constructions. In: Narendran, P., Rusinowitch, M. (eds.) RTA 1999. LNCS, vol. 1631, Springer, Heidelberg (1999)
9. Blanqui, F., Jouannaud, J.-P., Okada, M.: Inductive-data-type Systems. Theoretical Computer Science 272, 41–68 (2002)
10. Breazu-Tannen,V.: Combining algebra and higher-order types. In: Proceedings of the 3rd IEEE Symposium on Logic in Computer Science (1988)
11. Breazu-Tannen, V., Gallier, J.: Polymorphic rewriting conserves algebraic strong normalization. In: Della Rocca, S.R., Ausiello, G., Dezani-Ciancaglini, M. (eds.) ICALP 1989, LNCS, vol. 372, Springer, Heidelberg (1989)
12. Breazu-Tannen, V., Gallier, J.: Polymorphic rewriting conserves algebraic strong normalization. Theoretical Computer Science 83(1), 3–28 (1991)
13. Breazu-Tannen, V., Gallier, J.: Polymorphic rewriting conserves algebraic confluence. Information and Computation 114(1), 1–29 (1994)
14. Dershowitz, N.: Orderings for term rewriting systems. Theoretical Computer Science 17, 279–301 (1982)
15. Dershowitz, N., Jouannaud, J.-P.: Rewrite systems. In: van Leeuwen, J. (ed.) Handbook of Theoretical Computer Science, vol. B, ch.6. North-Holland, Amsterdam (1990)
16. Dougherty, D.: Adding algebraic rewriting to the untyped lambda calculus. In: Book, R.V. (ed.) RTA 1996, LNCS, vol. 488, Springer, Heidelberg (1991)
17. Dougherty, D.: Adding algebraic rewriting to the untyped lambda calculus. Information and Computation 101(2), 251–267 (1992)
18. Girard, J.-Y.: Une extension de l'interprétation de Gödel à l'analyse et son application à l'élimination des coupures dans l'analyse et la théorie des types. In: Fenstad, J. (ed) Proc. of the 2nd Scandinavian Logic Symposium. Studies in Logic and the Foundations of Mathematics, vol. 63. North-Holland, Amsterdam (1971)
19. Girard, J.-Y.: Interprétation fonctionelle et élimination des coupures dans l'arithmetique d'ordre supérieur. PhD thesis, Université Paris VII, France (1972)
20. Girard, J.-Y., Lafont, Y., Taylor, P.: Proofs and Types. Cambridge University Press, Cambridge (1988)
21. Jouannaud, J.-P., Kirchner, H.: Completion of a set of rules modulo a set of equations. SIAM Journal on Computing 15(4), 1155–1194 (1986)
22. Jouannaud, J.-P., Okada, M.: Executable higher-order algebraic specification languages. In: Proceedings of the 6th IEEE Symposium on Logic in Computer Science (1991)
23. Jouannaud, J.-P., Okada, M.: Abstract Data Type Systems. Theoretical Computer Science 173(2), 349–391 (1997)
24. Jouannaud, J.-P., Rubio, A.: Higher-order orderings for normal rewriting. In: Pfenning, F. (ed.) RTA 2006. LNCS, vol. 4098, Springer, Heidelberg (2006)
25. Jouannaud, J.-P., Rubio, A.: The Higher-Order Recursive Path Ordering. In: Proceedings of the 14th IEEE Symposium on Logic in Computer Science (1999)
26. Jouannaud, J.-P., Rubio, A.: A recursive path ordering for higher-order terms in eta-long beta-normal form. In: Ganzinger, H. (ed.) RTA 1996. LNCS, vol. 1103, Springer, Heidelberg (1996)
27. Khasidashvili, Z.: Expression Reduction Systems. In: Proc. of I. Vekua Institute of Applied Mathematics, vol. 36 (1990)
28. Klop, J. W.: Combinatory Reduction Systems PhD thesis, Utrecht Universiteit, The Netherlands, Published as Mathematical Center Tract 129 (1980)

29. Klop, J.W., van Oostrom, V., van Raamsdonk, F.: Combinatory reduction systems: introduction and survey. Theoretical Computer Science 121, 279–308 (1993)
30. Kruskal, J.B.: Well-quasi-ordering, the tree theorem, and vazsonyi's conjecture. Transactions of the American Mathematical Society 95, 210–225 (1960)
31. Loria-Saenz, C., Steinbach, J.: Termination of combined (rewrite and λ-calculus) systems. In: Rusinowitch, M., Remy, J.-L. (eds.) CTRS 1992, LNCS, vol. 656, Springer, Heidelberg (1992)
32. Lysne, O., Piris, J.: A termination ordering for higher order rewrite systems. In: Hsiang, J. (ed.) RTA 1995, LNCS, vol. 914, Springer, Heidelberg (1995)
33. Mayr, R., Nipkow, T.: Higher-order rewrite systems and their confluence. Theoretical Computer Science 192(2), 3–29 (1998)
34. Mendler, N. P.: Recursive types and type constraints in second order lambda calculus. In: Proceedings of the 2nd IEEE Symposium on Logic in Computer Science (1987)
35. Mendler, N.P.: Inductive types and type constraints in the second-order lambda calculus. Annals of Pure and Applied Logic 51(1-2), 159–172 (1991)
36. Miller, D.: A logic programming language with lambda-abstraction, function variables, and simple unification. In: Schroeder-Heister, P. (ed.) ELP 1989, LNCS, vol. 475, Springer, Heidelberg (1989)
37. Miller, D.: A logic programming language with lambda-abstraction, function variables, and simple unification. Journal of Logic and Computation 1(4), 497–536 (1991)
38. Miller, D., Nadathur, G.: An overview of λProlog. In: Proceedings of the 5th International Conference on Logic Programming. MIT Press, Cambridge, MA (1988)
39. Nipkow, T.: Higher-order critical pairs. In: Proceedings of the 6th IEEE Symposium on Logic in Computer Science (1991)
40. Okada, M.: Strong normalizability for the combined system of the typed lambda calculus and an arbitrary convergent term rewrite system. In: Proceedings of the 1989 International Symposium on Symbolic and Algebraic Computation. ACM Press, New York (1989)
41. Plaisted, D.A.: A recursively defined ordering for proving termination of term rewriting systems. Technical report, University of Illinois, Urbana-Champaign, United States (1978)
42. Sakai, M., Kusakari, K.: On new dependency pair method for proving termination of higher-order rewrite systems. In: Proceedings of the 1st International Workshop on Rewriting in Proof and Computation (2001)
43. Tait, W.W.: Intensional interpretations of functionals of finite type I. Journal of Symbolic Logic 32(2), 198–212 (1967)
44. Tait, W.W.: A realizability interpretation of the theory of species. In: Parikh, R. (eds.) Proceedings of the 1972 Logic Colloquium. Lecture Notes in Mathematics, vol. 453. Springer, Heidelberg (1975)
45. van de Pol, J.: Termination proofs for higher-order rewrite systems. In: Heering, J., Meinke, K., Möller, B., Nipkow, T. (eds.) HOA 1993. LNCS, vol. 816, Springer, Heidelberg (1993)
46. van Oostrom, V.: Development closed critical pairs. In: Dowek, G., Heering, J., Meinke, K., Möller, B. (eds.) HOA 1995. LNCS, vol. 1074, Springer, Heidelberg (1995)
47. van Oostrom, V.: Confluence for Abstract and Higher-Order Rewriting. PhD thesis, Vrije Universiteit Amsterdam, The Netherlands (1994)
48. Peterson, G., Stickel, M.: Complete sets of reductions for some equational theories. Journal of the ACM 28(2), 233–264 (1981)

49. van Raamsdonk, F.: Confluence and Normalization for Higher-Order Rewriting. PhD thesis, Vrije University Amsterdam, The Netherlands (1996)
50. Walukiewicz-Chrząszcz, D.: Termination of Rewriting in the Calculus of Constructions. PhD thesis, Warsaw University, Poland and Université d'Orsay, France (2003)
51. Walukiewicz-Chrząszcz, D.: Termination of rewriting in the Calculus of Constructions. Journal of Functional Programming 13(2), 339–414 (2003)

Reduction Strategies and Acyclicity

Jan Willem Klop[1,2,3], Vincent van Oostrom[4], and Femke van Raamsdonk[1]

[1] Vrije Universiteit, Department of Theoretical Computer Science,
De Boelelaan 1081a, 1081 HV Amsterdam, The Netherlands
[2] Radboud Universiteit Nijmegen, Department of Computer Science,
Toernooiveld 1, 6525 ED Nijmegen, The Netherlands
[3] CWI, P.O. Box 94079, 1090 GB Amsterdam, The Netherlands
[4] Universiteit Utrecht, Department of Philosophy,
Heidelberglaan 8, 3584 CS Utrecht, The Netherlands
jwk@cs.vu.nl, Vincent.vanOostrom@phil.uu.nl, femke@cs.vu.nl

Abstract. In this paper we review some well-known theory about reduction strategies of various kinds: normalizing, outermost-fair, cofinal, Church-Rosser. A stumbling block in the definition of such strategies is the presence of reduction cycles that may 'trap' a strategy as it is memory-free. We exploit a recently (re)discovered fact that there are no reduction cycles in orthogonal rewrite systems when each term has a normal form, in order to enhance some of the theorems on strategies, both with respect to their scope and the proof of their correctness.

Dedicated to Jean-Pierre Jouannaud
on the occasion of his 60th birthday

1 Introduction

The general objective of our note is to survey some fundamental theorems about reduction strategies in term rewriting, both first-order and higher-order. Some of these theorems are by now rather classical, and some are of a more recent date. The strategies serve various purposes: they may be normalizing, or outermost-fair, or cofinal, or Church-Rosser strategies, to name some of their more important properties. One liability they have in common: they may fall into a trap formed by a *reduction cycle*. This is so because the usual notion of a reduction strategy is such that no memory is involved: a reduction strategy $\mathbb{F}$ is just a function from terms to terms, such that for every term t that is not in normal form we have $t \to \mathbb{F}(t)$ in case $\mathbb{F}$ is a one-step strategy, and $t \twoheadrightarrow \mathbb{F}(t)$ in case $\mathbb{F}$ is a many-step strategy. Thus, if we have for a one-step strategy $\mathbb{F}$ that e.g. $\mathbb{F}^3(t) \equiv t$ (see Figure 1), then $\mathbb{F}$ will be forever trapped in this reduction cycle

$$t \to \mathbb{F}(t) \to \mathbb{F}(\mathbb{F}(t)) \to t$$

The danger of a strategy being trapped in a reduction cycle is apparent in the proofs of several theorems about strategies. E.g. avoiding cycles is prominent in

H. Comon-Lundh et al. (Eds.): Jouannaud Festschrift, LNCS 4600, pp. 89–112, 2007.
© Springer-Verlag Berlin Heidelberg 2007

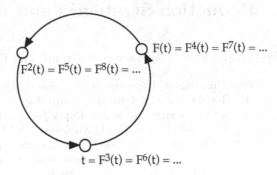

Fig. 1. Trap

the proof that there exists a computable many-step Church-Rosser strategy for λ-calculus [5,3], discussed in Section 6. And avoiding cycles is a major complicating factor in Statman's definition of a cofinal strategy for combinators [14].

Now recently it was found by Ketema et al. [7] that under very natural conditions there are no reduction cycles at all. Of course, if the rewrite system has the property SN, strong normalization (or termination), there are no reduction cycles. But this is a bit too strong. Ketema et al. [7] proved that for orthogonal term rewriting systems that are WN, weakly normalizing, there are already no cycles, a property that we indicate by AC (acyclicity). This theorem generalizes to a wide class of rewrite systems, namely the weakly orthogonal fully extended higher-order rewriting systems. Actually, this theorem was for the case of almost orthogonal combinatory reduction systems already proved in a rather implicit way in Kennaway [6], but there it has remained unnoticed until now.

Combining our first observation of the 'cycle trap' for strategies with this recent insight that we have WN $\Rightarrow$ AC for orthogonal rewrite systems, there arises a natural question: does the acyclicity of orthogonal systems that are WN facilitate the proofs of the theorems for reduction strategies that are in the literature?

The goal of our note is to show that the answer is affirmative. In doing so, we obtain a strengthening of some of the theorems known for strategies, and a simplification of some of their proofs. We also present some new theorems. Finally, we employ in our formulation a notion of strategy, based on abstract rewriting notions, that is more expressive than the classical (functional) notion.

2 Basic Notions

2.1 Abstract Rewriting

We start by introducing the necessary notions and notations concerning abstract rewriting, where the objects that are rewritten do not have any observable structure. One of the usual definitions of abstract rewriting is as a set equipped with a binary relation (as in [2, p.7], and as a special case of [15, Definition 1.1.1]). Here we take another approach, via the more expressive notion of ARS as in [15, Definition 8.2.2], where steps are first-class citizens.

Definition 1. An *abstract reduction system* (ARS) is defined as a quadruple

$$(A, \Phi, \text{source}, \text{target})$$

where A is a set of *objects*, Φ a set of *steps*, and $\text{source} : \Phi \to A$ and $\text{target} : \Phi \to A$ are functions mapping a step to its source and target. ARSs are denoted by $\to, \Rightarrow, \ldots$, and also by $\mathbb{A}, \mathbb{B}, \mathbb{S}, \mathbb{F}, \ldots$.

We can think of an ARS as a graph. There might be more than one step between two objects, so we can express more than binary relations on a set.

Example 1. See also Figure 2.

(i) The ARS $\mathbb{A}_1 = (A_1, \Phi_1, \text{source}_1, \text{target}_1)$ is defined by: $A_1 = \{a, b\}$, $\Phi_1 = \{\phi_1, \phi_2\}$, $\text{source}_1(\phi_1) = a$, $\text{target}_1(\phi_1) = a$, $\text{source}_1(\phi_2) = a$, $\text{target}_1(\phi_2) = b$.
(ii) The ARS $\mathbb{A}_2 = (A_2, \Phi_2, \text{source}_2, \text{target}_2)$ is defined by: $A_2 = \{a, b\}$, $\Phi_2 = \{\phi_1\}$, $\text{source}_2(\phi_1) = a$, $\text{target}_2(\phi_1) = a$.
So the underlying graph of an ARS is not necessarily connected.
(iii) The ARS $\mathbb{A}_3 = (A_3, \Phi_3, \text{source}_3, \text{target}_3)$ is defined by: $A_3 = \{a, b\}$, $\Phi_3 = \{\phi_2\}$, $\text{source}_3(\phi_2) = a$, $\text{target}_3(\phi_2) = b$.
(iv) The ARS $\mathbb{A}_4 = (A_4, \Phi_4, \text{source}_4, \text{target}_4)$ is defined by: $A_4 = \{a, b\}$, $\Phi_4 = \{\phi_2, \phi_3\}$, $\text{source}_4(\phi_2) = \text{source}_4(\phi_3) = a$, $\text{target}_4(\phi_2) = \text{target}_4(\phi_3) = b$.
In $\mathbb{A}_4$ there are two different steps from a to b, hence it cannot be given as a relation on a set. This phenomenon occurs for instance in λ-calculus with β-reduction: there are two different steps from $I(II)$ to II.
(v) The well-known counter-example against the implication 'local confluence implies confluence' is defined as the following ARS $\mathbb{A}_5$: $A = \{a, b, c, d\}$, $\Phi = \{\phi_1, \phi_2, \phi_3, \phi_4\}$, $\text{source}(\phi_1) = b$, $\text{target}(\phi_1) = a$, $\text{source}(\phi_2) = b$, $\text{target}(\phi_2) = c$, $\text{source}(\phi_3) = c$, $\text{target}(\phi_3) = b$, $\text{source}(\phi_4) = c$, $\text{target}(\phi_4) = d$.

In some of the examples in the paper, we will write ARSs in a simplified notation, namely as a set of arrows with source and target. It is then understood that the set of objects is the set of objects mentioned, and that source and target are as suggested by the explicit enumeration of the arrows. For instance the ARS $\mathbb{A}_5$ from Example 1 is then written as $\{b \to a, b \to c, c \to b, c \to d\}$.

The definition of strategy below employs the following definition of sub-ARS.

Definition 2. An ARS $\mathbb{A}_1 = (A_1, \Phi_1, \text{source}_1, \text{target}_1)$ is a *sub-ARS* of an ARS $\mathbb{A}_2 = (A_2, \Phi_2, \text{source}_2, \text{target}_2)$, notation $\mathbb{A}_1 \subseteq \mathbb{A}_2$, if the following holds:

(i) $A_1 \subseteq A_2$,
(ii) $\Phi_1 \subseteq \Phi_2$,
(iii) source_1 and target_1 are the restrictions of source_2 and target_2 to Φ_1.

If we think of an ARS as a graph, a sub-ARS is a sub-graph, with possibly less objects and less steps. The last condition of the definition of sub-ARS implies

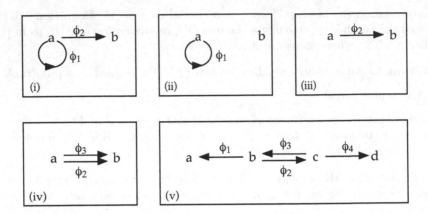

Fig. 2. The ARSs from Example 1

that $\mathsf{source}(\Phi_1) \subseteq A_1$ and also $\mathsf{target}(\Phi_1) \subseteq A_1$, that is, the sources and targets of steps in the small ARS must be present in its set of objects. Note that $\subseteq$ is a partial order on ARSs. The definition of sub-ARS used here is different from for instance [15, Definition 1.1.6]: there the set of objects of the 'small' ARS must be closed under the steps of the 'big' ARS. See also the example below.

Example 2.

(i) An ARS is a sub-ARS of itself: $\mathbb{A} \subseteq \mathbb{A}$.
(ii) For the ARSs defined of Example 1 we have: $\mathbb{A}_2 \subseteq \mathbb{A}_1$, $\mathbb{A}_3 \subseteq \mathbb{A}_1$, $\mathbb{A}_3 \subseteq \mathbb{A}_4$.
(iii) There is no sub-ARS of the ARS $\mathbb{A}_3$ from Example 1 with $\emptyset$ as set of objects, and $\{\phi_2\}$ as set of steps.
(iv) The ARS a without any steps is a sub-ARS of $a \rightarrow b$. So the set of objects of the 'small' ARS need not to be closed under the reduction of the 'big' ARS.

In the remainder of this subsection we assume an ARS $\mathbb{A} = (A, \Phi, \mathsf{source}, \mathsf{target})$.

A *reduction step* or *rewrite step* is an element of Φ, together with its source and target. Reduction steps are written as $\phi : a \rightarrow b$ or $a \rightarrow_\phi b$, for a step $\phi \in \Phi$. An object $a \in A$ is a *normal form* (or a is *in normal form*) if there is no reduction step $a \rightarrow$ with source a. A *reduction* or *rewrite sequence* starting in a_0 is a finite or infinite sequence of steps: $a_0 \rightarrow_{\phi_0} a_1 \rightarrow_{\phi_1} a_2 \rightarrow_{\phi_2} \ldots$. A finite reduction $a_0 \rightarrow_{\phi_0} \cdots \rightarrow_{\phi_{n-1}} a_n$ is said to be a *reduction from a_0 to a_n*. Such a reduction is also written as $a_0 \twoheadrightarrow a_n$. A reduction is said to be *maximal* if it cannot be extended, that is, either it ends in a normal form or it is infinite.

We sometimes omit irrelevant information from this notation, writing for instance $a \rightarrow$ to indicate that there is a step from a, or $a \twoheadrightarrow$ to indicate a finite or infinite reduction starting in a. If we want to stress that a step (or reduction) takes place in the ARS $\mathbb{A}$ we use $\mathbb{A}$ as subscript.

The *reduction graph of a in $\mathbb{A}$*, notation $\mathcal{G}(a, \mathbb{A})$, has as set of objects $\{b \mid a \twoheadrightarrow b\}$, and as set of steps all $\phi \in \Phi$ with $\mathsf{source}(\phi) \in \{b \mid a \twoheadrightarrow b\}$. Further, the source and target functions of $\mathcal{G}(a, \mathbb{A})$ are the appropriate restrictions of source and target. A reduction graph is a sub-ARS of $\mathbb{A}$.

An object $a \in A$ is *weakly normalizing in* $\mathbb{A}$, notation $a \in \mathsf{WN}(\mathbb{A})$, if there is a reduction sequence in $\mathbb{A}$ from a to a normal form of $\mathbb{A}$. The ARS $\mathbb{A}$ is *weakly normalizing*, notation $\mathbb{A} \in \mathsf{WN}$, if all objects $a \in A$ are weakly normalizing in $\mathbb{A}$. An object $a \in A$ is *strongly normalizing in* $\mathbb{A}$ or *terminating in* $\mathbb{A}$, notation $a \in \mathsf{SN}(\mathbb{A})$, if all reduction sequences starting in a are finite. The ARS $\mathbb{A}$ is *strongly normalizing* or *terminating*, notation $\mathbb{A} \in \mathsf{SN}$, if all objects $a \in A$ are strongly normalizing in $\mathbb{A}$. It may happen that an object is weakly normalizing in an ARS but not in a sub-ARS. For example, considering the ARSs of Example 1, we have $a \in \mathsf{WN}(\mathbb{A}_1)$, but a is not weakly normalizing in $\mathbb{A}_2 \subseteq \mathbb{A}_1$.

The ARS $\mathbb{A}$ is *confluent* if the endpoints of all pairs of co-initial reductions are joinable, so for all objects $a, b, b' \in A$: if $a \twoheadrightarrow b$ and $a \twoheadrightarrow b'$ then $b \downarrow_{\mathbb{A}} b'$.

2.2   Term Rewriting

We use the standard notions and notations from [2,15] for first-order term rewriting systems (TRSs). We also consider higher-order rewriting systems with patterns (HRSs), defined by Nipkow [11]. At some places in the literature these are called PRSs. The terms are simply typed λ-terms with constants, that are considered modulo $\alpha\beta\eta$. Rules satisfy the patterns restriction that guarantees matching (and unification) modulo $\beta\eta$ to be decidable. See also [15, Chapter 11] for definitions and notations.

A term rewriting system is *orthogonal* if all rewrite rules are left-linear and there are no critical pairs. A term rewriting system is *weakly orthogonal* if all rewrite rules are left-linear and all critical pairs are trivial (so overlapping steps yield the same result). Almost orthogonal is in between orthogonal and weakly orthogonal: trivial critical pairs are allowed but only if the overlap is at the top.

Definition 3. A rewrite rule is *fully extended* if in the left-hand side every free variable has as arguments exactly all variables that are bound at that position.

In fully extended systems, whether a rule is applicable does not depend on whether or not a bound variable occurs. The rewrite rule $f(\lambda x. z) \rightarrow a$ with z a free variable is not fully extended. The rule can only be applied to a term of the form $f(\lambda x.s)$ if x does not occur in s. Another example of a rule that is not fully extended is the η-reduction rule: $\lambda x.M\,x \rightarrow M$, with the side-condition that x should not occur in the free variables of M.

2.3   Reduction Strategies

A common approach in the literature is that a strategy, intuitively speaking, tells us how to reduce a term. That is, a strategy tells us how we *must* reduce a term. Then a strategy is a function from terms to terms, and hence deterministic, as in the Introduction. But we can also adopt a more general point of view: a strategy tells us how we *may* reduce a term. Following [15, Definition 9.1.1], see also [16], we take the latter approach.

Definition 4. A *strategy for an ARS* $\to$ is a sub-ARS of $\to$ having the same objects and normal forms.

So a strategy has the same objects as the original ARS, but possibly less arrows. Also, an object is a normal form in the strategy exactly if it is a normal form in the original ARS. The explanation for the requirement that a strategy has the same normal forms as the original ARS is that we want the strategy to be 'pushy': whenever there are still possibilities (steps, edges) to proceed, the strategy will select a positive number of them, and not discard them all. So a strategy can only stop in a normal form, but not before. Note that 'strategy for' is transitive: a strategy $\mathbb{S}$ for a strategy $\mathbb{S}'$ for an ARS $\mathbb{A}$ is again a strategy for $\mathbb{A}$. Thus we have a notion of *refinement* of strategies.

Example 3.

   (i) An ARS is a strategy for itself. In fact, this is the strategy of *exhaustive search*. This also shows that a strategy may be non-deterministic.
  (ii) We consider the following ARS $\mathbb{A}$ from [15, Example 9.1.2]: $a \overset{\leftrightarrow}{\to} b \to c$. Then $a \to b \to c$ is a strategy for $\mathbb{A}$. The sub-ARS $b \to c$ is not a strategy for $\mathbb{A}$, because it does not have the same objects as $\mathbb{A}$. The sub-ARS $a \leftarrow b \to c$ is not a strategy for $\mathbb{A}$ either, because a is not a normal form in $\mathbb{A}$.
 (iii) We reconsider the ARSs of Example 1. $\mathbb{A}_2$ and $\mathbb{A}_3$ are both strategies for $\mathbb{A}_1$. Also, $\mathbb{A}_3$ is a strategy for $\mathbb{A}_4$.
 (iv) Consider following ARS: $\mathbb{B} = \{a \to b, a \to c, a \to d, d \to d\}$. Then $\mathbb{S} = \{a \to b, a \to c, d \to d\}$ is a non-deterministic strategy for $\mathbb{B}$.

Properties of strategies. A strategy is usually employed to obtain a reduction with a certain property.

Definition 5. Let $\mathbb{S}$ be a strategy for $\mathbb{A} = (A, \Phi, \mathsf{source}, \mathsf{target})$.

   (i) $\mathbb{S}$ is *normalizing* if $a \in \mathsf{SN}(\mathbb{S})$ for every object $a \in \mathsf{WN}(\mathbb{A})$.
  (ii) $\mathbb{S}$ is *cofinal* if the following holds: for every $a \in A$, for every finite reduction $\mathcal{R} : a \twoheadrightarrow a'$ in $\mathbb{A}$, for every maximal reduction $\mathcal{S} : a \twoheadrightarrow$ in $\mathbb{S}$, there is an object c in $\mathcal{S}$ such that $a' \twoheadrightarrow c$ in $\mathbb{A}$. See Figure 3.

In Example 1, the ARS $\mathbb{A}_3$ is a normalizing strategy for $\mathbb{A}_1$. An ARS is not necessarily a cofinal strategy for itself. For instance, in the ARS $\mathbb{A}_1$ of Example 1 the final object b of the reduction $a \to b$ cannot be reduced to an object in the maximal reduction $a \to a \to a \to \ldots$. Also in this possibly non-deterministic setting cofinal strategies are normalizing [15, Proposition 9.1.16].

Proposition 1 ([15]). *Cofinal strategies are normalizing.*

Church-Rosser strategies. We now focus on a subclass of strategies. A strategy is said to be *deterministic* or *functional* if every object is the source of at most one arrow. Reconsidering the ARSs of Example 1, both $\mathbb{A}_2$ and $\mathbb{A}_3$ are functional strategies for $\mathbb{A}$. The ARS $\mathbb{A}_1$ is also a strategy for itself, which is not functional.

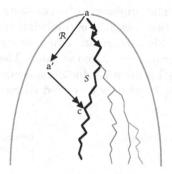

Fig. 3. A cofinal strategy

A function from terms to terms that maps a normal form to itself, and a term that is not in normal form to one of its one-step reducts, naturally induces a deterministic (or functional) strategy. Therefore we use in the setting of functional strategies also the notation $\mathbb{F}^n(a)$ for the object reached by performing n steps according to $\mathbb{F}$, starting in a (with $\mathbb{F}(a) \equiv a$ if a is in normal form).

Definition 6. A deterministic (or functional) strategy $\mathbb{F}$ for an ARS $\mathbb{A}$ is said to be a *Church-Rosser strategy for* $\mathbb{A}$, also called a *CR-strategy for* $\mathbb{A}$, if the following holds: if $a =_{\mathbb{A}} b$ then $\exists n, m \in \mathbb{N} : \mathbb{F}^n(a) \equiv \mathbb{F}^m(b)$. See also Figure 4.

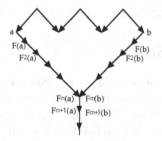

Fig. 4. One-step CR-strategy

In Section 6 we will also consider *many-step* functional Church-Rosser strategies, where intuitively a term not in normal form is mapped to some reduct (where the reduct is reached in at least one step).

Overview of properties of strategies. We conclude this section with a picture (Figure 5) of properties of reduction strategies, for abstract rewriting and term rewriting, and their interrelations. The notions fair and leftmost-fair are included for completeness and do not play a rôle in the remainder of the paper. The implication 'cofinal implies normalizing' is Proposition 1. The implication 'Church-Rosser implies cofinal' is Theorem 8, which is concerned with functional (or deterministic) strategies. The implication 'normalizing implies Church-Rosser' holds for functional strategies in weakly normalizing and confluent ARSs: a normalizing strategy then yields a common reduct of two convertible objects by computing their normal forms, which are the same. The implication 'outermost-fair implies normalizing' is Theorem 7, which is concerned with the more general setting of weakly orthogonal and fully extended HRSs.

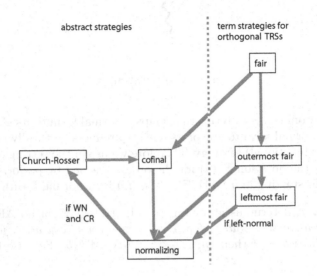

Fig. 5. Overview of reduction strategies

3　A Normalizing Strategy

A normalizing strategy is of interest in the case that a rewriting system has terms that can be rewritten to normal form, but are also the starting point of an infinite reduction. This happens for instance to the term $\mathsf{K\,I\,((S\,I\,I)\,(S\,I\,I))}$ in Combinatory Logic (CL) which is defined by the rewrite rules

$$
\begin{aligned}
\mathsf{I}\,x &\to x \\
\mathsf{K}\,x\,y &\to x \\
\mathsf{S}\,x\,y\,z &\to x\,z\,(y\,z)
\end{aligned}
$$

For (pure) CL the leftmost-outermost strategy is normalizing. But let us now consider CL extended with Gustave's term rewriting system which is defined by the following rules:

$$
\begin{aligned}
g(a,b,x) &\to c \\
g(x,a,b) &\to c \\
g(b,x,a) &\to c
\end{aligned}
$$

How should we evaluate a term of the form $g(l,m,r)$ with l, m, and r redexes of (pure) CL? Such a term intuitively seems to require parallel evaluation because it is undecidable whether a CL term has a (head) normal form. Nevertheless, Kennaway [6] proves, surprisingly, that there is a normalizing one-step strategy for the combination of CL and Gustave's TRS. More precisely, Kennaway proves that almost orthogonal Combinatory Reduction Systems (CRSs) have a computable one-step normalizing strategy. This means that also λ-calculus with parallel-or, defined by

$$(\lambda x.\, z)\, z' \rightarrow z[x := z']$$
$$\mathsf{por}(\mathsf{t}, z) \;\rightarrow\; \mathsf{t}$$
$$\mathsf{por}(z, \mathsf{t}) \;\rightarrow\; \mathsf{t}$$
$$\mathsf{por}(\mathsf{f}, \mathsf{f}) \;\rightarrow\; \mathsf{f}$$

has a computable one-step normalizing strategy, although intuitively it seems that a term $\mathsf{por}(M, N)$ with M and N λ-terms requires a parallel evaluation.

Antoy and Middeldorp [1] define a computable one-step strategy for almost orthogonal term rewriting systems, and show that it is normalizing via a reduction to normalization of outermost-fair rewriting. In this section we present two observations concerning their strategy. The first observation is that the definition of the strategy, and the proof of its normalization, can be extended to the case of fully extended weakly orthogonal higher-order rewriting. The second observation is that the definition of the strategy can be made substantially simpler for weakly normalizing systems, because then we do not have to deal with cycles.

The strategy $\mathbb{S}_F$. We define a non-deterministic strategy $\mathbb{S}_F$ for higher-order rewriting. The definition is a minor adaptation of the definition by Antoy and Middeldorp [1]. We use the notation $\mathbb{S}_F$ from [15]; the notation used in [1] is $\mathcal{S}_\omega$.

In the definition of $\mathbb{S}_F$ for higher-order rewriting we make use of the notion 'acyclicity-check'. In general, it is undecidable whether a term cycles. However, for finite systems, it is decidable whether a term t cycles within its own height, that is, is on a cycle where all terms are at most as big as t itself. More in particular, it is also decidable whether a terms cycles according to a strategy within its own height.

Definition 7. Assume a HRS $\mathbb{R}$. The strategy $\mathbb{S}_F$ and the property $\mathsf{AC}_{\mathbb{S}_F}$ of passing the $\mathbb{S}_F$-acyclicity-check are defined by induction on the structure of terms as follows:

(i) Given a term s, the strategy $\mathbb{S}_F$ can perform the following steps:
   (a) if s is a redex, then $\mathbb{S}_F$ can only contract a redex at the root,
   (a) otherwise, $\mathbb{S}_F$ is applied to a smallest direct argument satisfying $\mathsf{AC}_{\mathbb{S}_F}$,
   (a) otherwise, $\mathbb{S}_F$ can perform any step.
(ii) A term t satisfies $\mathsf{AC}_{\mathbb{S}_F}$, or otherwise said *passes the $\mathbb{S}_F$-acyclicity-check*, if it is not on a $\mathbb{S}_F$-cycle in which all terms are at most as big as t. Otherwise, it fails the acyclicity-check.

The strategy $\mathbb{S}_F$ is an outermost strategy that is only unfair to redexes that intuitively do not contribute to the normal form because they cycle. Below (Theorem 1) we show that $\mathbb{S}_F$ is normalizing.

Note that in the definition of $\mathbb{S}_F$-acyclicity-check for a term t, we only need the definition of $\mathbb{S}_F$ on terms smaller than t. Since overlap is allowed, a redex at the root is not necessarily unique.

Further, $\mathbb{S}_F$ is a non-deterministic strategy. If the first clause of the definition applies, then there is possibly a choice between overlapping root-redexes. If the second clause of the definition applies, there is a choice between all smallest reducible arguments that pass the $\mathbb{S}_F$-acyclicity-check. In addition, there might be a choice between overlapping redexes.

Example 4. We consider the orthogonal TRS defined by the following rules:

$$f(x, g'(y), h'(z)) \rightarrow b$$
$$a \qquad\qquad \rightarrow a$$
$$b \qquad\qquad \rightarrow g(g(b))$$
$$g(x) \qquad\quad \rightarrow g'(x)$$
$$h(x) \qquad\quad \rightarrow h'(x)$$

An example of a reduction according to $\mathbb{S}_F$:

$f(a, b, h(b)) \rightarrow$
 the argument a fails the acyclicity-check
 b is the smallest reducible argument passing the acyclicity-check
$f(a, g(g(b)), h(b)) \rightarrow$
 $h(b)$ is the smallest reducible argument passing the acyclicity-check
$f(a, g(g(b)), h'(b)) \rightarrow$
 $h'(b)$ is the smallest reducible argument passing the acyclicity-check
$f(a, g(g(b)), h'(g(g(b)))) \rightarrow$
 $g(g(b))$ is the smallest reducible argument passing the acyclicity-check
$f(a, g'(g(b)), h'(b)) \rightarrow$
 there is a root-redex
b

The strategy $\mathbb{S}_F$ skips arguments that are $\mathbb{S}_F$-cyclic within their own height. One might wonder whether we could skip more arguments, while remaining normalizing. The following examples shows that skipping arguments that are cyclic (but not necessarily $\mathbb{S}_F$-cyclic) destroys normalization of $\mathbb{S}_F$.

Example 5. We consider the orthogonal TRS defined by the following rules:

$$a \qquad \rightarrow b$$
$$c \qquad \rightarrow c$$
$$g(b, y) \rightarrow d$$
$$h(d, y) \rightarrow e$$

The term $h(g(a, c), c)$ has a normal form which is indeed found in the following $\mathbb{S}_F$-rewrite sequence:

$$h(g(a, c), c) \rightarrow h(g(b, c), c) \rightarrow h(d, c) \rightarrow e$$

However, if we adapt the definition of the strategy in the sense that we skip arguments that cycle within their own height, then we skip the argument $g(a, c)$

because $g(a,c) \to g(a,c)$, and we also skip the argument c because $c \to c$. In other words, both arguments are skipped, and the third clause of the definition of the strategy applies. That is, also

$$h(g(a,c),c) \to h(g(a,c),c) \to \ldots$$

is a rewrite sequence according to the strategy. So this adaptation yields a strategy that is not normalizing.

One might also wonder whether we could skip fewer arguments, while remaining normalizing. The following example shows that skipping arguments if all their reductions are cyclic within their own height (so an argument that is $\mathbb{S}_F$-cyclic within its own height but also has another reduction is not skipped anymore) destroys normalization of $\mathbb{S}_F$.

Example 6. We consider the orthogonal TRS defined by the following rules:

$$
\begin{aligned}
a &\to f(a) \\
g(x) &\to g(x) \\
h(x) &\to h'(x) \\
j(h'(x),y) &\to b
\end{aligned}
$$

The term $j(h(h(x)), g(a))$ has a normal form. Indeed the following $\mathbb{S}_F$-rewrite sequence finds the normal form:

$$j(h(h(x)), g(a)) \to j(h'(h(x)), g(a)) \to b$$

Note that the argument $g(a)$ is skipped because it is $\mathbb{S}_F$-cyclic within its own height. However, if we adapt the definition of the strategy by skipping arguments if all their reductions are cyclic within their own height, then the argument $g(a)$ is no longer skipped. In that case we obtain the following rewrite sequence:

$$j(h(h(x)), g(a)) \to j(h(h(x)), g(a)) \to \ldots$$

So this change in the condition on skipping arguments makes that the strategy is no longer normalizing.

Normalization via outermost-fair rewriting. One can show that if the strategy $\mathbb{S}_F$ fails to normalize a term s, then there is an infinite outermost-fair rewrite sequence starting from s. Section 5 is concerned with outermost-fair rewriting and in particular contains the theorem that outermost-fair rewriting is normalizing for HRSs that are fully extended and weakly orthogonal from [13].

Theorem 1. *Assume a fully extended and weakly orthogonal HRS. If there is an infinite $\mathbb{S}_F$-rewrite sequence starting from s, then there is an infinite outermost-fair rewrite sequence starting from s.*

Proof. We only give the idea of the proof. Suppose that there is an infinite $\mathbb{S}_F$-rewrite sequence starting in s. An outermost redex that is unfairly treated is on a $\mathbb{S}_F$-cycle. Also, it is disjoint from other such redexes. A $\mathbb{S}_F$-cycle can be made outermost-fair. Now interleave the original infinite $\mathbb{S}_F$-rewrite sequence repeatedly with extra reductions on the place of the cycles, to obtain an infinite outermost-fair reduction starting in s.

Corollary 1. *The strategy* $\mathbb{S}_F$ *is a computable one-step normalizing strategy for HRSs that are weakly orthogonal and fully extended.*

Acyclic rewriting. A second observation is that for weakly normalizing systems, the acyclicity-check can be omitted, thanks to Theorem 6. The definition of the strategy then becomes more simple, and applying the strategy becomes essentially easier.

Definition 8. Assume a weakly normalizing HRS $\mathbb{R}$. The strategy $\mathbb{S}_F^{AC}$ is defined by induction on the structure of terms as follows. Given a term s, the strategy $\mathbb{S}_F^{AC}$ can perform the following steps:

(i) if s is a redex, then $\mathbb{S}_F^{AC}$ can only contract a redex at the root,
(ii) otherwise, $\mathbb{S}_F^{AC}$ is applied to a smallest direct argument that is reducible.

We claim that $\mathbb{S}_F^{AC}$ is outermost-fair. Hence by Theorem 7 it is normalizing.

4   Acyclicity

As argued in this paper, for several strategies their computability is seen to rely on having a suitable cycle detection sub-routine available. As cycle detection is complex, it is interesting to look at rewrite systems which do not need it, i.e. which are acyclic. Then the sub-routine can simply answer: no, with a resulting simplification, as exemplified in Definition 8. In this section, we recapitulate some known acyclicity results and establish some new ones.

The following two classical acyclicity results for Combinatory Logic (CL) are due to [9] and [5] respectively. Here we consider CL with basis $\{S, K, I\}$ and the following applicative rewrite rules:

$$
\begin{aligned}
I\,x &\to x \\
K\,x\,y &\to x \\
S\,x\,y\,z &\to x\,z\,(y\,z)
\end{aligned}
$$

Theorem 2 ([9]). *In Combinatory Logic, every finite reduction graph is acyclic.*

This 'finite acyclicity' result is very much CL-specific. For instance, both the term a in the single-rule orthogonal TRS $\{a \to a\}$ as well as the term $\Omega = (\lambda x.xx)(\lambda x.xx)$ in the λ-calculus, have a single-node cyclic reduction graph. By the theorem, since the reduction graph of the direct translation $SII(SII)$ of Ω into CL is cyclic: $SII(SII) \twoheadrightarrow_{CL} SII(SII)$ it can no longer be finite, and indeed it is not: $SII(SII) \twoheadrightarrow_{CL} I(SII(SII)) \twoheadrightarrow_{CL} I(I(SII(SII))) \twoheadrightarrow_{CL} \cdots$.

Theorem 3 ([5]). *In Combinatory Logic, S-terms are acyclic.*

As it brings out nicely the minimal counter-example technique commonly employed in acyclicity proofs, we now present an alternative proof to this result.

Proof. For a proof by contradiction, suppose a cycle $\sigma : t \twoheadrightarrow t$ of minimal height would exist. By minimality σ is a *head* cycle, i.e. σ is of shape $t \twoheadrightarrow$ S$suv \rightarrow sv(uv) \twoheadrightarrow t$. Observe no S-step decreases size and only doesn't increase size if its third argument is an S. But then in the next head-step, the term size increases, because no term other than S reduces to S, in particular, uv does not reduce to S.

Remark 1. Neither of Theorems 2 and 3 entails the other; S-terms may not be terminating and thus have infinite reduction graphs, [1] and the example SII(SII) above shows that general CL-terms need not be acyclic. It could be difficult to find a common generalization, since the former result is even dependent on the particular basis chosen (here $\{S, K, I\}$) as noted in [5].

Next we present two results allowing to infer acyclicity of a system from that same property for its components. The first result is a special case of a more general result due to Middeldorp and Ohsaki [10, Theorem 6.7].

Theorem 4 ([10]). *The disjoint union $\mathbb{R}$ of two TRSs is acyclic if both components are and either $\mathbb{R}$ is non-collapsing, or $\mathbb{R}$ is non-duplicating, or one of the components is both non-collapsing and non-duplicating.*

Here we complement the above result by showing that acyclicity is preserved when combining orthogonal acyclic TRSs.

Theorem 5. *Acyclicity is modular for orthogonal TRSs.*

Proof. See Appendix A.

The proof method also yields modularity of absence of non-empty *fixed-point* reductions of shape $t \twoheadrightarrow C[t]$ for orthogonal TRSs.

Remark 2. Both non-overlappingness and left-linearity are essential for acyclicity to be modular, answering questions by Middeldorp: Let $\mathcal{R}_b$ either be the overlapping left-linear TRS with rules $\{g(x,y) \rightarrow x, g(x,y) \rightarrow y\}$ or the non-overlapping non-left-linear TRS with rules $\{g(x,y,z,z) \rightarrow x, g(x,y,z,S(z)) \rightarrow y, \infty \rightarrow S(\infty)\}$. In either case, $\mathcal{R}_b$ is acyclic since applying a g-rule decreases the number of g-symbols. Combining either with the acyclic orthogonal TRS $\mathcal{R}_w$ $\{f(0,1,x) \rightarrow f(x,x,x)\}$ yields a cyclic combination $\mathcal{R}_b \uplus \mathcal{R}_w$, as can be seen from $f(0,1,g(0,1))$ or $f(0,1,g(0,1,\infty,\infty))$, respectively.

Remark 3. First-orderness is also essential for modularity of acyclicity. The HRS (higher-order pattern rewriting system in the sense of Nipkow) consisting of the single rule

$$f(xyz.Z(x,y,z),W,V) \rightarrow Z(W,Z(V,W,f(xyz.Z(x,y,z),W,V)),V)$$

is acyclic (see below). The two-rule TRS

$$g(a,x,y) \rightarrow x$$
$$g(b,x,y) \rightarrow y$$

---

[1] Remarkably termination *is* decidable for S-terms [17].

is trivially acyclic. However, their combination is not as witnessed by

$$\frac{f(xyz.g(x,y,z),a,b)}{}$$
$$\to \underline{g(a,g(b,a,f(xyz.g(x,y,z),a,b)),b)}$$
$$\to \underline{g(b,a,f(xyz.g(x,y,z),a,b))}$$
$$\to f(xyz.g(x,y,z),a,b)$$

The main feat of the HRS is that the lhs of its rule is embeddable into its rhs, but only so in a non-empty context. If it were the case the context could be empty, then the term substituted for Z should collapse both to its second (y) and third (z) argument *only* depending on its first (x) argument, which is impossible using only the first rule (see Appendix B). It is exactly this feature which the two selection rules of the TRS bring.

Remark 4. We conjecture that the corresponding CRS rule (combinatory reduction system in the sense of Klop):

$$f([xyz]Z(x,y,z),W,V) \to Z(W,Z(V,W,f([xyz]Z(x,y,z),W,V)),V)$$

is acyclic as well. This does not follow directly from the above since the CRS contains 'spurious' terms, i.e. terms such as $f([x]f(x))$ which are not the image of a HRS term.

We conclude this section by discussing the relationship between normalization and acyclicity. Of course SN $\Rightarrow$ AC, i.e. termination trivially implies acyclicity. More interesting is that in the presence of orthogonality weak normalization implies acyclicity. This result was prefigured in Kennaway [6] and recently rediscovered [7, Theorem 5.1], and extended [8, Theorem 3.1] by Ketema, Klop, and van Oostrom.

Theorem 6. *Assume a fully extended and weakly orthogonal HRS* $\mathbb{R}$*. Then:*

$$\mathbb{R} \in \text{WN} \Rightarrow \mathbb{R} \in \text{AC}$$

We give a sketch of the proof as it again nicely illustrates the minimal counter example technique, as well as the rôle of normalization of the outermost-fair strategy.

Proof. Assume that the system is not acyclic. Take a minimal term t with a cycle. That cycle contains a head step. As a consequence, t admits an infinite reduction with infinitely many head steps. Clearly such a reduction is outermost-fair, and since the outermost-fair strategy is normalizing and the system is WN by assumption, the reduction ends in a normal form. Contradiction.

Remark 5. Weak normalization cannot be relaxed from *system* to *term* level, as witnessed by the weakly normalizing but cyclic term $f(a)$ in the orthogonal (but not WN) TRS $\{f(x) \to b, a \to a\}$.

5   Outermost-Fair Rewriting

Normalization of $\mathbb{S}_F$ is proved by a reduction to normalization of outermost-fair rewriting. This section is concerned with normalization of outermost-fair rewriting; it does not contain new results.

A rewrite sequence is *outermost-fair* if every outermost redex is eventually contracted. For instance, in Example 5 the rewrite sequence $h(g(a,c),c) \to h(g(a,c),c) \to \ldots$ is not outermost-fair because it is unfair to the outermost redex a. The rewrite sequence $j(h(h(x)),g(a)) \to j(h(h(x)),g(a)) \to \ldots$ of Example 6 is not outermost-fair because it is unfair to the outermost redex $h(h(x))$.

O'Donnell [12] shows that outermost-fair rewriting is normalizing for almost orthogonal TRSs. Van Oostrom [13] extends this in two directions: from first-order to higher-order, and from almost orthogonal to weakly orthogonal.

Theorem 7 ([13]). *Outermost-fair strategies are normalizing for HRSs that are fully extended and weakly orthogonal.*

We collect some observations concerning the limitations of possible extensions.

Remark 6.

(i)   In case rewrite rules with arbitrary overlapping patterns are allowed, then outermost-fair rewriting is not necessarily normalizing. Consider for instance the TRS from [13] defined by $\{a \to b, f(a) \to f(a)\}$. The term $f(a)$ can be reduced to the normal form $f(b)$, but the outermost-fair reduction $f(a) \to f(a) \to \ldots$ does not reach a normal form.

(ii) If non-fully-extended rewrite rules are allowed, then outermost-fair rewriting is not necessarily normalizing. Consider for example the HRS defined by $\{f(\lambda x.\, z) \to a, g(x) \to a, h(x) \to h(x)\}$. The term $f(\lambda x.\, h(g(x)))$ has a normal form: $f(\lambda x.\, h(g(x))) \to f(\lambda x.\, h(a)) \to a$. However, the outermost-fair reduction $f(\lambda x.\, h(g(x))) \to f(\lambda x.\, h(g(x))) \to \ldots$ contracting h-redexes does not reach the normal form. The reason is that the outermost f-redex is created only by contraction of the non-outermost g-redex.

(iii) Outermost-fair does not imply cofinal. Consider for instance the TRS defined by $\{f(x) \to f(x), a \to b\}$. The outermost-fair reduction $f(a) \to f(a) \to f(a) \to \ldots$ is not cofinal because the term $f(b)$ (which is a reduct of $f(a)$) cannot be reduced to a $f(a)$.

(iv) In [13] also head-normalization is considered. Using the proof method of Theorem 7, it is shown that outermost-fair strategies are head-normalizing for HRSs that are fully extended and almost orthogonal. Surprisingly, this cannot be extended to the *weakly* orthogonal case.

6   Church-Rosser Strategies

In a research seminar in 1975 with as outcome the set of notes [4], the question was raised whether there exists a computable one-step Church-Rosser strategy for the λ-calculus? Here a strategy was defined in the classical sense, so as a functional strategy, and the notion of a (functional) CR-strategy was defined as in Definition 6. As far as we know, the question above is still unsolved. In [5] some partial results were obtained.

Church-Rosser strategies are important for the following reason, stated in Barendregt [3, Lemma 13.1.4] (the assumption of confluence is superfluous there; it follows from the assumption of a CR-strategy).

Theorem 8 ([3]). *Let $\mathbb{F}$ be a one-step or many-step functional strategy for the ARS $\mathbb{A}$. Then:*

$$\mathbb{F} \text{ is a CR-strategy} \quad \Rightarrow \quad \mathbb{F} \text{ is cofinal} \quad \Rightarrow \quad \mathbb{F} \text{ is normalizing.}$$

Proof. The second implication is a special case of Proposition 1. We now prove the first implication. So suppose $\mathbb{F}$ is a CR-strategy for $\mathbb{A} = (A, \Phi, \text{source}, \text{target})$ and let $a \in A$. We claim that the reduction $a \to \mathbb{F}(a) \to \mathbb{F}^2(a) \to \ldots$ (in case $\mathbb{F}$ is a one-step strategy) or $a \twoheadrightarrow \mathbb{F}(a) \twoheadrightarrow \mathbb{F}^2(a) \twoheadrightarrow \ldots$ (in case $\mathbb{F}$ is a many-step strategy) is cofinal in $\mathcal{G}(a, \mathbb{A})$. Indeed, if $b \in \mathcal{G}(a, \mathbb{A})$, then $a =_\mathbb{A} b$, so since $\mathbb{F} \in \mathsf{CR}$, the trails $\mathbb{F}(a), \mathbb{F}^2(a), \mathbb{F}^3(a), \ldots$ and $\mathbb{F}(b), \mathbb{F}^2(b), \mathbb{F}^3(b), \ldots$ will intersect. This shows that $\mathbb{F}$ is a cofinal strategy.

Theorem 9 ([5]). *There exists a computable many-step CR-strategy for the lambda-calculus.*

One of the main problems in the proof of Theorem 9 is to avoid that the CR-strategy $\mathbb{F}$ to be defined, falls in the trap of a double $\mathbb{F}$-cycle which is linked, see Figure 6.

Suppose there are two different $\mathbb{F}$-cycles C_1 and C_2 containing points M_1 and M_2 such that $M_1 =_\mathbb{R} M_2$ (that is, M_1 and M_2 are convertible in $\mathbb{R}$).

Then we are in a contradictory situation: $\mathbb{F}$ cannot be a CR-strategy, because the $\mathbb{F}$-trails for M_1 and M_2 will keep cycling without ever intersecting.

An effective many-step CR strategy. We now show that under far more general circumstances a computable many-step CR-strategy exists.

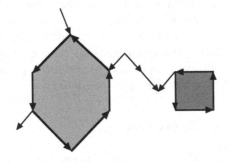

Fig. 6. Linked cycles

Definition 9. *An effective ARS is an ARS $\mathbb{A}$ with an injective computable function $\#$ from objects to natural numbers, and where the reduction relation is computable.*

So if $\mathbb{A}$ is Church–Rosser, we can compute a common reduct for any given finite set of convertible objects. Effective ARSs occur frequently, e.g. λ-calculus, or CL, or any TRS or HRS based on a finite signature and with a finite set of reduction rules. We will identify an object a with its corresponding natural number $\#a$, and with $\to_n$ the restriction of the reduction relation $\to$ of $\mathbb{A}$ to objects less than or equal to n is denoted. We show that if such an effective ARS $\to$ has the Church–Rosser property, then it has an effective many-step Church–Rosser strategy.

The core of our strategy is constituted by the following procedure which, for a given equivalence class of terms less than a given bound n, attempts to find a common reduct greater than that bound. Formally, for an object a and bound n with $\#a \leq n$ the object a_n is defined to be a common reduct of all (finitely many!) objects which are $\to_n$-convertible to a, such that that common reduct

(i) is greater than n, or else
(ii) is the greatest object of a strongly connected component of $\to_n$.

Here 'strongly connected' means that every pair of objects is related by $\to_n$. Note that by effectiveness of the ARS and the Church–Rosser property it is easy to turn the construction of a reduct a' common to the equivalence class, into a deterministic procedure. Next, by deterministically searching from a', going through the finitely many objects in the equivalence class, we will find a unique common reduct greater than n if it exists. Otherwise, the second item applies and one notes that the strongly connected component, and hence the common reduct computed, is unique by the Church–Rosser property (the strongly connected component may consist of a single object; a normal form).

The idea is then to repeat this procedure. But using what bounds? Using the number of the object itself as bound, i.e. from a compute $a_{\#a}$, may fail:

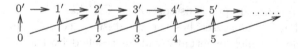

Fig. 7. Out-of-sync

Example 7. Consider the ARS of Figure 7, with the numbering $\#$ defined by $\#i = 2i$ and $\#i' = 2i + 1$. Then $0'_{\#0'} = 0'_1$ yields $2'$ (a common reduct of 0 and $0'$ and greater than both), $2'_{\#2'} = 2'_5$ yields $4'$, ... whereas $1'_{\#1'}$ yields $3'$, $3'_{\#3'}$ yields $5'$, etc.. A common reduct of $0'$ and $1'$ will never be reached.

One could think of the problem as arising from each object determining its own 'clock' and these staying 'out-of-sync' forever. To avoid this phenomenon, we inductively construct a (monotonically increasing) sequence of bounds $n(i)$, which one can think of as the 'ticks of a global clock'.

- $n(0) = 0$;
- $n(i+1)$ is the maximum of $n(i) + 1$ and all objects occurring in the construction of the common reducts $a_{n(i)}$, for a such that $\#a \leq n(i)$.

Now define $\mathbb{CR}(a) = a_{n(i)}$, with i least such that $\#a \leq n(i)$. Per construction $a \twoheadrightarrow_{n(i+1)} \mathbb{CR}(a)$, and if the first item applies $n(i) < \#\mathbb{CR}(a) \leq n(i+1)$, or else $\mathbb{CR}(a)$ is the greatest object of a strongly connected component.

Example 8. Consider the ARS of Figure 7 with the numbering $\#$ of Example 7.

- $n(0) = 0$,
- $n(1) = 1$, the number of $0'$, a (common) reduct of 0 greater than 0,
- $n(2) = 5$, the number of $2'$, a common reduct of 0 and $0'$,
- $n(3) = 9$, the number of $4'$, a common reduct of $0, \ldots, 2'$,
- $n(4) = 13$, $\ldots$

Thus $\mathbb{CR}(0') = 0'_1 = 2'$ and $\mathbb{CR}(2') = 2'_5 = 4'$ which is the same object as $\mathbb{CR}(1') = 1'_5 = 4'$ (since $2'$ and $1'$ are convertible within $\twoheadrightarrow_5$), as desired.

Remark 7. 'Ticks' of the 'global clock' need not have 'equal duration'. This can be seen by considering the multiplication ARS having positive natural numbers as objects (having themselves as number) and multiplication by a number as steps. Then $n(i+1)$ will be, for $i \geq 3$, the least common multiple of *all* numbers up to $n(i)$. Thus, in general, the 'duration' of the 'ticks' grows very fast.

Theorem 10. $\mathbb{CR}$ *is an effective many-step Church–Rosser strategy.*

Proof. That $\mathbb{CR}$ is an effective many-step strategy is clear from the above. To show it is a Church–Rosser strategy suppose a conversion between a and b exists, and let $n(i)$ bound the largest object in this conversion. By the above, if the first item always applies, then $a \twoheadrightarrow_{n(i)} \mathbb{CR}^k(a)$ and $b \twoheadrightarrow_{n(i)} \mathbb{CR}^{k'}(b)$ for some k and k', and since a and b were assumed to be convertible within $\twoheadrightarrow_{n(i)}$, so are $\mathbb{CR}^k(a)$ and $\mathbb{CR}^{k'}(b)$ and we conclude per construction of $\mathbb{CR}$ that $\mathbb{CR}^{k+1}(a) = \mathbb{CR}^{k'+1}(b)$. Otherwise, either sequence reaches the greatest object of some strongly connected component, which eventually will be reached by the other sequence of steps as well.

Remark 8. The strategy $\mathbb{CR}$ only avoids cycles which do have 'an exit'; a cycle without an exit (a strongly connected component) need not be avoided as it will be a common reduct (the unique sink of its connected component) due to the Church–Rosser property.

As a corollary of Theorem 10 we also have a computable cofinal and normalizing many-step strategy for this class of systems. Kennaway's theorem delivers a computable normalizing *one-step* strategy for the sub-class of almost orthogonal fully extended combinatory reduction systems (CRSs).

7 Cofinal Strategies

Using that CR-strategies are a fortiori cofinal, we have already some corollaries about the existence of cofinal strategies from the previous sections.

What we do not have as a corollary is the following noteworthy theorem:

Theorem 11 ([14]). *There exists a computable cofinal one-step strategy for Combinatory Logic.*

Also for CL, the question whether there is a computable one-step CR-strategy seems to be open.

In [15], Statman's strategy is given and shown to be cofinal in the setting of orthogonal TRSs. As remarked there, an extension to the higher-order case is not immediate, because the proof of cofinality essentially uses the fact that residuals of parallel redexes remain parallel, which is not true for the higher-order case. An extension to the weakly orthogonal case seems possible.

8 Concluding Remarks

The reduction strategies studied here are memory-free, or history-free. It will be interesting to study strategies with some form of memory. An abstract initial approach to add memory is described in [15, p.480, Definition 9.1.6], there called 'history-aware'.

References

1. Antoy, S., Middeldorp, A.: A sequential reduction strategy. Theoretical Computer Science 165(1), 75–95 (1996)
2. Baader, F., Nipkow, T.: Term Rewriting and All That. Cambridge University Press, Cambridge (1998)
3. Barendregt, H.P.: The Lambda Calculus, its Syntax and Semantic, of Studies in Logic and the Foundations of Mathematics. vol. 103, 2nd revised edn. North-Holland, Amsterdam (1984)
4. Barendregt, H.P., Bergstra, J.A., Klop, J.W., Volken, H.: Degrees, reductions and representability in the lambda calculus. Technical Report 22, Utrecht University (February 1976)
5. Bergstra, J.A., Klop, J.W.: Church-Rosser strategies in the lambda calculus. Theoretical Computer Science 9(1), 27–38 (1979)
6. Kennaway, J.R.: Sequential evaluation strategies for parallel-or and related reduction systems. Annals of Pure and Applied Logic 43, 31–56 (1989)
7. Ketema, J., Klop, J.W., van Oostrom, V.: Vicious circles in orthogonal term rewriting systems. In: Antoy, S., Toyama, Y. (eds.) (WRS'04). Proceedings of the 4th International Workshop on Reduction Strategies in Rewriting and Programming. Electronic Notes in Theoretical Computer Science, vol. 124, pp. 65–77. Elsevier, North-Holland, Amsterdam (2005)
8. Ketema, J., Klop, J.W., van Oostrom, V.: Vicious circles in rewriting systems. In: DiCosmo, R., Toyama, Y. (eds.): WRS'05. Proceedings of the 5th International Workshop on Reduction Strategies in Rewriting and Programming (2005)

9. Klop, J.W.: Reduction cycles in Combinatory Logic. In: Hindley, J.R., Seldin, J.P. (eds.) To H.B. Curry: Essays on Combinatory Logic, Lambda Calculus and Formalism, pp. 193–214. Academic Press, San Diego (1980) Also available via http://web.mac.com/janwillemklop/iWeb/Site/Bibliography.html
10. Middeldorp, A., Ohsaki, H.: Type introduction for equational rewriting. Acta Informatica 36(12), 1007–1029 (2000)
11. Nipkow, T.: Higher-order critical pairs. In: Proceedings of the 6th annual IEEE Symposium on Logic in Computer Science (LICS '91), pp. 342–349, Amsterdam, The Netherlands (July 1991)
12. O'Donnell, M.J.: Computing in Systems Described by Equations. LNCS, vol. 58. Springer, Heidelberg (1977)
13. van Oostrom, V.: Normalisation in weakly orthogonal rewriting. In: Narendran, P., Rusinowitch, M. (eds.) RTA 1999. LNCS, vol. 1631, pp. 60–74. Springer, Heidelberg (1999)
14. Statman, R.: Effective reduction and conversion strategies for combinators. In: Comon, H. (ed.) RTA 1997, LNCS, vol. 1232, pp. 203–213. Springer, Heidelberg (1997)
15. Terese.: Term Rewriting Systems. In: Cambridge Tracts in Theoretical Computer Science, vol. 55, Cambridge University Press, Cambridge, UK (2003)
16. Toyama, Y.: Reduction strategies for left-linear term rewriting systems. In: Middeldorp, A., van Oostrom, V., van Raamsdonk, F., de Vrijer, R. (eds.) Processes, Terms and Cycles: Steps on the Road to Infinity. LNCS, vol. 3838, pp. 198–223. Springer, Heidelberg (2005)
17. Waldmann, J.: The combinator S. Information and Computation 159, 2–21 (2000)

A   Proof of Modularity of Acyclicity

In this appendix we give a proof of Theorem 5 above. To that end, we first establish a lemma on standard reductions which is interesting in its own right.

Lemma 1 (Standard Prefix). *In an orthogonal TRS, the collection of standard reductions ending in a head step, is totally ordered by the prefix relation.*

Proof. In this proof we freely make use of Huet and Lévy's theory of standard/external reductions, for which we refer the reader to Sections 8.5 and 9.2.3 of [15].

First note that any standard reduction ending in a head step can be uniquely decomposed into a number of standard reductions such that *only* their final step is a head step. Thus to prove the lemma, it suffices to show that for any term there is *at most one* reduction of the latter type. We claim that a standard reduction of which only the final step is a head step is in fact an external reduction. The result then follows since supposing ρ and θ would be distinct such reductions from t, we may assume w.l.o.g. that they already differ in their first steps, say ϕ and ψ, and by totality of the textual order, we may assume w.l.o.g. that ϕ is to the left of ψ. Therefore, by externality of ϕ and standardness of θ, ϕ must have a unique residual up to the final step of θ. But that final step is a head step, so clearly it nests the residual of ϕ, contradicting externality of ϕ.

We prove the claim that any standard reduction of which only the final step is a head step, is an external reduction by induction on the lengh of the reduction. If the length is 1, it is trivial. Otherwise, we may write the reduction as $\phi \cdot \rho$ for some step ϕ. Since any suffix of a standard reduction is standard, the induction hypothesis yields that ρ is an external reduction.

For a proof by contradiction, suppose that ϕ contracting a redex-pattern at position p were not external. That is, a reduction θ co-initial to ρ would exist, consisting of steps disjoint from p and ending in a term allowing a step ψ at position q nesting p. By standardness of $\phi \cdot \rho$, the position p is in the redex-pattern of the first step above p in ρ (if any). As ρ ends in a head step such a step indeed exists, say it is ϕ' at position p' above p, and let ρ' be the prefix of ρ up to ϕ'.

Now consider the projections $\underline{\theta}$ of θ over ρ', and $\underline{\rho}'$ of ρ' over θ. Since by construction neither θ nor ρ' contracts redex-patterns on the path from the root to p, neither do their projections, hence the common reduct contains unique residuals of both ψ after $\underline{\rho}'$ and of ϕ' after $\underline{\theta}$, respectively at positions q and p' above p. Since the positions above p are totally ordered by the prefix relation, either of q and p' is above the other. We prove that neither is possible.

If q is properly above p', then the reduction $\underline{\theta}$ disjoint from p' and ending in a term containing a redex-pattern nesting p', shows that ϕ' is not external, contradicting the induction hypothesis. If p' is above q, then since q is above p and the redex-pattern at p' overlaps p, the redex-patterns of ϕ' and ψ must have overlap in the common reduct of $\overline{\theta}$ and $\overline{\rho}'$, contradicting orthogonality.   □

Remark 9. Although the lemma and its proof go through for higher-order rewriting systems, we have refrained from stating these since the next theorem doesn't generalise to the higher-order case (the result fails as shown in this paper, and its proof fails in it being based on the notion of rank).

Theorem 12. *Acyclicity is modular for orthogonal TRSs.*

Proof. In this proof we freely make use of the notions of modularity and tracing, for which we refer the reader to Sections 5.7.1 and 8.6.1 of [15].

Let $\mathcal{R}_b \uplus \mathcal{R}_w$ be the disjoint union of the orthogonal TRSs $\mathcal{R}_b$ and $\mathcal{R}_w$. To prove that acyclicity is a modular property is to prove that the underlying rewrite system $\to_{\mathcal{R}_b \uplus \mathcal{R}_w}$, which we will abbreviate to $\to$, is acyclic if both $\to_{\mathcal{R}_b}$ and $\to_{\mathcal{R}_w}$ are. For a proof by contradiction, assume that $\to_{\mathcal{R}_b \uplus \mathcal{R}_w}$ would allow a non-empty cycle σ on some term t, which we may w.l.o.g. assume to be of minimal rank. Since the rewrite systems $\to_{\mathcal{R}_b}$ and $\to_{\mathcal{R}_w}$ are acyclic by assumption, the rank of t must be positive, say it is $n + 1$. By minimality, at least a single step in σ must contract a redex-pattern in the top layer. Finally, w.l.o.g. we may assume t to have a minimal number, say $m + 1$, of principal subterms of maximal rank, i.e. of rank n.

Since rewriting does not increase the rank, the fact that σ is a cycle entails that the rank of all the terms along σ must be $n + 1$, so none of them has a principal subterm of rank greater than n. Now, let $\boldsymbol{p}$ be the vector of positions of principal subterms of maximal rank in t. We claim that for some index i

and some positive k, p_i is its own origin when tracing p_i *back* along the k-fold repetition σ^k of σ. The claim holds true by the Pigeon Hole Principle and the fact that a principal subterm of maximal rank has another such subterm as origin.[2] Let s be the principal subterm of maximal rank at the position p_i given by the claim. We show that from t we can obtain a term t' which also allows a non-empty cycle but has at most m principal subterms of rank n, yielding a contradiction. The term t' is obtained from t by replacing a number of principal subterms, the subterm s at position p_i inclusive, by a term s' the rank of which is less than that of s.

The replacement term s' is defined as follows. If s allows some reduction having a destructive step in its top layer, then as standardisation preserves this and a destructive step in the top layer is a head step, the Standard Prefix Lemma yields some standard reduction ρ from s ending in a destructive step, which is least among such in the prefix order, and we let s' be the target of ρ. Otherwise, we let s' be a fresh variable. Either way, the rank of s' is less than the rank of s.

To see which principal subterms, other than s at position p_i, of t are to be replaced by s', we proceed as follows. Consider tracing p_i *forward* along an infinite repetition of σ^k, where we only let a position trace as long as it is the position of a principal subterm.[3] Then we let $\boldsymbol{p'}$ be the collection of all descendants which occur in t after some repetititon of σ^k, and let t' be obtained from t by replacing all subterms at positions in $\boldsymbol{p'}$ by s'. Note that by the above, p_i itself is among the $\boldsymbol{p'}$, and that by construction the subterms of t at positions in $\boldsymbol{p'}$ are reachable from s.

Next, we show the non-empty cycle σ^k on t can be *simulated* by a non-empty cycle σ' on t', by simulating each step $\phi : u \to v$ by a *reduction* $\phi' : u' \twoheadrightarrow v'$ depending on the relative positions of the redex-pattern contracted in ϕ and the (pairwise disjoint) descendants of $\boldsymbol{p'}$ in u. The invariant is that u' is obtained from u by replacing all subterms at positions of descendants of $\boldsymbol{p'}$ by s'.

- If ϕ contracts a redex-pattern *outside*, i.e. in the context of, the descendants of $\boldsymbol{p'}$ in u, then we let $\phi' : u' \to v'$ be obtained by contracting the same redex-pattern in u'.
- If ϕ contracts a redex-pattern *inside* some descendant of $\boldsymbol{p'}$ and ϕ is not destructive at its top layer, then we let $\phi' : u' \twoheadrightarrow u'$ be the empty reduction.
- If ϕ is a destructive step at a descendant p of $\boldsymbol{p'}$, then the subterm $v_{|p}$ is reachable from s as noted above, hence per construction of s' and the Standard Prefix Lemma, there also exists some reduction from s to $v_{|p}$ *via* s', thus using $u' = u'[s']_p$ we may set $\phi' : u'[s']_p \twoheadrightarrow u'[v_{|p}]_p$.

That σ' is non-empty follows from the fact that σ contains at least one step in its top layer, which will be simulated by exactly one step in σ' according to the first item of the simulation. To show that σ' is a cycle, it suffices to show that

---

[2] Note that the claim need not hold when fixing k to 1. For instance, σ might swap two principal subterms (setting k to 2 then works).

[3] Per construction positions trace statically; a redex-pattern overlapping one would be polychrome *quod non*.

each position p among $\boldsymbol{p'}$ in t traces *back* along σ^k to some position in that set again, which is trivial per construction of the set.   □

B   Proof of Acyclicity of a PRS

Lemma 2. *The PRS consisting of the following rule is acyclic:*

$$f(xyz.Z(x,y,z),W,V) \to Z(W,Z(V,W,f(xyz.Z(x,y,z),W,V)),V)$$

Proof. By contradiction. To that end, suppose a non-empty cycle σ on t were to exist. W.l.o.g. we may assume such a t to be of minimal size among all terms admitting a non-empty cycle. Moreover, we may assume by the Standardisation Theorem for left-linear PRSs, that σ is standard.

We will employ the notion of *gripping* path due to Melliès. Say a position of an f-symbol in a term *grips* any position of an f-symbol which has a variable bound by the binders of the former, below it.

Note that a position only can grip positions inside its first argument, as only that argument has (three) binders. For instance, if we were to have a term $f^1(xyz.f^2(x'y'z'.a, f^3(x''y''z''.a, x, a), a, a), a, f^4(x'y'z'.a, a, a))$, where we have labelled the f-symbols for easy reference, then f^1 grips both f^2 and f^3 as both contain the variable x bound by f^1. Note that f^2 does not grip f^3.

Then a gripping path is a path w.r.t.. the gripping relation; in the example term there are just two non-trivial paths $f^1 f^2$ and $f^1 f^3$. Note that gripping paths are finite since successive positions are properly ordered by prefix. The property to be exploited is that gripping paths are preserved under taking their (position-wise) origin along any rewrite step, where we take as origin/descendant relation the usual (static) one [15], except that as origin of (all copies of) the f displayed in the right-hand side the head-f of the left-hand side is taken. The point is that if the path in the target of a step has some position below the contracted redex—which is the only interesting case—then the first such must either be the position of the head-symbol of the copy of the redex, or be in one of the copies of (the terms substituted for) the meta-variables in the rhs. In either case, the path must proceed completely inside that copy, by the variable convention. But then a corresponding path exists in the source of the step through the corresponding copy.

Now consider the origin of an arbitrary gripping path from the root of t along σ. This origin is again a gripping path in t by the above and by σ being a cycle. Distinguish cases depending on whether its first position, say p, is on some gripping path from the root of t or not.

If it is not, then consider the position q which is closest to the root and above p such that it is not on some gripping path from the root. Per construction, the subterm headed by q, say t', contains no variable bound by an f-symbol above it. Since p descends, also per construction, to the root of t along σ which was assumed to be standard, it follows that t reduces to t' somewhere along σ. Thus there would be a cylce on t' as well, contradicting minimality of t.

If it is, then a further case distinction is made depending on whether p is itself the root or it isn't.

If p is not the root, a contradiction is obtained since then for any gripping path from the root in t, one obtains a longer such path by prefixing its origin along σ by the (non-empty) gripping path from the root to p.

If p is the root, then first note that by the minimality assumption for t, σ must contain some head step. By standardness and the shape of the lhs—which is a pattern which cannot be created—also the first step of σ must be a head step, i.e.

$$\sigma : f([xyz]t', s, u) \to t'[x, y, z := s, t'[x, y, z := u, s, t], u] \twoheadrightarrow f([xyz]t', s, u)$$

and the root descends to the head f-symbol of a fresh copy of t in the rhs. Both y and z must occur in t' otherwise t would be erased. Therefore. by reasoning as above, the (instantiated) copies of t' above the f-symbol must be collapsable to their second respectively third arguments, depending on the respective substitutions s and u for its first argument. However, neither s nor u contains a variable bound outside it, and thus a collapsing reduction from t' could not depend on them. Contradiction.   □

Towards Rewriting in Coq[*]

Jacek Chrząszcz and Daria Walukiewicz-Chrząszcz

Institute of Informatics, Warsaw University
ul. Banacha 2, 02-097 Warsaw, Poland
{chrzaszcz,daria}@mimuw.edu.pl

This work is dedicated to Jean-Pierre Jouannaud who is unquestionably a spiritus movens of the research on bringing rewriting to Coq.

Abstract. Equational reasoning in Coq is not straightforward. For a few years now there has been an ongoing research process towards adding rewriting to Coq. However, there are many research problems on this way. In this paper we give a coherent view of rewriting in Coq, we describe what is already done and what remains to be done.

We discuss such issues as strong normalization, confluence, logical consistency, completeness, modularity and extraction.

1 Introduction

Large part of research in modern theoretical computer science is concerned with formalizing mathematical reasoning. On one hand various formal calculi are being developed which model mathematical notions and proofs. On the other hand computer programs are written which implement these formalisms together with tools which help the users formalize and solve their mathematical problems.

In this paper we concentrate on Coq [17], a proof assistant based on type theory and the Curry-Howard correspondence, which relates formulas to types and their proofs to terms of these types.

Calculus of constructions. The first version of Coq (which was called CoC at that time) was designed in the late 80s by Coquand and Huet. It implemented the calculus of constructions, i.e. the lambda calculus, equipped with a powerful typing discipline containing polymorphism, dependent types and type constructors. Let us mention one typing rule, conversion, which will be important to us in the rest of the paper.

$$\frac{E \vdash a : t \quad E \vdash t' : s}{E \vdash a : t'} \quad \text{if } t \approx t'$$

This rule says that a proof of t is also a proof of any correct formula t' which is convertible to t. In the pure calculus of constructions, the convertibility relation

---

[*] This work was partly supported by the Polish government grant 3 T11C 002 27 and the EU FP6 project IST-15905 Mobius.

$\approx$ is only β-equality, which due to normalization and confluence of β-reduction can be checked automatically. The latter property is also crucial for the decidability of type-checking.

In the calculus of constructions it is possible to define natural numbers, lists, booleans and other inductive types by using the so-called impredicative encoding. For example, natural numbers can be represented as polymorphic Church numerals with their type $Nat \equiv \forall C : \star, C \to (C \to C) \to C$. Nevertheless this coding has some important drawbacks concerning both logical and computational aspects. It is for example impossible to prove that 0 is different from 1, induction principles, for example on natural numbers, are not provable, and some trivial functions, like predecessor on natural numbers, cannot be computed in constant time.

Calculus of inductive constructions. In early 90s Coquand and Paulin proposed to extend the calculus with new kinds of syntactic objects: inductive definitions introducing a type and its constructors and elimination schemes for that type [19]. The elimination schemes come together with their reduction rules called ι-reduction, which extends convertibility. The real novelty in the calculus of inductive constructions is strong elimination, which allows one to build types by recursion over inductive types.

Using strong elimination one can show that 0 is different from 1. Other problems of impredicative encoding of inductive types are now also solved.

The calculus of inductive constructions preserves all essential meta-theoretical properties of the original system: it is terminating, confluent, logically consistent and has decidable type-checking [46].

Unfortunately using recursors to write function definitions is not very easy and the definitions, once written, are not very readable. A solution to these problems is to replace the elimination schemes by two separate mechanisms: one for pattern-matching (or case-analysis), and one for constructing well-founded recursive functions.

Definitions by pattern-matching were added to Martin-Löf's type theory by Coquand [18]. Consequently, constants may be defined not only explicitly, by giving a term, but also implicitly by a set of defining equations of the form $f(u_1, \ldots u_n) = e$, which must be exhaustive and unambiguous.

An adaptation of the above idea to the context of the calculus of constructions is due to Christine Paulin and was implemented in Coq in 1994. The problem of checking unambiguity and exhaustiveness is eliminated by choosing a simple format of case analysis using the `match` operator. The simple format was later extended to more complex patterns in [20]. The recursive definitions are built using the fixpoint operator `fix`. Normalization is guaranteed within the type-checking rule of `fix`. Every recursive call must operate on arguments that are structurally smaller than the original ones, i.e. are deconstructed from the original arguments by a `match`.

Although quite natural and general enough to encode many interesting functions, the `fix` rule with its guard condition causes problems, both at the practical and the theoretical levels: complicated meta-theory, non-incremental proof-checking, etc. For these reasons several versions of type annotations were proposed to hide the guardedness condition in the type system [25,36,26,9,5]. There is a running prototype implemented for the system [5].

In order to simplify writing definitions of functions, several authors consider direct translation of functional programs to Coq [35,39]. Another possibility is to include in Coq the style of pattern-matching definitions as proposed by Coquand. But pattern-matching equations are just a restricted form of rewrite rules.

Rewriting in the calculus of constructions. There is an ongoing research process aiming at adding rewriting into theorem provers based on type theory and Curry-Howard Isomorphism such as Coq. Jean-Pierre Jouannaud, who was supervisor of our PhD theses [15,42], is one of the people who actively pushed this research on.

Defining functions by rewriting is as simple and elegant as the definitions by pattern matching, but the user has a possibility to add more rules, that would otherwise have to be proved as axioms or lemmas in the form of Leibniz equalities or heterogeneous equalities. Moreover, rules can be ambiguous (their left-hand sides may overlap) as long as the rewriting system is confluent. By transforming equalities into rewrite rules, one makes the conversion richer and therefore proofs shorter and more automatic. Moreover more terms are now typable, so the calculus becomes more expressive.

As long as conversion is decidable, extending the conversion can be seen as a means to separate reasoning from computing in a similar manner that is used in Deduction Modulo [23]: while the proof term must record all deduction steps, the computation steps can be hidden away in conversion and performed automatically. This could be most helpful when working with axiomatic equational theories, like e.g. group theory, that can be transformed into confluent and terminating rewriting systems. There exist tools that assist users in performing such transformations (see e.g. [16]).

In order to maintain conversion and hence type-checking decidable one must be careful to add only rewrite rules which would not spoil subject reduction, strong normalization and confluence. The easiest and the most natural way to preserve subject-reduction is to require that the left- and right-hand sides of a rule have the same type. More flexible approaches allow for the left- and right-hand sides that do not need to be well-typed (see discussion about underscore variables in the next section). Since it is not possible to check automatically whether a given set of rewrite rules in strongly normalizing, one has to come up with decidable criteria ensuring strong normalization and flexible enough to accept most of the known and useful definitions by rewriting. In [1] it is shown that the calculus of constructions can be safely extended with any terminating and confluent first-order rewriting system. For the higher-order case, there are two such criteria: HORPO [42] by the second author and the General Schema [6] by Frédéric Blanqui. They are both discussed in detail in Section 3. In the paper of Blanqui, the second problem, confluence, is also discussed.

But ensuring termination and confluence is of course not enough. To trust theorems proved with the help of a proof assistant based on a formalism one needs logical consistency. Without rewriting, consistency is guaranteed for all developments without axioms. With rewriting, one can show it for all developments where rewriting systems are complete [10,45]. Practical way of checking completeness is also provided in [45] and discussed in Section 5.

In this paper we give a general vision of rewriting in Coq, how we think it will look and feel. We particularly care to maintain the important characteristics of Coq, such as decidable conversion and type-checking, interactive proof development, canonicity of inductive types, logical consistency etc. At the same time we aim to be able to express by rewriting the elimination schemes for inductive types and definitions by case-analysis and therefore to drop ι-reduction from the system.

2   Rewriting — Look and Feel

Let us imagine a future version of Coq with rewriting, where definitions by rewriting will be entered just as all other definitions:[1]

```
Welcome to Coq 10.1

Coq < Symbol + : nat → nat → nat
Rules
| 0 + y ⟶ y
| x + 0 ⟶ x
| (S x) + y ⟶ S (x + y)
| x + (S y) ⟶ S (x + y)
| x + (y + z) ⟶ (x + y) + z.
```

The above fragment defines addition on unary natural numbers. This function is defined by induction on both arguments simultaneously and the last rule expresses associativity.

Introducing a new definition by rewriting to an environment can be done just like for inductive definitions.

$$\frac{E \vdash \mathsf{ok} \qquad E \vdash \mathsf{Rew}(\Gamma; R) : \mathsf{correct}}{E; \mathsf{Rew}(\Gamma; R) \vdash \mathsf{ok}} \tag{1}$$

If the environment E is correct and if the new definition by rewriting is correct, then we can add it to the environment. The right premise stands for all tests that have to be performed before environment extension. First, the definition must be well-formed, e.g. the local environment Γ must contain function symbols only, their types must be correct etc. Second, the rewriting system must verify the chosen acceptance condition, which should guarantee subject reduction, strong normalization and confluence of the system after adding the given definition by rewriting.

Note that at this point we only require properties that are needed to keep type-checking decidable. The user is free to add a rewriting system which causes

---

[1] The syntax of the definition by rewriting is inspired by the experimental "recriture" branch of Coq developed by Frédéric Blanqui.

inconsistency, just as he is free to add an inconsistent axiom but not a non-terminating fixpoint definition in the current version of Coq. Consistency of environments containing definitions by rewriting is a separate issue which is discussed in Section 5.

Rewrite rules are to be used in the conversion rule, and since the set of available rules depends on the environment, so does the conversion relation. The correct version of conversion rule is:

$$\frac{E \vdash a : t \quad E \vdash t' : s \quad E \vdash t \approx t'}{E \vdash a : t'}$$

Going back to our example, the definition of + is well-typed, confluent and terminating, so we can assume that it is correct and safely add it to the environment. Our definition is also complete in the sense that for all pairs of canonical natural numbers (i.e. made of constructors), their sum computes into a canonical natural number.

With this definition, + becomes much more useful than the one usually defined using match and fix. Both lemmas $\forall x : nat.\ 0 + x = x$ and $\forall x : nat.\ x + 0 = x$ can be proved by $\lambda x : nat.\ refl\ nat\ x$, where $refl$ is the only constructor of the Leibniz equality inductive predicate. Since the definition of addition is now symmetric we do not have to use induction for any of the two lemmas.

By enriching conversion, we also make more terms typable. Hence the logical language becomes more expressive, especially when dependently typed programs and their properties are considered.

The most prominent example of this kind is the append function on lists with length. For the sake of simplicity, let us assume that we have a list of boolean values.

```
Inductive nlist : nat → Set :=
| nnil : nlist O
| ncons : bool → forall n:nat, nlist n → nlist (S n).

Symbol append : forall n m:nat, nlist n → nlist m → nlist (n+m).
Rules
| append O m nnil lm ⟶ lm
| append (S n) m (ncons b1 n ln) lm ⟶ ncons b1 (n+m) (append n m ln lm)
| append n O ln nnil ⟶ ln.
```

Note that without the symmetric + in the conversion, either the first two rules or the last rule would not be well-typed. Indeed, in the first rule, the type of the left hand side is nlist (O+m) and the type of the right hand side is nlist m and in the third rule the corresponding types are respectively nlist (n+O) and nlist n.

Thanks to the fact that associativity of + is in conversion, one could write and prove the following equational property of append.

```
append k (n+m) lk (append n m ln lm)=append (k+n) m (append k n lk ln) lm
```

The types of both sides are listn ((n+m)+k) and listn (n+(m+k)) respectively, and since standard Leibniz equality requires terms to compare to have convertible types, associativity of + must be in conversion.

Rewrite rules can also be used to define higher-order and polymorphic functions, like the map function on polymorphic lists.

```
Inductive list (A : Set) : Set :=
   nil : list A | cons : A → list A → list A.
```

```
Symbol map : forall A B:Set, (A → B) → list A → list B
Rules
  map A B f (nil A) ⟶ nil B
  map A B f (cons A a l) ⟶ cons B (f a) (map A B f l).
```

Even though we consider higher-order rewriting, we think that it is enough to choose the simple matching modulo α-conversion. Higher-order matching is useful for example to encode logical languages by higher-order abstract syntax, but it is not really used in Coq where modeling relies rather on inductive types.

Instead of higher-order matching, one rather needs the possibility to under-specify some arguments. Consider for example transforming the equation for associativity of append into a rewrite rule:

```
append k (n+m) lk (append n m ln lm)
     ⟶    append (k+n) m (append k n lk ln) lm
```

The (n+m) argument of append is needed there just for the sake of correct type-checking of the left-hand side, because the type of append n m ln lm is list (n+m). It has no meaning for actual matching of this rewrite rule against terms, because in all well-typed terms, the second argument of append is the length of the fourth argument anyway.

Besides, putting (n+m) in the rewrite rule creates many critical pairs with +, which cannot be resolved without adding many new rules (either by hand or through an automatic completion procedure) to make the rewriting system confluent.

Instead, we could replace (n+m) by a fresh variable (or by an underscore standing for a "don't care" variable) and write this rule as:

```
append k _ lk (append n m ln lm)
     ⟶    append (k+n) m (append k n lk ln) lm
```

This new rule matches all well-typed terms matched by the old rule, and more. Moreover, there is no critical pairs between this rule and the rules for + and the rule becomes left-linear, which is both easier to match and may help with confluence proof. The downside is that the left-hand side of the rule is not well-typed anymore which might make the proof of subject reduction harder.

This way of writing left-hand sides of rules was already used by Werner in [46] to define elimination rules for inductive types, making them orthogonal (the left-hand sides are of the form $I_{elim}\ P\ \vec{f}\ \vec{w}\ (c\ \vec{x})$, where P, $\vec{f}$, $\vec{w}$, $\vec{x}$ are distinct variables and c is a constructor of I). In [10], Blanqui gives a precise account of these omissions using them to make more rewriting rules left-linear. Later, the authors of [13] show that these redundant subterms can be completely removed from terms (in a calculus without rewriting however). In [4], a new optimized convertibility test algorithm is presented for Coq, which ignores testing equality of these redundant arguments.

It is also interesting to note that when the second argument of append is a fresh variable then we may say that this argument is matched modulo conversion and not syntactically.

3 Strong Normalization

In this section we concentrate on the part of acceptance criterion for rewrite rules which is supposed to guarantee strong normalization.

The first article about higher-order rewriting in the calculus of constructions is [2,3], where the authors extend the termination criterion called the General Schema, originally defined in [28]. This result is further extended in [11] by adding a powerful mechanism, called the computable closure and further on in [6,10,8,7,9] where rewriting on types, rewriting modulo AC, extended recursors and type-based termination are considered.

Another method for proving strong normalization of higher-order rewriting is the Higher Order Recursive Path Ordering (HORPO). HORPO was originally presented in [29], in the context of the simply typed lambda calculus. A version of HORPO for the calculus of constructions was first presented in [41] and its journal version [43]. An extended and elaborated version of the results can be found in [42].

The works on HORPO and the General Schema share the approach to rewriting in the calculus of constructions presented in the previous section. Rewriting is introduced by rewrite rules on function symbols that are constants added to the system. Function symbols can have dependent and polymorphic types. In [42] (HORPO approach) both sides of every rewrite rules must have the same type, in [6] (General Schema) they are meant to have the same type for any typable instance of the left-hand side.

In order to have strong normalization, the form of the rules is further restricted: it is required that all meaningful type parameters of the head function symbol of left-hand sides must be different variables.

Both termination criteria, the General Schema and HORPO, are based on a well-founded ordering on function symbols, called precedence. Inductive types are built from type constructors and constructors satisfying some positivity conditions, and elimination schemes are just function symbols with associated rewrite rules. It is shown that most elimination schemes can be accepted by the General Schema and HORPO.

In order to deal with elimination schemes, the structural ordering associated with inductive definitions is incorporated in both HORPO and General Schema. They share also the use of computable closure (first used in the context of the simply-typed λ-calculus [12]), which is a set of terms derived from the left-hand side by some syntactic reducibility-preserving operations.

While the General Schema consists essentially of the computable closure, its use in HORPO is just one of the possibilities. Nevertheless, it is not the case that all object level rules accepted by the General Schema are accepted by HORPO. Apart from some technical conditions, the reason is mainly hidden in the different approaches to inductive types and constructors; in [6], where the General Schema is used, every function symbol whose output type is an instance of an inductive type I is considered as a constructor of I, in [42], where HORPO is used, the standard vision of constructors as symbols that do not rewrite is adopted.

In both works, strong normalization is shown using the method of reducibility candidates. In [42] the proof is done not for a particular rewrite system accepted by HORPO, but for the whole HORPO itself. In other words, the calculus of constructions is extended with the rewrite relation generated by all valid HORPO judgments and it is shown that the resulting calculus is strongly normalizing. This implies strong normalization of any set of rewrite rules accepted by HORPO. In [6] the proof is done for any set of rules accepted by the General Schema.

An important characteristic of the General Schema is the possibility to define rewriting rules at the level of types and not only at the level of objects. This kind of rewriting enables to write, for example large elimination rules for inductive types.

To deal with type-level rewriting, confluence is needed. For that reason, all rules in [6] have to be left-linear (see Section 4). Extension to type-level rewriting for HORPO cannot be shown this way, since HORPO is obviously non confluent.

Practical issues. In order to be suitable for implementation, the termination criteria must have two important properties: decidability and compatibility with further extensions of environments.

Both, HORPO and General Schema, are decidable criteria for accepting rewrite rules. Putting aside the convertibility tests, checking a rewrite rule has a polynomial complexity.

Environment extension corresponds to rule 1 in Section 2 and accounts for building one rewriting system on the top of another. Originally proofs of strong normalizations for both criteria were done for the static setting: signature, precedence on function symbols, and set of rewrite rules were given in advance. But this can be adapted to the situation where a new set of rewrite rules is defined for symbols from the new signature, and type-checked with the calculus of construction extended with rewriting coming from all previous rewrite systems.

Examples. Let us end this section with some examples explaining the condition about different variables as type parameters of head function symbols of the left-hand sides and illustrating what more can be done concerning strong normalization.

The following identity rule for polymorphic `map: forall A B:Set, (A →` `B) →` `list A →` `list B` can be accepted neither by HORPO nor by the General Schema:

```
map C C λx.x l  ⟶  l
```

In the General Schema approach rules have to be left-algebraic (cannot contain abstractions) and this one is not. In HORPO, the condition on type parameters is not satisfied, as map has the same variable as the first and the second argument. Nevertheless, it is believed that it cannot break strong normalization.

The following rule for the function symbol J is not accepted either:

```
Symbol J : forall A B:Set, A → B → A
Rules
  J C C a b ⟶ b
```

But this time it can be shown that this innocent-looking rule leads to nonter-mination. This example derives from the one presented by J.-Y. Girard in [27] and was shown to authors by Christine Paulin (see Chapter 6 in [42] for details concerning nontermination).

An evident difference between the two rules presented above is that there exists a well-typed instance of J C _ a b the type of which is different from the type of the corresponding instance of b and that it is not possible for map. Nevertheless HORPO from [42] cannot deal with the rule map C _ λx.x l ⟶ l either since it requires both sides of the rules to have the same type.

On the other hand the identity rule for monomorphic mmap : forall A:Set, (A → A) → list A → list A:

```
  mmap C λx.x l ⟶ l
```

satisfies the condition about different type variables. It is accepted by HORPO and rejected by the General Schema, because it is not left-algebraic.

The next example concerns the heterogeneous equality JMeq.

```
Inductive JMeq (A:Set)(a:A) : forall B:Set, B → Set :=
  JMeq_refl : JMeq A a A a.
```

The standard elimination scheme for this rule (JMeq_std) does not satisfy the condition about different type parameters and hence is rejected by HORPO. But it is known to be terminating already from the works on CIC (see [46] and also [7]).

```
Symbol JMeq_std : forall (A:Set)(a:A)(P:(B:Set)B → Set),
  P A a → forall (B:Set)(b:B), JMeq A a B b → P B b
Rules
  JMeq_std A a P h A a (JMeq_refl A a) ⟶ h
```

However, its nonstandard (and more useful) elimination scheme JMeq_nstd sat-isfies the condition on type parameters and can be shown terminating by both HORPO and the General Schema.

```
Symbol JMeq_nstd : forall (A:Set)(a:A)(P:A → Set),
  P a → forall (b:A), JMeq A a A b → P b
Rules
  JMeq_nstd A a P h a (JMeq_refl A a) ⟶ h
```

4 Confluence

Confluence of the calculus of constructions with rewriting is less studied than strong normalization and it is known for two kinds of situations. First, if strong normalization can be established without confluence (it is the case for the object-level rewriting, see [6,42]), then confluence is a consequence of the strong normalization and local confluence, i.e. joinability of critical pairs. If confluence is needed before the strong normalization proof then the result of [33] can be used. It states that the sum of beta reduction with confluent left-linear and left-algebraic rewrite system R is confluent. Confluence of R (without beta reduction) is usually simpler to achieve; in [6] it is shown for every R being a combination of a first-order system that is strongly normalizing and nonduplicating with a set of first- and higher-order rules satisfying the General Schema and such that critical pairs of R are joinable.

Left-linearity may seem an important restriction when using dependent types, but it is not really the case. In fact, nonlinearities due to typing can be avoided using underscore variables, like described in Section 2. Nevertheless, if one aims to deal with type-level rewriting, both type- and object-level rules have to be left-linear and left-algebraic. In order to lift this restriction one should probably consider a simultaneous proof of strong normalization and confluence.

5 Logical Consistency, Completeness of Definitions and Inductive Consequences

Adding arbitrary rewrite rules to the calculus of constructions may easily lead to logical inconsistency, just like adding arbitrary axioms. It is of course possible to put the responsibility on the user, but it is contrary to the current Coq policy to guarantee consistency of a large class of developments, namely those which do not contain axioms. Since we plan on using rewriting as a principal means of defining functions, we have to come up with a large decidable class of rewriting systems that are guaranteed not to violate consistency.

Logical consistency for the calculus of constructions with rewriting was first studied in [10]. It was shown under an assumption that for every symbol f defined by rewriting, $f(t_1, \ldots, t_n)$ is reducible if $t_1 \ldots t_n$ are terms in normal form in the environment consisting of one type variable. But there were no details how to satisfy the assumption of the consistency lemma.

In [45] it is shown that logical consistency is an easy consequence of canonicity, which can be proved from completeness of definitions by rewriting (discussed below), provided that termination and confluence are proved first. More precisely, it can be shown that in every environment consisting only of inductive definitions and complete definitions by rewriting, every term of an inductive type can be reduced to a canonical form. This, by an easy analysis of normal forms, implies that there is no proof of $\Pi x\!:\!*.x$.

Completeness of definitions by rewriting. Informally, a definition by rewriting of a function symbol f is *complete* if the goal $f(x_1, \ldots, x_n)$ is covered, which means that all its canonical instances are head-reducible. In [45] the definition of completeness is precised in such a way that it guarantees logical consistency and there exist a sound and terminating algorithm for checking completeness of definitions.

If we adopt the view that properties of a rewriting system should be checked when it is being introduced to an environment (see typing rule 1 in Section 2), then completeness of the function symbol f has to be checked much earlier than it is used: one uses it in an environment $E = E_1; \mathsf{Rew}(f, R); E_2$ but it has to be checked when f is added to the environment, i.e. in the environment E_1. It follows that completeness checking has to account for environment extension and can be performed only with respect to arguments of such types which guarantee that their set of normal inhabitants would not change in the future. This is the case for inductive types whose normal inhabitants are always terms built from constructors.

In [45] there is also an algorithm for checking completeness. It checks that a goal is covered using successive splitting, i.e. replacement of variables of inductive types by constructor patterns. In presence of dependent types not all constructors can be put in every place. The head function below is completely defined since nnil can never be of type nlist (S n).

```
Symbol head : forall (n:nat) nlist (S n) → bool
Rules
    head n (ncons b n l) ——→ b
```

The algorithm is necessarily incomplete, since in the presence of dependent types emptiness of types trivially reduces to completeness and the former is undecidable. The algorithm accepts all definitions that follow dependent pattern matching schemes presented by Coquand and studied by McBride in his PhD thesis. Extended with the second run, it deals with all usual definitions by case analysis in Coq. It also accepts many definitions by rewriting containing rules which depart from standard pattern matching.

The rewriting systems for +, append, map, JMeq_std, JMeq_nstd presented earlier can be easily proved complete by the algorithm. This is also true for Streicher's axiom K:

```
Symbol K : forall (A:Set) (a:A) (P:eq A a a → Set),
    P (refl A a) → forall p: eq A a a, P p
Rules
    K A a P h (refl A a) ——→ h
```

Another method for checking completeness of pattern matching equations in the Calculus of Constructions is presented in [34]. It consists in computing approximations of inductive types and is not based on splitting; for that reason it accepts some of the examples not accepted by the algorithm described above. Fortunately, it seems that the approximation method can be easily added to the algorithm from [45] as another phase, if the original version fails to show completeness.

Inductive consequences. During the completeness check of a definition by rewriting only some of the rules are used; usually they correspond to the pattern matching definition of a given symbol. An interesting question is how much the rules outside this part extend the conversion.

For first-order rewriting it is known that these rules are inductive consequences of the pattern matching ones, i.e. all their canonical instances are satisfied as equalities (see e.g. Theorem 7.6.5 in [40]). It is also true for higher-order and dependent rewriting in the calculus of constructions as long as there is no rewriting under a binder in the rewrite steps needed to join the critical pairs [44]. For example, the identity rule for the monomorphic `mmap` function from Section 3 is clearly an inductive consequence of the basic rules for `nil` and `cons`.

Unfortunately, the problem is more difficult for higher-order rules over inductive types with functional arguments. The defined function symbol might get under a binder and might be applied to a bound variable instead of a canonical term on which it is always reducible. Here is an example:

```
Inductive ord : Set :=
   o : ord
 | s : ord → ord
 | lim : (nat → ord) → ord.

Rewriting n2o : nat → ord
Rules
   n2o 0 ⟶ o
   n2o (S x) ⟶ S (n2o x)

Rewriting id : ord → ord
Rules
   id o ⟶ o
   id (s x) ⟶ s (id x)
   id (lim f) ⟶ lim (fun n => id (f n))

   id (id x) ⟶ id x
```

The last rewriting system is confluent (unlike the one in which the last rule is replaced with `id x ⟶ x` because the critical pair for `x=(lim f)` needs eta to be joinable). Now, for $l =$ `id (id x)`, $r =$ `id x`, $\sigma = \{x \mapsto$ `lim (fun n ⇒ n2o n)`$\}$ one has:

```
lσ = id (id (lim (fun n ⇒ n2o n)))
   ⟶   id (lim (fun n' ⇒ id ((fun n ⇒ n2o n) n')))
   ⟶   id (lim (fun n' ⇒ id (n2o n')))
   ⟶   lim (fun n'' ⇒ id ((fun n' ⇒ id (n2o n')) n''))
   ⟶   lim (fun n'' ⇒ id (id (n2o n'')))

rσ = id (lim (fun n ⇒ n2o n))
   ⟶   lim (fun n' ⇒ id ((fun n ⇒ n2o n) n'))
   ⟶   lim (fun n' ⇒ id (n2o n'))
```

and they are not equal.

It seems that in case when critical pairs are joinable using rewriting under a binder, rules that are outside definitional part can also be considered as inductive consequences of the definition, but then the conversion needs to be functionally extensional (similarly to [34]) and some special care should be payed to the contexts under which rewriting occurs.

Summarizing, in many rewriting systems, especially simple ones, defining functions over non-functional inductive types, additional rules are inductive consequences of the complete subsystem. In other rewriting systems, even if we are not sure that this is the case, by [10,45], a terminating, confluent and complete rewriting system cannot lead to inconsistency.

In practice it would be best to have two different keywords for complete and "not necessarily complete" definitions by rewriting. For example, the keyword `Complete Symbol` would mean that the set of rules must be checked for completeness by Coq and rejected if its completeness cannot be proved. The keyword `Symbol` (without `Complete`) would not incur any completeness checking and the user would understand that the responsibility for consistency in entirely in his hands.

6   Modularity

A very important issue in an interactive system like Coq is modularity. Coq developments are usually composed of many files and use the standard library or some libraries developed by third parties.

Once the given library file is checked, Coq metatheory guarantees that the compiled library can be read and included in any development without risking undecidability or logical inconsistency (the latter provided that there are no axioms in the library or the development).

In order to retain this status once rewriting is added to Coq one must be very careful to ensure good modularity properties on the rewriting systems included in library files.

In particular it should be impossible to define a rewrite rule $f(x) \longrightarrow g(x)$ in one file and $g(x) \longrightarrow f(x)$ in another one, because loading these two files together would break strong normalization. Although it is possible to design a new version of Coq in such a way that the whole set of rewriting rules is rechecked every time a new library is loaded, it would be very time consuming and therefore it is not a good solution.

Instead, the acceptance criteria for rewrite rules should take modularity into consideration. In other words, the following lemma should hold even if there are some definitions by rewriting in E_1, E_2 and/or $\mathcal{J}$:

For all judgments $\mathcal{J}$, if $E; E_1 \vdash \mathcal{J}$ and $E; E_2 \vdash \mathsf{ok}$ then $E; E_1; E_2 \vdash \mathcal{J}$.

In practice, many modularity problems are avoided by allowing only rewrite definitions $\mathsf{Rew}(\Gamma, R)$ whose head symbols of the left hand sides of rules come from Γ. It is the case in all examples given in Section 2.

The module system. Additional modularity requirements for definitions by rewriting come from the module system. The Coq module system [14,15] was designed with adding rewriting in mind. In particular, even though more theoretically advanced module systems existed at the time it was implemented (first-class modules, anonymous modules [38,21,22]), a simple named version was chosen, similar to [30], where each module construct must be given a name before being used in terms. Thanks to that, existing syntactic acceptance criteria (see Section 3) can be easily adapted to modules.

The module language resembles a simply typed lambda calculus with records and record types. A very important feature is module subtyping, with its subsumption rule permitting to give a less precise type to a module.

$$\frac{E \vdash M : T \qquad E \vdash T <: T'}{E \vdash M : T'}$$

This rule is useful in two cases. First, it permits to hide some implementation details of a module in order to be able to change them in the future without affecting other parts of the project. Second, it permits to define a functor with minimal requirements to its arguments and then apply it to a module at hand with more elements and more precise interface.

Once rewriting is added to Coq, definitions by rewriting will be allowed in module interfaces and in particular in argument types of functors.

Since functors can be applied to all modules whose interface is a subtype of the functor argument type, the subtyping on module interfaces has to be extended to interfaces containing definitions by rewriting.

It is clear that the convertibility properties required by the functor argument interface must be satisfied by the actual parameter's interface. Otherwise the functor result would not be well-typed.

In [15] no other restrictions on "rewriting-subtyping" are imposed. Note however, that such liberal definition of subtyping implies very strict modularity properties for the acceptance condition for definitions by rewriting. This means that the definition by rewriting must be guaranteed not only to be terminating and confluent in the current environment, but also in an environment, where some module type is replaced by a subtype. For example consider the following module type and functor:

```
Module Type T.
   Symbol g : bool → bool
   Rules
      g true → true.
End T.

Module F(X:T).
   Symbol f : bool → nat.
   Rules
      f true  ⟶ 0
      f false ⟶ 0
      f (X.g false) ⟶ 1.
End F.
```

The definition of f inside the functor F is confluent, because no reduction rules are associated with g false and hence there are no critical pairs. Consider a possible implementation M of the module type T and the application of F to M.

```
Module M <: T.
  Symbol g : bool → bool
  Rules
    g true  ⟶ true
    g false ⟶ false.
End M.

Module Z := F M.
```

Now, the signature of Z is the same as the body of F, but the formal parameter X is replaced by the actual parameter M. This gives the following set of rules defining Z.f:

```
f true  ⟶ 0
f false ⟶ 0
f (M.g false) ⟶ 1
```

which is non-confluent, because on one hand f (M.g false) ⟶ 1 and on the other hand f (M.g false) ⟶ f false ⟶ 0.

It turns out that in presence of modules and subtyping, rewrite rules where left-hand sides mentions external symbols whose specification may still be completed is very dangerous. The easiest way to prevent this danger is to restrict the left-hand sides of the rewrite rules to contain only the symbols declared by the given rewrite definition. This is, again, the case in all examples from Section 2.

Such restriction however turns out to be quite severe. Consider for example defining mathematical functions over natural numbers. It might be a good idea to add a rule defining how this function behaves for the arguments of the form (a+b), but since + is not defined at the same time, this is impossible. Since + is already completely defined it is unlikely to introduce a new definition of + which would create more critical pairs.

This question, whether it is safe to allow external but completely defined symbols in left hand sides of rewrite rules, definitely needs to be studied further.

7 Extraction

The possibility to extract executable Ocaml, Haskell or Scheme code from Coq developments is one of the key features of Coq [37,31,32]. In this section we try to analyze the impact of introducing rewriting to Coq on the extraction mechanism.

The general problem with rewriting is that it does not immediately correspond to any mechanism present in functional languages. To extract a definition of a symbol defined by rewriting it is important to check whether this symbol is completely defined or not. If it is not, this means that the symbol is like an axiom and its successful extraction is impossible.

If it is complete then, as we explained in Section 5, its definition can be divided into two parts. The first part, which is a complete subset containing the rules used by the completeness checking procedure, usually consists of pattern matching rules. The second part is the remaining set of rules which, in most cases, are inductive consequences of the first part. These rules can also be called *shortcut* rules and they are only really important if the function's arguments are not ground terms, which is never the case when a functional program is executed.

So it is enough to just translate those rules which have the pattern-matching form and simply leave out all the others. The resulting definition will include the complete definition and some of the shortcut rules which have a pattern-matching form. Other shortcut rules should simply be dropped or they can be transformed into rewrite rules for optimization, available e.g. in the Glasgow Haskell Compiler.

For example the definition of + from Section 2 could be extracted to the following Ocaml code:

```
(** val plus : nat → nat → nat **)

let rec plus n m =
  match n, m with
  | 0, y → y
  | x, 0 → x
  | S x, y → S (plus x y)
  | x, S y → S (plus x y);;
```

The second and fourth lines are not necessary for the completeness of the translation. However, the second line can speed up the definition if the second argument is 0. Unfortunately, the fourth line is never used, even though it could also speed the computation up. Indeed, any natural number which does not match the first and the second rule, does match the third one. The associativity rule for + is not extracted, as it is not in the pattern-matching form.

The definition of append is extracted in the following way:

```
(** val append : nat → nat → nlist → nlist → nlist **)

let rec append n m ln lm =
  match n, m, ln, lm with
  | 0, m, Nnil, lm → lm
  | (S n0), m, Ncons (b, n0', n1), lm →
        Ncons (b, (plus n0 m), (append n0 m n1 lm))
  | n, 0, ln, Nnil → ln;;
```

A smart extraction procedure should also change the order of the second and third rule, because otherwise one of the first two rules always applies and the expected speed up from the third rule can never be achieved. Note also, that an extracted function has the same number of arguments as the original one, but the dependencies between them are broken. Consequently, while `append` is complete in the Coq world, its extracted version contains non-exhaustive pattern-matching, corresponding to unexpected cases when the list and its declared length do not match. Note however that the same problem it is already present for the extracted version of definitions by `fix` and `match` in the current Coq.

8   Conclusions

The goal of this paper was to present our vision of rewriting in Coq and to summarize the results already known in the field. We started from an incremental character of the calculus of constructions with rewriting, the form of the definitions by rewriting and matching used to apply rewrite rules to terms. Then we discussed such issues as strong normalization, confluence, logical consistency, completeness of definitions by rewriting, modularity and extraction.

We hope that this paper can be a basis for a deeper/more detailed discussion about rewriting in Coq, its future and its alternative views. Moreover we hope that it can serve for comparisons with conceptually different extensions of Coq, for example the one described in [24] aiming at extending Coq with decision procedures.

Acknowledgements. We would like to thank Paweł Urzyczyn, Frédéric Blanqui and the anonymous referees for their comments on the first version of our paper.

References

1. Barbanera, F.: Adding algebraic rewriting to the calculus of constructions: Strong normalization preserved. In: Proceedings of the Second International Workshop on Conditional and Typed Rewriting (1990)
2. Barbanera, F., Fernández, M., Geuvers, H.: Modularity of strong normalization and confluence in the λ-algebraic-cube. In: Proceedings of the Ninth Annual IEEE Symposium on Logic in Computer Science, Paris, France, pp. 406–415. IEEE Comp. Soc. Press, Washington, DC, USA (1994)
3. Barbanera, F., Fernández, M., Geuvers, H.: Modularity of strong normalization in the algebraic-λ-cube. Journal of Functional Programming 7(6), 613–660 (1997)
4. Barras, B., Grégoire, B.: On the role of type decorations in the calculus of inductive constructions. In: Ong, L. (ed.) CSL 2005. LNCS, vol. 3634, pp. 151–166. Springer, Heidelberg (2005)
5. Barthe, G., Grégoire, B., Pastawski, F.: CIC^: Type-based termination of recursive definitions in the Calculus of Inductive Constructions. In: Hermann, M., Voronkov, A. (eds.) LPAR 2006. LNCS (LNAI), vol. 4246, pp. 257–271. Springer, Heidelberg (2006)
6. Blanqui, F.: Théorie des Types et Récriture. PhD thesis, Université Paris-Sud (2001)
7. Blanqui, F.: Inductive types in the Calculus of Algebraic Constructions. In: Hofmann, M. (ed.) TLCA 2003. LNCS, vol. 2701, Springer, Heidelberg (2003)
8. Blanqui, F.: Rewriting modulo in Deduction modulo. In: Nieuwenhuis, R. (ed.) RTA 2003. LNCS, vol. 2706, Springer, Heidelberg (2003)
9. Blanqui, F.: A Type-Based Termination Criterion for Dependently-Typed Higher-Order Rewrite Systems. In: van Oostrom, V. (ed.) RTA 2004. LNCS, vol. 3091, pp. 24–39. Springer, Heidelberg (2004)
10. Blanqui, F.: Definitions by rewriting in the Calculus of Constructions. Mathematical Structures in Computer Science 15(1), 37–92 (2005)
11. Blanqui, F., Jouannaud, J.-P., Okada, M.: The Calculus of Algebraic Constructions. In: Narendran, P., Rusinowitch, M. (eds.) RTA 1999. LNCS, vol. 1631, Springer, Heidelberg (1999)

12. Blanqui, F., Jouannaud, J.-P., Okada, M.: Inductive data type systems. Theoretical Computer Science 272(1–2), 41–68 (2002)
13. Brady, E., McBride, C., McKinna, J.: Inductive families need not store their indices. In: Berardi, S., Coppo, M., Damiani, F. (eds.) TYPES 2003. LNCS, vol. 3085, pp. 115–129. Springer, Heidelberg (2004)
14. Chrząszcz, J.: Implementation of modules in the Coq system. In: Basin, D., Wolff, B. (eds.) TPHOLs 2003. LNCS, vol. 2758, pp. 270–286. Springer, Heidelberg (2003)
15. Chrząszcz, J.: Modules in Type Theory with Generative Definitions. PhD thesis, Warsaw Univerity and University of Paris-Sud (January 2004)
16. Contejean, E., Marché, C., Monate, B., Urbain, X.: CiME version 2 (2000). Available at http://cime.lri.fr/
17. The Coq proof assistant. http://coq.inria.fr/
18. Coquand, T.: Pattern matching with dependent types. In: Proceedings of the Workshop on Types for Proofs and Programs, pp. 71–83, Båstad, Sweden (1992)
19. Coquand, T., Paulin-Mohring, C.: Inductively defined types. In: Martin-Löf, P., Mints, G. (eds.) COLOG-88. LNCS, vol. 417, Springer, Heidelberg (1990)
20. Cornes, C.: Conception d'un langage de haut niveau de répresentation de preuves. PhD thesis, Université Paris VII (1997)
21. Courant, J.: A Module Calculus for Pure Type Systems. In: de Groote, P., Hindley, J.R. (eds.) TLCA 1997. LNCS, vol. 1210, pp. 112–128. Springer, Heidelberg (1997)
22. Courant, J.: Un calcul de modules pour les systèmes de types purs. Thèse de doctorat, Ecole Normale Supérieure de Lyon (1998)
23. Dowek, G., Hardin, T., Kirchner, C.: Theorem proving modulo. Journal of Automated Reasoning 31(1), 33–72 (2003)
24. Jouannaud, J.-P., Blanqui, F., Strub, P.-Y.: Building decision procedures in the calculus of inductive constructions (Submitted)
25. Giménez, E.: Un Calcul de Constructions Infinies et son Application à la Vérification des Systèmes Communicants. PhD thesis, Ecole Normale Supérieure de Lyon (1996)
26. Giménez, E.: Structural recursive definitions in type theory. In: Larsen, K.G., Skyum, S., Winskel, G. (eds.) ICALP 1998. LNCS, vol. 1443, pp. 397–408. Springer, Heidelberg (1998)
27. Girard, J.-Y.: Une extension de l'interprétation de Gödel à l'analyse, et son application à l'élimination des coupures dans l'analyse et la téorie des types. In: Proceedings of the 2nd Scandinavian Logic Symposium, pp. 63–92. North-Holland (1971)
28. Jouannaud, J.-P., Okada, M.: Executable higher-order algebraic specification languages. In: Proceedings of the Sixth Annual IEEE Symposium on Logic in Computer Science, pp. 350–361. IEEE Comp. Soc. Press, Washington, DC, USA (1991)
29. Jouannaud, J.-P., Rubio, A.: The higher-order recursive path ordering. In: Longo, G. (ed.) Fourteenth Annual IEEE Symposium on Logic in Computer Science, Trento, Italy, IEEE Comp. Soc. Press, Washington, DC, USA (1999)
30. Leroy, X.: Manifest types, modules, and separate compilation. In: Conference Record of the 21st Symposium on Principles of Programming Languages, Portland, Oregon, pp. 109–122. ACM Press, New York (1994)
31. Letouzey, P.: A New Extraction for Coq. In: Geuvers, H., Wiedijk, F. (eds.) TYPES 2002. LNCS, vol. 2646, Springer, Heidelberg (2003)
32. Letouzey, P.: Programmation fonctionnelle certifiée – L'extraction de programmes dans l'assistant Coq. PhD thesis, Université Paris-Sud (2004)
33. Müller, F.: Confluence of the lambda calculus with left-linear algebraic rewriting. Information Processing Letters 41(6), 293–299 (1992)

34. Oury, N.: Égalité et filtrage avec types dépendants dans le Calcul des Constructions Inductives. PhD thesis, Université Paris-Sud (2006)
35. Parent, C.: Developing certified programs in the system Coq - the Program tactic. In: Barendregt, H., Nipkow, T. (eds.) TYPES 1993. LNCS, vol. 806, pp. 291–312. Springer, Heidelberg (1994)
36. Paulin-Mohring, C.: Définitions inductives en théorie des types d'ordre supérieur. Thèse d'habilitation, Ecole Normale Supérieure de Lyon (1996)
37. Paulin-Mohring, C., Werner, B.: Synthesis of ML programs in the system Coq. Journal of Symbolic Computation 15, 607–640 (1993)
38. Pollack, R.: Dependently typed records in type theory. Formal Aspects of Computing 13, 386–402 (2002)
39. Sozeau, M.: Subset coercions in coq. In: Types for Proofs and Programs, TYPES 2006. LNCS, vol. 4502, Springer, Heidelberg (To appear, 2007)
40. Terese (ed.): Term Rewriting Systems. Cambridge Tracts in Theoretical Computer Science, vol. 55. Cambridge University Press, New York (2003)
41. Walukiewicz-Chrząszcz, D.: Termination of rewriting in the calculus of constructions. In: Despeyroux, J. (ed.) Termination of rewriting in the calculus of constructions. Proceedings of the 2nd Workshop on Logical Frameworks and Meta-Languages, Santa Barbara, California (2000)
42. Walukiewicz-Chrząszcz, D.: Termination of Rewriting in the Calculus of Constructions. PhD thesis, Warsaw University and University Paris XI (2003)
43. Walukiewicz-Chrząszcz, D.: Termination of rewriting in the calculus of constructions. Journal of Functional Programming 13(2), 339–414 (2003)
44. Walukiewicz-Chrząszcz, D., Chrząszcz, J.: Inductive consequences in the calculus of constructions. Draft available at http://www.mimuw.edu.pl/~chrzaszcz/papers/
45. Walukiewicz-Chrząszcz, D., Chrząszcz, J.: Consistency and completeness of rewriting in the calculus of constructions. In: Furbach, U., Shankar, N. (eds.) IJCAR 2006. LNCS (LNAI), vol. 4130, pp. 619–631. Springer, Heidelberg (2006)
46. Werner, B.: Méta-théorie du Calcul des Constructions Inductives. PhD thesis, Université Paris VII (1994)

Superdeduction at Work

Paul Brauner[1], Clément Houtmann[2], and Claude Kirchner[3]

[1] INPL & LORIA*
[2] ENS Cachan & LORIA
[3] INRIA & LORIA

Dedicated to Jean-Pierre Jouannaud on the occasion of his 60th birthday

Abstract. Superdeduction is a systematic way to extend a deduction system like the sequent calculus by new deduction rules computed from the user theory. We show how this could be done in a systematic, correct and complete way. We prove in detail the strong normalisation of a proof term language that models appropriately superdeduction. We finaly examplify on several examples, including equality and noetherian induction, the usefulness of this approach which is implemented in the lemuridæ system, written in TOM.

1 Introduction

Our objective is twofold:
– to scale up by an order of magnitude the size of the problems we can deal with;
– to downsize by an order of magnitude the time needed for a given development.
To this end, we started studying a new version of the calculus of constructions in which user-defined computations expressed by rewrite rules can be made transparent in proof terms.

Jean-Pierre Jouannaud [Towards Engineering Proofs, 1999]

The design, verification and communication of formal proofs are central in informatics and mathematics. In the later, the notion of proofs has a long and fruitful history which now becomes even richer with a century of experience in its formalization. In informatics, formal proofs are in particular essential to formaly assess safety as well as security properties of digital systems. In this context, proof engineering becomes crucial and relies on a semi-interactive design where human interaction is unavoidable. Moreover, to be well designed, proofs have to be well understood and built. As the size of critical softwares increases dramatically, typically a "simple" automotive cruise control software consists of more than one hundred thousand lines of code, proof methods and tools should also scale-up.

This proof engineering process is now mastered with the use of proof assistants like Coq [The04], Isabelle [Pau94], PVS [ORS92], HOL [HOL93], Mizar [Rud92] and large libraries of formalised theories ease this task.

---

* UMR 7503 CNRS-INPL-INRIA-Nancy2-UHP. Campus Scientifique, BP 239, 54506 Vandoeuvre-lès-Nancy Cedex, France.

H. Comon-Lundh et al. (Eds.): Jouannaud Festschrift, LNCS 4600, pp. 132–166, 2007.
© Springer-Verlag Berlin Heidelberg 2007

In this context one has to deal with at least two main difficulties. First, proof engineering should scale-up as the theories describing the context become huge and may consist of thousand of axioms and definitions, some of them being quite sophisticated. Second, the proof assistant needs to provide the user with appropriate ways to understand and to guide the proof construction. Both concerns are currently tackled by making libraries available, by providing specific tactics, tacticals or strategies (see typically coq.inria.fr), by integration rewriting [BJO02] and decision procedures [NKK02, Alv00, MQP06] safely into the proof assistants, or by interfacing first-order automated theorem provers with proof assistants like [BHdN02] or like the use of Zenon in Focal [Pre05].

Indeed these approaches raise the question of structuring the theories of interest. For instance one would like to identify the subtheory of lists or of naturals to apply specific decision procedures, *e.g.* [KRRT06] and of course finding a good modular structure is one of the first steps in an engineering process.

> ... *the role of higher-order rewriting is to design a type theoretic frameworks in which computation and deduction are integrated by means of higher-order rewrite rules, while preserving decidability of typing and coherence of the underlying logic ...*
>
> *Jean-Pierre Jouannaud [Jou05]*

In this context, we have proposed in [BHK07] a foundational framework making use of three complementary dimensions. First, as pioneered by *deduction modulo*, the computational axioms should be identified. Typically the definition of addition on naturals ought to be embedded into a congruence modulo which deduction is performed [DHK03]. In this case, the deduction rules like the one of natural deduction or of the sequent calculus are not modified but they are applied modulo a congruence embedding part of the theory. Second, we are proposing a complementary approach where *new deduction rules* are inferred from part of the theory in a correct, systematic and complete way. Third, the rest of the theory will be used as the context on which all the standard and new deduction rules will act, possibly modulo some congruence.

To sum up, a theory is split in three parts $Th = Th_1 \cup Th_2 \cup Th_3$ and instead of seeking for a proof of $Th_1 \cup Th_2 \cup Th_3 \vdash \varphi$, we are building a proof of $Th_3 \vdash^{+Th_2}_{\sim Th_1} \varphi$, *i.e.* we use the theory Th_3 to prove φ using the extended deduction system modulo the congruence $\sim_{Th_1}$. We assume that the propositions in Th_2 are all proposition rewrite rules, *i.e.* are of the form $\forall \overline{x}.(P \Leftrightarrow \varphi)$, where P is atomic.

To ease the presentation of the main ideas, we will not consider in this paper the case of deduction modulo even if in addition to simplicity it admits unbounded proof size speed-up [Bur07]. We call *superdeduction* the new deduction system embedding the newly generated deduction rules, and the extended entailment relation is denoted $\vdash^{+Th}$ or simply $\vdash^+$.

Intuitively, a superdeduction rule supplants the *folding* of an atomic proposition P by its definition φ, as done by Prawitz [Pra65], followed by as much introductions as possible of the connectives appearing in φ. For instance, the axiom

$$\text{TRANS} : \forall x. \forall z. (x \leq z \Leftrightarrow \exists y. (x \leq y \wedge y \leq z))$$

is translated into a left deduction rule by first applying the rules of the classical sequent calculus to $\Gamma, \exists y.(x \leq y \wedge y \leq z) \vdash \Delta$. Then by collecting the premises and the side conditions, we get the *new* deduction rule:

$$\leq_{\text{TRANS}_L} \frac{\Gamma, x \leq y, y \leq z \vdash \Delta}{\Gamma, x \leq z \vdash \Delta} \quad y \notin \mathcal{FV}(\Gamma, \Delta)$$

The right rule:

$$\leq_{\text{TRANS}_R} \frac{\Gamma \vdash x \leq y, \Delta \quad \Gamma \vdash y \leq z, \Delta}{\Gamma \vdash x \leq z, \Delta}$$

is similarly obtained by applying deduction rules to $\Gamma \vdash \exists y.(x \leq y \wedge y \leq z), \Delta$.

These new deduction rules are quite natural and translate the usual mathematical reasoning *w.r.t.* this axiom. Let us see on a simple example the difference between a proof in sequent calculus and the corresponding one in the extended deduction system. The proof that $\text{TRANS} \vdash a \leq b \Rightarrow b \leq c \Rightarrow a \leq c$ is the following:

$$
\begin{array}{c}
\text{AX} \dfrac{}{a \leq b, b \leq c \vdash a \leq b, a \leq c} \quad \text{AX} \dfrac{}{a \leq b, b \leq c \vdash b \leq c, a \leq c} \\[2mm]
\wedge_R \dfrac{}{a \leq b, b \leq c \vdash a \leq b \wedge b \leq c, a \leq c} \\[2mm]
\exists_R \dfrac{}{a \leq b, b \leq c \vdash \exists y.(a \leq y \wedge y \leq c), a \leq c} \\
\vdots \qquad \text{AX} \dfrac{}{a \leq c, a \leq b, b \leq c \vdash a \leq c} \\[2mm]
\Rightarrow_L \dfrac{}{\exists y.(a \leq y \wedge y \leq c) \Rightarrow a \leq c, a \leq b, b \leq c \vdash a \leq c} \\[2mm]
\wedge_L \dfrac{}{a \leq c \Leftrightarrow \exists y.(a \leq y \wedge y \leq c), a \leq b, b \leq c \vdash a \leq c} \\[2mm]
\forall_L \dfrac{}{\forall z.(a \leq z \Leftrightarrow \exists y.(a \leq y \wedge y \leq z)), a \leq b, b \leq c \vdash a \leq c} \\[2mm]
\forall_L \dfrac{}{\forall x.\forall z.(x \leq z \Leftrightarrow \exists y.(x \leq y \wedge y \leq z)), a \leq b, b \leq c \vdash a \leq c} \\[2mm]
\Rightarrow_R \dfrac{}{\forall x.\forall z.(x \leq z \Leftrightarrow \exists y.(x \leq y \wedge y \leq z)), a \leq b \vdash b \leq c \Rightarrow a \leq c} \\[2mm]
\Rightarrow_R \dfrac{}{\forall x.\forall z.(x \leq z \Leftrightarrow \exists y.(x \leq y \wedge y \leq z)) \vdash a \leq b \Rightarrow b \leq c \Rightarrow a \leq c}
\end{array}
$$

Using superdeduction, the axiom TRANS has been used to generate the new deduction rules above and the proof becomes simply:

$$
\begin{array}{c}
\text{AX} \dfrac{}{a \leq b, b \leq c \vdash b \leq c, a \leq c} \quad \text{AX} \dfrac{}{a \leq b, b \leq c \vdash a \leq b, a \leq c} \\[2mm]
\leq_{\text{TRANS}_R} \dfrac{}{a \leq b, b \leq c \vdash a \leq c} \\[2mm]
\Rightarrow_R \dfrac{}{a \leq b \vdash b \leq c \Rightarrow a \leq c} \\[2mm]
\Rightarrow_R \dfrac{}{\vdash a \leq b \Rightarrow b \leq c \Rightarrow a \leq c}
\end{array}
$$

It is important to notice that these new rules are not just "macros" collapsing a sequence of introductions into a single one: they apply to a predicate, not a connector, and therefore do not solely contain purely logical informations. This therefore raises non trivial questions solved in [BHK07] and in this paper, like the conditions under which the system is complete or consistent and sufficient conditions to get cut-elimination.

Superdeduction is based on previous works on supernatural deduction, a deduction system introduced by Benjamin Wack in [Wac05] and providing a logical interpretation of the ρ-calculus [CK01, CLW03]. Preliminary presentation of superdeduction for the sequent calculus has been given in [Bra06] and the consistency of such systems is studied in [Hou06]. The superdeduction principle has been presented in [BHK07].

In this context, our contributions are the following:

- We first summarize in the next section the general principle defined in [BHK07]: a systematic extension of the classical sequent calculus by new deduction rules inferred from the axioms of the theory that are proposition rewrite rules; We prove in detail that this is correct and complete taking into account permutability problems; Building on Urban's proof-term language for the sequent calculus [Urb01], we present the simple and expressive calculus proposed in [BHK07] that we show to provide a Curry-Howard-de Bruijn correspondence for superdeduction; Assuming the proposition rewrite system used to extend deduction to be weakly normalising and confluent, we prove in detail that the calculus is strongly normalising and therefore that the theory is consistent since the superdeduction system has the cut-elimination property.
- Then, we investigate in Section 3 the consequence of these principles and results for the foundation of a new generation of proof assistants for which we have a first downloadable prototype, lemuridæ (rho.loria.fr). In particular we show how convenient and natural proofs become for instance in higher-order logic, mathematical induction, equational logic. We also examplify the current limitations set to get the general results of previous section.
- Finally, we provide in Section 4 the detailed proofs of the results summarized in Section 2.

2   Super Sequent Calculus

In this section we recall the principles of superdeduction.

$$\text{AX} \frac{}{\Gamma, \varphi \vdash \varphi, \Delta} \qquad \text{CONTR}_R \frac{\Gamma \vdash \varphi, \varphi, \Delta}{\Gamma \vdash \varphi, \Delta} \qquad \text{CONTR}_L \frac{\Gamma, \varphi, \varphi \vdash \Delta}{\Gamma, \varphi \vdash \Delta} \qquad \bot_L \frac{}{\Gamma, \bot \vdash \Delta}$$

$$\wedge_L \frac{\Gamma, \varphi_1, \varphi_2 \vdash \Delta}{\Gamma, \varphi_1 \wedge \varphi_2 \vdash \Delta} \qquad \wedge_R \frac{\Gamma \vdash \varphi_1, \Delta \quad \Gamma \vdash \varphi_2, \Delta}{\Gamma \vdash \varphi_1 \wedge \varphi_2, \Delta} \qquad \top_R \frac{}{\Gamma \vdash \top, \Delta}$$

$$\vee_L \frac{\Gamma, \varphi_1 \vdash \Delta \quad \Gamma, \varphi_2 \vdash \Delta}{\Gamma, \varphi_1 \vee \varphi_2 \vdash \Delta} \qquad \vee_R \frac{\Gamma \vdash \varphi_1, \varphi_2, \Delta}{\Gamma \vdash \varphi_1 \vee \varphi_2, \Delta} \qquad \Rightarrow_R \frac{\Gamma, \varphi_1 \vdash \varphi_2, \Delta}{\Gamma \vdash \varphi_1 \Rightarrow \varphi_2, \Delta}$$

$$\forall_R \frac{\Gamma \vdash \varphi, \Delta}{\Gamma \vdash \forall x.\varphi, \Delta} x \notin \mathcal{FV}(\Gamma, \Delta) \qquad \forall_L \frac{\Gamma, \varphi[t/x] \vdash \Delta}{\Gamma, \forall x.\varphi \vdash \Delta} \qquad \Rightarrow_L \frac{\Gamma \vdash \varphi_1, \Delta \quad \Gamma, \varphi_2 \vdash \Delta}{\Gamma, \varphi_1 \Rightarrow \varphi_2 \vdash \Delta}$$

$$\exists_R \frac{\Gamma \vdash \varphi[t/x], \Delta}{\Gamma \vdash \exists x.\varphi, \Delta} \qquad \exists_L \frac{\Gamma, \varphi \vdash \Delta}{\Gamma, \exists x.\varphi \vdash \Delta} x \notin \mathcal{FV}(\Gamma, \Delta) \qquad \text{CUT} \frac{\Gamma \vdash \varphi, \Delta \quad \Gamma, \varphi \vdash \Delta}{\Gamma \vdash \Delta}$$

Fig. 1. Classical sequent calculus

As mentioned in the introduction and similarly as in deduction modulo, we focus our attention to formulæ of the form $\forall \overline{x}.(P \Leftrightarrow \varphi)$ where P is atomic:

Definition 1 (Propositions rewrite rule). *The notation* $R : P \to \varphi$ *denotes the axiom* $\forall \overline{x}.(P \Leftrightarrow \varphi)$ *where* R *is a name for it,* P *is an atomic proposition,* φ *some proposition and* $\overline{x}$ *their free variables.*

Notice that P may contain first-order terms and therefore that such an axiom is not just a definition. For instance, $isZero(succ(n)) \to \bot$ is a proposition rewrite rule.

For the classical sequent calculus, let us now describe how the computation of the superdeduction new inference rules is performed.

Definition 2 (Super sequent calculus rules computation). *Let* $Calc$ *be a set of rules composed by the subset of the sequent calculus deduction rules formed of* AX, $\bot_L$, $\top_R$, $\vee_L$, $\vee_R$, $\wedge_L$, $\wedge_R$, $\Rightarrow_L$, $\Rightarrow_R$, $\forall_L$, $\forall_R$, $\exists_L$ *and* $\exists_R$, *as well as of the two following rules* $\top_L$ *and* $\bot_R$

$$\top_L \; \frac{\Gamma \vdash \Delta}{\Gamma, \top \vdash \Delta} \qquad\qquad \bot_R \; \frac{\Gamma \vdash \Delta}{\Gamma \vdash \bot, \Delta}$$

Let $R : P \to \varphi$ *be a proposition rewrite rule.*

1. *To get the right rule associated with* R, *initialise the procedure with the sequent* $\Gamma \vdash \varphi, \Delta$. *Next, apply the rules of* $Calc$ *until no more open leave remain on which they can be applied. Then, collect the premises, the side conditions and the conclusion and replace* φ *by* P *to obtain the right rule* R_R.
2. *To get the left rule* R_L *associated with* R, *initialise the procedure with the sequent* $\Gamma, \varphi \vdash \Delta$. *apply the rules of* $Calc$ *and get the new left rule the same way as for the right one.*

Definition 3 (Super sequent calculus). *Given a proposition rewrite system* $\mathcal{R}$, *the super sequent calculus associated with* $\mathcal{R}$ *is formed of the rules of classical sequent calculus and the rules built upon* $\mathcal{R}$. *The sequents in such a system are written* $\Gamma \vdash^{+\mathcal{R}} \Delta$.

To ensure good properties of the system, we need to put some restrictions on the axioms though. Although the deduction rules of the classical sequent calculus propositional fragment may be applied in any order to reach axioms, the application order of rules concerning quantifiers is significant. Let us consider the following cases:

$$\forall_R \; \frac{\forall_L \; \dfrac{AX \; \dfrac{}{P(x_0) \vdash P(x_0)}}{\forall x.P(x) \vdash P(x_0)}}{\forall x.P(x) \vdash \forall x.P(x)} \qquad\qquad \forall_L \; \frac{P(t) \vdash \forall x.P(x)}{\forall x.P(x) \vdash \forall x.P(x)}$$

The left-hand side proof succeeds because the early application of the $\forall_R$ rule provides the appropriate term for instantiating the variable of the proposition present in the context. On the other hand, the second proof cannot be completed since the $\forall_R$ side condition requires the quantified variable to be substituted for a fresh one. Such a situation may occur when building the super sequent calculus custom rules and therefore may break its completeness *w.r.t.* classical predicate logic. This common permutability problem of automated proof search appears here since superdeduction systems are in fact embedding a part of compiled automated deduction. Thereby we apply an idea inspired by focusing techniques [And92, AM99, And01], namely replacing every sub-formula of φ leading to a permutability problem by a fresh predicate symbol parame-terised by the free variables of the subformula. To formalise this, we first need to recall the polarity notion:

Definition 4 (Polarity of a subformula). *The polarity $pol_\varphi(\psi)$ of ψ in φ where ψ is a subformula occurrence of φ is a boolean defined as follows:*

- *if $\varphi = \psi$, then $pol_\varphi(\psi) = 1$;*
- *if $\varphi = \varphi_1 \wedge \varphi_2$ or $\varphi_1 \vee \varphi_2$, then $pol_\varphi(\psi) = pol_{\varphi_1}(\psi)$ if ψ is a subformula occur-rence of φ_1, $pol_{\varphi_2}(\psi)$ otherwise;*
- *if $\varphi = \forall x.\varphi_1$ or $\exists x.\varphi_1$, then $pol_\varphi(\psi) = pol_{\varphi_1}(\psi)$;*
- *if $\varphi = \varphi_1 \Rightarrow \varphi_2$, then $pol_\varphi(\psi) = \neg pol_{\varphi_1}(\psi)$ if ψ is a subformula occurrence of φ_1, $pol_{\varphi_2}(\psi)$ otherwise.*

Definition 5 (Set of permutability problems). *A formula ψ is in the set $PP(\varphi)$ of φ permutability problems if there exists φ' a subformula of φ such that ψ is a subformula occurrence of φ' and one of these propositions holds:*

- *$\varphi' = \forall x.\varphi_1'$, $\psi = \forall x.\psi_1'$ and $pol_{\varphi'}(\psi) = 0$*
- *$\varphi' = \exists x.\varphi_1'$, $\psi = \exists x.\psi_1'$ and $pol_{\varphi'}(\psi) = 0$*
- *$\varphi' = \forall x.\varphi_1'$, $\psi = \exists x.\psi_1'$ and $pol_{\varphi'}(\psi) = 1$*
- *$\varphi' = \exists x.\varphi_1'$, $\psi = \forall x.\psi_1'$ and $pol_{\varphi'}(\psi) = 1$*

This allows us to define the most appropriate generalisation of a proposition rewrite rule $R : P \to \varphi$:

Definition 6 (Set of delayed proposition rewrite rules). *This is the set:*

$$Dl(R : P \to \varphi) = \{P \to C[Q_1(\overline{x_1}), \dots, Q_n(\overline{x_n})]\} \bigcup_{i=1\dots n} Dl(Q_i \to \varphi_i)$$

such that:

- *C is the largest context in φ with no formula in $PP(\varphi)$ such that $\varphi = C[\varphi_1 \dots \varphi_n]$;*
- *$\forall i \in \{1 \dots n\}$, $\overline{x_i}$ is the vector of φ_i free variables;*
- *$Q_1 \dots Q_n$ are fresh predicate symbols.*

As an example, let us consider the proposition rewrite rule defining the natural num-bers as the set of terms verifying the inductive predicate:

$$\in_\mathbb{N} \; : \; \mathbb{N}(n) \to \forall P.(0 \in P \Rightarrow \forall m.(m \in P \Rightarrow s(m) \in P) \Rightarrow n \in P)$$

This axiom can be found in [DW05] which introduces an axiomatisation of constructive arithmetic with rewrite rules only. It uses a simple second-order encoding by expressing quantification over propositions by quantification over classes; $x \in P$ should therefore be read as $P(x)$. The delayed set $Dl(\in_\mathbb{N})$ of proposition rewrite rules derived from the rules above is:

$$\in_\mathbb{N} \; : \; \mathbb{N}(n) \to \forall P.(0 \in P \Rightarrow H(P) \Rightarrow n \in P)$$
$$hered \; : \; H(P) \to \forall m.(m \in P \Rightarrow s(m) \in P)$$

Let us notice that the proposition $H(P)$ revealed by the elimination of permutability problems expresses heredity, a well-known notion. Focussing on parts of the propositions which raise some non-trivial choice at some phase on the proof has been naturally done by mathematicians. Then we obtain the following deduction rules for the natural numbers definition:

$$\in_{\mathbb{N}_L} \frac{\Gamma \vdash^+ 0 \in P, \Delta \quad \Gamma \vdash^+ H(P), \Delta \quad \Gamma, n \in P \vdash^+ \Delta}{\Gamma, \mathbb{N}(n) \vdash^+ \Delta}$$

$$\in_{\mathbb{N}_R} \frac{0 \in P, H(P) \vdash^+ n \in P, \Delta}{\Gamma \vdash^+ \mathbb{N}(n), \Delta} \quad P \notin \mathcal{FV}(\Gamma, \Delta)$$

The left rule translates exactly the usual induction rule. The *hered* proposition rewrite rule generates new deduction rules too:

$$hered_L \frac{\Gamma \vdash^+ m \in P, \Delta \quad \Gamma, s(m) \in P \vdash^+ \Delta}{\Gamma, H(P) \vdash^+ \Delta}$$

$$hered_R \frac{\Gamma, m \in P \vdash^+ s(m) \in P, \Delta}{\Gamma \vdash^+ H(P), \Delta} \quad m \notin \mathcal{FV}(\Gamma, \Delta)$$

Once again, the right rule corresponds to the usual semantics of heredity.

Main properties of the super sequent calculus associated with a delayed set of axioms are its soundness and completeness *w.r.t.* classical predicate logic.

Theorem 1 (Soundness and completeness of super sequent calculus). *Given Th an axiomatic theory made of axioms of the form $\forall \overline{x}.(P \Leftrightarrow \varphi)$ with P atomic and $\mathcal{R}$ the associated proposition rewrite rules, every proof of $\Gamma \vdash_{Dl(\mathcal{R})} \Delta$ in super sequent calculus can be translated into a proof of $\Gamma, Th \vdash \Delta$ in sequent calculus (soundness) and conversely (completeness).*

Proof. **Soundness.** This is easily proved by replacing every occurrence of a superrule R_R obtained from $P \rightarrow \varphi$ by the partial proof derived during its computation. Then by translating the unfolding step by an application of $\Rightarrow_L$.

$$
\begin{array}{c}
\Rightarrow_L \dfrac{\text{AX} \dfrac{}{\Gamma, Th, P \vdash P, \Delta} \qquad \dfrac{\pi_R}{\Gamma, Th, \varphi \vdash \Delta}}{\wedge_L \dfrac{\Gamma, Th, P \Rightarrow \varphi \vdash P, \Delta}{\forall_L \dfrac{\Gamma, Th, P \Leftrightarrow \varphi, P \vdash \Delta}{\forall_L \dfrac{\cdots}{\text{CONTR}_L \dfrac{\Gamma, Th, \forall \overline{x}.(P \Leftrightarrow \varphi), P \vdash \Delta}{\Gamma, Th, P \vdash \Delta}}}}}
\end{array}
$$

The left case is symmetric.

Completeness. Let π be the proof of $\Gamma, Th \vdash \Delta$. By cutting the conclusion on Th, the problem is brought down to proving the axioms of Th in the super sequent calculus.

$$\text{CUT} \frac{\overset{\cdots}{\Gamma \vdash^{+_{\mathcal{R}}} Th, \Delta} \qquad \overset{\pi}{\Gamma, Th \vdash^{+_{\mathcal{R}}} \Delta}}{\Gamma \vdash^{+_{\mathcal{R}}} \Delta}$$

This is done by induction on the derivations of R_R and R_L for each rewrite rule R of $\mathcal{R}$. The full proof is in [Bra06]. □

A proof-term language for superdeduction has been designed in [BHK07] together with a cut-elimination procedure shown to be strongly normalising under appropriate properties. We will recall its definition now and the full proofs of the strong normalisation property will be written in Section 4. This proof-term language is based upon Christian Urban's work on cut-elimination for classical sequent calculus [Urb00, Urb01, UB01, Len03, vBLL05]. The main difference between Urban's proof-terms and other approaches such as Hugo Herbelin's $\bar{\lambda}\mu\tilde{\mu}$-calculus [Her95, CH00, Wad03] is that no focus is made on a particular formula of a sequent $\Gamma \vdash \Delta$, and thus a proof-term M always annotate the full sequent. Such typing judgements are denoted $M \rhd \Gamma \vdash \Delta$. It is explained in [BHK07] why this difference between Urban's and Herbelin's approaches made us choose the first one to base our proof-terms for superdeduction upon.

Urban's proof-term language for classical sequent calculus makes no use of the first-class objects of the λ-calculus such as *abstractions* or *variables*. Variables are replaced by *names* and *conames*. Let X and A be respectively the set of *names* and the set of *conames*. Symbols $x, y, \dots$ will range over X while symbols $a, b, \dots$ will range over A. Symbols x, y, $\dots$ will range over the set of first-order variables. Left-contexts and right-contexts are sets containing respectively pairs $x : \varphi$ and pairs $a : \varphi$. Symbol Γ will range over left-contexts and symbol Δ will range over the right-contexts. Moreover, contexts cannot contain more than one occurrence of a name or coname. We will never omit the 'first-order' in 'first-order term' in order to avoid confusion with 'terms' (*i.e.* proof-terms). The set of terms is defined as follows.

$$M, N ::= \text{Ax}(x, a) \mid \text{Cut}(\widehat{a}M, \widehat{x}N) \mid \text{False}_L(x) \mid \text{True}_R(a)$$
$$\mid \text{And}_R(\widehat{a}M, \widehat{b}N, c) \mid \text{And}_L(\widehat{x}\widehat{y}M, z) \mid \text{Or}_R(\widehat{a}\widehat{b}M, c) \mid \text{Or}_L(\widehat{x}M, \widehat{y}N, z)$$
$$\mid \text{Imp}_R(\widehat{x}\widehat{a}M, b) \mid \text{Imp}_L(\widehat{x}M, \widehat{a}N, y) \mid \text{Exists}_R(\widehat{a}M, t, b) \mid \text{Exists}_L(\widehat{x}\text{x}M, y)$$
$$\mid \text{Forall}_R(\widehat{a}\text{x}M, b) \mid \text{Forall}_L(\widehat{x}M, t, y)$$

Names and conames are not called *variables* and *covariables* such as in $\bar{\lambda}\mu\tilde{\mu}$-calculus since they do not represent places where terms might be inserted. They still may appear bound: the symbol «$\widehat{}$» is the unique binder of the calculus and thus we can compute the sets of free and bound names, conames and first-order variables in any term. We consequently adopt Barendregt's convention on names, conames and first-order variables: in a term or in a statement a name, a coname or a first-order variable is never both bound and free in the same context.

The type system is expressed in Figure 2. The differences with Urban's type system is the use of $\qquad \vee_R \dfrac{\Gamma \vdash \varphi_1, \varphi_2, \Delta}{\Gamma \vdash \varphi_1 \vee \varphi_2, \Delta}$ instead of $\qquad \vee_{R\text{-}i} \dfrac{\Gamma \vdash \varphi_i, \Delta}{\Gamma \vdash \varphi_1 \vee \varphi_2, \Delta} \quad$ for $i \in \{1, 2\}$

and similarly for $\wedge$. A comma in a conclusion stands for the set union and a comma in a premise stands for the *disjoint* set union. This allows our type inference rules to contain *implicit* contraction.

A term M *introduces* the name z if it is of the form $\mathsf{Ax}(z,a)$, $\mathsf{False}_L(z)$, $\mathsf{And}_L(\widehat{x}\widehat{y}M, z)$, $\mathsf{Or}_L(\widehat{x}M, \widehat{y}N, z)$, $\mathsf{Imp}_L(\widehat{x}M, \widehat{a}N, z)$, $\mathsf{Exists}_L(\widehat{x}\widehat{x}M, z)$, $\mathsf{Forall}_L(\widehat{x}M, t, z)$, and it *introduces* the coname c is it is of the form $\mathsf{Ax}(x,c)$, $\mathsf{True}_R(c)$, $\mathsf{And}_R(\widehat{a}M, \widehat{b}N, c)$, $\mathsf{Or}_R(\widehat{a}\widehat{b}M, c)$, $\mathsf{Imp}_R(\widehat{x}\widehat{a}M, c)$, $\mathsf{Exists}_R(\widehat{a}M, t, c)$, $\mathsf{Forall}_R(\widehat{a}\widehat{x}M, c)$. A term M *freshly* introduces a name or a coname if it introduces it, but none of its proper subterms. It means that the corresponding formula is introduced at the top-level of the proof, but not implicitly contracted and consequently introduced in some subproof.

Figure 3 presents a (non-confluent) cut-elimination procedure denoted $\xrightarrow{\mathsf{cut}}$ proven to be strongly normalising on well-typed terms in [Urb00, UB01]. It is *complete* in the sense that irreducible terms are cut-free. $M[b \mapsto a]$ stands for the term M where every free occurrence of the coname b is rewritten to a (and similarly for $Q[y \mapsto x]$). Besides, the proof substitution operation denoted $M[a := \widehat{x}N]$ and its dual $M[x := \widehat{a}N]$ are defined in Figure 4.

$$\mathsf{AX}\ \frac{}{\mathsf{Ax}(x,a) \triangleright \Gamma, x:\varphi \vdash a:\varphi, \Delta} \qquad \mathsf{CUT}\ \frac{M \triangleright \Gamma \vdash a:\varphi, \Delta \qquad N \triangleright \Gamma, x:\varphi \vdash \Delta}{\mathsf{Cut}(\widehat{a}M, \widehat{x}N) \triangleright \Gamma \vdash \Delta}$$

$$\perp_L\ \frac{}{\mathsf{False}_L(x) \triangleright \Gamma, x:\perp \vdash \Delta} \qquad \top_R\ \frac{}{\mathsf{True}_R(a) \triangleright \Gamma \vdash a:\top, \Delta}$$

$$\wedge_R\ \frac{M \triangleright \Gamma \vdash a:\varphi_1, \Delta \qquad N \triangleright \Gamma \vdash b:\varphi_2, \Delta}{\mathsf{And}_R(\widehat{a}M, \widehat{b}N, c) \triangleright \Gamma \vdash c:\varphi_1 \wedge \varphi_2, \Delta} \qquad \wedge_L\ \frac{M \triangleright \Gamma, x:\varphi_1, y:\varphi_2 \vdash \Delta}{\mathsf{And}_L(\widehat{x}\widehat{y}M, z) \triangleright \Gamma, z:\varphi_1 \wedge \varphi_2 \vdash \Delta}$$

$$\vee_R\ \frac{M \triangleright \Gamma \vdash a:\varphi_1, b:\varphi_2, \Delta}{\mathsf{Or}_R(\widehat{a}\widehat{b}M, c) \triangleright \Gamma \vdash c:\varphi_1 \vee \varphi_2, \Delta} \qquad \vee_L\ \frac{M \triangleright \Gamma, x:\varphi_1 \vdash \Delta \qquad N \triangleright \Gamma, y:\varphi_2 \vdash \Delta}{\mathsf{Or}_L(\widehat{x}M, \widehat{y}N, z) \triangleright \Gamma, z:\varphi_1 \vee \varphi_2 \vdash \Delta}$$

$$\Rightarrow_R\ \frac{M \triangleright \Gamma, x:\varphi_1 \vdash a:\varphi_2, \Delta}{\mathsf{Imp}_R(\widehat{x}\widehat{a}M, b) \triangleright \Gamma \vdash b:\varphi_1 \Rightarrow \varphi_2, \Delta} \qquad \Rightarrow_L\ \frac{M \triangleright \Gamma, x:\varphi_2 \vdash \Delta \qquad N \triangleright \Gamma \vdash a:\varphi_1, \Delta}{\mathsf{Imp}_L(\widehat{x}M, \widehat{a}N, y) \triangleright \Gamma, y:\varphi_1 \Rightarrow \varphi_2 \vdash \Delta}$$

$$\exists_L\ \frac{M \triangleright \Gamma, x:\varphi \vdash \Delta}{\mathsf{Exists}_L(\widehat{x}\widehat{x}M, y) \triangleright \Gamma, y:\exists x.\varphi \vdash \Delta}\ x \notin \mathcal{FV}(\Gamma, \Delta)$$

$$\exists_R\ \frac{M \triangleright \Gamma \vdash a:\varphi[x:=t], \Delta}{\mathsf{Exists}_R(\widehat{a}M, t, b) \triangleright \Gamma \vdash b:\exists x.\varphi, \Delta} \qquad \forall_L\ \frac{M \triangleright \Gamma, x:\varphi[x:=t] \vdash \Delta}{\mathsf{Forall}_L(\widehat{x}M, t, y) \triangleright \Gamma, y:\forall x.\varphi \vdash \Delta}$$

$$\forall_R\ \frac{M \triangleright \Gamma \vdash a:\varphi, \Delta}{\mathsf{Forall}_R(\widehat{a}\widehat{x}M, b) \triangleright \Gamma \vdash b:\forall x.\varphi, \Delta}\ x \notin \mathcal{FV}(\Gamma, \Delta)$$

Fig. 2. Type system

Now let us extend Urban's proof-term language for superdeduction. During the computation of the deduction rules for some proposition rewrite rule, the procedure computes an *open* derivation where two kinds of information still need to be provided:

Logical Cuts:

$$\mathsf{Cut}(\widehat{a}M, \widehat{x}\mathsf{Ax}(x, b)) \xrightarrow{\text{cut}} M[a \mapsto b] \qquad \text{if } M \text{ freshly introduces } a$$

$$\mathsf{Cut}(\widehat{a}\mathsf{Ax}(y, a), \widehat{x}M) \xrightarrow{\text{cut}} M[x \mapsto y] \qquad \text{if } M \text{ freshly introduces } x$$

$$\mathsf{Cut}(\widehat{a}\mathsf{True}_R(a), \widehat{x}M) \xrightarrow{\text{cut}} M \qquad \text{if } M \text{ freshly introduces } x$$

$$\mathsf{Cut}(\widehat{a}M, \widehat{x}\mathsf{False}_L(x)) \xrightarrow{\text{cut}} M \qquad \text{if } M \text{ freshly introduces } a$$

$$\mathsf{Cut}(\widehat{a}\mathsf{And}_R(\widehat{b}M_1, \widehat{c}M_2, a), \widehat{x}\mathsf{And}_L(\widehat{yz}N, x)) \xrightarrow{\text{cut}} \begin{cases} \mathsf{Cut}(\widehat{b}M_1, \widehat{y}\mathsf{Cut}(\widehat{c}M_2, \widehat{z}N)) \\ \mathsf{Cut}(\widehat{c}M_2, \widehat{z}\mathsf{Cut}(\widehat{b}M_1, \widehat{y}N)) \end{cases}$$

$$\text{if } \mathsf{And}_R(\widehat{b}M_1, \widehat{c}M_2, a) \text{ and } \mathsf{And}_L(\widehat{yz}N, x) \text{ freshly introduce } a \text{ and } x$$

$$\mathsf{Cut}(\widehat{a}\mathsf{Or}_R(\widehat{bc}M, a), \widehat{x}\mathsf{Or}_L(\widehat{y}N_1, \widehat{z}N_2, x)) \xrightarrow{\text{cut}} \begin{cases} \mathsf{Cut}(\widehat{b}\mathsf{Cut}(\widehat{c}M, \widehat{z}N_2), \widehat{y}N_1) \\ \mathsf{Cut}(\widehat{c}\mathsf{Cut}(\widehat{b}M, \widehat{y}N_1), \widehat{z}N_2) \end{cases}$$

$$\text{if } \mathsf{Or}_R(\widehat{bc}M, a) \text{ and } \mathsf{Or}_L(\widehat{y}N_1, \widehat{z}N_2, x) \text{ freshly introduce } a \text{ and } x$$

$$\mathsf{Cut}(\widehat{a}\mathsf{Imp}_R(\widehat{xb}M, a), \widehat{y}\mathsf{Imp}_L(\widehat{z}N_1, \widehat{c}N_2, y)) \xrightarrow{\text{cut}} \begin{cases} \mathsf{Cut}(\widehat{b}\mathsf{Cut}(\widehat{c}N_2, \widehat{x}M), \widehat{z}N_1) \\ \mathsf{Cut}(\widehat{c}N_2, \widehat{x}\mathsf{Cut}(\widehat{b}M, \widehat{z}N_1)) \end{cases}$$

$$\text{if } \mathsf{Imp}_R(\widehat{xb}M, a) \text{ and } \mathsf{Imp}_L(\widehat{z}N_1, \widehat{c}N_2, y) \text{ freshly introduce } a \text{ and } y$$

$$\mathsf{Cut}(\widehat{a}\mathsf{Exists}_R(\widehat{b}M, t, a), \widehat{x}\mathsf{Exists}_L(\widehat{yx}N, x)) \xrightarrow{\text{cut}} \mathsf{Cut}(\widehat{b}M, \widehat{y}N[\mathsf{x} := t])$$

$$\text{if } \mathsf{Exists}_R(\widehat{b}M, t, a) \text{ and } \mathsf{Exists}_L(\widehat{yx}N, x) \text{ freshly introduce } a \text{ and } x$$

$$\mathsf{Cut}(\widehat{a}\mathsf{Forall}_R(\widehat{bx}M, a), \widehat{x}\mathsf{Forall}_L(\widehat{y}N, t, x)) \xrightarrow{\text{cut}} \mathsf{Cut}(\widehat{b}M[\mathsf{x} := t], \widehat{y}N)$$

$$\text{if } \mathsf{Forall}_R(\widehat{bx}M, a) \text{ and } \mathsf{Forall}_L(\widehat{y}N, t, x) \text{ freshly introduce } a \text{ and } x$$

Commuting Cuts: $\mathsf{Cut}(\widehat{a}M, \widehat{x}N) \xrightarrow{\text{cut}} \begin{cases} M[a := \widehat{x}N] & \text{if } M \text{ does not freshly introduce } a, \text{ or} \\ N[x := \widehat{a}M] & \text{if } M \text{ does not freshly introduce } x \end{cases}$

Fig. 3. Urban's cut-reductions

(1) premises that remain to be proved and (2) first-order terms written at a metalevel by rules $\exists_R$ and $\forall_L$ that still remain to be instantiated. In order to represent these, we use a formal notion of *open-terms*: terms that contains (1) open leaves that represent premises that remain to be proved and are denoted $\square$, and (2) placeholders for first-order terms that represent uninstantiated first-order terms and are denoted by $\alpha, \beta, \ldots$ Substitutions over placeholder-terms are written $[\alpha := t, \ldots]$ and are defined over first-order terms, formulæ, sequents, and terms. The syntax of open-terms is then:

$$C, D ::= \square \rhd \Gamma \vdash \Delta \mid \mathsf{Ax}(x, a) \mid \mathsf{Cut}(\widehat{a}C, \widehat{x}D)$$
$$\mid \ \ldots$$
$$\mid \ \mathsf{Exists}_R(\widehat{a}C, \alpha, b) \mid \mathsf{Exists}_L(\widehat{xx}C, y)$$
$$\mid \ \mathsf{Forall}_R(\widehat{ax}C, b) \mid \mathsf{Forall}_L(\widehat{x}C, \alpha, y)$$

Urban's cut-elimination procedure is extended to open-terms in the obvious way. Typing is also extended to open-terms by adding the following rule to the type inference rules of Figure 2.

$$\frac{}{(\square \rhd \Gamma \vdash \Delta) \rhd \Gamma \vdash \Delta}$$

$$\mathsf{Ax}(x,c)[c := \widehat{y}M] \triangleq M[y \mapsto x]$$
$$\mathsf{Ax}(y,a)[y := \widehat{c}M] \triangleq M[c \mapsto a]$$
$$\mathsf{And}_R(\widehat{a}M_1,\widehat{b}M_2,c)[c := \widehat{y}N] \triangleq \mathsf{Cut}(\widehat{c}\mathsf{And}_R(\widehat{a}M_1[c := \widehat{y}N],\widehat{b}M_2[c := \widehat{y}N],c),\widehat{y}N)$$
$$\mathsf{And}_L(\widehat{x}\widehat{y}M,z)[z := \widehat{a}N] \triangleq \mathsf{Cut}(\widehat{a}N,\widehat{z}\mathsf{And}_L(\widehat{x}\widehat{y}M[z := \widehat{a}N],z))$$

$$\cdots$$

$$\mathsf{Exists}_R(\widehat{a}M,t,b)[b := \widehat{x}N] \triangleq \mathsf{Cut}(\widehat{b}\mathsf{Exists}_R(\widehat{a}M[b := \widehat{x}N],t,b),\widehat{x}N)$$
$$\mathsf{Exists}_L(\widehat{x}\widehat{x}M,y)[y := \widehat{a}N] \triangleq \mathsf{Cut}(\widehat{a}N,\widehat{y}\mathsf{Exists}_L(\widehat{x}\widehat{x}M[y := \widehat{a}N],y))$$

$$\cdots$$

Otherwise :
$$\mathsf{Ax}(x,a)[\vartheta] \triangleq \mathsf{Ax}(x,a)$$
$$\mathsf{Cut}(\widehat{a}M,\widehat{x}N)[\vartheta] \triangleq \mathsf{Cut}(\widehat{a}M[\vartheta],\widehat{x}N[\vartheta])$$
$$\mathsf{And}_R(\widehat{a}M_1,\widehat{b}M_2,c)[\vartheta] \triangleq \mathsf{And}_R(\widehat{a}M_1[\vartheta],\widehat{b}M_2[\vartheta],c)$$
$$\mathsf{And}_L(\widehat{x}\widehat{y}M,z)[\vartheta] \triangleq \mathsf{And}_L(\widehat{x}\widehat{y}M[\vartheta],z)$$

$$\cdots$$

$$\mathsf{Exists}_R(\widehat{a}M,t,b)[\vartheta] \triangleq \mathsf{Exists}_R(\widehat{a}M[\vartheta],t,b)$$
$$\mathsf{Exists}_L(\widehat{x}\widehat{x}M,y)[\vartheta] \triangleq \mathsf{Exists}_L(\widehat{x}\widehat{x}M[\vartheta],y)$$

$$\cdots$$

Fig. 4. Proof Substitution

These leaves will be denoted for short $\overline{\square \triangleright \Gamma \vdash \Delta}$. Type inference derivation for open-terms are called open type inference derivations. Their *open leaves* are the later leaves, *i.e.* the *open leaves* of the open-term. For some open-term C, its number of occurrences of $\square$ is denoted n_C. Then for some placeholder-term substitution $\sigma = [\alpha_1 := t_1, \ldots, \alpha_p := t_p]$ where all placeholder-terms appearing in C are substituted by σ (we say that σ *covers* C) and for $M_1, \ldots, M_{n_C}$ some terms, we define the term $\sigma C[M_1, \ldots, M_{n_C}]$ as follows.

- if C is a term and $n_C = 0$ then trivially $\sigma C[] \triangleq \sigma C$;
- if $C = \square \triangleright \Gamma \vdash \Delta$ and $n_C = 1$ then $\sigma C[M] \triangleq M$;
- if $C = \mathsf{And}_R(\widehat{a}C_1,\widehat{b}C_2,c)[M_1, \ldots, M_{n_C}]$ then

$$\sigma C[M_1, \ldots, M_{n_C}] \triangleq \mathsf{And}_R(\widehat{a}\sigma C_1[M_1, \ldots, M_{n_{C_1}}],\widehat{b}\sigma C_2[M_{n_{C_1}+1}, \ldots, M_{n_C}],c);$$

- if $C = \mathsf{Exists}_L(\widehat{x}\widehat{x}C_1,y)$, then

$$\sigma C[M_1, \ldots, M_{n_C}] \triangleq \mathsf{Exists}_L(\widehat{x}\widehat{x}\sigma C_1[M_1, \ldots, M_{n_C}],y) ;$$

- if $C = \mathsf{Exists}_R(\widehat{a}C_1,\alpha,b)$, then

$$\sigma C[M_1, \ldots, M_{n_C}] \triangleq \mathsf{Exists}_R(\widehat{a}\sigma C_1[M_1, \ldots, M_{n_C}],\sigma\alpha,b) ;$$

- the other remaining cases are similar.

Let us define now the extended terms and reduction rules associated with the proposition rewrite rule $\mathsf{R} : P \to \varphi$. For some formula φ, for x and a some name and coname, the open-terms denoted $\langle\!\langle \vdash a : \varphi \,\rangle\!\rangle$ and $\langle\!\langle\, x : \varphi \vdash \rangle\!\rangle$ are defined as follows.

$$\begin{aligned}
(\, \Gamma \vdash \Delta \,) & \triangleq \quad \Box \rhd \Gamma \vdash \Delta \quad \text{if } \Gamma \text{ and } \Delta \text{ only contain atomic formulæ} \\
(\, \Gamma, x : \varphi \vdash a : \varphi, \Delta \,) & \triangleq \quad \mathsf{Ax}(x, a) \\
(\, \Gamma \vdash a : \varphi_1 \Rightarrow \varphi_2, \Delta \,) & \triangleq \quad \mathsf{Imp}_R(\widehat{xb}(\, \Gamma, x : \varphi_1 \vdash b : \varphi_2, \Delta \,), a) \\
(\, \Gamma, x : \varphi_1 \Rightarrow \varphi_2 \vdash \Delta \,) & \triangleq \quad \mathsf{Imp}_L(\widehat{y}(\, \Gamma, y : \varphi_2 \vdash \Delta \,), \widehat{a}(\, \Gamma \vdash a : \varphi_1, \Delta \,), x) \\
(\, \Gamma \vdash a : \varphi_1 \vee \varphi_2, \Delta \,) & \triangleq \quad \mathsf{Or}_R(\widehat{bc}(\, \Gamma \vdash b : \varphi_1, c : \varphi_2, \Delta \,), a) \\
(\, \Gamma, x : \varphi_1 \vee \varphi_2 \vdash \Delta \,) & \triangleq \quad \mathsf{Or}_L(\widehat{y}(\, \Gamma, y : \varphi_1 \vdash \Delta \,), \widehat{z}(\, \Gamma, z : \varphi_2 \vdash \Delta \,), x) \\
(\, \Gamma \vdash a : \varphi_1 \wedge \varphi_2, \Delta \,) & \triangleq \quad \mathsf{And}_R(\widehat{b}(\, \Gamma \vdash b : \varphi_1, \Delta \,), \widehat{c}(\, \Gamma \vdash c : \varphi_2, \Delta \,), a) \\
(\, \Gamma, x : \varphi_1 \vee \varphi_2 \vdash \Delta \,) & \triangleq \quad \mathsf{And}_L(\widehat{yz}(\, \Gamma, y : \varphi_1, z : \varphi_2 \vdash \Delta \,), x) \\
(\, \Gamma \vdash a : \exists x.\varphi, \Delta \,) & \triangleq \quad \mathsf{Exists}_R(\widehat{b}(\, \Gamma \vdash b : \varphi[x := \alpha], \Delta \,), \alpha, a) \quad \alpha \text{ is fresh} \\
(\, \Gamma, x : \exists x.\varphi \vdash \Delta \,) & \triangleq \quad \mathsf{Exists}_L(\widehat{yx}(\, \Gamma, y : \varphi \vdash \Delta \,), x) \quad \text{if } x \notin \mathcal{FV}(\Gamma, \Delta) \\
(\, \Gamma \vdash a : \forall x.\varphi, \Delta \,) & \triangleq \quad \mathsf{Forall}_R(\widehat{bx}(\, \Gamma \vdash b : \varphi, \Delta \,), a) \quad \text{if } x \notin \mathcal{FV}(\Gamma, \Delta) \\
(\, \Gamma, x : \forall x.\varphi \vdash \Delta \,) & \triangleq \quad \mathsf{Forall}_L(\widehat{y}(\, \Gamma, y : \varphi[x := \alpha] \vdash \Delta \,), \alpha, x) \quad \alpha \text{ is fresh}
\end{aligned}$$

The definition is non-deterministic just as the definition of new deduction rules in super sequent calculus systems. We may pick any of the possibilities just as we do for the computation of new deduction rules.

We prove the following lemma, which states the adequacy of the typing of $(\, \vdash a : \varphi \,)$ (resp. $(\, x : \varphi \vdash)$) with the right (resp. left) superdeduction rule associated with a proposition rewrite rule $P \to \varphi$.

Lemma 1. *Let* $R : P \to \varphi$ *be some proposition rewrite rule and let C be the open-term* $(\, \vdash a : \varphi \,)$. *Then, for any instance of the right rule* R_R *having* $\Gamma \vdash a : P, \Delta$ *as its conclusion,* $C \rhd \Gamma \vdash a : \varphi, \Delta$ *is well-typed, and moreover there exists some substitution σ for placeholder-terms covering C such that the sequents in the premises of C substituted by σ are the premises of this instance of* R_R.

Proof. By construction, an instance of R_R can be transformed into a decomposition of the logical connectors of φ, and thus into some open type inference of $C \rhd \Gamma \vdash a : \varphi, \Delta$, by construction of C. The substitution σ substitutes for the placeholder-terms in this open type inference derivation the terms that are used in this instance of R_R. We obtain thus that the sequents in the premises of C substituted by σ are the premises of this instance of R_R. $\qquad\square$

An analogous version of Lemma 1 can be proven for the introduction of P on the left. We propose the type inference rules presented as follows for introducing P on the left and on the right.

$$R_R \dfrac{\left(\, M_i \rhd \Gamma, x_1^i : A_1^i, \ldots, x_{p_i}^i : A_{p_i}^i \vdash a_1^i : B_1^i, \ldots, a_{q_i}^i : B_{q_i}^i, \Delta \, \right)_{1 \leqslant i \leqslant n}}{R_R \left(\widehat{x_1} \ldots \widehat{x_p}, \left(\widehat{x_1^i \ldots x_{p_i}^i a_1^i \ldots a_{q_i}^i} \, M_i \right)_{1 \leqslant i \leqslant n}, \alpha_1, \ldots, \alpha_q, a \right) \rhd \Gamma \vdash a : P, \Delta} \; C$$

n is the number of open leaves of $(\, \vdash a : \varphi \,)$. The side condition C is the side condition of the corresponding rule in the super sequent calculus. The first-order variables $x_1, \ldots, x_p$ are the variables concerned by this side condition and by Lemma 1, they are the bound first-order variables of $(\, \vdash a : \varphi \,)$. The $\alpha_1, \ldots, \alpha_q$ are the placeholder-terms appearing in this later open-term. When using this type inference rule, these placeholder-terms are to be instantiated by first-order terms in the proof-terms as in the formulæ.

$$R_L \frac{\left(N_j \rhd \Gamma, y_1^j : C_1^j, \ldots, y_{r_j}^j : C_{r_j}^j \vdash b_1^j : D_1^j, \ldots, b_{s_j}^j : D_{s_j}^j, \Delta \right)_{1 \leqslant j \leqslant m}}{R_L \left(\widehat{y_1} \ldots \widehat{y_r}, \left(\widehat{y_1^j} \ldots \widehat{y_{r_j}^j} \widehat{b_1^j} \ldots \widehat{b_{s_j}^j} N_j \right)_{1 \leqslant j \leqslant m} \right), \beta_1, \ldots, \beta_s, x \rhd \Gamma, x : P \vdash \Delta} C'$$

m is the number of open leaves of $\langle\!|\ x : \varphi \vdash\!|\rangle$. The side condition C' is the side condition of the corresponding rule in the super sequent calculus. The first-order variables $y_1, \ldots, y_r$ are the variables concerned by this side condition and by the version of Lemma 1 for introducing P on the left, they are the bound first-order variables of $\langle\!|\ x : \varphi \vdash\!|\rangle$. The $\beta_1, \ldots, \beta_s$ are the placeholder-terms appearing in this later open-term. By duality it is expected that $p = s$ and $q = r$. When using this type inference rule, these placeholder-terms are to be instantiated by first-order terms in the proof-terms as in the formulæ.

We obtain the extended proof-terms for a super sequent calculus system. Proofs substitutions are extended in the obvious way on proof-terms.

The extended cut-elimination associated with $\xrightarrow{\text{cut}}$, denoted $\xrightarrow{\text{excut}}$, is defined as follows. For each proposition rewrite rule R : $P \to \varphi$, for each reduction

$$\text{Cut}(\widehat{a}\langle\!|\vdash a : \varphi\ |\rangle, \widehat{x}\langle\!|\ x : \varphi \vdash\!|\rangle) \xrightarrow{\text{cut}}{}^+ C$$

where C is a normal form for $\xrightarrow{\text{cut}}$, we add to $\xrightarrow{\text{cut}}$ the following rewrite rule:

$$\sigma\text{Cut}\left(\widehat{a}R_R \left(\widehat{x_1} \ldots \widehat{x_p}, \left(\widehat{x_1^i} \ldots \widehat{x_{p_i}^i} \widehat{a_1^i} \ldots \widehat{a_{q_i}^i} M_i \right)_{1 \leqslant i \leqslant n}, \alpha_1 \ldots \alpha_q, a \right), \right.$$
$$\left. \widehat{x}R_L \left(\widehat{y_1} \ldots \widehat{y_r}, \left(\widehat{y_1^j} \ldots \widehat{y_{r_j}^j} \widehat{b_1^j} \ldots \widehat{b_{s_j}^j} N_j \right)_{1 \leqslant j \leqslant m}, \beta_1 \ldots \beta_s, x \right) \right)$$

$$\xrightarrow{\text{excut}} \sigma C[M_1, \ldots, N_m]$$

if $R_R(\ldots)$ and $R_L(\ldots)$ freshly introduce a and x

Here σ substitutes for each placeholder-term a first-order term. However these terms are *meta* just as the symbol t in the eighth and ninth rules of Figure 2.

The cut-elimination $\xrightarrow{\text{excut}}$ is *complete*: any instance of a cut is a redex and thus a normal form for $\xrightarrow{\text{excut}}$ is cut-free.

An important result of [BHK07] is the following theorem.

Theorem 2 (Strong Normalisation). *Let us suppose that the set of proposition rewrite rules $\mathcal{R}$ is such that for each of its rules R : $P \to \varphi$:*

- *P contains only first-order variables (no function symbol or constant);*
- *$\mathcal{FV}(\varphi) \subseteq \mathcal{FV}(P)$;*

and such that the rewrite relation $\xrightarrow{\text{prop}}$ *associated with* $\mathcal{R}$ *is weakly normalising and confluent. Then* $\xrightarrow{\text{excut}}$ *is strongly normalising on well-typed extended terms.*

The proof of this theorem is detailed in Section 4. It uses the normal forms of formulæ through the rewrite relation $\xrightarrow{\text{prop}}$ to translate proofs in superdeduction into proofs in usual sequent calculus and thus requires that $\xrightarrow{\text{prop}}$ is weak normalising and confluent. Besides the translation of existential/universal rules requires the two other hypothesis, as it will be explained by a precise counter-example in Section 3.

It is interesting to notice that since Hypothesis 1 implies the cut-admissibility in the super sequent calculus system, and since this system is sound and complete *w.r.t.* predicate logic, it implies the consistency of the corresponding first-order theory.

3   A Foundation for New Proof Assistants

The first strong argument in favour of proof assistants based on superdeduction is the representation of proofs. Indeed, existing proof assistants such as COQ, Isabelle or PVS are based on the proof planning paradigm, where proofs are represented by a succession of applications of tactics and of tacticals. COQ also builds a proof-term, in particular to bring the proof check down to a micro kernel. In these approaches, the witness of the proof is bound to convince the user that the proof is correct but not to actually *explain* it, as usual mathematical proofs often also do. Even if the proof-terms of COQ are displayed as trees or under the form of natural language text, the main steps of the proof are drown in a multitude of usually not expressed logical arguments due to both the underlying calculus and the presence of purely computational parts, *e.g.* the proof that $2 + 3$ equals 5.

Deduction modulo is a first step forward addressing this later issue by internalising computational aspects of a theory inside a congruence. With the canonical rewrite system on naturals, $P(2 + 3) \vdash P(5)$ becomes an axiom. However a congruence defined by proposition rewrite rules whose right-hand side is not atomic does not bring the expected comfort to interactive proving: the choice of a proposition representative in the congruence introduces some nondeterminism which is neither useful nor wanted. Superdeduction solves this problem by narrowing the choice of a deduction rule to the presence in the goal of one of the extended deduction rules conclusions and goes a step further by also eliminating trivial logical arguments in a proof. Thereby, superdeduction provides a framework for naturally building but also communicating and understanding the essence of proofs.

Notice that extended deduction rules contain only atomic premises and conclusions, thus proof building in this system is like plugging in theorems, definitions and axioms together. This points out the fact that logical arguments of proofs are actually encoded by the structure of theorems, which explains why they are usually not mentionned.

Another important aspect of superdeduction is its potential ability to naturally encode custom reasoning schemes. Let us see how superdeduction behaves in practice when confronted to common situations of theorem proving.

3.1 Higher-Order Logic

An interesting case is the encoding of other logics like higher-order logic which has been expressed through proposition rewrite rules in [Dow97]. As an example, the proposition rewrite rule $\epsilon(\alpha(\dot{\forall}, x)) \to \forall y.\epsilon(\alpha(x, y))$ is translated into the following deduction rules which mimic the deduction rules of higher-order logic.

$$\frac{\Gamma \vdash^+ \epsilon(\alpha(x,y)), \Delta}{\Gamma \vdash^+ \epsilon(\alpha(\dot{\forall}, x)), \Delta} \; (y \notin \mathcal{FV}(\Gamma)) \qquad \frac{\Gamma, \epsilon(\alpha(x,t)) \vdash^+ \Delta}{\Gamma, \epsilon(\alpha(\dot{\forall}, x)) \vdash^+ \Delta}$$

The interesting point is that this behaviour is not encoded inside the underlying logic but is the result of the chosen theory which is only a parameter of the system.

3.2 Induction

Another application field of superdeduction is the handling of induction schemes, introduced in Section 2 with the example of structural induction over Peano naturals. Let us carry on this by proving that every natural number is either odd or even in the super sequent calculus. We start by defining the predicates *even* and *odd* with the following three proposition rewrite rules.

$$\begin{aligned} zero: & \quad Even(0) \to \top \\ even: & \quad Even(s(n)) \to Odd(n) \\ odd: & \quad Odd(s(n)) \to Even(n) \end{aligned}$$

This leads to six simple *folding* and *unfolding* rules.

$$zero_L \; \frac{\Gamma \vdash^{+R} \Delta}{\Gamma, Even(0) \vdash^{+R} \Delta} \qquad\qquad zero_R \; \frac{}{\Gamma \vdash^{+R} Even(0), \Delta}$$

$$even_L \; \frac{\Gamma, Odd(n) \vdash^{+R} \Delta}{\Gamma, Even(s(n)) \vdash^{+R} \Delta} \qquad even_R \; \frac{\Gamma \vdash^{+R} Odd(n), \Delta}{\Gamma \vdash^{+R} Even(s(n)), \Delta}$$

$$odd_L \; \frac{\Gamma, Even(n) \vdash^{+R} \Delta}{\Gamma, Odd(s(n)) \vdash^{+R} \Delta} \qquad odd_R \; \frac{\Gamma \vdash^{+R} Even(n), \Delta}{\Gamma \vdash^{+R} Odd(s(n)), \Delta}$$

Finally, let us recall that the derived inference rules for induction encode second-order reasoning by the use of *classes*, *i.e.* constants standing for propositions. For instance, assuming that the *odd* class represents the *Odd* predicate, we add the following axiom to the context of the proof : $\forall x.(x \in odd \Leftrightarrow Odd(x))$. Here, since we want to prove that every natural is either odd or even, we introduce the *oöe* class which encodes the latter proposition. This is done through a proposition rewrite rule:

$$oddoreven : \; n \in o\dot{o}e \to Odd(n) \vee Even(n)$$

This leads to the creation of two new deduction rules for the super sequent calculus.

$$oddoreven_L \; \frac{\Gamma, Odd(n) \vdash^{+R} \Delta \qquad \Gamma, Even(n) \vdash^{+R} \Delta}{\Gamma, n \in o\dot{o}e \vdash^{+R} \Delta}$$

$$oddoreven_R \; \frac{\Gamma \vdash^{+R} Odd(n), Even(n), \Delta}{\Gamma \vdash^{+R} n \in o\dot{o}e, \Delta}$$

We finally can build a proof of $n \in \mathbb{N} \vdash^{+\mathcal{R}} Odd(n) \vee Even(n)$, which is depicted by Figure 5 (some weakening steps are left implicit to lighten the proof tree). Let us call respectively Π_1, Π_2 and Π_3 the premises of the $\in_{\mathbb{N}_L}$ rule. The proof appears to be rather readable compared to a proof of the same proposition in classical sequent calculus: we start by proving that zero is even or odd (Π_1), then that the *even or odd* property is hereditary (Π_2) by using the deduction rules translating the definitions of even, odd and zero. Then we prove that the proposition holds for every integer by using the induction principle expressed by rule $\in_{\mathbb{N}_L}$. The subproof Π_3 is purely axiomatic and would be typically automated in a proof assistant.

$$
\cfrac{\text{AX} \cfrac{}{Odd(n) \vdash^{+\mathcal{R}} Odd(n), Even(n)} \qquad \text{AX} \cfrac{}{Even(n) \vdash^{+\mathcal{R}} Odd(n), Even(n)}}{n \in \dot{oo}e \vdash^{+\mathcal{R}} Odd(n), Even(n)} \; oddoreven_L
$$

$$
\cfrac{\text{AX} \cfrac{}{Odd(m) \vdash^{+\mathcal{R}} Odd(m)}}{Odd(m) \vdash^{+\mathcal{R}} Odd(s(m)), Even(s(m))} \; even_R
$$

$$
\cfrac{\text{AX} \cfrac{}{Even(m) \vdash^{+\mathcal{R}} Even(m)}}{Even(m) \vdash^{+\mathcal{R}} Odd(s(m)), Even(s(m))} \; odd_R
$$

$$
\cfrac{m \in \dot{oo}e \vdash^{+\mathcal{R}} Odd(s(m)), Even(s(m))}{\cfrac{m \in \dot{oo}e \vdash^{+\mathcal{R}} s(m) \in \dot{oo}e}{\vdash^{+\mathcal{R}} H(\dot{oo}e), Odd(n), Even(n)} \; hered_R} \; oddoreven_R
$$

$$
\cfrac{zero_R \cfrac{}{\vdash^{+\mathcal{R}} Odd(0), Even(0)}}{\cfrac{\vdash^{+\mathcal{R}} 0 \in \dot{oo}e, Odd(n), Even(n)}{\cfrac{n \in \mathbb{N} \vdash^{+\mathcal{R}} Odd(n), Even(n)}{n \in \mathbb{N} \vdash^{+\mathcal{R}} Odd(n) \vee Even(n)} \; \vee_R} \; \in_{\mathbb{N}_L}} \; oddoreven_R
$$

Fig. 5. Proof of $n \in \mathbb{N} \vdash^{+\mathcal{R}} Odd(n) \vee Even(n)$

Let us remark that in a framework mixing superdeduction and deduction modulo, Π_3 would be immediately closed by an axiom, while the encoding of second order by classes could hardly disappear everywhere in the proof tree. Indeed, the proposition $m \in \dot{oo}e$ for instance would be equal to $Odd(m) \vee Even(m) \vdash^{+\mathcal{R}} Odd(s(m)) \vee Even(s(m))$ modulo $\mathcal{R}$, which would hide the explicit decoding by the successive applications of $oddoreven_R$ and $oddoreven_L$. The study of such a deduction system is an active research topic.

One may argue that this approach is not viable within the framework of proof assistants because it requires to virtually provide a class for each constructible proposition of the language. This would lead to the introduction of an infinite number of constants symbols, as well as an infinity of associated "decoding" axioms. This problem is addressed in [Kir06] which proposes a finite axiomatisation of the theory of classes. The basic idea is to introduce a constant symbol along with its decoding axiom for each predicate symbol of the discourse. They shall be a finite number of them. As an example, let us encode *Odd* and *Even*:

$$decodeeven : x \in even \rightarrow Even(x)$$
$$decodeodd :\;\; x \in odd \rightarrow Odd(x)$$

However this time, classes encoding complex propositions are *built* over this finite set of constants using function symbols encoding logical connectors. For instance, the $\cup$ function symbol encodes the $\vee$ connector:

$$decodeunion :\; x \in a \cup b \rightarrow x \in a \vee x \in b$$

This entails the encoding of the proposition $Odd(x) \vee Even(x)$ by the $x \in odd \cup even$ one. The difficulty of such an approach is the handling of bound variables and predicates arities. This is achieved via the use of De Bruijn indices and axioms distributing variables *a la* explicit substitutions. The latter proposition is eventually encoded by the following term, whose derivation using the decoding axioms is provided here as an example (see [Kir06] for more details):

$$x::nil \in odd(1) \cup even(1)$$
$$\rightarrow\quad x::nil \in odd(1) \vee x::nil \in even(1)$$
$$\rightarrow\quad Odd(1[x::nil]) \vee x::nil \in even(1)$$
$$\rightarrow\quad Odd(x) \vee x::nil \in even(1)$$
$$\rightarrow\quad Odd(x) \vee Even(1[x::nil])$$
$$\rightarrow\quad Odd(x) \vee Even(x)$$

This powerful mechanism enables the simulation of higher-order behaviour in proof assistants in a natural way. Indeed, decoding is only calculus, which therefore is well handled by both deduction modulo and superdeduction. Once again, a system mixing the two approaches would totally hide the encoding part to the user through deduction modulo while providing a natural way of expressing the induction reasoning via an extended deduction rule.

3.3 Equality

Let us see now how superdeduction handles equality. Taken back to the previously discussed higher-order encoding, the Leibniz definition of equality is expressed as follows:

$$eq :\; x = y \rightarrow \forall p.(x::nil \in p \Rightarrow y::nil \in p)$$

This leads to the derivation of the following new inference rules:

$$eq_L \;\frac{\Gamma \vdash^{+\mathcal{R}} x::nil \in p, \Delta \qquad \Gamma, y::nil \in p \vdash^{+\mathcal{R}} \Delta}{\Gamma, x = y \vdash^{+\mathcal{R}} \Delta}$$

$$eq_R \;\frac{\Gamma, x::nil \in p \vdash^{+\mathcal{R}} y::nil \in p, \Delta}{\Gamma \vdash^{+\mathcal{R}} x = y, \Delta} \; p \notin \mathcal{FV}(\Gamma, \Delta)$$

The right rule is rather intuitive and is used to prove the reflexivity of equality in two proof steps:

$$\forall_R \cfrac{eq_L \cfrac{\text{AX}\cfrac{}{x::nil \in p \vdash^{+R} x::nil \in p}}{\vdash^{+R} x = x}}{\vdash^{+R} \forall x. x = x}$$

The left rule requires a class term encoding a proposition and is typically used to prove extensionality of function symbols. For instance, given a function symbol f, let us prove that $x = y \Rightarrow f(x) = f(y)$ for any x and y. The appropriate proposition to feed the axiom of Leibniz with would then be $f(x) = f(\alpha)$, parameterized by α. Let us translate this into a class term and prove the proposition:

$$eq_L \cfrac{eq_R \cfrac{\text{AX}\cfrac{}{f(x)::nil \in p \vdash^{+R} f(x)::nil \in p}}{\vdash^{+R} f(x) = f(x)} \qquad \text{AX}\cfrac{}{f(x) = f(y) \vdash^{+R} f(x) = f(y)}}{}$$

$$eq_L \cfrac{\cfrac{\vdots}{\vdash^{+R} x::nil \in f(S(x)) \doteq 1} \qquad \cfrac{\vdots}{y::nil \in f(S(x)) \doteq 1 \vdash^{+R} f(x) = f(y)}}{x = y \vdash^{+R} f(x) = f(y)}$$

The dots stands for decoding steps using axioms of [Kir06]. The S function symbol should be read as "shift" and is part of the explicit substitution mechanism.

Thus, while Leibniz' definition is adapted to proofs of equality metaproperties, simple notions like extensionality require some deduction steps. A natural use of superdeduction would then be to translate this theorem into an inference rule:

$$f_R \cfrac{\Gamma \vdash^{+R} x = y, \Delta}{\Gamma \vdash^{+R} f(x) = f(y), \Delta}$$

However, this goes beyond the scope of superdeduction since the proved proposition is not a proposition rewrite rule (*i.e.* an equivalence). A reasonable extension of superdeduction would be the creation of only-right inference rules to translate axioms of the shape $\forall \overline{x}.(P \Rightarrow \varphi)$. Nevertheless, the price to pay would be the loss of the cut-elimination result. The question of extending the cut-elimination procedure to this case is still open.

3.4 Cut-Elimination as a Translation

An interesting cut-reduction is the following. Let us consider the following proposition rewrite rule:

$$\text{INC} : \forall A. \forall B. (A \subseteq B \rightarrow \forall x. (x \in A \Rightarrow x \in B))$$

First of all we construct the proof π_1 of $\vdash^{+\text{INC}}$ INC depicted in Figure 6 (in fact for any theory Th, there is a proof of $\vdash^{+Th} Th$ by completeness of superdeduction). The proofterm associated with this proof is

$$\pi_1 = \text{Forall}_R(\widehat{a_2}X\text{Forall}_R(\widehat{a_3}Y\text{And}_R(\widehat{a_4}\nu_1, \widehat{a_9}\nu_2, a_3), a_2), a_1)$$

$$
\text{INC}_L \cfrac{
\text{AX} \cfrac{}{x \in Y, x \in X \vdash^{+\text{INC}} x \in Y} \quad
\text{AX} \cfrac{}{x \in X \vdash^{+\text{INC}} x \in Y, x \in X}
}{
\Rightarrow_R \cfrac{X \subseteq Y, x \in X \vdash^{+\text{INC}} x \in Y}{
\forall_R \cfrac{X \subseteq Y \vdash^{+\text{INC}} x \in X \Rightarrow x \in Y}{
\Rightarrow_R \cfrac{X \subseteq Y \vdash^{+\text{INC}} \forall x.(x \in X \Rightarrow x \in Y)}{
\vdash^{+\text{INC}} X \subseteq Y \Rightarrow (\forall x.(x \in X \Rightarrow x \in Y))}}}}
$$

$$
\wedge_R \cfrac{
\forall_R \cfrac{
\forall_R \cfrac{
\Rightarrow_R \cfrac{
\text{INC}_R \cfrac{
\forall_L \cfrac{
\Rightarrow_L \cfrac{
\text{AX} \cfrac{}{x \in X \vdash^{+\text{INC}} x \in Y, x \in X} \quad
\text{AX} \cfrac{}{x \in Y, x \in X \vdash^{+\text{INC}} x \in Y}
}{x \in X \Rightarrow x \in Y, x \in X \vdash^{+\text{INC}} x \in Y}
}{\forall x.(x \in X \Rightarrow x \in Y), x \in X \vdash^{+\text{INC}} x \in Y}
}{\forall x.(x \in X \Rightarrow x \in Y) \vdash^{+\text{INC}} X \subseteq Y}
}{\vdash^{+\text{INC}} (\forall x.(x \in X \Rightarrow x \in Y)) \Rightarrow X \subseteq Y}
}{\vdash^{+\text{INC}} X \subseteq Y \Leftrightarrow \forall x.(x \in X \Rightarrow x \in Y)}
}{\vdash^{+\text{INC}} \forall Y.(X \subseteq Y \Leftrightarrow \forall x.(x \in X \Rightarrow x \in Y))}
}{\vdash^{+\text{INC}} \forall X.\forall Y.(X \subseteq Y \Leftrightarrow \forall x.(x \in X \Rightarrow x \in Y))}
$$

Fig. 6. The proof π_1

with

$$
\nu_1 = \text{Imp}_R(\widehat{x_1}\widehat{a_5}\text{Forall}_R(\widehat{a_6}\text{x}\text{Imp}_R(\widehat{x_2}\widehat{a_7}\text{INC}_L(\widehat{x_3}\text{Ax}(x_3, a_7),
$$
$$
\widehat{a_8}\text{Ax}(x_2, a_8), \text{x}, x_1), a_6), a_5), a_4)
$$

and

$$
\nu_2 = \text{Imp}_R(\widehat{x_4}\widehat{a_{10}}\text{INC}_R(\widehat{x}\widehat{x_5}\widehat{a_{11}}\text{Forall}_L(\widehat{x_6}\text{Imp}_L(\widehat{x_7}\text{Ax}(x_7, a_{11}),
$$
$$
\widehat{a_{12}}\text{Ax}(x_5, a_{12}), x_6), \text{x}, x_4), a_{10}), a_9)
$$

Besides we propose the following proof of $\text{INC} \vdash A \subseteq A$, denoted π_2, in raw classical sequent calculus.

$$
\forall_L \cfrac{
\forall_L \cfrac{
\wedge_L \cfrac{
\Rightarrow_L \cfrac{
\text{AX} \cfrac{}{\ldots, A \subseteq A \vdash A \subseteq A}
}{} \quad
\forall_R \cfrac{
\Rightarrow_R \cfrac{
\text{AX} \cfrac{}{\ldots, x \in A \vdash A \subseteq A, x \in A}
}{\ldots \vdash A \subseteq A, x \in A \Rightarrow x \in A}
}{\ldots \vdash A \subseteq A, \forall x.(x \in A \Rightarrow x \in A)}
}{\ldots, (\forall x.(x \in A \Rightarrow x \in A)) \Rightarrow A \subseteq A \vdash A \subseteq A}
}{(A \subseteq A) \Leftrightarrow \forall x.(x \in A \Rightarrow x \in A) \vdash A \subseteq A}
}{\forall Y.(A \subseteq Y) \Leftrightarrow \forall x.(x \in A \Rightarrow x \in Y) \vdash A \subseteq A}
}{\text{INC} \vdash A \subseteq A}
$$

The proofterm associated with this proof is

$$
\pi_2 = \text{Forall}_L(\widehat{x_9}\text{Forall}_L(\widehat{x_{10}}\text{And}_L(\widehat{x_{11}}\widehat{x_{12}}\nu_3, x_{10}), A, x_9), A, x_8)
$$

with

$$\nu_3 = \mathsf{Imp}_L(\widehat{x_{13}}\mathsf{Ax}(x_{13}, a_{14}),$$
$$\widehat{a_{15}}\mathsf{Forall}_R(\widehat{a_{16}}\widehat{x}\mathsf{Imp}_R(\widehat{x_{14}}\widehat{a_{17}}\mathsf{Ax}(x_{14}, a_{17}), a_{16}), a_{15}), x_{12})$$

Now we wish to express the proof π_2 in superdeduction. The corresponding proof denoted π_3 is

$$\mathsf{INC}_R \frac{\mathsf{AX} \dfrac{}{x \in A \vdash^{+\mathrm{INC}} x \in A}}{\vdash^{+\mathrm{INC}} A \subseteq A}$$

We will now obtain it directly from π_2 (and from π_1 whose construction only depends on the axiom INC). Let us consider the proofterm $\mathsf{Cut}(\widehat{a_1}\pi_1, \widehat{x_8}\pi_2)$ which represents the proof

$$\mathsf{CUT} \frac{\begin{array}{cc} \pi_1 & \pi_2 \\ \vdash^{+\mathrm{INC}} \mathrm{INC} & \mathrm{INC} \vdash A \subseteq A \end{array}}{\vdash^{+\mathrm{INC}} A \subseteq A}$$

This proof can also be seen as the *translation* of the proof π_2 in superdeduction: a cut is used to delete the axiom INC from the context. Now it is interesting to understand that the elimination of this cut will actually propagate the superdeduction inference rules contained by π_1 into the proof π_2 and translate the (cut-free) proof of $\mathrm{INC} \vdash A \subseteq A$ into a (cut-free) proof of $\vdash^{+\mathrm{INC}} A \subseteq A$ replacing any use of the axiom INC by a superdeduction rule. An elimination of this cut is depicted in Figure 7. Its result represents the proof π_3.

$$\mathsf{Cut}(\widehat{a_1}\pi_1, \widehat{x_1}\pi_2)$$
$$= \quad \mathsf{Cut}(\widehat{a_1}\mathsf{Forall}_R(\widehat{a_2}\widehat{\mathsf{X}}\mathsf{Forall}_R(\widehat{a_3}\widehat{\mathsf{Y}}\mathsf{And}_R(\widehat{a_4}\nu_1, \widehat{a_9}\nu_2, a_3), a_2), a_1),$$
$$\widehat{x_8}\mathsf{Forall}_L(\widehat{x_9}\mathsf{Forall}_L(\widehat{x_{10}}\mathsf{And}_L(\widehat{x_{11}}\widehat{x_{12}}\nu_3, x_{10}), A, x_9), A, x_8))$$
$$\xrightarrow{\mathrm{excut}^+} \mathsf{Cut}(\widehat{a_9}\nu_2, \widehat{x_{12}}\nu_3)$$
$$= \quad \mathsf{Cut}(\widehat{a_9}\mathsf{Imp}_R(\widehat{x_4}\widehat{a_{10}}\mathsf{INC}_R(\dots), a_9),$$
$$\widehat{x_{12}}\mathsf{Imp}_L(\widehat{x_{13}}\mathsf{Ax}(x_{13}, a_{14}), \widehat{a_{15}}\mathsf{Forall}_R(\dots), \widehat{x_{12}}))$$
$$\xrightarrow{\mathrm{excut}} \mathsf{Cut}(\widehat{a_{10}}\mathsf{Cut}(\widehat{a_{15}}\mathsf{Forall}_R(\dots), \widehat{x_4}\mathsf{INC}_R(\dots)), \widehat{x_{13}}\mathsf{Ax}(x_{13}, a_{14}))$$
$$\xrightarrow{\mathrm{excut}} \mathsf{Cut}(\widehat{a_{15}}\mathsf{Forall}_R(\dots), \widehat{x_4}\mathsf{INC}_R(\widehat{x x_5}\widehat{a_{11}}\mathsf{Forall}_L(\dots), a_{14}))$$
$$\xrightarrow{\mathrm{excut}} \mathsf{INC}_R(\widehat{x x_5}\widehat{a_{11}}\mathsf{Cut}(\widehat{a_{15}}\mathsf{Forall}_R(\dots), \widehat{x_4}\mathsf{Forall}_L(\dots)), a_{14})$$
$$\xrightarrow{\mathrm{excut}} \mathsf{INC}_R(\widehat{x x_5}\widehat{a_{11}}\mathsf{Cut}(\widehat{a_{16}}\mathsf{Imp}_R(\dots), \widehat{x_6}\mathsf{Imp}_L(\dots)), a_{14})$$
$$\xrightarrow{\mathrm{excut}} \mathsf{INC}_R(\widehat{x x_5}\widehat{a_{11}}\mathsf{Cut}(\widehat{a_{12}}\mathsf{Ax}(x_5, a_{12}),$$
$$\widehat{x_{14}}\mathsf{Cut}(\widehat{a_{17}}\mathsf{Ax}(x_{14}, a_{17}), \widehat{x_7}\mathsf{Ax}(x_7, a_{11}))), a_{14})$$
$$\xrightarrow{\mathrm{excut}^+} \mathsf{INC}_R(\widehat{x x_5}\widehat{a_{11}}\mathsf{Ax}(x_5, a_{11}), a_{14})$$

Fig. 7. A cut-elimination of INC

3.5 Crabbe's Counterexample

The (counter)example we consider now is known as *Crabbe's counterexample* and consists in R $: A \to B \wedge (A \Rightarrow \perp)$. The open-terms associated with it are:

$$\langle\!| \vdash a : B \wedge (A \Rightarrow \perp) |\!\rangle = \mathsf{And}_R(\widehat{b}M_1, \widehat{c}\mathsf{Imp}_R(\widehat{x}\widehat{b'}M_2, c), a)$$
$$\langle\!| x : B \wedge (A \Rightarrow \perp) \vdash |\!\rangle = \mathsf{And}_L(\widehat{y}\widehat{z}\mathsf{Imp}_L(\widehat{y'}\mathsf{False}_L(y'),$$
$$\widehat{a}M, z), x)$$

The reduction

$$\mathsf{Cut}(\widehat{a}\mathsf{And}_R(\widehat{b}M_1, \widehat{c}\mathsf{Imp}_R(\widehat{x}\widehat{b'}M_2, c), a),$$
$$\widehat{x}\mathsf{And}_L(\widehat{y}\widehat{z}\mathsf{Imp}_L(\widehat{y'}\mathsf{False}_L(y'), \widehat{a}M, z), x))$$
$$\overset{\mathsf{cut}}{\longrightarrow}{}^* \mathsf{Cut}(\widehat{b}M_1, \widehat{y}\mathsf{Cut}(\widehat{a}M, \widehat{x}M_2))$$

is replaced by

$$\mathsf{Cut}(\widehat{a}\mathsf{R}_R(\widehat{b}M_1, \widehat{x}\widehat{b'}M_2, a), \widehat{x}\mathsf{R}_L(\widehat{y}\widehat{a}M, x))$$
$$\to \mathsf{Cut}(\widehat{b}M_1, \widehat{y}\mathsf{Cut}(\widehat{a}M, \widehat{x}M_2))$$

with *ad hoc* conditions on freshly introduced variables. Let us define the two following terms.

$$\delta \triangleq \mathsf{R}_L(\widehat{y}\widehat{a}\mathsf{Ax}(x, a), x)$$
$$\Delta \triangleq \mathsf{R}_R(\widehat{b}\mathsf{Ax}(z, b), \widehat{x}\widehat{b'}\delta, c)$$

The following reduction does not terminate:

$$\mathsf{Cut}(\widehat{c}\Delta, \widehat{x}\delta)$$
$$= \mathsf{Cut}(\widehat{c}\Delta, \widehat{x}\mathsf{R}_L(\widehat{y}\widehat{a}\mathsf{Ax}(x, a), x))$$
$$\quad \mathsf{R}_L(\widehat{y}\widehat{a}\mathsf{Ax}(x, a), x) \text{ does not freshly introduce } x$$
$$\to \mathsf{R}_L(\widehat{y}\widehat{a}\mathsf{Ax}(x, a), x)[x := \widehat{c}\Delta]$$
$$= \mathsf{Cut}(\widehat{c}\Delta, \widehat{x}\mathsf{R}_L(\widehat{y}\widehat{a}\mathsf{Ax}(x, a)[x := \widehat{c}\Delta], x))$$
$$= \mathsf{Cut}(\widehat{c}\Delta, \widehat{x}\mathsf{R}_L(\widehat{y}\widehat{a}\Delta[c \mapsto a], a))$$
$$=_\alpha \mathsf{Cut}(\widehat{c}\Delta, \widehat{x}\mathsf{R}_L(\widehat{y}\widehat{c}\Delta, a))$$
$$= \mathsf{Cut}(\widehat{c}\mathsf{R}_R(\widehat{b}\mathsf{Ax}(z, b), \widehat{x}\widehat{b'}\delta, c), \widehat{x}\mathsf{R}_L(\widehat{y}\widehat{c}\Delta, a))$$
$$\to \mathsf{Cut}(\widehat{c}\mathsf{Cut}(\widehat{b}\mathsf{Ax}(z, b), \widehat{y}\Delta), \widehat{x}\delta)$$
$$\quad \Delta \text{ does not freshly introduces } y$$
$$\to \mathsf{Cut}(\widehat{c}\Delta[y := \widehat{b}\mathsf{Ax}(z, b)], \widehat{x}\delta)$$
$$= \mathsf{Cut}(\widehat{c}\Delta, \widehat{x}\delta)$$
$$\to \ldots$$

This proposition rewrite rules thus breaks cut-elimination. It obviously does not satisfy Hypothesis 1.

3.6 A Convergent Presentation of Russel's Paradox

This interesting example has first been exposed for deduction modulo in [DW03]. It will be adapted here for superdeduction. Let us consider these two proposition rewrite rules.

$$\mathsf{R}^1 : R \in R \quad \to \quad \forall y.(y \simeq R \Rightarrow (R \in y \Rightarrow \perp))$$
$$\mathsf{R}^2 : y \simeq z \quad \to \quad \forall y.(x \in y \Rightarrow z \in y)$$

The associated inference rules are

$$R_R^1 \; \frac{\Gamma, y \simeq R, R \in y \vdash \Delta}{\Gamma \vdash R \in R, \Delta} \; y \notin \mathcal{FV}(\Gamma, \Delta) \qquad R_L^1 \; \frac{\Gamma \vdash R \in t, \Delta \qquad \Gamma \vdash t \simeq R, \Delta}{\Gamma, R \in R \vdash \Delta}$$

$$R_R^2 \; \frac{\Gamma, x \in t_1 \vdash x \in t_2, \Delta}{\Gamma \vdash t_1 \simeq t_2, \Delta} \; x \notin \mathcal{FV}(\Gamma, \Delta) \qquad R_L^2 \; \frac{\Gamma, t \in t_2 \vdash \Delta \qquad \Gamma \vdash t \in t_1, \Delta}{\Gamma, t_1 \simeq t_2 \vdash \Delta}$$

Then we can prove $\vdash \bot$.

$$R_L^2 \; \cfrac{\text{Ax} \; \cfrac{}{R \in R, R \in y \vdash R \in R, \bot} \qquad \text{Ax} \; \cfrac{}{R \in y \vdash R \in y, R \in R, \bot}}{y \simeq R, R \in y \vdash R \in R, \bot}$$

$$R_L^1 \; \cfrac{\text{Ax} \; \cfrac{}{R \in R \vdash R \in R, \bot} \qquad R_L^2 \; \cfrac{\text{Ax} \; \cfrac{}{R \in R, x \in R \vdash x \in R, \bot}}{R \in R \vdash R \simeq R, \bot}}{R \in R \vdash \bot}$$

$$\text{CUT} \; \cfrac{y \simeq R, R \in y, R \in R \vdash \bot \qquad \cdots\cdots\cdots\cdots\cdots}{}$$

$$R_R^1 \; \cfrac{y \simeq R, R \in y \vdash \bot}{\vdash R \in R, \bot}$$

$$\text{CUT} \; \cfrac{}{\vdash \bot}$$

The deduction system is not consistent and since there is no cut-free proof of $\vdash \bot$, strong normalisation of the cut-reduction does not hold. The set of proposition rewrite rules $\{R^1, R^2\}$ does not satisfy the hypothesis of Theorem 2 because of the constant R in $R \in R$ which also plays a central role in the proof of $\vdash \bot$.

3.7 Lemuridæ

All these properties led us to develop a proof assistant based on the super sequent calculus: lemuridæ. It features extended deduction rules derivation with focussing, rewriting on first-order terms, proof building with the associated superdeduction system, as well as some basic automatic tactics. It is implemented with the TOM [MR06] language, which provides powerful (associative) rewriting capabilities and strategic programmation on top of JAVA. The choice of the TOM language has several beneficial consequences. First of all, the expressiveness of the language allows for clean and short code. This is in particular the case of the micro proofchecker, whose patterns faithfully translate deduction rules of sequent calculus. Thus, the proofchecker is only one hundred lines long and it is therefore more realistic to convince everyone that it is actually sound.

The other main contribution of TOM to lemuridæ is the expression of tacticals by strategies. The TOM strategy language is directly inspired from early research on ELAN [VB98] and ρ-calculus and allows to compose basic strategies to express complex programs using strategies combinators. In this formalism, a naive proof search tactical is simply expressed by $topdown(elim)$, where $topdown$ is a "call-by-name" strategy and $elim$ has the usual semantics of the corresponding command.

4   Full Proofs of the Principles

In this section we provide the full proofs of Theorem 2. Let us prove first the following simple result.

Lemma 2. *For some well-typed open-term* $C \triangleright \Gamma \vdash \Delta$ *whose open leaves are* $\square \triangleright \Gamma_i \vdash \Delta_i$ *for* $1 \leqslant i \leqslant n_C$, *for some* σ *covering* C, *if for all* $1 \leqslant i \leqslant n_C$, $M_i \triangleright \sigma\Gamma_i \vdash \sigma\Delta_i$ *is a well-typed term, then* $\sigma C[M_1, \ldots, M_{n_C}] \triangleright \sigma\Gamma \vdash \sigma\Delta$ *is a well-typed term.*

Proof. We proceed by induction on the context C.

– If it is $\square \triangleright \Gamma \vdash \Delta$, typed by $\Gamma \vdash \Delta$, then its type inference derivation is the single leaf

$$\overline{\square \triangleright \Gamma \vdash \Delta}$$

and $n_C = 1$. As by hypothesis $M_1 \triangleright \sigma\Gamma \vdash \sigma\Delta$ is well-typed, and as by definition $\sigma C[M_1] = M_1$, $\sigma C[M_1] \triangleright \sigma\Gamma \vdash \sigma\Delta$ is well-typed.

– If it is $\mathsf{Ax}(x, a)$, typed by $\Gamma', x : \varphi \vdash a : \varphi, \Delta'$. then its type inference derivation has no leaf since it is

$$\mathrm{AX} \; \overline{\mathsf{Ax}(x, a) \triangleright \Gamma', x : \varphi \vdash a : \varphi, \Delta'}$$

Then $C = \sigma C[]$ is a term and $\sigma C[] \triangleright \sigma\Gamma \vdash \sigma\Delta$ is a well-typed term.

– If it is $\mathsf{And}_R(\widehat{b}C_1, \widehat{c}C_2, a)$, the type inference is

$$\wedge_R \; \frac{\cdots \quad\quad\quad\quad\quad\quad\quad \cdots}{\dfrac{C_1 \triangleright \Gamma \vdash b : \varphi_1, \Delta' \quad\quad C_2 \triangleright \Gamma \vdash c : \varphi_2, \Delta'}{\mathsf{And}_R(\widehat{b}C_1, \widehat{c}C_2, a) \triangleright \Gamma \vdash a : \varphi_1 \wedge \varphi_2, \Delta'}}$$

By induction hypothesis,

$$\sigma C_1[M_1, \ldots, M_{n_{C_1}}] \triangleright \sigma\Gamma, b : \sigma\varphi_1, \sigma\Delta'$$

and

$$\sigma C_2[M_{n_{C_1}+1}, \ldots, M_{n_{C_1}+n_{C_2}}] \triangleright \sigma\Gamma, c : \sigma\varphi_2, \sigma\Delta'$$

are well-typed. Then

$$\sigma C[M_1, \ldots, M_{n_C}] \triangleright \sigma\Gamma \vdash a : \sigma\varphi_1 \wedge \sigma\varphi_2, \sigma\Delta'$$

is well-typed.

– If it is $\mathsf{Exists}_R(\widehat{a}C_1, \alpha, b)$, the type inference is

$$\exists_R \; \frac{\cdots}{\dfrac{C_1 \triangleright \Gamma \vdash a : \varphi[\mathsf{x} := \alpha], \Delta'}{\mathsf{Exists}_R(\widehat{a}C_1, \alpha, b) \triangleright \Gamma \vdash b : \exists\mathsf{x}.\varphi, \Delta'}}$$

By induction hypothesis,

$$\sigma C_1[M_1, \ldots, M_{n_C}] \triangleright \sigma\Gamma \vdash a : (\sigma\varphi)[\mathsf{x} := \sigma\alpha], \sigma\Delta'$$

is well-typed and then

$$\sigma C[M_1, \ldots, M_{n_C}] \rhd \sigma \Gamma \vdash b : \exists x.\sigma \varphi, \sigma \Delta'$$

is well-typed.

– If it is $\mathsf{Exists}_L(\widehat{x}\widehat{x}C_1, y)$, the type inference is

$$\exists_L \frac{C_1 \rhd \Gamma, x : \varphi \vdash \Delta'}{\mathsf{Exists}_L(\widehat{x}\widehat{x}C_1, y) \rhd \Gamma, y : \exists x.\varphi \vdash \Delta'} \, x \notin \mathcal{FV}(\Gamma, \Delta')$$

By induction hypothesis,

$$\sigma C_1[M_1, \ldots, M_{n_C}] \rhd \sigma \Gamma, x : \sigma \varphi \vdash \sigma \Delta'$$

is well-typed, and then

$$\sigma C[M_1, \ldots, M_{n_C}] \rhd \sigma \Gamma, y : \exists x.\sigma \varphi \vdash \sigma \Delta'$$

is well-typed.

– other cases are similar.

$\square$

Subject reduction is implied by Lemmas 2 and 1.

Lemma 3 (Subject Reduction). *If* $M \xrightarrow{\mathsf{excut}^*} M'$ *and* $M \rhd \Gamma \vdash \Delta$ *is well-typed, then* $M' \rhd \Gamma \vdash \Delta$ *is well-typed.*

Proof. By inspection of the rules defining $\xrightarrow{\mathsf{excut}}$. $\square$

We define a rewrite system denoted $\xrightarrow{\mathsf{prop}}$ on propositions by turning each proposition rewrite rule into a rewrite rule in the standard way (see for example [DHK03]). We define a rewrite system denoted $\xrightarrow{\mathsf{term}}$ on extended proof-terms as follows. It contains for each $\mathsf{R} : P \to \varphi$ the rewrite rule

$$\sigma \mathsf{R}_R \left(\widehat{x}_1 \ldots \widehat{x}_p, \left(\widehat{x_1^i} \ldots \widehat{x_{p_i}^i} \widehat{a_1^i} \ldots \widehat{a_{q_i}^i} M_i \right)_{1 \leqslant i \leqslant n}, \alpha_1 \ldots \alpha_q, a \right) \xrightarrow{\mathsf{term}} \sigma \langle\!| \vdash a : \varphi |\!\rangle [M_1, \ldots, M_n]$$

where σ is a substitution over placeholder-terms covering $\langle\!| \vdash a : \varphi |\!\rangle$ (here the bound names and conames of this later open-term are supposed different from the free and bound names and conames of $\mathsf{R}_R(\ldots)$) and the rewrite rule

$$\sigma \mathsf{R}_L \left(\widehat{y}_1 \ldots \widehat{y}_r, \left(\widehat{y_1^j} \ldots \widehat{y_{r_j}^j} \widehat{b_1^j} \ldots \widehat{b_{s_j}^j} N_j \right)_{1 \leqslant j \leqslant m}, \beta_1 \ldots \beta_s, x \right) \xrightarrow{\mathsf{term}} \sigma \langle\!| x : \varphi \vdash |\!\rangle [N_1, \ldots, N_m]$$

where σ is a substitution over placeholder-terms covering $\langle\!| x : \varphi \vdash |\!\rangle$ (here the bound names and conames of this later open-term are supposed different from the free and bound names and conames of $\mathsf{R}_L(\ldots)$).

As $\xrightarrow{\text{term}}$ is orthogonal, it is confluent. Besides if $\xrightarrow{\text{term}}$ is confluent and weakly normalising, then the unique normal form of an extended term M is denoted $M \downarrow^{\text{t}}$. Similarly if $\xrightarrow{\text{prop}}$ is confluent and weakly normalising, then the unique normal form of a formula φ is denoted $\varphi \downarrow^{\text{p}}$. This notation is extended to contexts and sequents. It is also extended to open-terms, since they also contain sequents through the $\square \triangleright \Gamma \vdash \Delta$ constructor.

Let us prove now that $\xrightarrow{\text{excut}}$ is strongly normalising on well-typed extended terms under the following hypothesis.

Hypothesis 1. *For a set of proposition rewrite rules $\mathcal{R}$, the rewrite relation $\xrightarrow{\text{prop}}$ associated with $\mathcal{R}$ is weakly normalising and confluent and for each of its rule $\mathsf{R} : P \to \varphi$:*

- *P contains only first-order variables (no function or constant);*
- *$\mathcal{FV}(\varphi) \subseteq \mathcal{FV}(P)$.*

The second hypothesis restricts the use of first-order constants and functions in particular to avoid counterexamples such as the presentation of Russel's paradox from [DW03] and presented in Section 3 for which the set of proposition rewrite rules terminates but the cut-elimination does not.

Now let us begin our strong normalisation proof with the following lemmas. First, if no proper subterm of M introduces some name or coname and if $M \xrightarrow{\text{term}}^* M'$, then no proper subterm of M' introduces this name of coname. This remark allows to prove the following lemma.

Lemma 4. *If $M \xrightarrow{\text{term}} M'$ then M freshly introduces some name or coname is equivalent to M' freshly introduces this name of coname.*

By definition of $\xrightarrow{\text{term}}$ with respect to substitutions over first-order variables, the following lemma is straightforward.

Lemma 5. *If $M \xrightarrow{\text{term}} M'$, then for all substitution $[x := t]$, $M[x := t] \xrightarrow{\text{term}} M'[x := t]$. This result extends obviously to $\xrightarrow{\text{term}}^*$.*

This allows to prove the following corollary.

Corollary 1. *If $\xrightarrow{\text{term}}$ is weakly normalising, for all M and $[x := t]$, $(M[x := t]) \downarrow^{\text{t}} = (M \downarrow^{\text{t}})[x := t]$.*

Proof. By Lemma 5 and since $M \xrightarrow{\text{term}}^* M \downarrow^{\text{t}}$, then $M[x := t] \xrightarrow{\text{term}}^* (M \downarrow^{\text{t}})[x := t]$. Moreover it is to be noticed that by definition of $\xrightarrow{\text{term}}$ and for all term N, N contains a redex for $\xrightarrow{\text{term}}$ implies that $N[x := t]$ contains a redex. Therefore $(M \downarrow^{\text{t}})[x := t]$ is a normal form for $\xrightarrow{\text{term}}$ and it is $(M[x := t]) \downarrow^{\text{t}}$. $\qquad\square$

We supposed that in any proposition rewrite rule $\mathsf{R} : P \to \varphi$, P (which is a predicate) only contains first-order variables, and no first-order constant or function. Thus it implies the following lemma.

Lemma 6. *Let φ and φ' be some first-order formulæ such that $\varphi \xrightarrow{\text{prop}} \varphi'$. Let $\times$ be some first-order variable and t be some first-order term. Then $\varphi[\times := t] \xrightarrow{\text{prop}} \varphi'[\times := t]$*

Proof. We first suppose that the reduction $\varphi \xrightarrow{\text{prop}} \varphi'$ is done at the head of φ. If the reduction takes place inside a context, we proceed by induction on this context. □

This result is extended to $\xrightarrow{\text{prop}}^*$ in the obvious way. Besides, it implies the following corollary.

Corollary 2. *Let φ be some first-order formula. Let x be some first-order variable and t be some first-order term. Then $(\varphi[x := t]) \downarrow^P = \varphi \downarrow^P [x := t]$.*

Proof. As $\varphi \xrightarrow{\text{prop}}^* \varphi \downarrow^P$, by Lemma 6, $\varphi[x := t] \xrightarrow{\text{prop}}^* \varphi \downarrow^P [x := t]$. If this later formula contains some redex, this redex is an instance of $P(x_1, \ldots, x_n)$. Then $\varphi \downarrow^P$ also contains an instance of $P(x_1, \ldots, x_n)$. This is a contradiction to the fact that $\varphi \downarrow^P$ is a normal form for $\xrightarrow{\text{prop}}$. Thus $\varphi \downarrow^P [x := t] = (\varphi[x := t]) \downarrow^P$. □

We can also prove a result similar to Corollary 2 on placeholder-terms substitutions.

Lemma 7. *Let φ be some first-order formula. Let σ be some placeholder-terms substitution. Then $(\sigma\varphi) \downarrow^P = \sigma(\varphi \downarrow^P)$.*

Proof. Similar to Corollary 2, with a lemma similar to Lemma 6. □

The last hypothesis we did on the set of proposition rewrite rule is that for each R : $P \to \varphi$, we have $\mathcal{FV}(\varphi) \subseteq \mathcal{FV}(P)$. It allows to prove the following lemma.

Lemma 8. *Let φ_1 and φ_2 be some formulæ such that $\varphi_1 \xrightarrow{\text{prop}} \varphi_2$. Then $\mathcal{FV}(\varphi_2) \subseteq \mathcal{FV}(\varphi_1)$.*

Proof. – If the reduction $\varphi_1 \xrightarrow{\text{prop}} \varphi_2$ takes place at the head of φ_1. Then for some R : $P(x_1, \ldots, x_p) \to \varphi$, φ_1 is $P(t_1, \ldots, t_p)$ where the t_i are first-order terms. Then φ_2 is $\varphi[(x_i := t_i)_{1 \leqslant i \leqslant p}]$. As the free variables of φ are by hypothesis included in $\{x_1, \ldots, x_p\}$, the free variables of φ_2 are included in $\mathcal{FV}(t_1) \cup \cdots \cup \mathcal{FV}(t_p)$, which is the set $\mathcal{FV}(\varphi_1)$.
 – If the reduction $\varphi_1 \xrightarrow{\text{prop}} \varphi_2$ takes place inside a context, we proceed by induction on this context.

□

This result is extended to $\xrightarrow{\text{prop}}^*$ in the obvious way.

Lemma 9. *Any open type inference derivation of $C \triangleright \Gamma \vdash \Delta$ with open leaves $\Box \triangleright \Gamma_i \vdash \Delta_i$ for $1 \leqslant i \leqslant n_C$ may be turned into an open type inference derivation of $C \downarrow^P \triangleright \Gamma \downarrow^P \vdash \Delta \downarrow^P$ with premises $\Box \triangleright \Gamma_i \downarrow^P \vdash \Delta_i \downarrow^P$.*

Proof. By induction on the open type inference derivation.

 – One of the base cases is for instance the axiom case : if $C = \text{Ax}(x, a)$, and $C \triangleright \Gamma', x : \varphi \vdash a : \varphi, \Delta'$ well-typed (by the axiom rule), then it is straightforward that $C \downarrow^P \triangleright \Gamma' \downarrow^P, x : \varphi \downarrow^P \vdash a : \varphi \downarrow^P, \Delta' \downarrow^P$ is well-typed.

– Let us treat the case of an open leaf : if $C = \square \triangleright \Gamma \vdash \Delta$, then $C \downarrow^P = \square \triangleright \Gamma \downarrow^P \vdash \Delta \downarrow^P$ is also well-typed.

$$\frac{(\square \triangleright \Gamma \downarrow^P \vdash \Delta \downarrow^P)}{\triangleright \Gamma \downarrow^P \vdash \Delta \downarrow^P}$$

– Let us treat the case of $\wedge_R$. In this case C is $\mathsf{And}_R(\widehat{b}C_1, \widehat{c}C_2, a)$ and the type inference derivation has the following form

$$\wedge_R \frac{\dfrac{(\square \triangleright \Gamma_i \vdash \Delta_i)_{i \in \{1,\dots,n_{C_1}\}}}{\cdots} \qquad \dfrac{(\square \triangleright \Gamma_i \vdash \Delta_i)_{i \in \{n_{C_1}+1,\dots,n_C\}}}{\cdots}}{C_1 \triangleright \Gamma \vdash b : \varphi_1, \Delta' \qquad C_2 \triangleright \Gamma \vdash c : \varphi_2, \Delta'}$$
$$\overline{C \triangleright \Gamma \vdash a : \varphi_1 \wedge \varphi_2, \Delta'}$$

Then by induction hypothesis on the open type inference derivations of C_1 and C_2, we obtain open type inference derivations of $C_1 \downarrow^P \triangleright \Gamma \downarrow^P \vdash b : \varphi_1 \downarrow^P, \Delta' \downarrow^P$ and of $C_2 \downarrow^P \triangleright \Gamma \downarrow^P \vdash c : \varphi_2 \downarrow^P, \Delta' \downarrow^P$ with open leaves $\square \triangleright \Gamma_i \downarrow^P \vdash \Delta_i \downarrow^P$. Finally as $(\varphi_1 \wedge \varphi_2) \downarrow^P = \varphi_1 \downarrow^P \wedge \varphi_2 \downarrow^P$ and $C \downarrow^P = \mathsf{And}_R(\widehat{b}C_1 \downarrow^P, \widehat{c}C_2 \downarrow^P, a)$ this gives using the rule $\wedge_R$ an open type inference derivation of $C \downarrow^P \triangleright \Gamma \downarrow^P \vdash \Delta \downarrow^P$.

– Let us treat the case of $\exists_R$. In this case C is $\mathsf{Exists}_R(\widehat{b}C_1, \alpha, a)$ and the type inference derivation has the following form.

$$\exists_R \frac{\dfrac{(\square \triangleright \Gamma_i \vdash \Delta_i)_{1 \leqslant i \leqslant n_C}}{\cdots}}{C_1 \triangleright \Gamma \vdash b : \varphi[x := \alpha], \Delta'}$$
$$\overline{C \triangleright \Gamma \vdash a : \exists x.\varphi, \Delta'}$$

Then by induction hypothesis on the open type inference derivations of C_1, we obtain an open type derivation of $C_1 \downarrow^P \triangleright \Gamma \downarrow^P \vdash (\varphi[x := \alpha]) \downarrow^P, \Delta' \downarrow^P$ with open leaves $\square \triangleright \Gamma_i \downarrow^P \vdash \Delta_i \downarrow^P$. By Corollary 2 $(\varphi[x := \alpha]) \downarrow^P$ is equal to $\varphi \downarrow^P [x := \alpha]$. Finally as $(\exists x.\varphi) \downarrow^P = \exists x.(\varphi) \downarrow^P$ and as $C \downarrow^P = \mathsf{Exists}_R(\widehat{b}C_1, \alpha, a) \downarrow^P$, this give an open type inference derivation of $C \downarrow^P \triangleright \Gamma \downarrow^P \vdash \Delta \downarrow^P$.

– Let us treat the case of $\exists_L$. In this case C is $\mathsf{Exists}_L(\widehat{y}xC_1, x)$ and the type inference derivation has the following form.

$$\exists_L \frac{\dfrac{(\square \triangleright \Gamma_i \vdash \Delta_i)_{1 \leqslant i \leqslant n_C}}{\cdots}}{C_1 \triangleright \Gamma', y : \varphi \vdash \Delta} \quad x \notin \mathcal{FV}(\Gamma', \Delta)$$
$$\overline{\mathsf{Exists}_L(\widehat{y}xC_1, x) \triangleright \Gamma', x : \exists x.\varphi \vdash \Delta}$$

Then by induction hypothesis on the open type inference derivation of C_1, we obtain an open type inference derivation of $C_1 \downarrow^P \triangleright \Gamma' \downarrow^P, y : \varphi \downarrow^P \vdash \Delta \downarrow^P$ with open leaves $\square \triangleright \Gamma_i \downarrow^P \vdash \Delta_i \downarrow^P$. First of all by Lemma 8 and as $x \notin \mathcal{FV}(\Gamma', \Delta)$, x is not in $\mathcal{FV}(\Gamma' \downarrow^P, \Delta \downarrow^P)$. Furthermore $(\exists x.\varphi) \downarrow^P = \exists x.(\varphi) \downarrow^P$. Since $C \downarrow^P = \mathsf{Exists}_L(\widehat{y}xC_1 \downarrow^P, x)$, we can build an open type inference derivation of $C \downarrow^P \triangleright \Gamma \downarrow^P \vdash \Delta \downarrow^P$.

– other cases are similar.

$\square$

Lemma 10. *If $M \rhd \Gamma \vdash \Delta$ is well-typed, then there exists M' such that $M' \rhd \Gamma \downarrow^{\mathsf{P}} \vdash \Delta \downarrow^{\mathsf{P}}$ is well-typed. Besides $M \xrightarrow{\text{term}} M'$ and M' is a normal form, denoted $M \xrightarrow{\text{term!}} M'$.*

Proof. By induction on the type inference derivation of $M \rhd \Gamma \vdash \Delta$.

- If the bottom rule of the derivation is for instance the Ax rule. M is $\mathsf{Ax}(x, a)$ and the derivation is

$$\text{AX} \; \frac{}{\mathsf{Ax}(x, a) \rhd \Gamma', x : \varphi \vdash a : \varphi, \Delta'}$$

Then we can build the following derivation.

$$\text{AX} \; \frac{}{\mathsf{Ax}(x, a) \rhd \Gamma' \downarrow^{\mathsf{P}}, x : \varphi \downarrow^{\mathsf{P}} \vdash a : \varphi \downarrow^{\mathsf{P}}, \Delta' \downarrow^{\mathsf{P}}}$$

Finally we can check that $M \xrightarrow{\text{term!}} \mathsf{Ax}(x, a)$.

- If the bottom rule of the derivation is for instance the $\wedge_R$ rule. M is $\mathsf{And}_R(\widehat{b}M_1, \widehat{c}M_2, c)$ and the derivation is

$$\wedge_R \; \frac{M_1 \rhd \Gamma \vdash b : \varphi_1, \Delta' \qquad M_2 \rhd \Gamma \vdash c : \varphi_2, \Delta'}{M \rhd \Gamma \vdash a : \varphi_1 \wedge \varphi_2, \Delta'}$$

By induction hypothesis there exists M_1' and M_2' such that $M_1' \rhd \Gamma \downarrow^{\mathsf{P}} \vdash b : \varphi_1 \downarrow^{\mathsf{P}}, \Delta' \downarrow^{\mathsf{P}}$ and $M_2' \rhd \Gamma \downarrow^{\mathsf{P}} \vdash c : \varphi_2 \downarrow^{\mathsf{P}}, \Delta' \downarrow^{\mathsf{P}}$ are well-typed. Then we can build the following derivation.

$$\wedge_R \; \frac{M_1' \rhd \Gamma \downarrow^{\mathsf{P}} \vdash b : \varphi_1 \downarrow^{\mathsf{P}}, \Delta' \downarrow^{\mathsf{P}} \qquad M_2' \rhd \Gamma \downarrow^{\mathsf{P}} \vdash c : \varphi_2 \downarrow^{\mathsf{P}}, \Delta' \downarrow^{\mathsf{P}}}{M' \rhd \Gamma \downarrow^{\mathsf{P}} \vdash a : \varphi_1 \downarrow^{\mathsf{P}} \wedge \varphi_2 \downarrow^{\mathsf{P}}, \Delta' \downarrow^{\mathsf{P}}}$$

where M' stands for $\mathsf{And}_R(\widehat{b}M_1', \widehat{c}M_2', c)$. Finally as $\varphi_1 \downarrow^{\mathsf{P}} \wedge \varphi_2 \downarrow^{\mathsf{P}} = (\varphi \wedge \varphi_2) \downarrow^{\mathsf{P}}$ we have found M' such that $M' \rhd \Gamma \downarrow^{\mathsf{P}} \vdash \Delta \downarrow^{\mathsf{P}}$ is well-typed and such that $M \xrightarrow{\text{term!}} M'$.

- If the bottom rule of the derivation is for instance $\exists_R$, M is $\mathsf{Exists}_R(\widehat{b}M_1, t, a)$ and the derivation is

$$\exists_R \; \frac{M_1 \rhd \Gamma \vdash a : \varphi[\mathsf{x} := t], \Delta'}{M \rhd \Gamma \vdash a : \exists \mathsf{x}.\varphi, \Delta'}$$

By induction hypothesis there exists M_1' such that $M_1' \rhd \Gamma \downarrow^{\mathsf{P}} \vdash a : \varphi[\mathsf{x} := t] \downarrow^{\mathsf{P}}, \Delta' \downarrow^{\mathsf{P}}$ is well-typed. By Corollary 2, $\varphi[\mathsf{x} := t] \downarrow^{\mathsf{P}} = \varphi \downarrow^{\mathsf{P}} [\mathsf{x} := t]$ and then we can build the derivation.

$$\exists_R \; \frac{M_1' \rhd \Gamma \downarrow^{\mathsf{P}} \vdash a : \varphi \downarrow^{\mathsf{P}} [\mathsf{x} := t], \Delta' \downarrow^{\mathsf{P}}}{M' \rhd \Gamma \downarrow^{\mathsf{P}} \vdash a : \exists \mathsf{x}.\varphi \downarrow^{\mathsf{P}}, \Delta' \downarrow^{\mathsf{P}}}$$

where M' stands for $\mathsf{Exists}_R(\widehat{b}M_1', t, a)$. Finally as $(\exists \mathsf{x}.\varphi) \downarrow^{\mathsf{P}} = \exists \mathsf{x}.\varphi \downarrow^{\mathsf{P}}$, we have found M' such that $M' \rhd \Gamma \downarrow^{\mathsf{P}} \vdash \Delta \downarrow^{\mathsf{P}}$ is well-typed and $M \xrightarrow{\text{term!}} M'$.

– If the bottom rule of the derivation is for instance $\exists_L$, M is $\mathsf{Exists}_L(\widehat{y}\mathsf{x}M_1, x)$ and the derivation is

$$\exists_L \frac{\cdots}{M \rhd \Gamma', x : \exists \mathsf{x}.\varphi \vdash \Delta} \, x \notin \mathcal{FV}(\Gamma', \Delta)$$

By induction hypothesis there exists M_1' such that $M_1' \rhd \Gamma' \downarrow^\mathsf{P}, x : \varphi \downarrow^\mathsf{P}\vdash \Delta \downarrow^\mathsf{P}$ is well-typed. As $x \notin \mathcal{FV}(\Gamma', \Delta)$ and by Lemma 8, $x \notin \mathcal{FV}(\Gamma' \downarrow^\mathsf{P}, \Delta \downarrow^\mathsf{P})$, we can build the following derivation.

$$\exists_L \frac{\cdots \quad M_1' \rhd \Gamma' \downarrow^\mathsf{P}, y : \varphi \downarrow^\mathsf{P}\vdash \Delta \downarrow^\mathsf{P}}{M' \rhd \Gamma' \downarrow^\mathsf{P}, x : \exists \mathsf{x}.\varphi \downarrow^\mathsf{P}\vdash \Delta \downarrow^\mathsf{P}} \, x \notin \mathcal{FV}(\Gamma' \downarrow^\mathsf{P}, \Delta \downarrow^\mathsf{P})$$

where M' stands for $\mathsf{Exists}_L(\widehat{y}\mathsf{x}M_1', x)$. Finally as $\exists \mathsf{x}.\varphi \downarrow^\mathsf{P}= \exists \mathsf{x}.\varphi \downarrow^\mathsf{P}$, we have found M' such as $M' \rhd \Gamma \downarrow^\mathsf{P}\vdash \Delta \downarrow^\mathsf{P}$ is well-typed and $M \xrightarrow{\text{term!}} M'$.

– If the bottom rule of the derivation is not an extended rule, other cases are similar.
– If the bottom rule of the derivation is an extended rule, say R_R for $R : P \to \varphi$, it has the form

$$\mathsf{R}_R \frac{(M_i \rhd \Gamma_i \vdash \Delta_i)_i}{\mathsf{R}_R(\ldots, (\ldots M_i)_i, \ldots, a) \rhd \Gamma \vdash a : P, \Delta'} \, \mathcal{C}$$

Let us denote $\mathcal{C} = \langle\!\vert \vdash a : \varphi \vert\!\rangle$. By induction hypothesis there exists $M_1', \ldots, M_{n_\mathcal{C}}'$ such that for all i, $M_i' \rhd \Gamma_i \downarrow^\mathsf{P}\vdash \Delta_i \downarrow^\mathsf{P}$ is well-typed and $M_i \xrightarrow{\text{term!}} M_i'$. Besides by Lemma 1, there exists a substitution for placeholder-terms σ and an open type inference derivation whose open leaves are the $\square \rhd \Gamma_i' \vdash \Delta_i'$ with $\sigma\Gamma_i' = \Gamma_i$ and $\sigma\Delta_i' = \Delta_i$ for all i and whose conclusion is $\mathcal{C} \rhd \Gamma \vdash a : \varphi, \Delta'$. By Lemma 9, this open type inference derivation can be turned into one with open leaves $\square \rhd \Gamma_i' \downarrow^\mathsf{P}\vdash \Delta_i' \downarrow^\mathsf{P}$ and with conclusion $\mathcal{C} \downarrow^\mathsf{P} \rhd\Gamma \downarrow^\mathsf{P}\vdash a : \varphi \downarrow^\mathsf{P}, \Delta' \downarrow^\mathsf{P}$. Let us notice that for all i and by Lemma 7, $\Gamma_i \downarrow^\mathsf{P}= (\sigma\Gamma_i') \downarrow^\mathsf{P}= \sigma(\Gamma_i' \downarrow^\mathsf{P})$ and $\Delta_i \downarrow^\mathsf{P}= (\sigma\Delta_i') \downarrow^\mathsf{P}= \sigma(\Delta_i' \downarrow^\mathsf{P})$. Thus by Lemma 2, $\sigma\mathcal{C} \downarrow^\mathsf{P} [(M_i')_i] \rhd \sigma(\Gamma \downarrow^\mathsf{P}) \vdash a : \sigma(\varphi \downarrow^\mathsf{P}), \sigma(\Delta' \downarrow^\mathsf{P})$ is well-typed. Since $\sigma\Gamma \downarrow^\mathsf{P}= \Gamma \downarrow^\mathsf{P}$, $\sigma\varphi \downarrow^\mathsf{P}= \varphi \downarrow^\mathsf{P}$ and $\sigma\Delta' \downarrow^\mathsf{P}= \Delta' \downarrow^\mathsf{P}$ (Γ, φ and Δ' appear in a derivation in the super sequent calculus and therefore do not contain placeholder-terms !) and since $P \downarrow^\mathsf{P}= \varphi \downarrow^\mathsf{P}$, this is a type inference of $\sigma\mathcal{C} \downarrow^\mathsf{P} [(M_i')_i] \rhd \Gamma \downarrow^\mathsf{P}\vdash a : P \downarrow^\mathsf{P}, \Delta' \downarrow^\mathsf{P}$. Finally as for all i, $M_i \xrightarrow{\text{term!}} M_i'$, then

$$\begin{aligned} M &= \mathsf{R}_R(\ldots, (\ldots M_i)_i, \ldots, a) \\ &\xrightarrow{\text{term}} \sigma\mathcal{C}[(M_i)_i] = \sigma\mathcal{C} \downarrow^\mathsf{P} [(M_i)_i] \\ &\xrightarrow{\text{term}} \sigma\mathcal{C} \downarrow^\mathsf{P} [(M_i')_i] \end{aligned}$$

As this later term is a normal form, $M \xrightarrow{\text{term!}} \sigma\mathcal{C} \downarrow^\mathsf{P} [(M_i')_i]$.

$\square$

Corollary 3. $\xrightarrow{\text{term}}$ *is weakly normalising on well-typed extended terms. Moreover for all* $M \rhd \Gamma \vdash \Delta$ *well-typed,* $M \downarrow^\mathsf{t} \rhd \Gamma \downarrow^\mathsf{P}\vdash \Delta \downarrow^\mathsf{P}$ *is well-typed in Urban's type system.*

Proof. From Lemma 10.   □

Lemma 11. *If* $M \xrightarrow{\text{excut}} M'$, *then* $M \downarrow^{\text{t}} \xrightarrow{\text{cut}}^{+} M' \downarrow^{\text{t}}$.

Proof. Let us suppose first that the reduction $M \xrightarrow{\text{excut}} M'$ is done at the head of M. We can distinguish two cases.

– if the reduction is a $\xrightarrow{\text{cut}}$ reduction, then M is a redex for the $\xrightarrow{\text{cut}}$ reduction. Let us consider for instance the $\wedge$ case. Thus M has the form

$$\text{Cut}(\widehat{a}\text{And}_R(\widehat{b}M_1, \widehat{c}M_2, a), \widehat{x}\text{And}_L(\widehat{y}\widehat{z}N, x))$$

where $\text{And}_R(\widehat{b}M_1, \widehat{c}M_2, a)$ and $\text{And}_L(\widehat{y}\widehat{z}N, x)$ freshly introduces a and x and M' may have the form

$$\text{Cut}(\widehat{b}M_1, \widehat{y}\text{Cut}(\widehat{c}M_2, \widehat{z}N)) \text{ (case 1)}$$

or the form

$$\text{Cut}(\widehat{c}M_2, \widehat{z}\text{Cut}(\widehat{b}M_1, \widehat{y}N)) \text{ (case 2)}$$

Then $M \downarrow^{\text{t}}$ is

$$\text{Cut}(\widehat{a}\text{And}_R(\widehat{b}M_1 \downarrow^{\text{t}}, \widehat{c}M_2 \downarrow^{\text{t}}, a), \widehat{x}\text{And}_L(\widehat{y}\widehat{z}N \downarrow^{\text{t}}, x))$$

where $\text{And}_R(\widehat{b}M_1 \downarrow^{\text{t}}, \widehat{c}M_2 \downarrow^{\text{t}}, a)$ and $\text{And}_L(\widehat{y}\widehat{z}N \downarrow^{\text{t}}, x)$ freshly introduces a and x (Lemma 4) and reduces in one step into

$$\text{Cut}(\widehat{b}M_1 \downarrow^{\text{t}}, \widehat{y}\text{Cut}(\widehat{c}M_2 \downarrow^{\text{t}}, \widehat{z}N \downarrow^{\text{t}}))$$

and also into

$$\text{Cut}(\widehat{c}M_2 \downarrow^{\text{t}}, \widehat{z}\text{Cut}(\widehat{b}M_1 \downarrow^{\text{t}}, \widehat{y}N \downarrow^{\text{t}}))$$

The first is $M' \downarrow^{\text{t}}$ in case 1, the second is $M' \downarrow^{\text{t}}$ in case 2. So in both cases, $M \downarrow^{\text{t}} \xrightarrow{\text{cut}}^{+} M' \downarrow^{\text{t}}$.

– If the reduction is a $\xrightarrow{\text{cut}}$ reduction, let us consider for instance the $\exists$ case. Thus M has the form

$$\text{Cut}(\widehat{a}\text{Exists}_R(\widehat{b}M, t, a), \widehat{x}\text{Exists}_L(\widehat{y}\widehat{x}N, x))$$

where $\text{Exists}_R(\widehat{b}M, t, a)$ freshly introduces a and M' is

$$\text{Cut}(\widehat{b}M, \widehat{y}N[x := t])$$

Then $M \downarrow^{\text{t}}$ is

$$\text{Cut}(\widehat{a}\text{Exists}_R(\widehat{b}M \downarrow^{\text{t}}, t, a), \widehat{x}\text{Exists}_L(\widehat{y}\widehat{x}N \downarrow^{\text{t}}, x))$$

where $\text{Exists}_R(\widehat{b}M \downarrow^{\text{t}}, t, a)$ freshly introduces a (Lemma 4) and reduces in one step into

$$\text{Cut}(\widehat{b}M, \widehat{y}N \downarrow^{\text{t}} [x := t])$$

By Corollary 1, $N \downarrow^{\text{t}} [x := t] = (N[x := t]) \downarrow^{\text{t}}$ and we obtain that the later one-step reduct of $M \downarrow^{\text{t}}$ is in fact $M' \downarrow^{\text{t}}$.

– If the reduction is a $\xrightarrow{\text{cut}}$ reduction, let us consider the case where M is

$$\mathsf{Cut}(\widehat{a}M_1, \widehat{x}M_2)$$

with M_1 does not freshly introduce a (the case where M_2 does not freshly introduce x is symmetrical) and M' is

$$M_1[a := \widehat{x}M_2]$$

Then $M \downarrow^{\text{t}}$ is

$$\mathsf{Cut}(\widehat{a}M_1 \downarrow^{\text{t}}, \widehat{x}M_2 \downarrow^{\text{t}})$$

and since $M_1 \downarrow^{\text{t}}$ does not freshly introduce a (Lemma 4), we deduce that it reduces to

$$M_1 \downarrow^{\text{t}} [a := \widehat{x}M_2 \downarrow^{\text{t}}]$$

As this later is a normal form and a reduct of M' for $\xrightarrow{\text{term}}$, it is $M' \downarrow^{\text{t}}$.

– Other cases of $\xrightarrow{\text{cut}}$ reductions are similar.
– If the reduction is a $\xrightarrow{\text{excut}}$ reduction, then M is of the form

$$\mathsf{Cut}(\widehat{a}\mathsf{R}_R(\ldots, (\ldots M_i)_i, \ldots, a), \widehat{x}\mathsf{R}_L(\ldots, (\ldots N_j)_j, \ldots, x))$$

with $\mathsf{R} : P \to \varphi$. Let us denote C_R and C_L respectively $\langle\!\vdash a : \varphi \,\rangle$ and $\langle\, x : \varphi \vdash\!\rangle$. Thus we may write the following reduction in $\xrightarrow{\text{term}}$.

$$\begin{aligned}
M &= \mathsf{Cut}(\widehat{a}\mathsf{R}_R((\ldots M_i)_i, a), \widehat{x}\mathsf{R}_L((\ldots N_j)_j, x)) \\
&\xrightarrow{\text{term}} \mathsf{Cut}(\widehat{a}\sigma C_R[(M_i)_i], \widehat{x}\sigma' C_L[(N_j)_j]) \\
&\xrightarrow{\text{term}} \mathsf{Cut}(\widehat{a}\sigma C_R[(M_i \downarrow^{\text{t}})_i], \widehat{x}\sigma' C_L[(N_j \downarrow^{\text{t}})_j])
\end{aligned}$$

where σ and σ' are *ad hoc* placeholder-term substitutions. As this later term is a normal form for $\xrightarrow{\text{term}}$, it is in fact $M \downarrow^{\text{t}}$. Besides by definition of $\xrightarrow{\text{excut}}$, there exists an open-term C such that $\mathsf{Cut}(\widehat{a}C_R, \widehat{x}C_L) \xrightarrow{\text{cut}^+} C$ with $M' = \sigma'' C[M_1, \ldots, N_p]$, and thus $M' \downarrow^{\text{t}} = \sigma'' C[M_1 \downarrow^{\text{t}}, \ldots, N_p \downarrow^{\text{t}}]$. As $\mathsf{Cut}(\widehat{a}C_R, \widehat{x}C_L) \xrightarrow{\text{cut}^+} C$, we deduce finally that $M \downarrow^{\text{t}} \xrightarrow{\text{cut}^+} M' \downarrow^{\text{t}}$.

Now let us suppose that the reduction $M \xrightarrow{\text{excut}} M'$ is done under some context. We reason by induction on this context. We just treated the case of an empty context.

– Let us consider now for instance the case of R_R. M is of the form $\mathsf{R}_R(\ldots, (\ldots, M_i)_i, \ldots, a)$ and M' is $\mathsf{R}_R(\ldots, (\ldots, M_i')_i, \ldots, a)$ with some k such that $M_k \xrightarrow{\text{excut}} M_k'$ and for all $i \neq k$, $M_i' = M_i$. By induction hypothesis, $M_k \downarrow^{\text{t}} \xrightarrow{\text{cut}^+} M_k' \downarrow^{\text{t}}$ and then

$$\begin{aligned}
M \downarrow^{\text{t}} &= \sigma C[(M_i \downarrow^{\text{t}})_i] \\
&\xrightarrow{\text{cut}^+} \sigma C[(M_i' \downarrow^{\text{t}})_i] \\
&= M' \downarrow^{\text{t}}
\end{aligned}$$

- Let us consider now for instance the case of And_R. M is of the form $\mathsf{And}_R(\widehat{b}M_1, \widehat{c}M_2, a)$ and M' is of the form $\mathsf{And}_R(\widehat{b}M_1', \widehat{c}M_2', a)$ with some i in $\{1, 2\}$ such that $M_i \xrightarrow{\text{excut}} M_i'$ and $M_k = M_k'$ for $k \neq i$. By induction hypothesis, $M_i \downarrow^{\text{t}} \xrightarrow{\text{cut}}^+ M_i' \downarrow^{\text{t}}$ and thus

$$
\begin{aligned}
M \downarrow^{\text{t}} &= \mathsf{And}_R(\widehat{b}M_1 \downarrow^{\text{t}}, \widehat{c}M_2 \downarrow^{\text{t}}, a) \\
&\xrightarrow{\text{cut}}^+ \mathsf{And}_R(\widehat{b}M_1' \downarrow^{\text{t}}, \widehat{c}M_2' \downarrow^{\text{t}}, a) \\
&= M' \downarrow^{\text{t}}
\end{aligned}
$$

- Let us consider now for instance the case Exists_R. M is of the form $\mathsf{Exists}_R(\widehat{b}M_1, t, a)$ and M' is of the form $\mathsf{Exists}_R(\widehat{b}M_1', t, a)$ with $M_1 \xrightarrow{\text{excut}} M_1'$. By induction hypothesis, $M_1 \downarrow^{\text{t}} \xrightarrow{\text{cut}}^+ M_1' \downarrow^{\text{t}}$ and thus

$$
\begin{aligned}
M \downarrow^{\text{t}} &= \mathsf{Exists}_R(\widehat{b}M_1 \downarrow^{\text{t}}, t, a) \\
&\xrightarrow{\text{cut}}^+ \mathsf{Exists}_R(\widehat{b}M_1' \downarrow^{\text{t}}, t, a) \\
&= M' \downarrow^{\text{t}}
\end{aligned}
$$

- Let us consider now for instance the case Exists_L. M is of the form $\mathsf{Exists}_L(\widehat{y}\widehat{x}M_1, x)$ and M' is $\mathsf{Exists}_L(\widehat{y}\widehat{x}M_1', x)$ with $M_1 \xrightarrow{\text{excut}} M_1'$. By induction hypothesis, $M_1 \downarrow^{\text{t}} \xrightarrow{\text{cut}}^+ M_1' \downarrow^{\text{t}}$ and thus

$$
\begin{aligned}
M \downarrow^{\text{t}} &= \mathsf{Exists}_L(\widehat{y}\widehat{x}M_1 \downarrow^{\text{t}}, x) \\
&\xrightarrow{\text{cut}} \mathsf{Exists}_L(\widehat{y}\widehat{x}M_1' \downarrow^{\text{t}}, x) \\
&= M' \downarrow^{\text{t}}
\end{aligned}
$$

- Other cases are similar.

$\square$

Now we can prove the main result:

Theorem 2 (Strong Normalisation). *If the set of proposition rewrite rules satisfies Hypothesis 1, then* $\xrightarrow{\text{excut}}$ *is strongly normalising on well-typed extended terms.*

Proof. Let us suppose that $\xrightarrow{\text{prop}}$ is convergent. Let $M \rhd \Gamma \vdash \Delta$ be some well-typed extended term. Let us suppose that there exists an infinite reduction

$$
M = M_0 \xrightarrow{\text{excut}} M_1 \xrightarrow{\text{excut}} M_2 \ldots
$$

First by Corollary 3, $\xrightarrow{\text{term}}$ is weakly normalising and $M \downarrow^{\text{t}} \rhd \Gamma \downarrow^{\text{p}} \vdash \Delta \downarrow^{\text{p}}$. Besides by Lemma 11, there is an infinite reduction

$$
M \downarrow^{\text{t}} = M_0 \downarrow^{\text{t}} \xrightarrow{\text{cut}}^+ M_1 \downarrow^{\text{t}} \xrightarrow{\text{cut}}^+ M_2 \downarrow^{\text{t}} \ldots
$$

This is impossible since $M \downarrow^{\text{t}}$ is well-typed in Urban's calculus and $\xrightarrow{\text{cut}}$ is strongly normalising on well-typed terms [Urb00]. $\square$

5   Conclusion

We have motivated and presented superdeduction, a powerful systematic way of extending deduction systems with rules derived from an axiomatic theory. First, we have presented its application to classical sequent calculus along with its properties. After having exhibited a proof-term language associated with this deduction system along with a cut-elimination procedure, we have shown in details its strong normalisation under non-trivial hypothesis, therefore ensuring the consistency of a large class of theories, as well as of the corresponding instances of the system. We have shown on significative examples including higher-order logic, induction and equality why superdeduction could be a grounding framework for a new generation of interactive proof environments. A prototype of this framework, lemuridæ, has been presented and can be actually downloaded.

The very promising results obtained when using lemuridæ, first in term of proof discovery agility and second in the close relationship between human constructed proofs and superdeduction ones, are all very encouraging and trigger the further development of the concepts and implementation. This leads to new questions, since, as seen in Section 3, the behavior of superdeduction systems with propositions considered modulo a congruence is important to study now in details. This will for instance allow building proofs modulo the symmetry of equality. Another promising point of further research is program extraction from lemuridæ proof-terms along with a computational interpretation of extended deduction rules. We anticipate the extracted programs to have modular structures inherited from the superdeduction proof.

The link, studied in [BDW07], between supernatural deduction (e.g. superdeduction applied to natural deduction) and natural deduction modulo, shows the equivalence between strong normalisation of cut elimination in supernatural deduction and in natural deduction modulo for the implicational fragment of predicate logic. The links between cut elimination in superdeduction and deduction modulo for the sequent calculus have still to be worked out. However, we already can import theories expressed by proposition rewrite rules for deduction modulo to super sequent calculus systems. This is in particular the case of Peano's arithmetic [DW05], but also of Zermelo-Frænkel axiomatization of set theory [DM07].

Finally, let us stress out the recent encoding of pure types systems in $\lambda\Pi$-calculus modulo [CD07]. Indeed, since recent works by G. Burel show that the $\lambda\Pi$-calculus can be naturally encoded in the super sequent calculus, this globally confirms the legitimacy of superdeduction as a foundation for high-level proof assistants. It opens also new questions on the global architecture of proof systems as well as on the interaction with users, either humans or programs.

Acknowledgments. Many thanks to Benjamin Wack for inspiring discussions and his seminal work on this topics, to Horatiu Cirstea for his detailed and crisp comments on previous version this work, to Dan Dougherty for helpful discussions, to the Modulo meetings and the Protheo team for many interactions.

References

[Alv00]   Alvarado, C.: Reflection for rewriting in the calculus of inductive constructions. In: Proceedings of TYPES 2000, Durham, United Kingdom (December 2000)

[AM99]   Andreoli, J.-M., Maieli, R.: Focusing and proof-nets in linear and non-commutative logic. In: Ganzinger, H., McAllester, D., Voronkov, A. (eds.) LPAR 1999. LNCS, vol. 1705, pp. 321–336. Springer, Heidelberg (1999)

[And92]   Andreoli, J.-M.: Logic programming with focusing proofs in linear logic. Journal of Logic and Computation 2(3), 297–347 (1992)

[And01]   Andreoli, J.-M.: Focussing and proof construction. Annals Pure Applied Logic 107(1-3), 131–163 (2001)

[BDW07]   Brauner, P., Dowek, G., Wack, B.: Normalization in supernatural deduction and in deduction modulo (2007) Available at
             http://hal.inria.fr/inria-00141720

[BHdN02]   Bezem, M., Hendriks, D., de Nivelle, H.: Automated proof construction in type theory using resolution. Journal of Automated Reasoning 29(3-4), 253–275 (2002)

[BHK07]   Brauner, P., Houtmann, C., Kirchner, C.: Principles of superdeduction. In: Proceedings of LICS (July 2007)

[BJO02]   Blanqui, F., Jouannaud, J.-P., Okada, M.: Inductive Data Type Systems. Theoretical Computer Science 272(1-2), 41–68 (2002)

[Bra06]   Brauner, P.: Un calcul des séquents extensible. Master's thesis, Université Henri Poincaré – Nancy 1 (2006)

[Bur07]   Burel, G.: Unbounded proof-length speed-up in deduction modulo. Technical report, INRIA Lorraine (2007) Available at
             http://hal.inria.fr/inria-00138195

[CD07]   Cousineau, D., Dowek, G.: Embedding pure type systems in the lambda-pi-calculus modulo. In: TLCA 2007. LNCS, vol. 4583. Springer, Heidelberg (To appear, 2007)

[CH00]   Curien, P.-L., Herbelin, H.: The duality of computation. In: ICFP '00: Proceedings of the fifth ACM SIGPLAN international conference on Functional programming, pp. 233–243. ACM Press, New York, NY, USA (2000)

[CK01]   Cirstea, H., Kirchner, C.: The rewriting calculus — Part I and II. Logic Journal of the Interest Group in Pure. and Applied Logics 9(3), 427–498 (2001)

[CLW03]   Cirstea, H., Liquori, L., Wack, B.: Rewriting calculus with fixpoints: Untyped and first-order systems. In: Berardi, S., Coppo, M., Damiani, F. (eds.) TYPES 2003. LNCS, vol. 3085, Springer, Heidelberg (2004)

[DHK03]   Dowek, G., Hardin, T., Kirchner, C.: Theorem proving modulo. Journal of Automated Reasoning 31(1), 33–72 (2003)

[DM07]   Dowek, G., Miquel, A.: Cut elimination for Zermelo's set theory. Available on author's web page (2007)

[Dow97]   Dowek, G.: Proof normalization for a first-order formulation of higher-order logic. In: Gunter, E.L., Felty, A.P. (eds.) TPHOLs 1997. LNCS, vol. 1275, pp. 105–119. Springer, Heidelberg (1997)

[DW03]   Dowek, G., Werner, B.: Proof normalization modulo. Journal of Symbolic Logic 68(4), 1289–1316 (2003)

[DW05]   Dowek, G., Werner, B.: Arithmetic as a theory modulo. In: Giesl, J. (ed.) RTA 2005. LNCS, vol. 3467, pp. 423–437. Springer, Heidelberg (2005)

[Her95]   Herbelin, H.: Séquents qu'on calcule. PhD thesis, Université Paris 7 (January 1995)

[HOL93]   University of Cambridge, DSTO, SRI Internatioal. Description of the HOL-System (1993)

[Hou06]   Houtmann, C.: Cohérence de la déduction surnaturelle. Master's thesis, École Normale Supérieure de Cachan (2006)

[Jou05]   Jouannaud, J.-P.: Higher-order rewriting: Framework, confluence and termination. In: Middeldorp, A., van Oostrom, V., van Raamsdonk, F., de Vrijer, R.C. (eds.) Processes, Terms and Cycles, pp. 224–250 (2005)

[Kir06]   Kirchner, F.: A finite first-order theory of classes (2006) http://www.lix.polytechnique.fr/Labo/Florent.Kirchner/

[KRRT06]   Kirchner, H., Ranise, S., Ringeissen, C., Tran, D.-K.: Automatic combinability of rewriting-based satisfiability procedures. In: Hermann, M., Voronkov, A. (eds.) LPAR 2006. LNCS (LNAI), vol. 4246, pp. 542–556. Springer, Heidelberg (2006)

[Len03]   Lengrand, S.: Call-by-value, call-by-name, and strong normalization for the classical sequent calculus. Electronic Notes in Theoretical Computer Science, vol. 86(4) (2003)

[MQP06]   Meng, J., Quigley, C., Paulson, L.C.: Automation for interactive proof: First prototype. Information and Computation 204(10), 1575–1596 (2006)

[MR06]   Moreau, P.-E., Reilles, A.: The tom home page (2006) http://tom.loria.fr

[NKK02]   Nguyen, Q.-H., Kirchner, C., Kirchner, H.: External rewriting for skeptical proof assistants. Journal of Automated Reasoning 29(3-4), 309–336 (2002)

[ORS92]   Owre, S., Rushby, J.M., Shankar, N.: PVS: A prototype verification system. In: Kapur, D. (ed.) Automated Deduction - CADE-11. LNCS, vol. 607, pp. 748–752. Springer, Heidelberg (1992)

[Pau94]   Paulson, L.: Isabelle: A Generic Theorem Prover. LNCS, vol. 828. Springer, Heidelberg (1994)

[Pra65]   Prawitz, D.: Natural Deduction. A Proof-Theoretical Study, vol. 3 of Stockholm Studies in Philosophy. Almqvist & Wiksell, Stockholm (1965)

[Pre05]   Prevosto, V.: Certified mathematical hierarchies: the focal system. In: Coquand, T., Lombardi, H., Roy, M.-F. (eds.) Mathematics, Algorithms, Proofs, number 05021 in Dagstuhl Seminar Proceedings, Dagstuhl, Germany, Internationales Begegnungs- und Forschungszentrum (IBFI), Schloss Dagstuhl, Germany (2005)

[Rud92]   Rudnicki, P.: An overview of the Mizar project. Notes to a talk at the workshop on Types for Proofs and Programs (June 1992)

[The04]   The Coq development team. The Coq proof assistant reference manual. LogiCal Project, Version 8.0 (2004)

[UB01]   Urban, C., Bierman, G.M.: Strong normalisation of cut-elimination in classical logic. Fundam. Inform. 45(1-2), 123–155 (2001)

[Urb00]   Urban, C.: Classical Logic and Computation. PhD thesis, University of Cambridge, (October 2000)

[Urb01]   Urban, C.: Strong normalisation for a gentzen-like cut-elimination procedure. In: Abramsky, S. (ed.) TLCA 2001. LNCS, vol. 2044, pp. 415–430. Springer, Heidelberg (2001)

[VB98]   Visser, E., Benaissa, Z.-e.-A.: A core language for rewriting. In: Kirchner, C., Kirchner, H. (eds.) WRLA, Pont-à-Mousson, France, September 1998. Electronic Notes in Theoretical Computer Science, vol. 15, Elsevier, North-Holland (1998)

[vBLL05]   van Bakel, S., Lengrand, S., Lescanne, P.: The language $\mathcal{X}$: circuits, computations and classical logic. In: van Bakel, S., Lengrand, S., Lescanne, P. (eds.) ICTCS'05. Proceedings of Ninth Italian Conference on Theoretical Computer Science. LNCS, vol. 3701, pp. 81–96. Springer, Heidelberg (2005)

[Wac05]   Wack, B.: Typage et déduction dans le calcul de réécriture. PhD thesis, Université Henri Poincaré, Nancy 1 (October 2005)

[Wad03]   Wadler, P.: Call-by-value is dual to call-by-name. In: ICFP '03: Proceedings of the eighth ACM SIGPLAN international conference on Functional programming, September 2003, pp. 189–201. ACM Press, New York (2003)

Remarks on
Semantic Completeness for Proof-Terms
with Laird's Dual Affine/Intuitionistic
λ-Calculus

Mitsuhiro Okada and Ryo Takemura*

Department of Philosophy, Keio University,
2-15-45 Mita, Minato-ku, Tokyo 108-8345, Japan
{mitsu, takemura}@abelard.flet.keio.ac.jp

Abstract. The purpose of this note is to give a demonstration of the completeness theorem of type assignment system for λ-terms of [Hindley 83] and [Coquand 05] with two directions of slight extensions. Firstly, using the idea of [Okada 96], [Okada-Terui 99] and [Hermant-Okada 07], we extend their completeness theorem to a stronger form which implies a normal form theorem. Secondly, we extend the simple type (the implicational fragment of intuitionistic logic) framework of [Hindley 83] and [Coquand 05] to a linear (affine) types (the $\{-\circ, \&, \to\}$-fragment of affine logic) framework of [Laird 03, 05].

1 Introduction

Using the traditional Tarskian or Kripke model, Hindley [1983] and Coquand [2005] showed completeness at the level of "proof-terms" (λ-terms), in place of the traditional completeness for "provability," with the implicational fragment of intuitionistic logic. Compared with some recent works on full completeness and full abstraction employing Scott-Plotkin's denotational semantics or game semantics (e.g., [O'Hearn-Riecke 95], [Hyland-Ong 00]), their completeness proofs can be considered natural extensions of traditional completeness proofs for provability. On the other hand, in our previous work [Okada 96, 02] and [Okada-Terui 99], we remarked that a slight change in the phase semantic completeness proof of [Girard 87] leads to the cut-elimination theorem (or, existence theorem of a normal proof) for "provability." In this note we combine these two ideas to show that a slight change in the setting of Hindley-Coquand's semantic completeness proof for "proof-terms" leads to the normal form theorem for "proof-terms." We demonstrate this for Laird's dual affine/intuitionistic λ-calculus.

* This work is partly supported by Grants-in-Aid for Scientific Research of MEXT, a JST-Franco-Japanese collaborative grant, 21 COE-Humanity Science grant, and Oogata Kenkyu Josei grant of Keio University. The second author is also partly supported by Research Fellowships of the Japan Society for the Promotion of Science for Young Scientists.

H. Comon-Lundh et al. (Eds.): Jouannaud Festschrift, LNCS 4600, pp. 167–181, 2007.

Girard proved, in his completeness proof in [Girard 87] at the level of provability, a lemma of the form

$$A^* = [\![A]\!],$$

where A^* (called the inner-value of A in [Okada 02]) is the interpretation of a formula A in the canonical model, and $[\![A]\!] = \{\Gamma \mid \Gamma \vdash A$ is provable$\}$ (called the outer-value). We remarked in [Okada 96], [Okada-Terui 99] (cf. also [Hermant-Okada 07] for higher order cases) that the cut-elimination theorem can be obtained by changing this lemma slightly into the following form:

$$A \in A^* \subseteq [\![A]\!],$$

where $[\![A]\!] = \{\Gamma \mid \Gamma \vdash A$ is provable without the cut-rule $\}$. Indeed, the completeness proofs for "proof-terms" in [Hindley 83] and [Coquand 05] use the same form $A^* = [\![A]\!]$ as in [Girard 87], where A^* and $[\![A]\!]$ are adapted to a semantics for "proof-terms." We shall remark in this note that a modification of the lemma similar to [Okada 96, 02] and [Okada-Terui 99] can show the normal form theorems for "proof-terms," with a suitable change in the definition of $[\![A]\!]$.

As was mentioned above, we also extend completeness of [Hindley 83] and [Coquand 05] for the simple type (the implicational fragment of intuitionistic logic) framework to a linear (affine) types (the $\{-\!\circ, \&, \rightarrow\}$-fragment of affine logic) framework. In order to do this, we consider dual affine/intuitionistic λ-calculus (λ_{Aff}) of [Laird 05, 03], which is a fragment of Dual Intuitionistic Linear Logic (**DILL**) of Barber and Plotkin (see [Barber 96]). Based on the linear types of the forms $A -\!\circ B$ and $A \& B$, λ_{Aff} has a part of the exponential as the intuitionistic function type of the form $A \rightarrow B$, which corresponds to $!A -\!\circ B$ with the exponential $!$. (Hasegawa [2002b] also considers a similar system in the framework of classical logic.) In [Laird 05, 03], λ_{Aff} is introduced as a target language of Continuation-Passing-Style (CPS) translation of simple types of the call-by-value λ-calculus. Introducing game semantics for λ_{Aff}, Laird gives a semantic analysis of λ_{Aff} and CPS translation. CPS translation is developed as an evaluation-order independent λ-encoding of λ-terms (see [Plotkin 75], [Fischer 93] etc.). Although the standard call-by-value CPS translation has been shown to be equationally sound and complete, it is not *full*: there are inhabitants of the interpreted types which are not in the image of the transformation. (See [Hasegawa 02a].) Using game semantics, Laird showed the fullness of CPS translation by adopting λ_{Aff} as the target language.

Our completeness proof for "proof-terms" could be understood as a variant of the well-known Tait-Girard's computability/reducibility argument of proof-terms normalization.

The rest of this note is organized as follows. In Section 2, we mainly concern ourselves with the level of "provability" of Laird's dual affine/intuitionistic λ-calculus (λ_{Aff}) ([Laird 05, 03]) and its phase semantics. In Section 3, we first review the type assignment system of Laird's λ_{Aff}, and then we introduce phase semantics for proof-terms of this system. We prove, in Section 4, the soundness and the completeness theorems of λ_{Aff}. Using completeness, we show a normal form theorem of λ_{Aff}.

2   Phase Semantics for the Provability of λ_{Aff}

In this section, we first briefly review the logic of Laird's dual affine/intuitionistic λ-calculus (λ_{Aff}) ([Laird 05, 03]). Then we introduce phase semantics for the provability of this system for the preparation of phase semantics for proof-terms, which will be developed in Section 3.2.

λ_{Aff} takes dual contexts of linear and non-linear in the style of Barber-Plotkin's Dual Intuitionistic Linear Logic (**DILL**) (see [Barber 96]). A sequent in this system has the form $\Phi \, ; \, \Gamma \vdash A$, where Φ is a set of formulas (types) called "intuitionistic context", and Γ is a multiset of formulas (types) called "linear context", with A a formula (type). The symbol " ; " is used to distinguish an intuitionistic context and a linear context. We call $\Phi \, ; \, \Gamma$ a dual context. We write $\emptyset$ for the empty sequent.

Syntactical notions such as formulas (types) and contexts of λ_{Aff} are defined as the type assignment system for λ-terms in Section 3.1, and we only indicate the inference rules in Table 1 in this section.

Table 1. Inference rules of λ_{Aff}

$$\frac{}{\Phi \, ; \, \Gamma, A \vdash A} \; ax \qquad\qquad \frac{\Phi \, ; \, \Gamma, A \vdash B}{\Phi, A \, ; \, \Gamma \vdash B} \; der$$

$$\frac{\Phi \, ; \, \Gamma, A \vdash B}{\Phi \, ; \, \Gamma \vdash A \multimap B} \; \multimap I \qquad\qquad \frac{\Phi \, ; \, \Gamma \vdash A \multimap B \quad \Phi \, ; \, \Delta \vdash A}{\Phi \, ; \, \Gamma, \Delta \vdash B} \; \multimap E$$

$$\frac{\Phi, A \, ; \, \Gamma \vdash B}{\Phi \, ; \, \Gamma \vdash A \to B} \; \to I \qquad\qquad \frac{\Phi \, ; \, \Gamma \vdash A \to B \quad \Phi \, ; \, \emptyset \vdash A}{\Phi \, ; \, \Gamma \vdash B} \; \to E$$

$$\frac{\Phi \, ; \, \Gamma \vdash A \quad \Phi \, ; \, \Gamma \vdash B}{\Phi \, ; \, \Gamma \vdash A \, \& \, B} \; \& I \qquad\qquad \frac{\Phi \, ; \, \Gamma \vdash A_1 \, \& \, A_2}{\Phi \, ; \, \Gamma \vdash A_i} \; \& E_i \quad i = 1, 2$$

We introduce phase semantics for the provability of λ_{Aff}. First for comparison, we briefly recall operations of usual phase semantics for the provability. See [Okada 02] for details. Phase semantics for the provability of the $\{\multimap, \&\}$-fragment of intuitionistic linear logic is based on commutative monoid M and the following operations: For any $\alpha, \beta \subseteq M$,

- $\alpha \multimap \beta = \{m \mid \text{for any } n \in \alpha, \ m \cdot n \in \beta\}$,
- $\alpha \, \& \, \beta = \alpha \cap \beta$.

We now introduce phase semantics for the provability of λ_{Aff}, based on intuitionistic phase semantics of [Okada 02]. See also [Okada-Terui 99] on phase semantics for affine logic.

Definition 1 (Phase space for the provability). A *phase space* $\mathcal{M}$ *for the provability of* λ_{Aff} is defined as follows.

- Start with a structure $(M, \star, \cdot, \varepsilon)$ where M is a set equipped with two binary commutative associative operators $\star$ and $\cdot$ which share the same unit ε, and such that $\star$ is also idempotent. Then the phase space which is used is the set of subsets of $\mathcal{M} = (M, \star, \varepsilon) \times (M, \cdot, \varepsilon)$ with the following operations for any $\alpha, \beta \subseteq \mathcal{M}$. We denote an element of $\mathcal{M}$ as $(n \; ; \; l)$ instead of (n, l).

  - $\alpha \multimap \beta = \{(n \; ; \; l) \mid \text{for any } (n' \; ; \; l') \in \alpha, \; (n \star n' \; ; \; l \cdot l') \in \beta\}$
  - $\alpha \to \beta = \{(n \; ; \; l) \mid \text{for any } (n' \; ; \; \varepsilon) \in \alpha, \; (n \star n' \; ; \; l) \in \beta\}$
  - $\alpha \,\&\, \beta = \alpha \cap \beta$.

- $\alpha \subseteq \mathcal{M}$ is called *closed* if it satisfies the following *monotonicity* condition:

(*Monotonicity*) If $(n \; ; \; l \cdot l') \in \alpha$, then $(n \star l' \star m \; ; \; l \cdot k) \in \alpha$ for any $m, k \in M$.

This condition is a combination of *Weakening* and *Dereliction* (*der*-rule).

Definition 2 (Phase model for the provability). A *phase model* $(\mathcal{M}, *)$ *for the provability of* λ_{Aff} consists of a phase space $\mathcal{M}$ for the provability and an interpretation function $*$ from the set of atoms to the set of closed sets of $\mathcal{M}$.

We write $\mathfrak{l}$ for $l_1 \cdots l_k$ in a linear context, and $\mathfrak{n}$ for $n_1 \star \cdots \star n_l$ and $\mathfrak{m}$ for $m_1 \star \cdots \star m_k$ in an intuitionistic context.

Definition 3 (Interpretation of sequents)
A sequent $C_1, \ldots, C_l \; ; \; D_1, \ldots, D_k \vdash A$ is *true* (denoted as $C_1, \ldots, C_l \; ; \; D_1, \ldots, D_k \models A$) in a phase model $(\mathcal{M}, *)$ for the provability of λ_{Aff}, if, for any $(n_i \; ; \; \varepsilon) \in C_i^*$ and $(m_j \; ; \; l_j) \in D_j^*$, we have $(\mathfrak{n} \star \mathfrak{m} \; ; \; \mathfrak{l}) \in A^*$.

In the above definition of phase semantics, if we define an order relation in a monoid as $m \leq n$ *iff* $\exists l(m \cdot l = n)$, then we obtain a linear (affine) Kripke semantics naturally (see [Okada 04]). Hence our framework can be also considered as a framework of Kripke semantics as [Coquand 05].

Using the method of [Okada 96, 02] and [Okada-Terui 99], we have completeness of λ_{Aff} with respect to phase semantics for the provability. We shall also show that these theorems are obtained by proofs for corresponding theorems in Section 4.

Theorem 1 (Soundness for the provability)
If $C_1, \ldots, C_l \; ; \; D_1, \ldots, D_k \vdash A$ *is provable in* λ_{Aff}, *then* $C_1, \ldots, C_l \; ; \; D_1, \ldots, D_k \models A$ *in any phase model for the provability of* λ_{Aff}.

In order to show completeness for the provability of λ_{Aff}, we construct a canonical model $(\mathcal{M}_S, *)$ as follows. See Section 4.2 for the detail.

- $\mathcal{M}_S$ is the set of dual contexts, where binary operators $\star$ and $\cdot$ are " , " in intuitionistic contexts (set-union) and " , " in linear contexts (multiset-union), respectively, and the unit is the empty sequent $\emptyset$.

- On this set, we consider the following outer-value:

  - $[\![A]\!] = \{ \Phi \; ; \; \Gamma \mid \Phi \; ; \; \Gamma \vdash A$ is provable with a normal proof $\}$

- We define an interpretation function $*$ as $X^* = [\![X]\!]$.

Then we have the following main lemma by the induction on the complexity of A as [Okada 96, 02]. See Section 4.2 for the detail.

Lemma 1 (Main lemma). *In $(\mathcal{M}_S, *)$, for any type A,*

$$(\emptyset \; ; \; A) \in A^* \subseteq [\![A]\!].$$

The following completeness is a direct consequence of the main lemma.

Theorem 2 (Completeness for the provability)
If $C_1, \ldots, C_l \; ; \; D_1, \ldots, D_k \models A$ in any phase model for the provability of λ_{Aff}, then $C_1, \ldots, C_l \; ; \; D_1, \ldots, D_k \vdash A$ is provable with a normal proof in λ_{Aff}.

Then with the soundness theorem, the following normal form theorem is obtained.

Theorem 3 (Normal form theorem for λ_{Aff})
If $C_1, \ldots, C_l \; ; \; D_1, \ldots, D_k \vdash A$ is provable in λ_{Aff}, then it is provable with a normal proof.

3 Phase Semantics for Proof-Terms of λ_{Aff}

In this section, we review the type assignment system of Laird's dual affine/intuitionistic λ-calculus (λ_{Aff}) ([Laird 05, 03]), and we introduce phase semantics for proof-terms of this system.

3.1 Type Assignment System for λ_{Aff}

Although Barber [1996] and others, who study **DILL** or linear CPS-translation, introduce the linear λ-terms, we take, following [Laird 05, 03], the usual (non linear) untyped λ-terms with pairs for λ_{Aff}: Variables $x, y, z, \ldots$; abstraction $\lambda x.s$; application (st); pair $\langle s, t \rangle$; and projection $\pi_1(s), \pi_2(s)$.

We write $s[x := t]$ for the substitution of a λ-term t for the free occurrences of x in a λ-term s.

Definition 4 (Types). The linear types of λ_{Aff} is defined as follows:

- Atomic types $X, Y, \ldots, X_1, X_2, \ldots$ are types.
- If A and B are types, then $A \multimap B, A \to B$ and $A \,\&\, B$ are also types.

We now define the type assignment rules of Laird's λ_{Aff}.

Definition 5 (Type asignment rules)

- A *declaration* (*assumption*) is of the form $x\colon A$ with a variable x and a type A.
- A *dual context* is of the form $y_1\colon C_1,\ldots,y_l\colon C_l$; $x_1\colon D_1,\ldots,x_k\colon D_k$ where the left of " ; " $(y_1\colon C_1,\ldots,y_l\colon C_l)$ is a finite *set* of declarations called an "intuitionistic context" and the right of " ; " $(x_1\colon D_1,\ldots,x_k\colon D_k)$ is a finite *multiset* of declarations called a "linear context". We write $\Phi,\Psi,\ldots$ for any intuitionistic contexts and $\Gamma,\Delta,\ldots$ for any linear contexts. We write $\emptyset$ for the empty context.
- A λ-term s is *typable* as type A if a sequent Φ ; $\Gamma\vdash s\colon A$ is derivable for some dual context Φ ; Γ by the type assignment rules of Table 2.

Table 2. Type assignment rules of λ_{Aff}

$$\frac{}{\Phi\ ;\ \Gamma,x\colon A\vdash x\colon A}\ ax \qquad \frac{\Phi\ ;\ \Gamma,x\colon A\vdash s\colon B}{\Phi,x\colon A\ ;\ \Gamma\vdash s\colon B}\ der$$

$$\frac{\Phi\ ;\ \Gamma,x\colon A\vdash s\colon B}{\Phi\ ;\ \Gamma\vdash \lambda x.s\colon A\multimap B}\ \multimap I$$
where s contains at most one free occurrence of x.
$$\frac{\Phi\ ;\ \Gamma\vdash s\colon A\multimap B \quad \Phi\ ;\ \Delta\vdash t\colon A}{\Phi\ ;\ \Gamma,\Delta\vdash (st)\colon B}\ \multimap E$$

$$\frac{\Phi,x\colon A\ ;\ \Gamma\vdash s\colon B}{\Phi\ ;\ \Gamma\vdash \lambda x.s\colon A\to B}\ \to I \qquad \frac{\Phi\ ;\ \Gamma\vdash s\colon A\to B \quad \Phi\ ;\ \emptyset\vdash t\colon A}{\Phi\ ;\ \Gamma\vdash (st)\colon B}\ \to E$$

$$\frac{\Phi\ ;\ \Gamma\vdash s\colon A \quad \Phi\ ;\ \Gamma\vdash t\colon B}{\Phi\ ;\ \Gamma\vdash \langle s,t\rangle\colon A\mathbin{\&}B}\ \&I \qquad \frac{\Phi\ ;\ \Gamma\vdash s\colon A_1\mathbin{\&}A_2}{\Phi\ ;\ \Gamma\vdash \pi_i(s)\colon A_i}\ \&E_i \quad i=1,2$$

We introduce the $\beta\eta$-equality relation $\simeq_{\beta\eta}$ on λ-terms as the usual conversion relation, see [Hindley-Seldin 86], [Barendregt 92]. A λ-term is in *normal form*, if it contains no redex of the form $(\lambda x.st)$, $\pi_i(\langle s,t\rangle)$ for $i=1$ and 2, $\lambda x.(sx)$ for $x\notin FV(s)$, or $\langle\pi_1(s),\pi_2(s)\rangle$, where $FV(s)$ means the set of free variables of the λ-term s.

Note that there is a slight difference between our λ_{Aff} and Barber-Plotkin's **DILL**-style λ_{Aff}. In **DILL**-style λ_{Aff}, it is assumed that Φ and Γ are disjoint in a dual context Φ ; Γ, and further that Γ and Δ are disjoint in a linear context Γ,Δ. (See [Barber 96].) In our λ_{Aff}, in place of this assumption, we assume that $\multimap I$-rule of Table 2 is applicable when s contains at most one free occurrence of x. This change does not affect the type assignment system of λ_{Aff}, which can be stated in Proposition 1 bellow.

Note first that, if a sequent Φ ; $\Gamma\vdash s\colon A$ is derivable in **DILL**-style λ_{Aff}, then the variables of the linear context Γ occur at most once in s due to the assumption of disjointness of linear contexts (see [Barber 96]). Hence $\multimap I$-rule of **DILL**-style system satisfies the restriction of $\multimap I$-rule of our λ_{Aff}.

On the other hand, the following proposition means that any derivation of our λ_{Aff} can be simulated in **DILL**-style λ_{Aff} by considering duplicated formulas in a linear context of our λ_{Aff} as an intuitionistic assumption of **DILL**-style λ_{Aff}.

Proposition 1 (Simulation). *Let* $x_i\colon\vec{A}_i$ *be a sequence* $x_i\colon A_i,\ldots,x_i\colon A_i$ *of the same assumptions. Assume that no variable appears twice in a sequence of assumptions* $\Phi,\Gamma,x_1\colon A_1,\ldots,x_n\colon A_n$. *For* $0 \le k \le n$,
if $\Phi,x_1\colon A_1,\ldots,x_k\colon A_k$; $\Gamma,x_1\colon\vec{A}_1,\ldots,x_n\colon\vec{A}_n \vdash s\colon B$ *is derivable in our* λ_{Aff}, *then* $\Phi,x_1\colon A_1,\ldots,x_n\colon A_n$; $\Gamma \vdash s\colon B$ *is derivable in* **DILL**-*style* λ_{Aff}.

This proposition is obtained by the following lemma of **DILL**-style λ_{Aff}.

Lemma 2 (Environment strengthening (Cf. [?]))
If $\Phi,x\colon A$; $\Gamma \vdash s\colon B$ *is derivable in* **DILL**-*style* λ_{Aff} *and* s *contains at most one free occurrence of* x, *then* Φ ; $\Gamma,x\colon A \vdash s\colon B$ *is derivable in* **DILL**-*style* λ_{Aff}.

Let us consider the following example of an application of $\multimap I$

$$\frac{\Phi \ ; \ \Gamma, x\colon A, x\colon A \vdash s\colon B}{\Phi \ ; \ \Gamma, x\colon A \vdash \lambda x.s\colon A \multimap B} \ \multimap I \quad \text{in our } \lambda_{\text{Aff}}.$$

For simplicity, we assume that no variable other than x occurs twice in the dual context.

This form of $\multimap I$-rule is simulated by **DILL**-style λ_{Aff} as follows: First we consider the duplicated assumptions $(x\colon A, x\colon A)$ in the linear context of the upper sequent as an intuitionistic assumption as

$$\Phi, x\colon A \ ; \ \Gamma \vdash s\colon B$$

in **DILL**-style λ_{Aff}. Note that by the definition of $\multimap I$-rule of our λ_{Aff}, the λ-term s contains at most one free occurrence of x. Hence by Lemma 2, we have Φ ; $\Gamma, x\colon A \vdash s\colon B$. Thus by applying $\multimap I$-rule of **DILL**-style λ_{Aff}, we have the following derivation:

$$\frac{\Phi \ ; \ \Gamma, x\colon A \vdash s\colon B}{\Phi \ ; \ \Gamma \vdash \lambda x.s\colon A \multimap B} \ \multimap I \quad \text{in } \textbf{DILL}\text{-style } \lambda_{\text{Aff}}.$$

Then by Weakening (cf. [Barber 96]) we have $\Phi, x\colon A$; $\Gamma \vdash \lambda x.s\colon A \multimap B$ in **DILL**-style λ_{Aff}.

3.2   Phase Semantics for Proof-Terms of λ_{Aff}

In this subsection, we introduce phase semantics for proof-terms of λ_{Aff}. The domain of our model consists of untyped λ-terms with dual contexts, which corresponds to [Coquand 05]'s model. The operations $\multimap$, $\to$ and $\&$ are based on the $\multimap$, $\to$ elimination rules and the set theoretical intersection operation, which are natural extensions of those operations of phase semantics for the provability of λ_{Aff} (Definition 1). The following phase space for proof-terms is obtained by augmenting proof-terms (λ-terms) to a phase space for the provability of λ_{Aff}.

Definition 6 (Phase space for proof-terms). A *phase space for proof-terms* of λ_{Aff} is $(\mathcal{M}, \mathcal{P})$ where

- $\mathcal{M}$ is a phase space for the provability of λ_{Aff}.
- $\mathcal{P} = \{((n ; l), s) \mid (n ; l) \in \mathcal{M} \text{ and } s \text{ is a } \lambda\text{-term}\}$.
  We write $(n ; l \rhd s)$ for $((n ; l), s)$.

  There are the following operations for any $\alpha, \beta \subseteq \mathcal{P}$:

  - $\alpha \multimap \beta = \{(n ; l \rhd s) \mid \text{for any } (n' ; l' \rhd t) \in \alpha, (n \star n' ; l \cdot l' \rhd (st)) \in \beta\}$
  - $\alpha \to \beta = \{(n ; l \rhd s) \mid \text{for any } (n' ; \varepsilon \rhd t) \in \alpha, (n \star n' ; l \rhd (st)) \in \beta\}$
  - $\alpha \, \& \, \beta = \pi_1(\alpha) \cap \pi_2(\beta)$,
    where $\pi_i(\alpha) = \{(n ; l \rhd s) \mid (n ; l \rhd \pi_i(s)) \in \alpha\}$ for $i = 1, 2$.

- We call $\alpha \subseteq \mathcal{P}$ *closed* if it satisfies the following *equality-closed* and *monotonicity* conditions:
  (*Equality-closed*) If $t \simeq_{\beta\eta} s$ and $(n ; l \rhd s) \in \alpha$, then $(n ; l \rhd t) \in \alpha$;
  (*Monotonicity*) If $(n ; l \cdot l' \rhd s) \in \alpha$, then $(n \star m \star l' ; l \cdot k \rhd s) \in \alpha$ for any $m, k \in M$.

These two conditions are collectively called the *closure condition*.

Note that, in the above definition of phase space for proof-terms of λ_{Aff}, if we forget λ-terms (proof-terms), then (1) $\mathcal{P}$ coincides with $\mathcal{M}$, (2) operations $\{\multimap, \to, \&\}$ exactly correspond to those of Definition 1 of phase space for the provability of λ_{Aff}, and (3) only monotonicity remains as the closure condition. Hence a phase space for the provability is obtained by forgetting λ-terms of a phase space for proof-terms.

It is easily shown that the closure condition is preserved under $\{\multimap, \to, \&\}$-operations.

Lemma 3. *For any $\alpha, \beta \subseteq \mathcal{P}$, if β is closed then $\alpha \multimap \beta$ and $\alpha \to \beta$ are closed; if α and β are closed then $\alpha \, \& \, \beta$ is closed.*

Definition 7 (Phase model for proof-terms). A *phase model $(\mathcal{M}, \mathcal{P}, *)$ for proof-terms* of λ_{Aff} consists of

- a phase space $(\mathcal{M}, \mathcal{P})$ for proof-terms of λ_{Aff};
- an interpretation function $*$ form the set of atomic types to the set of closed sets of $(\mathcal{M}, \mathcal{P})$ such that
  $(A \multimap B)^* = A^* \multimap B^*$, $(A \to B)^* = A^* \to B^*$, $(A \, \& \, B)^* = A^* \, \& \, B^*$.

Note that any interpretation A^* of a type is closed from Lemma 3.

Notation: We write $s[\mathfrak{t}, \mathfrak{s}]$ for $s[y_1 := t_1, \ldots, y_l := t_l, x_1 := s_1, \ldots, x_k := s_k]$. We also write $\mathfrak{l}$ for $l_1 \cdots \cdot l_k$ in a linear context, and $\mathfrak{n}$ for $n_1 \star \cdots \star n_l$ and $\mathfrak{m}$ for $m_1 \star \cdots \star m_k$ in an intuitionistic context.

Definition 8 (Interpretation of sequents)
A sequent $y_1 \colon C_1, \ldots, y_l \colon C_l \; ; \; x_1 \colon D_1, \ldots, x_k \colon D_k \vdash s \colon A$ is *true* (denoted as $y_1 \colon C_1, \ldots, y_l \colon C_l \; ; \; x_1 \colon D_1, \ldots, x_k \colon D_k \models s \colon A$) in a phase model $(\mathcal{M}, \mathcal{P}, *)$ for

proof-terms of λ_{Aff}, if, for any $(n_i \; ; \; \varepsilon \rhd t_i) \in C_i^*$ and $(m_j \; ; \; l_j \rhd s_j) \in D_j^*$, we have $(\mathfrak{n} \star \mathfrak{m} \; ; \; \mathfrak{l} \rhd s[\mathfrak{t}, \mathfrak{s}]) \in A^*$.

4   Soundness and Completeness of λ_{Aff}

In this section, we prove the soundness and the completeness theorems. Our proof below is an extension of the completeness proof in [Okada 96, 02] for phase semantics for the provability of intuitionistic linear logic. Using completeness, we show a normal form theorem of λ_{Aff}: *if a λ-term s is typable in λ_{Aff}, then there is a λ-term t in normal form such that $s \simeq_{\beta\eta} t$* .

By the following completeness proof for proof-terms (λ-terms), we obtain completeness for the provability if we ignore the part related to λ-terms.

4.1   Soundness Theorem

We first show the soundness theorem.

Theorem 4 (Soundness for proof-terms)

If $y_1 \colon C_1, \ldots, y_l \colon C_l \; ; \; x_1 \colon D_1, \ldots, x_k \colon D_k \vdash s \colon A$ is derivable in λ_{Aff}, then $y_1 \colon C_1, \ldots, y_l \colon C_l \; ; \; x_1 \colon D_1, \ldots, x_k \colon D_k \models s \colon A$ in any phase model for proof-terms of λ_{Aff}.

Proof. By induction on the construction of derivation. As for elimination rules, the assertion is more or less immediate by the induction hypothesis since the corresponding operations in our phase model are defined based on the elimination rules. Further, since $\to E$-rule is a particular case of $\multimap I$-rule, it is treated by the same way as $\multimap I$ case. Thus we show only for $\multimap I$ and $\& I$ rules.

In the following, Φ denotes $y_1 \colon C_1, \ldots, y_l \colon C_l$, and Γ denotes $x_1 \colon D_1, \ldots, x_k \colon D_k$.

Case $\dfrac{\Phi \; ; \; \Gamma, x \colon A \vdash s \colon B}{\Phi \; ; \; \Gamma \vdash \lambda x.s \colon A \multimap B} \; \multimap I$.

Let $(n_i \; ; \; \varepsilon \rhd t_i) \in C_i^*$ and $(m_j \; ; \; l_j \rhd s_j) \in D_j^*$ for each $1 \le i \le l$ and $1 \le j \le k$. Then by the induction hypothesis, for any $(n \; ; \; l \rhd u) \in A^*$, we have $(\mathfrak{n} \star \mathfrak{m} \star n \; ; \; \mathfrak{l} \cdot l \rhd s[\mathfrak{t}, \mathfrak{s}, x := u]) \in B^*$. Since B^* is closed, we have $(\mathfrak{n} \star \mathfrak{m} \star n \; ; \; \mathfrak{l} \cdot l \rhd (\lambda x.su)[\mathfrak{t}, \mathfrak{s}]) \in B^*$. That is $(\mathfrak{n} \star \mathfrak{m} \; ; \; \mathfrak{l} \rhd \lambda x.s[\mathfrak{t}, \mathfrak{s}]) \in A^* \multimap B^*$ by the definition of $\multimap$.

Case $\dfrac{\Phi \; ; \; \Gamma \vdash s \colon A \quad \Phi \; ; \; \Gamma \vdash t \colon B}{\Phi \; ; \; \Gamma \vdash \langle s, t \rangle \colon A \& B} \; \& I$.

Let $(n_i \; ; \; \varepsilon \rhd t_i) \in C_i^*$ and $(m_j \; ; \; l_j \rhd s_j) \in D_j^*$. Then by the induction hypothesis, we have $(\mathfrak{n} \star \mathfrak{m} \; ; \; \mathfrak{l} \rhd s[\mathfrak{t}, \mathfrak{s}]) \in A^*$ and $(\mathfrak{n} \star \mathfrak{m} \; ; \; \mathfrak{l} \rhd t[\mathfrak{t}, \mathfrak{s}]) \in B^*$. Since both A^* and B^* are closed, we have $(\mathfrak{n} \star \mathfrak{m} \; ; \; \mathfrak{l} \rhd \pi_1 \langle s, t \rangle [\mathfrak{t}, \mathfrak{s}]) \in A^*$ and $(\mathfrak{n} \star \mathfrak{m} \; ; \; \mathfrak{l} \rhd \pi_2 \langle s, t \rangle [\mathfrak{t}, \mathfrak{s}]) \in B^*$. Thus, from the definition of $\&$, we have $(\mathfrak{n} \star \mathfrak{m} \; ; \; \mathfrak{l} \rhd \langle s, t \rangle [\mathfrak{t}, \mathfrak{s}]) \in A^* \& B^*$. ∎

Note that the soundness theorem (Theorem 1) for the provability is a direct corollary of this soundness theorem for proof-terms.

4.2 Completeness Theorem

In this subsection, we present the completeness theorem. For the sake of a normal form theorem, we consider the following form of main lemma for completeness:

$$(\emptyset \; ; \; x{:}\,A \rhd x) \in A^* \subseteq [\![A]\!]$$

for any variable x and any type A, where A^* is the interpretation of A in the canonical model, and $[\![A]\!] = \{(\varPhi \; ; \; \varGamma \rhd s) \mid \varPhi \; ; \; \varGamma \vdash s{:}\,A$ and there is t in normal form such that $s \simeq_{\beta\eta} t\}$ (called the outer-value of A). This is a modification of the lemma of [Coquand 05] following the method of [Okada 96, 02].

In order to show completeness of λ_{Aff}, we add the following *equality*-rule:

$$\frac{\varPhi \; ; \; \varGamma \vdash s : A \quad s \simeq_{\beta\eta} t}{\varPhi \; ; \; \varGamma \vdash t{:}\,A} \; eq$$

This type of equality-rule is used in [Hindley 83] and [Coquand 05] to show completeness.

Now we construct a canonical model $(\mathcal{M}_S, \mathcal{P}_S, *)$ as follows.

- $\mathcal{M}_S$ is the set of dual contexts, where binary operators $\star$ and $\cdot$ are " , " in intuitionistic contexts (set-union) and " , " in linear contexts (multiset-union), respectively, and the unit is the empty sequent $\emptyset$.

- $\mathcal{P}_S = \{(\varPhi \; ; \; \varGamma \rhd s) \mid (\varPhi \; ; \; \varGamma) \in \mathcal{M}_S$ and s is a λ-term $\}$.

- On this set, we consider the following outer-value:

  - $[\![A]\!] = \{(\varPhi \; ; \; \varGamma \rhd s) \mid \varPhi \; ; \; \varGamma \vdash s{:}\,A$ and there is t in normal form such that $s \simeq_{\beta\eta} t\}$.

- Then we define an interpretation function $*$ as $X^* = [\![X]\!]$.

Note that we can define another outer-value as $[\![A]\!]_T = \{(\varPhi \; ; \; \varGamma \rhd s) \mid \varPhi \; ; \; \varGamma \vdash s{:}\,A\}$ without referring any normal form nor equality relation on λ-terms. The completeness theorem of [Coquand 05] is obtained by this outer-value.

The above construction indeed produces a phase model for proof-terms.

Lemma 4. $(\mathcal{M}_S, \mathcal{P}_S, *)$ *is a phase model for proof-terms of* λ_{Aff}.

Now we prove the following main lemma for our completeness theorem.

Lemma 5 (Main lemma). *In* $\mathcal{M}_S$, *for any variable x and any type A,*

$$(\emptyset \; ; \; x{:}\,A \rhd x) \in A^* \subseteq [\![A]\!].$$

Proof. In order to prove this lemma, we first introduce the following meta expression for a type and a λ-term.

For any type $B_1, \ldots, B_n$, we first define, by the induction on n, a meta expression $E(B_1, \ldots, B_n)$ of a type as follows:

$(n = 1)$ $E(B_1)$ means B_1;
$(n > 1)$ $E(B_1, \ldots, B_n)$ means one of the followings;
  - $E(B_1, \ldots, B_{n-2}, (B_{n-1} \multimap B_n))$ or;
  - $E(B_1, \ldots, B_{n-2}, (B_{n-1} \to B_n))$ or;
  - $E(B_1, \ldots, B_{n-2}, (B_n \,\&\, B_{n-1}))$ or;
  - $E(B_1, \ldots, B_{n-2}, (B_{n-1} \,\&\, B_n))$.

Next, for any term $s_1, \ldots, s_n$ which have types $B_1, \ldots, B_n$ respectively, we introduce a meta expression $E(s_n, s_1, \ldots, s_{n-1})$ of a λ-term, which depends on the form of a type $E(B_1, \ldots, B_n)$ as follows:
$E(s_n)$ is s_n;
$E(s_n, s_1, \ldots, s_{n-1})$ is one of the following:

- an application $(E(s_n, s_1, \ldots, s_{n-2})s_{n-1})$
    if $E(B_1, \ldots, B_{n-1}, B_n)$ is $E(B_1, \ldots, (B_{n-1} \multimap B_n))$ or $E(B_1, \ldots, (B_{n-1} \to B_n))$;
- a projection $\pi_1(E(s_n, s_1, \ldots, s_{n-2}))$
    if $E(B_1, \ldots, B_{n-1}, B_n)$ is $E(B_1, \ldots, (B_n \,\&\, B_{n-1}))$;
- a projection $\pi_2(E(s_n, s_1, \ldots, s_{n-2}))$
    if $E(B_1, \ldots, B_{n-1}, B_n)$ is $E(B_1, \ldots, (B_{n-1} \,\&\, B_n))$.

If we consider only $\{\multimap, \to\}$-fragment, then a λ-term $E(x, s_1, \ldots, s_n)$ is just an application $(\cdots (x s_1) \cdots s_n)$, and from a proof-theoretical point of view, it correspond to a proof structure whose main branch consists only of $\{\multimap, \to\}$-elimination rules. (Cf. [Martin-Löf 71].)

Then we prove, by induction on the complexity of A, the conjunction of the following two statements (1) and (2), which is a generalized form of the main lemma.

(1) $A^* \subseteq [\![A]\!]$;
(2) *For any type $E(B_1, \ldots, B_n, A)$,*
    if $(\Phi \,;\, \Gamma_i \rhd s_i) \in [\![B_i]\!]$ for any $i \leq n$ such that $E(B_1, \ldots, B_{i-1}, (B_i \multimap D))$; and
    if $(\Phi \,;\, \emptyset \rhd s_j) \in [\![B_j]\!]$ for any $j \leq n$ such that $E(B_1, \ldots, B_{j-1}, (B_j \to D))$,
    then we have $(\Phi \,;\, \vec{\Gamma_i}, x\!:\!E(B_1, \ldots, B_n, A) \rhd E(x, s_1, \ldots, s_n)) \in A^*$,
    where $\vec{\Gamma_i}$ is a sequence of contexts appearing in the premise of the statement.

In particular, we have $(\emptyset \,;\, x\!:\!A \rhd x) \in A^*$ from the case $n = 0$ of (2).

We write $E(\vec{B_n}, A)$ for the type $E(B_1, \ldots, B_n, A)$, and write $E(x, \vec{s_n})$ for the λ-term $E(x, s_1, \ldots, s_n)$.

(Case $A \equiv X$)
(1) $X^* \subseteq [\![X]\!]$ is obvious from the definition.

(2) By the assumption we have Φ ; $\Gamma_i \vdash s_i : B_i$ for each i and Φ ; $\emptyset \vdash s_j : B_j$ for each j, hence from the axiom of the form

$$\frac{}{\Phi \; ; \; x : E(\vec{B_n}, X) \vdash x : E(\vec{B_n}, X)} \; ax \; ,$$

by applying n-times of the following form of elimination rules:

$$\frac{\Phi \; ; \; \vec{\Gamma_l}, x : E(\vec{B_n}, X) \vdash E(x, \vec{s_i}) : B_{i+1} \Rightarrow E(B_{i+2}, \dots, B_n, X) \quad \Phi \; ; \; \Gamma_{i+1} \vdash s_{i+1} : B_{i+1}}{\Phi \; ; \; \vec{\Gamma_l}, \Gamma_{i+1}, x : E(\vec{B_n}, X) \vdash (E(x, \vec{s_i}) s_{i+1}) : E(B_{i+2}, \dots, B_n, X)} \Rightarrow E$$

where $\Rightarrow$ is $\multimap$ or $\to$, and Γ_{i+1} is $\emptyset$ if $\Rightarrow$ is $\to$,

or

$$\frac{\Phi \; ; \; \vec{\Gamma_l}, x : E(\vec{B_n}, X) \vdash E(x, \vec{s_i}) : E(B_{i+2}, \dots, B_n, X) \& B_{i+1}}{\Phi \; ; \; \vec{\Gamma_l}, x : E(\vec{B_n}, X) \vdash \pi_1(E(x, \vec{s_i})) : E(B_{i+2}, \dots, B_n, X)} \& E_1$$

similar for $\& E_2$,

we obtain Φ ; $\vec{\Gamma_i}, x : E(\vec{B_n}, X) \vdash E(x, \vec{s_n}) : X$.

On the other hand there are λ-terms $u_1, \dots, u_n$ in normal forms such that $s_k \simeq u_k$ for each $1 \le k \le n$ by the assumption. Hence we have $E(x, s_1, \dots, s_n) \simeq_{\beta\eta} E(x, u_1, \dots, u_n)$ where $E(x, u_1, \dots, u_n)$ is in normal form.

Thus we obtain $(\Phi \; ; \; \vec{\Gamma_i}, x : E(\vec{B_n}, X) \triangleright E(x, s_1, \dots, s_n)) \in [\![X]\!] = X^*$.

(Case $A \equiv B \multimap C$)
(1) We show $B^* \multimap C^* \subseteq [\![B \multimap C]\!]$. Let $(\Phi \; ; \; \Gamma \triangleright s) \in B^* \multimap C^*$. Then for any $(\Psi \; ; \; \Delta \triangleright t) \in B^*$, we have $(\Phi, \Psi \; ; \; \Gamma, \Delta \triangleright (st)) \in C^*$. Since we have $(\emptyset \; ; \; x : B \triangleright x) \in B^*$ for any x by the induction hypothesis on B of the case $n = 0$, we have $(\Phi \; ; \; \Gamma, x : B \triangleright (sx)) \in C^*$ for $x \notin FV(s)$. Then by the induction hypothesis on C, we have Φ ; $\Gamma, x : B \vdash (sx) : C$ and there is u in normal form such that $(sx) \simeq_{\beta\eta} u$. Then by applying the following $\multimap I$-rule

$$\frac{\Phi \; ; \; \Gamma, x : B \vdash (sx) : C}{\Phi \; ; \; \Gamma \vdash \lambda x.(sx) : B \multimap C} \multimap I \; ,$$

we have Φ ; $\Gamma \vdash \lambda x.(sx) : B \multimap C$ and $\lambda x.(sx) \simeq_{\beta\eta} \lambda x.u$.

Note that $\lambda x.u$ is not necessarily in normal form even if u is in normal form. Thus we divide the following two cases depending on u.
(i) If u is of the form (vx), then we have $s \simeq_\eta \lambda x.(sx) \simeq \lambda x.u \equiv \lambda x.(vx) \simeq_\eta v$. Note that v is in normal form since u is in normal form, and that we have Φ ; $\Gamma \vdash s : B$ by the equality-rule.
(ii) If otherwise, $\lambda x.u$ is in normal form since u is in normal form. Hence from $(sx) \simeq u$, we have $s \simeq_\eta \lambda x.(sx) \simeq \lambda x.u$, and we have Φ ; $\Gamma \vdash s : B$ by the equality-rule.
Hence in either case, we have $(\Phi \; ; \; \Gamma \triangleright s) \in [\![B \multimap C]\!]$.

(2) We show that for any $(\Phi \; ; \; \Gamma \triangleright t) \in B^*$, we have $(\Phi \; ; \; \vec{\Gamma_i}, \Gamma, x : E(B_1, \dots, B_n, (B \multimap C)) \triangleright (E(x, s_1, \dots, s_n) t)) \in C^*$. ¿From the assumption $(\Phi \; ; \; \Gamma \triangleright t) \in B^*$, we

have $(\Phi \; ; \; \Gamma \rhd t) \in [\![B]\!]$ by the induction hypothesis on B. Since $E(B_1, \ldots, B_n, (B \multimap C))$ is expressed as $E(B_1, \ldots, B_n, B, C)$ and $(E(x, s_1, \ldots, s_n)t)$ is $E(x, s_1, \ldots, s_n, t)$, we have the assertion by the induction hypothesis on C.

(Case $A \equiv B \to C$)

We omit a proof for this case since it is treated by the similar way as $\multimap$.

(Case $A \equiv B \& C$)

(1)   We show $B^* \& C^* \subseteq [\![B \& C]\!]$. Let $(\Phi \; ; \; \Gamma \rhd s) \in B^* \& C^*$. Then we have $(\Phi \; ; \; \Gamma \rhd \pi_1(s)) \in B^*$ and $(\Phi \; ; \; \Gamma \rhd \pi_2(s)) \in C^*$. Then by the induction hypothesis on B and C respectively, we have $\Phi \; ; \; \Gamma \vdash \pi_1(s) : B$ and there is u in normal form such that $\pi_1(s) \simeq_{\beta\eta} u$, and we have $\Phi \; ; \; \Gamma \vdash \pi_2(s) : C$ and there is v in normal form such that $\pi_2(s) \simeq_{\beta\eta} v$. Thus by the following $\& I$-rule

$$\frac{\Phi \; ; \; \Gamma \vdash \pi_1(s) : B \quad \Phi \; ; \; \Gamma \vdash \pi_2(s) : C}{\Phi \; ; \; \Gamma \vdash \langle \pi_1(s), \pi_2(s) \rangle : B \& C} \; \& I \; ,$$

we have $\Phi \; ; \; \Gamma \vdash \langle \pi_1(s), \pi_2(s) \rangle : B \& C$ and $\langle \pi_1(s), \pi_2(s) \rangle \simeq_{\beta\eta} \langle u, v \rangle$.

Thus we divide the following two cases depending on u and v.

(i)   If u is of the form $\pi_1(t)$ and v is of the form $\pi_2(t)$, then we have $s \simeq_\eta \langle \pi_1(s), \pi_2(s) \rangle \simeq \langle u, v \rangle \equiv \langle \pi_1(t), \pi_2(t) \rangle \simeq_\eta t$. Note that t is in normal form since u and v are in normal forms, and that we have $\Phi \; ; \; \Gamma \vdash s : B \& C$ by the equality-rule.

(ii)   If otherwise, $\langle u, v \rangle$ is in normal form since u and v are in normal forms. Hence from $\pi_1(s) \simeq u$ and $\pi_2(s) \simeq v$, we have $s \simeq_\eta \langle \pi_1(s), \pi_2(s) \rangle \simeq \langle u, v \rangle$, and $\Phi \; ; \; \Gamma \vdash s : B \& C$ by the equality-rule.

Hence in either case, we have $(\Phi \; ; \; \Gamma \rhd s) \in [\![B \& C]\!]$.

(2)   We show that $(\Phi \; ; \; \vec{\Gamma_i}, x : E(B_1, \ldots, B_n, (B \& C)) \rhd \pi_1(E(x, s_1, \ldots, s_n))) \in B^*$ and $(\Phi \; ; \; \vec{\Gamma_i}, x : E(B_1, \ldots, B_n, (B \& C)) \rhd \pi_2(E(x, s_1, \ldots, s_n))) \in C^*$.

Since $E(B_1, \ldots, B_n, (B \& C))$ is expressed as $E(B_1, \ldots, B_n, B, C)$ and $\pi_i(E(x, s_1, \ldots, s_n))$ for $i = 1, 2$ are $E(x, s_1, \ldots, s_n, s_{n+1})$ respectively, we have the assertion by the induction hypothesis on B and C respectively.   ∎

Assume that, for any $(n_i \; ; \; \varepsilon \rhd t_i) \in C_i^*$ and $(m_j \; ; \; l_j \rhd s_j) \in D_j^*$, we have $(\mathfrak{n} \star \mathfrak{m} \; ; \; \mathfrak{l} \rhd s[\mathfrak{t}, \mathfrak{s}]) \in A^*$ in any phase mode for proof-terms. Then we have $(y_1 : C_1, \ldots, y_l : C_l \; ; \; x_1 : D_1, \ldots, x_k : D_k \rhd s) \in A^*$ in the canonical model, since $(y_i : C_i \; ; \; \emptyset) \in C_i^*$ and $(\emptyset \; ; \; x_j : D_j) \in D_j^*$ for any C_i and D_j by the main lemma and the monotonicity. Hence by the main lemma $A^* \subseteq [\![A]\!]$, the sequent $y_1 : C_1, \ldots, y_l : C_l \; ; \; x_1 : D_1, \ldots, x_k : D_k \vdash s : A$ is derivable in λ_{Aff} and there is t in normal form such that $s \simeq_{\beta\eta} t$. Thus we obtain the following completeness theorem for proof-terms of λ_{Aff}.

Theorem 5 (Completeness for proof-terms)

If $y_1 : C_1, \ldots, y_l : C_l \; ; \; x_1 : D_1, \ldots, x_k : D_k \models s : A$ in any phase model for proof-terms of λ_{Aff}, then $y_1 : C_1, \ldots, y_l : C_l \; ; \; x_1 : D_1, \ldots, x_k : D_k \vdash s : A$ is derivable in λ_{Aff}, and there is t in normal form such that $s \simeq_{\beta\eta} t$.

Note that the completeness theorem (Theorem 2) for provability is a direct corollary of this completeness theorem for proof-terms.

If a λ-term s is typable in λ_{Aff}, then by the soundness, the premise of the completeness is satisfied. Hence by the completeness, we have the following normal form theorem of λ_{Aff}.

Corollary 1 (Normal form theorem). *If a λ-term s is typable in λ_{Aff}, then there is a λ-term t in normal form such that $s \simeq_{\beta\eta} t$.*

5   Concluding Remarks

We remarked that the completeness theorem of type assignment system of [Coquand 05] in the simple type framework can be extended to a stronger form which implies a normal form theorem in a linear (affine) types framework with Laird's dual affine/intuitionistic λ-calculus.

In order to prove completeness, we introduced, following [Hindley 83] and [Coquand 05], an equality-rule. This equality-rule makes some usually untypable λ-terms typable. It seems that this equality-rule is essential to prove completeness in our framework of λ_{Aff} which has η-rule for &, since the subject reduction property fails for this reduction. We remark that, in the framework without & nor η-rule, the following weaker form of completeness holds without having the additional equality-rule: *If $(\Gamma \rhd s) \in A^*$ for any model, then there is a λ-term t such that $s \simeq t$ and $\Gamma \vdash t : A$ is derivable*, which naturally implies completeness at the level of the provability.

¿From the phase semantic point of view, the $\{\multimap, \&, \rightarrow\}$-fragment of **ILL** is complete with respect to intuitionistic phase semantics without any closure condition, which is a generalization of the double negation operation $(\;)^{\perp\perp}$. Cf. [Abrusci 90] and [Okada 02] for the phase semantic closure. Hence our *closure condition* (the equality-closed and the monotonicity conditions) is not related to the closure condition of intuitionistic phase semantics for the provability. As future work, we investigate whether or not our closure condition in phase semantics for proof-terms can be considered as an extension of the closure condition of intuitionistic phase semantics for the provability.

References

[Abrusci 90] Michele, V.: Abrusci, Sequent calculus for intuitionistic linear propositional logic, Mathematical Logic, Plenum, New York, pp. 223–242 (1990)

[Barber 96] Barber, A.: Dual Intuitionistic Linear Logic, Technical Report ECS-LFCS-96-347, University of Edinburgh (1996)

[Barendregt 92] Barendregt, H.P.: Lambda Calculi with Types. In: Abramsky, S., Gabbay, D.M., Maibaum, T.S.E. (eds.) Handbook of logic in computer science, vol. 2, pp. 117–309. Oxford University Press, Oxford (1992)

[Coquand 05] Coquand, T.: Completeness Theorems and lambda-Calculus. In: Urzyczyn, P. (ed.) TLCA 2005. LNCS, vol. 3461, pp. 1–9. Springer, Heidelberg (2005)

[Fischer 93] Michael, J.: Lambda-Calculus Schemata. Lisp. and Symbolic Computation 6(3-4), 259–288 (1993)

[Girard 87] Girard, J.-Y.: Linear Logic, Theoretical Computer Science, vol. 50 (1987)

[Hasegawa 02a] Hasegawa, M.: Linearly used effects: monadic and CPS transformations into the linear lambda calculus. In: Hu, Z., Rodríguez-Artalejo, M. (eds.) FLOPS 2002. LNCS, vol. 2441, pp. 167–182. Springer, Heidelberg (2002)

[Hasegawa 02b] Hasegawa, M.: Classical linear logic of implications. In: Bradfield, J.C. (ed.) CSL 2002 and EACSL 2002. LNCS, vol. 2471, pp. 458–472. Springer, Heidelberg (2002)

[Hermant-Okada 07] Hermant, O., Okada, M.: A semantics for cut elimination in intensional higher-order Linear Logic (In preparation) (2007)

[Hindley 83] Hindley, J.R.: The Completeness Theorem for Typing lambda-Terms. Theoretical Computer Science 22, 1–17 (1983)

[Hindley-Seldin 86] Hindley, J.R., Seldin, J.P.: Introduction to Combinators and Lambda-Calculus. Cambridge University Press, Cambridge (1986)

[Hyland-Ong 00] Hyland, J.M.E., Luke, C.-H.: On Full Abstraction for PCF: I, II, and III. Information and Computation 163(2), 285–408 (2000)

[Laird 03] Laird, J., Game, A.: Semantics of Linearly Used Continuations. In: Gordon, A.D. (ed.) ETAPS 2003 and FOSSACS 2003. LNCS, vol. 2620, pp. 313–327. Springer, Heidelberg (2003)

[Laird 05] Laird, J.: Game Semantics and linear CPS interpretation. Theoretical Computer Science 333, 199–224 (2005)

[Martin 71] Martin-Löf, P.: Hauptsatz for the intuitionistic theory of iterated inductive definitions, In: Fenstad, J.E. (ed.) Proceedings of the Second Scandinavian Logic Symposium, North-Holland, pp. 179–216 (1971)

[Mitchell 90] Mitchell, J.C.: Type Systems for Programming Languages, Handbook of Theoretical Computer Science, vol. B, pp. 365–458 (1990)

[O'Hearn-Riecke] O'Hearn, P.W., Riecke, J.G.: Kripke Logical Relations and PCF. Information and Computation 120(1), 107–116 (1995)

[Okada 96] Okada, M.: Phase semantics for higher order completeness, cut-elimination and normalization proofs (Extended Abstract). Electronic Notes in Theoretical Computer Science 3, 22 (1996)

[Okada 99] Okada, M.: Phase semantic cut-elimination and normalization proofs of first- and higher-order linear logic. Theoretical Computer Science 227, 333–396 (1999)

[Okada 02] Okada, M.: A Uniform semantic proof for cut-elimination and completeness of various first and higher order logics. Theoretical Computer Science 281, 471–498 (2002)

[Okada 04] Okada, M.: Intuitionistic logic and linear logic. La. revue internationale de philosophie, special issue "Intuitionism" 230, 449–481 (2004)

[Okada-Terui 99] Okada, M., Terui, K.: The Finite Model Property for Various Fragments of Intuitionistic Linear Logic. Journal of Symbolic Logic 64, 790–802 (1999)

[Plotkin 75] Plotkin, G.D.: Call-by-Name, Call-by-Value and the lambda-Calculus. Theoretical Computer Science 1(2), 125–159 (1975)

Linear Recursive Functions[*]

Sandra Alves[1][**], Maribel Fernández[2], Mário Florido[1], and Ian Mackie[3][***]

[1] University of Porto, Department of Computer Science & LIACC, R. do Campo
Alegre 823, 4150-180, Porto, Portugal
[2] King's College London, Department of Computer Science, Strand, London
WC2R 2LS, UK
[3] LIX, CNRS UMR 7161, École Polytechnique, 91128 Palaiseau Cedex, France

Abstract. With the recent trend of analysing the process of computation through the linear logic looking glass, it is well understood that the ability to copy and erase data is essential in order to obtain a Turing-complete computation model. However, erasing and copying don't need to be explicitly included in Turing-complete computation models: in this paper we show that the class of partial recursive functions that are syntactically linear (that is, partial recursive functions where no argument is erased or copied) is Turing-complete.

Keywords: Recursion theory, linear calculi, iteration, computable functions.

1 Introduction

In the definition of recursive functions, together with recursion, a key mechanism in the process of computation is the ability for functions to duplicate and to discard their arguments (i.e., management of resources: erase and copy). In this paper we focus on this aspect of computation, which has attracted a great deal of attention in recent years. We say that a function is *linear* if it uses its arguments exactly once.

Primitive recursive functions, which we shall call PR, are a class of functions which form an important building block on the way to a full formalisation of computability. Intuitively speaking, (partial) recursive functions are those that can be computed by some Turing machine. Primitive recursive functions can be computed by a specific class of Turing machines that always halt. Many of the functions normally studied in number theory, and approximations to real-valued functions, are primitive recursive: addition, division, factorial, exponential, finding the nth prime, and so on [9]. In fact, it is difficult to devise a function that

---

[*] Research partially supported by the Treaty of Windsor Grant: "Linearity: Programming Languages and Implementations", and by funds granted to *LIACC* through the *Programa de Financiamento Plurianual, Fundação para a Ciência e Tecnologia* and *FEDER/POSI*.
[**] Programa Gulbenkian de Estímulo à Investigação.
[***] Projet Logical, Pôle Commun de Recherche en Informatique du plateau de Saclay, CNRS, École Polytechnique, INRIA, Université Paris-Sud.

H. Comon-Lundh et al. (Eds.): Jouannaud Festschrift, LNCS 4600, pp. 182–195, 2007.
© Springer-Verlag Berlin Heidelberg 2007

is not primitive recursive; Ackermann's function is a well-known example of a non-primitive recursive function.

The class of PR functions is the least set including the zero, successor and projection functions, and closed under the operations of composition and primitive recursion. In the definition of PR, zero and successor give access to the natural numbers and the projection functions are useful for erasing, copying and permuting arguments. Copying and erasing (i.e., the ability for functions to duplicate and to discard their arguments) are key operations in the definition of all interesting functions by primitive recursion, and in particular in the definition of the two operations used to define PR itself: composition and the primitive recursive scheme.

In this context the following question arises: can we define the class of primitive recursive functions without explicitly relying on copying and erasing? In this paper we show that the answer is yes; more precisely, we show that any primitive recursive function can be defined using a syntactically *linear* system. Furthermore, we show that any computable function can be defined using a single minimisation operator and linear functions. This yields an alternative formulation of the theory of recursive functions, where each function is linear; we call this class of functions *linear recursive functions*.

To define linear primitive recursive functions, which we shall call LPR, we start by specifying a set of linear initial functions (projections are not linear, so we will use natural numbers and the identity function), together with composition of linear functions and a linear primitive recursive scheme (i.e., primitive recursion where each function uses its arguments exactly once). Linear primitive recursive functions offer an *implicit* approach to copying and erasing. We can express both the process of copying a number and the process of erasing a number, as linear primitive recursive functions. Thus, the classes PR and LPR coincide.

Summarising, our main contributions are:

- Definition of linear primitive recursive functions (LPR)—a class of functions defined by the initial functions zero, successor, and identity, together with linear composition and *pure* iteration.
- Simulation of erasing and copying in LPR, in particular, projections can be simulated by permutation followed by a linear erasing. Using this result, we show that LPR and PR are exactly the same class of functions.
- Any general recursive function (i.e., any computable function) can be obtained if we add a minimisation operator working on linear primitive recursive functions.

This work exhibits a redundancy in the definition of recursive functions, and shows that a minimalistic definition of primitive recursion, based on linear functions, is sufficient. This is one more indication of the power of linear functions.

Related work: There are several alternative definitions of the primitive recursion scheme [22,15,16,21,10]. In some of these works, for instance [16,10], primitive recursion was replaced by *pure iteration*. Pure iteration is a linear scheme, in the sense that arguments of functions are used exactly once. Gladstone [16] gave a definition of primitive recursion using the standard initial functions and composition, but replaced primitive recursion by pure iteration. Here we refine this definition by replacing also the initial functions (by linear initial functions) and the composition scheme (by a linear composition scheme). We then show that this defines a set of linear functions that corresponds exactly to the primitive recursive functions.

Burroni [10] defined a category of primitive recursive functions with rather intuitive graphic descriptions of its objects. The definition of PR in this category is very close to ours (in particular iteration is also used instead of primitive recursion). The main difference from our work is the underlying approach: Burroni uses a categorical approach, while we use a standard recursion theory approach in the definition of PR. As an example of this, in [10], the construction of natural numbers uses an axiom similar to the Peano-Lawvere [19] axiom (more suitable in a categorical approach), instead of the Peano axioms which build numbers using the successor function.

There are several formalisms based on the notion of linearity that limit the use of copy and erasing. This includes languages based on a version of the λ-calculus with a type system corresponding to intuitionistic linear logic [12]. This calculus (which can be seen as a minimal functional programming language) provides *explicit* syntactical constructs for copying and erasing terms (corresponding to the exponentials in linear logic) [1].

From another perspective there have been a number of calculi, again many based on linear logic, for capturing specific complexity classes ([6,11,14,7,18,25,8]). One of the main examples is that of *bounded linear logic* [14], which captures the class of polynomial time computable functions.

This paper is part of a research project which aims at studying the notion of linearity in computation, and at analysing the computation power of linear systems. The results described here provide the foundations for a series of results, including the definition of a linear version of Gödel's System $\mathcal{T}$ [2] with a decidable typing system for polymorphic iteration [4]. Current research in this area includes the definition of an alternative version of System $\mathcal{T}$ which uses the linear λ-calculus and pure iteration with standard (monomorphic) linear types, without losing any of the computational power of Gödel's original definition. This paper is also a starting point for studying the connection between cartesian closed categories and symmetric monoidal closed categories. This work, which began in [20], studies this question using the internal languages (which are respectively the λ-calculus and the linear λ-calculus).

In the next section we recall the background material. In Section 3 we define the linear primitive recursive functions, and in Section 4 we show how any PR function can be encoded as an LPR function and vice versa. In Section 5 we define linear recursive functions and show that any computable function can be written as a linear recursive function. Section 6 briefly discusses higher-order primitive recursion. Finally we conclude the paper in Section 7.

2   Background

We assume familiarity with recursion theory, and recall some basic notions along the lines presented in [23]. We refer to reader to [23] for more details.

2.1   Primitive Recursive Functions

Notation: We use $x_1, \ldots, y_1, \ldots$ to represent natural numbers, f, g, h to represent functions and $X_1, \ldots$ to represent sequences of the form $x_1, \ldots, x_n$. We only have tuples on natural numbers, thus we will work modulo associativity for simplicity: $(X_1, (x_1, x_2), X_2) = (X_1, x_1, x_2, X_2)$.

Definition 1 (Primitive recursive functions). *A function $f : \mathsf{Nat}^k \to \mathsf{Nat}$ is primitive recursive if it can be defined from a set of initial functions using composition and the primitive recursive scheme defined as:*

- *Initial functions:*
    1. *The natural numbers, built from 0 and the successor function S. (We write n or S^n 0 for $\underbrace{\mathsf{S} \ldots (\mathsf{S}\ 0)}_{n}$.)*

    2. *Projection functions: $pr_i^n(x_1, \ldots, x_n) = x_i$ ($1 \le i \le n$); we omit the superindex when there is no ambiguity.*
- *Composition, which allows us to define a primitive recursive function h using auxiliary functions f, $g_1, \ldots, g_n$ where $n \ge 0$: $h(X) = f(g_1(X), \ldots, g_n(X))$.*
- *The primitive recursive scheme, which allows us to define a recursive function h using two auxiliary primitive recursive functions f, g:*

$$h(X, 0) \quad = f(X)$$
$$h(X, \mathsf{S}\ n) = g(X, h(X, n), n).$$

In [16] it was shown that primitive recursion could be replaced by a more restricted recursion scheme, called *pure iteration*:

$$h_g(X, 0) \quad = X$$
$$h_g(X, \mathsf{S}\ n) = g(h_g(X, n)).$$

The function $h_g(X, n)$, obtained by the last scheme, is the result of applying the function g n times to X. Hence we may write $h_g(X, n)$ to denote the function $g^n(X)$. In the sequel we sometimes use the notation h_f for the operator that iterates f (using the pure iteration scheme).

We do not have constant functions of the form $C(X) = x$ as initial functions. However, we can see 0 as a constant function with no arguments, and every other constant function can be built by composition of 0 and S, and projections. For instance, the constant function $zero(x, y) = 0$ is defined as an instance of composition (using the initial, 0-ary function 0) and $one(x, y) = \mathsf{S}(zero(x, y))$, again as an instance of the composition scheme.

Note also, that functions obtained from primitive recursive functions by introducing "dummy" variables, permuting variables, or repeating variables, are also primitive recursive functions. To keep our definitions simple, we will sometimes omit the definition of those functions. We give some examples below.

Example 1. Consider the standard functions add and mul from Nat^2 to Nat:

$$\mathsf{add}(x, y) = x + y \quad \mathsf{mul}(x, y) = x * y$$

The function add can be defined by primitive recursion as follows:

$$\mathsf{add}(x, 0) \quad = f(x)$$
$$\mathsf{add}(x, \mathsf{S}\ n) = g(x, n, \mathsf{add}(x, n))$$

where

$$f(x) \qquad = pr_1(x) \qquad\qquad = x$$
$$g(x_1, x_2, x_3) = \mathsf{S}(pr_3(x_1, x_2, x_3)) = \mathsf{S}(x_3)$$

The primitive recursive function mul is defined by:

$$\mathsf{mul}(x, 0) \quad = f(x)$$
$$\mathsf{mul}(x, \mathsf{S}\ n) = g(x, n, \mathsf{mul}(x, n))$$

where

$$f(x) \qquad = 0$$
$$g(x_1, x_2, x_3) = \mathsf{add}(pr_1(x_1, x_2, x_3), pr_3(x_1, x_2, x_3)) = \mathsf{add}(x_1, x_3)$$

In the sequel, we consider primitive recursive functions from Nat^k to Nat^l, since every primitive recursive function from Nat^k to Nat^l can be transformed into a primitive recursive function from Nat^k to Nat, and vice versa (see [24] for details).

2.2   Recursive Functions

Definition 2 (Minimisation). *Let f be a total function from Nat^{n+1} to Nat. The function g from Nat^n to Nat is called the* minimisation *of f and is defined as: $g(X) = \min\{y \mid f(X, y) = 0\}$. We denote g as $\mu_y(f)$.*

Definition 3 (Recursive functions). *The set of (partial) recursive functions is defined as the smallest set of functions containing the natural numbers (built from 0 and the successor function S) and the projection functions, and closed by composition, primitive recursion and minimisation.*

In particular, every primitive recursive function is recursive (since in both definitions we use the same initial functions, composition and primitive recursive scheme). Closure by minimisation implies that for every $n \geq 0$ and every total recursive function $f : \mathsf{Nat}^{n+1} \to \mathsf{Nat}$, the function $M_f : \mathsf{Nat}^n \to \mathsf{Nat}$ defined by $M_f = \mu_y(f)$ is a recursive function.

We recall the following result from Kleene [17].

Theorem 1 (The Kleene normal form). *Let h be a partial recursive function on Nat^k. Then, a number n can be found such that*

$$h(x_1, \ldots, x_k) = f(\mu_y(g(n, x_1, \ldots, x_k, y)))$$

where f and g are primitive recursive functions.

3   Linear Primitive Recursive Functions

Definition 4. *A function $f : \mathsf{Nat}^k \to \mathsf{Nat}^j$ is linear primitive recursive if it can be defined from a set of linear initial functions using linear composition and the linear primitive recursive scheme defined as follows:*

- *Initial functions:*
  1. *The natural numbers, built from 0 and the successor function S. We write n or $\mathsf{S}^n\, 0$ for $\underbrace{\mathsf{S} \ldots (\mathsf{S}\, 0)}_{n}$.*
  2. *The identity function* (`Id`).
- *Linear composition, which allows us to define a function h using auxiliary linear primitive recursive functions $f,\, g_1, \ldots, g_k$:*

$$h(x_1, \ldots, x_n) = f(g_1(X_1), \ldots, g_k(X_k)),$$

  where $(X_1, \ldots, X_k) = (x_1, \ldots, x_n)$.
- *Pure iteration, which allows us to define a recursive function h_g using an auxiliary linear primitive recursive function g:*

$$
\begin{aligned}
h_g(X, 0) &= X \\
h_g(X, \mathsf{S}\, n) &= g(h_g(X, n)).
\end{aligned}
$$

Note that the condition $(X_1, \ldots, X_k) = (x_1, \ldots, x_n)$ in the definition of linear composition above is simply a concise way of saying that each argument of the function h must be used exactly once in the composition (it may seem that this condition also restricts the order in which arguments are used, but we will show below that permutations can be defined as primitive recursive functions).

Example 2. A simple example of a linear primitive recursive function is addition. It can be defined as follows, where $g(x) = \mathsf{S}(x)$:

$$
\begin{aligned}
\mathsf{add}_g(x, 0) &= x \\
\mathsf{add}_g(x, \mathsf{S}\, n) &= g(\mathsf{add}_g(x, n)).
\end{aligned}
$$

Gladstone [16] defined the primitive recursive functions using the standard initial functions and composition, with pure iteration as a recursion scheme (indeed the name comes from [16]). Burroni [10], from a categorical approach, gave a definition of PR that is very close to ours, except that a different construction of natural numbers is given.

3.1   Some Useful Linear Primitive Recursive Functions

Erasing the last element of a tuple. The function $\mathcal{E}_{\mathsf{last}}$, which erases the last element of a tuple, is defined as:

$$
\begin{aligned}
\mathcal{E}_{\mathsf{last}}(X, 0) &= X \\
\mathcal{E}_{\mathsf{last}}(X, \mathsf{S}\, n) &= \mathtt{Id}(\mathcal{E}_{\mathsf{last}}(X, n))
\end{aligned}
$$

Lemma 1. *For any X and number n, $\mathcal{E}_{\mathsf{last}}(X, n) = X$.*

Proof. By induction: $\mathcal{E}_{\mathsf{last}}(X, 0) = X$ and $\mathcal{E}_{\mathsf{last}}(X, \mathsf{S}\ n) = \mathtt{Id}(\mathcal{E}_{\mathsf{last}}(X, n)) = \mathtt{Id}(X) = X$.

We can use the fact that we can erase the last element of a tuple, to erase at any position. We define $\mathcal{E}_i$, the function that erases element i of a tuple as:

$$\mathcal{E}_i(x_1, \ldots, x_n) = \mathtt{Id}(\mathcal{E}_{\mathsf{last}}(x_1, \ldots, x_i), \mathtt{Id}(x_{i+1}, \ldots, x_n))$$

Lemma 2. $\mathcal{E}_i(x_1, \ldots, x_n) = (x_1, \ldots, x_{i-1}, x_{i+1}, \ldots, x_n)$.

Proof. Follows from the correctness of $\mathcal{E}_{\mathsf{last}}$.

The zero function. Using the function that erases the last element one can define a function **zero**, such that $\mathtt{zero}(X) = 0$. The function **zero** is defined as:

$$\mathtt{zero}(x_1, \ldots, x_n) = \underbrace{\mathcal{E}_{\mathsf{last}} \cdots \mathcal{E}_{\mathsf{last}}}_{n}(0, x_1, \ldots, x_n)$$

Lemma 3. *For any X, $\mathtt{zero}(X) = 0$.*

Proof. By induction on the length of the tuple X.

Linear copying. We now define copying using pure iteration. The function C_k^1 produces k copies of a number:

$$\begin{aligned} f(x_1, \ldots, x_k) &= \mathtt{Id}(\mathsf{S}x_1, \ldots, \mathsf{S}x_k) \\ C_k^1(n) &= h_f(\underbrace{(0, \ldots, 0)}_{k}, n), \end{aligned}$$

where h_f denotes the function obtained by using the pure iteration scheme with the auxiliary function f.

Lemma 4. *For any number n, and any $k > 0$, $C_k^1(n) = \underbrace{(n, \ldots, n)}_{k}$.*

Proof. By induction: $C_k^1(0) = h_f(\underbrace{(0, \ldots, 0)}_{k}, 0) = \underbrace{(0, \ldots, 0)}_{k}$, and

$$C_k^1(\mathsf{S}\ n) = h_f(\underbrace{(0, \ldots, 0)}_{k}, \mathsf{S}\ n) = f(h_f(\underbrace{(0, \ldots, 0)}_{k}, n)) = f(\underbrace{n, \ldots, n}_{k}) = (\underbrace{\mathsf{S}\ n, \ldots, \mathsf{S}\ n}_{k}).$$

This can be generalised to copy tuples. We use C_j^i to denote copying j times a tuple with i elements. We first show how to define C_2^2, then after encoding permutations we define C_j^i.

$$C_2^2(x_1, x_2) = h(C'(C_2^1(x_1)), x_2)$$

where

$$h(x_1, x_2, x_3, x_4, 0) = (x_1, x_2, x_3, x_4)$$
$$h(x_1, x_2, x_3, x_4, \mathsf{S}\ n) = C''(h(x_1, x_2, x_3, x_4))$$

$$C'(x_1, x_2) = \mathtt{Id}(\mathtt{putZero}(x_1), \mathtt{putZero}(x_2))$$
$$\mathtt{putZero}(x_1) = \mathtt{Id}(x_1, 0)$$
$$C''(x_1, x_2, x_3, x_4) = \mathtt{Id}(\mathtt{Id}(x_1), \mathsf{S}(x_2), \mathtt{Id}(x_3), \mathsf{S}(x_4))$$

Lemma 5. $C_2^2(x_1, x_2) = (x_1, x_2, x_1, x_2)$.

Proof. Using the definition, $C_2^2(x_1, x_2) = h((x_1, 0, x_1, 0), x_2)$. The result follows by induction on x_2.

Permutations. We now define the swapping function $\pi(x, y) = (y, x)$, as follows:

$$\pi(x, y) = \mathcal{E}_1(\mathcal{E}_4(C_2^2(x, y)))$$

Permutations on any tuple can be obtained from composition of swappings and the identity. We will use π to denote permutation functions.

Having defined permutations, we define C_j^i as:

$$C_j^i(x_1, \ldots, x_i) = \pi(C_j^1(x_1), \ldots, C_j^1(x_i))$$

where $\pi(\underbrace{x_1, \ldots, x_1}_{j}, \ldots, \underbrace{x_i, \ldots, x_i}_{j}) = (x_1, \ldots, x_i, \ldots, x_1, \ldots, x_i)$.

To simplify notation, we use C to denote C_j^i, when there is no ambiguity.

Example 3. Using the erasing and copying functions, we can define multiplication as a linear primitive recursive function.

$$\mathtt{mul}(x, y) = \mathcal{E}_{\mathsf{last}}(\mathtt{mul}'_g(0, x, y))$$
$$\mathtt{mul}'_g(x_1, x_2, 0) = (x_1, x_2)$$
$$\mathtt{mul}'_g(x_1, x_2, \mathsf{S}\ n) = g(\mathtt{mul}'_g(x_1, x_2, n))$$

where $g(x_1, x_2) = f(x_1, C(x_2))$, and $f(x_1, x_2, x_3) = (\mathtt{add}(x_1, x_2), x_3)$.

Using these ideas we will define a systematic translation of primitive recursive definitions into linear primitive recursive functions.

4   From Linear Primitive to Primitive and Back

In this section we show that every primitive recursive function is linear primitive recursive. We also show that linear primitive recursive functions do not add any power to primitive recursive functions, i.e., the two classes coincide.

4.1   Primitive Recursive Functions Are Linear Primitive Recursive

A summary of the encoding of primitive recursive functions using linear primitive recursive functions is given as follows:

Primitive recursive	Linear primitive recursive
0 and S	0 and S
projections	permutations + linear erasing
composition	linear composition + linear copying + linear erasing
recursive scheme	pure iteration + linear copying + linear erasing

Projections. There are many alternative definitions of projections using linear primitive recursive functions, for instance:

$$pr_i(x_1, \ldots, x_n) = \underbrace{\mathcal{E}_{\mathsf{last}} \cdots \mathcal{E}_{\mathsf{last}}}_{n-1}(x_i, x_1, \ldots, x_{i-1}, x_{i+1}, \ldots, x_n)$$

where $(x_i, x_1, \ldots, x_{i-1}, x_{i+1}, \ldots, x_n) = \pi(x_1, \ldots, x_n)$.

Lemma 6. *For any* $(x_1, \ldots, x_n)$: $pr_i(x_1, \ldots, x_n) = x_i$.

Proof. By induction on n.

- Basis: $pr_1(x_1) = x_1$.
- Induction:

$$pr_i(x_1, \ldots, x_n) = \underbrace{\mathcal{E}_{\mathsf{last}} \cdots \mathcal{E}_{\mathsf{last}}}_{n-1}(x_i, x_1, \ldots, x_{i-1}, x_{i+1}, \ldots, x_n)$$

$$= \underbrace{\mathcal{E}_{\mathsf{last}} \cdots \mathcal{E}_{\mathsf{last}}}_{n-2}(x_i, x_1, \ldots, x_{i-1}, x_{i+1}, \ldots, x_{n-1}) = x_i.$$

Multiple projection can be defined as follows:

$$pr_I(X) = \underbrace{\mathcal{E}_{\mathsf{last}} \cdots \mathcal{E}_{\mathsf{last}}}_{n-k}(X_1, X_2)$$

where $I = \{i_1, \ldots, i_k\} \subseteq \{1, \ldots, n\}$, $(x_{i_1}, \ldots, x_{i_k}, X_2) = \pi(X)$.

Lemma 7. $pr_{\{i_1, \ldots, i_k\}}(x_1, \ldots, x_n) = (x_{i_1}, \ldots, x_{i_k})$.

Proof. By induction on $n - k$.

- $pr_{\{1, \ldots, n\}}(x_1, \ldots, x_n) = (x_1, \ldots, x_n)$.
- Induction:

$$pr_{\{i_1, \ldots, i_k\}}(x_1, \ldots, x_n) = \underbrace{\mathcal{E}_{\mathsf{last}} \cdots \mathcal{E}_{\mathsf{last}}}_{n-k}(x_{i_1}, \ldots, x_{i_k}, x_{j_1}, \ldots, x_{j_{n-k}})$$

$$= \underbrace{\mathcal{E}_{\mathsf{last}} \cdots \mathcal{E}_{\mathsf{last}}}_{n-k-1}(x_{i_1}, \ldots, x_{i_k}, x_{j_1}, \ldots, x_{j_{n-k-1}})$$

$$= (x_{i_1}, \ldots, x_{i_k}).$$

Composition. We now define composition (see Definition 1), using linear primitive recursive functions. Let $h(X) = f(g_1(X), \ldots, g_k(X))$ where $X = x_1, \ldots, x_n$, and assume there are linear primitive recursive functions f^L, and $g_1^L, \ldots, g_k^L$ such that

$$f^L(Y) = f(Y)$$
$$g_i^L(Z) = g_i(Z), \ (1 \le i \le k).$$

Then we define h using the linear composition scheme as follows:
$h(X) = f'_L(\pi(C_k(x_1), \ldots, C_k(x_n)))$, where

$$f'_L(X') = f^L(g_1^L(X_1), \ldots, g_k^L(X_k)) \text{ and}$$
$$X' = (X_1, \ldots, X_k) = (\underbrace{x_1, \ldots, x_n}_{X_1}, \ldots, \underbrace{x_1, \ldots, x_n}_{X_k}) = \pi(\underbrace{x_1, \ldots, x_1}_{k}, \ldots, \underbrace{x_n, \ldots, x_n}_{k}).$$

Primitive recursive scheme. We now define the primitive recursive scheme of Definition 1, using linear primitive recursive functions. Let f^L and g^L be such that for the auxiliary functions f and g in the primitive recursive scheme we have:

$$f^L(X) \quad = f(X)$$
$$g^L(X, x, n) = g(X, x, n).$$

We define h^L in the following way: $h^L(X, n) = pr_1(h_{g_1}(f_1(C(X)), 0, n))$, where

$$
\begin{aligned}
f_1(X_1, X_2) &= (f^L(X_1), X_2) \\
f_2(X, x, n) &= (X, x, n, X, n) &&= \pi(C(X), x, C(n)) \\
g_2(X, x, n, X, n) &= (g^L(X, x, n), X, \mathsf{S}\,n) \\
g_1(x, X, n) &= g_2(f_2(X, x, n)) &&(x, X, n) = \pi(X, x, n).
\end{aligned}
$$

Lemma 8. *For any X, and number n, $h_{g_1}(f_1(C(X)), 0, n) = (h(X, n), X, n)$.*

Proof. By induction: $h_{g_1}(f_1(C(X)), 0, 0) = (f^L(X), X, 0) = (h(X, 0), X, 0)$ and

$$
\begin{aligned}
h_{g_1}(f_1(C(X)), 0, \mathsf{S}\,n) &= g_1(h_{g_1}(f_1(C(X)), 0, n)) \\
&= g_1(h(X, n), X, n) \\
&= g_2(f_2(X, h(X, n), n)) \\
&= (g^L(X, h(X, n), n), X, \mathsf{S}\,n) = (h(X, \mathsf{S}\,n), X, \mathsf{S}\,n).
\end{aligned}
$$

Lemma 9. *For any X, and number n: $h^L(X, n) = h(X, n)$.*

Proof. $h^L(X, n) = pr_1(h_{g_1}(f_1(C(X)), 0, n)) = pr_1(h(X, n), X, n) = h(X, n)$.

Example 4. The primitive recursive function mul defined in Example 1, can be encoded as the following linear primitive recursive function:

$$\mathsf{mul}^L(x_1, x_2) = pr_1(h_{g_1}(f_1(C(x_1)), 0, x_2))$$

with

$$
\begin{aligned}
f_1(x_1, x_2) &= (f^L(x_1), x_2) \\
g_1(x_1, x_2, x_3) &= g_2(f_2(x_1, x_2, x_3)) \\
f_2(x_1, x_2, x_3) &= \pi(C(x_1), x_2, C(x_3)) = (x_1, x_2, x_3, x_1, x_3) \\
g_2(x_1, x_2, x_3, x_4, x_5) &= (g^L(x_1, x_2, x_3), x_4, \mathsf{S}\,x_5)
\end{aligned}
$$

Assuming g^L to be the encoding of $\mathsf{add}(pr_1(x_1, x_2, x_3), pr_3(x_1, x_2, x_3))$ and $f^L(x) = \mathcal{E}(x)$. Notice that a more simple encoding of this function is possible as was shown in Example 3.

4.2 Linear Primitive Recursive Functions Are Primitive Recursive

A summary of the encoding of linear primitive recursive functions using primitive recursive functions is given as follows:

Linear primitive recursive	Primitive recursive
0 and S	0 and S
Id	projection
linear composition	composition + projection
pure iteration	recursive scheme + projection

Identity. This is just a trivial projection $\mathsf{Id}(x) = pr_1^1(x)$.

Linear composition. We now define linear composition, using primitive recursive functions. Let f^P, and $g_1^P, \ldots, g_k^P$ be such that

$$f^P(X) = f(X)$$
$$g_i^P(X_i) = g_i(X_i), \ (1 \le i \le k).$$

and $(X_1, \ldots, X_k) = \pi(X)$. Then we define linear composition as

$$h(X) = f^P(g_1'(X), \ldots, g_k'(X))$$

where $g_i'(X) = g_i^P(pr_{I_i}(X))$, with $I_i = \{i_1, \ldots, i_m\} \subseteq \{1, \ldots, n\}$, and if $X = x_1, \ldots, x_n$, then $X_i = x_{j_{i_1}}, \ldots, x_{j_{i_m}}$.

Pure Iteration. Let g^P be a primitive recursive function from Nat^k to Nat^l, such that for the auxiliary function g in the pure iteration scheme we have: $g^P(X) = g(X)$.

We define h^P in the following way: $h^P(X, n) = h_{g_1}(X, n)$, where, if $X = x_1, \ldots, x_n, Y = y_1, \ldots, y_l$

$$f^P(X) \quad = X$$
$$g_1(X, Y, n) = g^P(pr_{\{n+1, \ldots, n+l\}}(X, Y, n)) = g^P(Y).$$

Lemma 10. *For any* $X = x_1, \ldots, x_k$, *and number* n, $h^P(X, n) = h_g(X, n)$.

Proof. By induction on n.

- Basis: $h^P(X, 0) = f(X) = X = h_g(X, 0)$.
- Induction:

$$
\begin{aligned}
h^P(X, \mathsf{S}n) &= g_1(X, h(X, n), n) \\
&= g^P(pr_{\{n+1, \ldots, n+l\}}(X, h_{g_1}(X, n), n)) \\
&= g^P(pr_{\{n+1, \ldots, n+l\}}(X, h^P(X, n), n)) \\
&= g^P(h^P(X, n)) \\
&= g(h_g(X, n)) \\
&= h_g(X, \mathsf{S}\, n).
\end{aligned}
$$

Using the encodings described above, we define the following translation functions:

Definition 5. – *Let f be a primitive recursive function. Then $[\![f]\!]_L$ will denote a linear primitive recursive function such that: $f(X) = [\![f]\!]_L(X)$.*
– *Let f be a linear primitive recursive function. Then $[\![f]\!]_P$ will denote a primitive recursive function such that: $f(X) = [\![f]\!]_P(X)$.*

We thus obtain the main result of this section:

Theorem 2. *Every PR function is LPR, and vice versa. That is $PR = LPR$.*

5 Minimisation of Linear Functions

5.1 Partial Linear Recursive Functions

The minimisation operator defined in Section 2 (see Definition 2) can also be applied to linear functions.

Definition 6 (Minimisation). *Let f be a linear recursive function from Nat^{n+1} to Nat. The minimisation of f, written $\mu_y(f)$, is the function from Nat^n to Nat defined as: $\mu_y(f)(X) = \min\{y \mid f(X, y) = 0\}$.*

Definition 7 (Linear recursive functions). *The set of linear recursive functions (LRF) is the smallest set containing the initial functions 0, S and Id (that is, natural numbers and the identity function, as in Definition 4) and closed by linear composition, pure iteration, and minimisation.*

In particular, every linear primitive recursive function is linear recursive, and for every $n \geq 0$ and every total linear recursive function $f : \mathsf{Nat}^{n+1} \to \mathsf{Nat}$, the function $M_f : \mathsf{Nat}^n \to \mathsf{Nat}$ defined by $M_f = \mu_y(f)$ is a linear recursive function.

5.2 From Recursive to Linear Recursive

Theorem 3. *Let h be a (partial) recursive function on Nat^k. Then there exists a linear recursive function h^L on Nat^k, such that: $h(x_1, \ldots, x_k) = h^L(x_1, \ldots, x_k)$.*

Proof. Let h be a recursive function on Nat^k. Then, by Kleene's theorem, there exists f and g primitive recursive, and a number n, such that $h(x_1, \ldots, x_k) = f(\mu_y(g(n, x_1, \ldots, x_k, y)))$.

Consider then the function $h^L(x_1, \ldots, x_k) = [\![f]\!]_L(\mu_y([\![g]\!]_L(n, x_1, \ldots, x_k, y)))$. Notice that

$$
\begin{aligned}
g(n, x_1, \ldots, x_k, y) &= [\![g]\!]_L(n, x_1, \ldots, x_k, y) \\
\Rightarrow \mu_y(g(n, x_1, \ldots, x_k, y)) &= \mu_y([\![g]\!]_L(n, x_1, \ldots, x_k, y)) \\
\Rightarrow f(\mu_y(g(n, x_1, \ldots, x_k, y))) &= [\![f]\!]_L(\mu_y([\![g]\!]_L(n, x_1, \ldots, x_k, y))).
\end{aligned}
$$

Thus

$$
\begin{aligned}
h(x_1, \ldots, x_k) &= f(\mu_y(g(n, x_1, \ldots, x_k, y))) \\
&= [\![f]\!]_L(\mu_y([\![g]\!]_L(n, x_1, \ldots, x_k, y))) \\
&= h^L(x_1, \ldots, x_k).
\end{aligned}
$$

The function h^L is linear recursive.

An alternative proof could be written using the fact that closing isomorphic sets of functions with the same minimisation functor gives isomorphic sets.

Corollary 1. *All computable functions are linear recursive.*

6 Primitive Recursion at Higher Types

It is well known that a primitive recursion scheme at higher types permits the representation of all the functions that are provably total in Peano Arithmetic (see e.g., [13]). The most commonly known formalism for this is Gödel's System $\mathcal{T}$. Using and extending techniques similar to the ones shown in Section 4 we can also prove that:

Theorem 4. *All functions provably total in Peano Arithmetic are linear.*

The essential points in the proof of this theorem are the mechanisms for copying and erasing functions; we refer the reader to [3] for the technical details.

7 Conclusion

The aim of this paper is to demonstrate that linear computations are powerful: linear recursive functions can express copying and erasing, thus all Turing computable functions are linear recursive. Moreover, without minimisation but with the addition of higher-order constructs, any function definable in Gödel's System $\mathcal{T}$ is linear.

Acknowledgements

We thank Yves Lafont for pointing out [10] to us, and Andrew Pitts for comments on a previous version of this paper. A preliminary version of this paper was presented at [5].

References

1. Abramsky, S.: Computational Interpretations of Linear Logic. Theoretical Computer Science 111(3), 3–57 (1993)
2. Alves, S., Fernández, M., Florido, M., Mackie, I.: The power of linear functions. In: Ésik, Z. (ed.) CSL 2006. LNCS, vol. 4207, pp. 119–134. Springer, Heidelberg (2006)
3. Alves, S., Fernández, M., Florido, M., Mackie, I.: Gödel's System T revisited. Technical Report TR-07-02, King's College London (2007)
4. Alves, S., Fernández, M., Florido, M., Mackie, I.: Iterator types. In: Seidl, H. (ed.) FOSSACS 2007, vol. 4423, pp. 17–31. Springer, Heidelberg (2007)

5. Alves, S., Fernández, M., Florido, M., Mackie, I.: Very primitive recursive functions. In: Computation and Logic in the Real World, CiE 2007, Quaderni del Dipartimento di Scienze Matematiche e Informatiche Roberto Magari (2007)
6. Asperti, A.: Light affine logic. In: Proc. Logic in Computer Science (LICS'98), pp. 300–308. IEEE Computer Society, Washington (1998)
7. Asperti, A., Roversi, L.: Intuitionistic light affine logic. ACM Transactions on Computational Logic 3(1), 137–175 (2002)
8. Baillot, P., Mogbil, V.: Soft lambda-calculus: a language for polynomial time computation. In: Walukiewicz, I. (ed.) FOSSACS 2004. LNCS, vol. 2987, pp. 27–41. Springer, Heidelberg (2004)
9. Brainerd, W.S., Landweber, L.H.: Theory of Computation. John Wiley and Sons, Inc, New York, NY, USA (1974)
10. Burroni, A.: Récursivité graphique, I: Catégorie des fonctions récursives primitives formelles. Cahiers de topologie et géométrie différentielle catégoriques, XXVII:49 (1986)
11. Girard, J.-Y.: Light linear logic. Information and Computation 143(2), 175–204 (1998)
12. Girard, J.-Y.: Linear Logic. Theoretical Computer Science 50(1), 1–102 (1987)
13. Girard, J.-Y., Lafont, Y., Taylor, P.: Proofs and Types. Cambridge Tracts in Theoretical Computer Science, vol. 7. Cambridge University Press, Cambridge (1989)
14. Girard, J.-Y., Scedrov, A., Scott, P.J.: Bounded linear logic: A modular approach to polynomial time computability. Theoretical Computer Science 97, 1–66 (1992)
15. Gladstone, M.: A reduction of the recursion scheme. J. Symb. Logic, vol. 32 (1967)
16. Gladstone, M.: Simplification of the recursion scheme. J. Symb. Logic, vol. 36 (1971)
17. Kleene, S.C.: Introduction to Metamathematics. North-Holland (1952)
18. Lafont, Y.: Soft linear logic and polynomial time. Theoretical Computer Science 318(1-2), 163–180 (2004)
19. Lawvere, F.: An elementary theory of the category of sets. Proc. Nat. Acad. Sci. vol. 52 (1964)
20. Mackie, I., Román, L., Abramsky, S.: An internal language for autonomous categories. Journal of Applied Categorical Structures 1(3), 311–343 (1993)
21. Odifreddi, P.: Classical recursion theory. Elsevier Science, Amsterdam (1999)
22. Robinson, R.: Primitive recursive functions. Bull. Am. Math. Soc., vol. 53 (2004)
23. Shoenfield, J.: Recursion Theory. Springer, Heidelberg (1993)
24. Stern, J.: Fondements Mathematiques de L'Informatique. Ediscience International, Paris (1994)
25. Terui, K.: Light affine calculus and polytime strong normalization. In: Proc. Logic in Computer Science (LICS'01), IEEE Computer Society, Washington (2001)

Deducibility Constraints, Equational Theory and Electronic Money*

Sergiu Bursuc[1], Hubert Comon-Lundh[1], and Stéphanie Delaune[2]

[1] Laboratoire Spécification & Vérification
ENS de Cachan & CNRS UMR 8643, France
{bursuc,comon,delaune}@lsv.ens-cachan.fr
[2] INRIA & LORIA**

Abstract. The starting point of this work is a case study (from France Télécom) of an electronic purse protocol. The goal was to prove that the protocol is secure or that there is an attack. Modeling the protocol requires algebraic properties of a fragment of arithmetic, typically containing modular exponentiation. The usual equational theories described in papers on security protocols are too weak: the protocol cannot even be executed in these models. We consider here an equational theory which is powerful enough for the protocol to be executed, and for which unification is still decidable.

Our main result is the decidability of the so-called intruder deduction problem, *i.e.* security in presence of a passive attacker, taking the algebraic properties into account. Our equational theory is a combination of several equational theories over non-disjoint signatures.

1   Introduction

The formal verification of security protocols is now a well-established area of research. One of the main challenges during the past years was to refine the models, taking into account some algebraic properties of the cryptographic primitives. Representing messages as terms in a free algebra, which is known as the *perfect cryptography assumption*, allows to find some logical attacks, but fails to find some of them, which rely on the algebraic properties. Even worse, for some protocols, the local program of an honest agent may itself rely on some algebraic properties. In such a case, the protocol does not have any honest execution in the perfect cryptography model.

More precise models of protocols are therefore needed. They assume that messages are terms modulo an equational theory. A list of some relevant equational theories is proposed in [9] (see also [18] for a list of protocols and comments on possible attacks).

---

* This work has been partly supported by the RNTL project PROUVÉ and POSÉ.
** UMR 7503 CNRS-INPL-INRIA-Nancy2-UHP. Campus Scientifique, BP 239, 54506 Vandoeuvre-lès-Nancy Cedex, France.

H. Comon-Lundh et al. (Eds.): Jouannaud Festschrift, LNCS 4600, pp. 196–212, 2007.

Proving the security for a bounded number of sessions in such formal models deserved a lot of articles, which we cannot all cite here. Let us mention [16], in which the authors proved that the security problem is co-NP complete in the perfect cryptography case. The extension to several equational theories has been considered: exclusive-or [7,2], Abelian groups [17], some properties of modular exponentiation [3,15], homomorphisms and exclusive-or [10],... All these works rely on solving *deducibility constraints* modulo equational theories, an approach that we will follow in the present paper.

On the other side, if we put too much of arithmetic in the equational theory, getting a more precise model, the security problem becomes undecidable: a necessary condition is the decidability of unification. A typical problem is: which properties of modular exponentiation do we want to keep? As shown in [13], the boundary between decidability and undecidability is tight.

We are interested here in yet other properties of modular exponentiation. In a case study of an electronic purse protocol (whose some parts will be described in Section 2) submitted by France Télécom, the protocol cannot be even executed if we don't have both the properties $(x^y)^z = x^{y \times z}$ and $x^y \times x^z = x^{y+z}$, as well as some other properties described later. However, having both multiplication and addition of exponents, together with the usual distributivity laws, yields undecidability of unification by an easy encoding of integer arithmetic. Nevertheless, we managed to design some equational theory for which unification is decidable and the protocol can be executed. The theory will be described in detail in Section 2. It is a union of three Abelian group theories and some rules for exponentiation.

Our equational theory does not fall in any class for which the security problem is known to be decidable. In view of the number of symbols and rules, it is worth trying to use combination results. Unfortunately, we cannot use directly the results of [4], as our theories are not disjoint. Further (closer) results are those of Y. Chevalier and M. Rusinowitch in [5], in which the authors give combination results for non-disjoint signatures, with applications to some security issues in presence of modular exponentiation. However, again, we cannot apply these results, as our theory can not be split into two equational theories satisfying the hypotheses of [5].

We were left to develop a new decision procedure. An important step towards this result is to decide the so-called *intruder deduction problem*: Given a finite set of messages T and a given message m, is it possible for the intruder to retrieve m from T by using his deduction capabilities? This corresponds to the security decision problem in presence of a passive eavesdropper, *i.e.* an intruder who is only able to listen messages that pass over the network. In particular it is assumed that he can not intercept messages and send some fake messages over the network. In this paper, we propose a decision procedure to decide this problem in presence of an intruder having complex deduction capabilities which are modeled through an equational theory. This is achieved by using a locality lemma from which it follows that the intruder deduction problem can be decided in polynomial time.

2   Intruder Deduction Problem

In this section, we describe our case study and the equational theory allowing us to model the protocol. Then, we formally describe the problem we are interested in. Our main result is stated in Theorem 1.

2.1   The Electronic Purse Protocol

The protocol involves three possible agents: the electronic purse EP, a server S and a trusted authority A. We will not consider here the authority A, who is involved only in case of claims of either party (and we also simplify several parts in the following). We denote by b and r two positive integers, which are public. The public key of EP is b^s mod r whereas s is its private key.

First, there is a phase during which the server authenticates itself. We skip this phase here, which does not make use of algebraic properties. After this phase, S and EP agree on a session nonce N_s and S owes the (certified) public key b^s mod r of EP. Then

1. The purse EP generates a nonce N, builds a message M (which is only used in case of conflict and whose content is not relevant here) and sends to the server S: hash(b^N mod r, S, N_s, M, X), where X is the amount payed.
2. The server S challenges EP sending a nonce N_c.
3. The purse EP sends back $N - s \times N_c, M, X$ and subtract X from his account.
4. The server S checks that the message received at step 1 is consistent with the message received at step 3 and then increases his account from the amount X.

The important and difficult part is the last step: S should be able to complete this verification. Here are the operations performed by S at this stage:

$$\mathsf{hash}((b^s)^{N_c} \times b^{N-s \times N_c} \mathsf{mod}\ r, S, N_s, M, X) = \mathsf{hash}(b^N \mathsf{mod}\ r, S, N_s, M, X)$$

The server S raises b^{-s} to the power N_c (b^s is public and N_c is known), raises b to the power $N - s \times N_c$ (which is the message sent at step 3), and multiply the two results. We can see that the following equational properties are used:

$$\mathsf{exp}(\mathsf{exp}(b, y), z) = \mathsf{exp}(b, y \times z) \quad \mathsf{exp}(b, x) \times \mathsf{exp}(b, y) = \mathsf{exp}(b, y + z)$$

as well as Abelian group properties of both $\times$ and $+$.

2.2   The Equational Theory

The problem now is that if we put together the above properties and the Abelian group properties of $+$ and $\times$, we can derive the distributivity of $\times$ w.r.t. $+$, in which case unification (hence security) becomes undecidable (see e.g. [9]). That is why we used a first trick: we introduce a unary function symbol h, whose meaning is $h(x) = \mathsf{exp}(b, x)$. We also use two distinct multiplication symbols: $\bullet$ and $\star$, with the following equational axioms EP: $\mathsf{AG}(+, J_+, e_+)$, $\mathsf{AG}(\star, J_\star, e_\star)$, $\mathsf{AG}(\bullet, J_\bullet, e_\bullet)$

(where AG are the axioms of Abelian Groups, which will be discussed later) as well as:

$$\exp(h(x), y) = h(x \star y) \qquad h(x) \bullet h(y) = h(x + y)$$
$$\exp(\exp(x, y), z) = \exp(x, y \star z)$$

These equational axioms suffice for the verification at the last step of the protocol. The distinction of the two multiplication symbols is not necessary for the purpose of the present paper: everything holds if we equate $\bullet$ and $\star$. However, we try here to meet the conditions of [5] for the combination results: the distinction between the two multiplication symbols might be useful when extending the results of this paper to the active intruder case.

It remains to show that unification is decidable modulo this theory. This is the subject of Section 3.

2.3 Security Problem

The most widely used deduction relation representing the deduction abilities of an intruder is often referred to as the Dolev-Yao model [12]. However, we want to give to the intruder the power to use equational reasoning modulo the set EP of equational axioms. The resulting set of deduction rules, denoted by $\mathcal{I}_{\mathsf{EP}}$ is given in Figure 1 where $\mathcal{F} = \{+, J_+, \star, J_\star, \bullet, J_\bullet, \exp, h\}$. This is the now classical approach, using explicit destructors. When f is associative and commutative, the number of premises of such a rule is unbounded; the set of intruder deduction rules is recursive (but might be infinite).

$$\frac{T \vdash u_1 \quad \dots \quad T \vdash u_n}{T \vdash f(u_1, \dots, u_n)} \text{ where } f \in \mathcal{F} \qquad (\mathsf{Eq}) \ \frac{T \vdash u}{T \vdash v} \ u =_{\mathsf{EP}} v$$

Fig. 1. Inference system — $\mathcal{I}_{\mathsf{EP}}$

Assume given an intruder theory. The problem whether an intruder can gain certain information s from a set of knowledge T, *i.e.* whether there is a proof of $T \vdash s$, is called the *intruder deduction problem*.

INPUT: a finite set of terms T, a term s (the secret).
OUTPUT: Does there exist a proof of $T \vdash s$?

Theorem 1. *The intruder deduction problem is decidable in polynomial time for the inference system $\mathcal{I}_{\mathsf{EP}}$.*

To prove this result, we will first introduce a new inference system that is equivalent from the point of view of deduction. Indeed, the proof system given in Figure 1 is not appropriate for automated proof search: the rule (Eq) allows equational reasoning at any moment of a proof. To define a more effective model, we represent the equational theory by an AC-convergent rewrite system. The rewriting system together with some of its properties are given in Section 3. Moreover, in order to make easier some reasoning we will split the rule about exp into three different inference rules. This new inference system will be fully described at the beginning of Section 4.

3 Properties of the Equational Theory

In this section we study the equational theory we have introduced in Section 2.2. We show that this theory can be represented by an AC-convergent rewriting system and we establish that unification modulo EP is decidable. Lastly, we prove some technical lemmas which will be useful to establish our locality result stated in Proposition 2. We rely on classical results on rewriting modulo equations (in particular modulo AC). See [11] for the definitions and notations.

3.1 Rewriting System Associated to the Equational Theory EP

For simplicity, our alphabet will contain a finite number of free constant symbols and the associative-commutative symbols $\{\star, \bullet, +\}$, the binary symbol exp, the unary symbols $h, J_\star, J_+, J_\bullet$ and the 3 neutral elements. We could also add other symbols, such as encryption, hashing,... and use then combination results of [1] allowing us to conclude in the case of disjoint theories.

The equational theory EP can actually be presented by a finite convergent rewrite system $\mathcal{R}$ (modulo associativity and commutativity (AC) of $+$, $\star$ and $\bullet$), which has actually even stronger properties. First, for each $\circ \in \{+, \star, \bullet\}$ $\mathcal{R}_{\mathsf{AG}(\circ)}$ is the rewrite system modulo AC for $\circ$:

$$
\begin{aligned}
x \circ e_\circ &\to x & x \circ J_\circ(x) &\to e_\circ \\
J_\circ(x) \circ J_\circ(y) &\to J_\circ(x \circ y) & J_\circ(e_\circ) &\to e_\circ \\
J_\circ(J_\circ(x)) &\to x & J_\circ(x) \circ x \circ y &\to y \\
J_\circ(x) \circ J_\circ(y) \circ z &\to J_\circ(x \circ y) \circ z & J_\circ(x \circ y) \circ x &\to J_\circ(y) \\
J_\circ(x \circ y) \circ x \circ z &\to J_\circ(y) \circ z & J_\circ(J_\circ(x) \circ y) &\to x \circ J_\circ(y)
\end{aligned}
$$

where $e_\circ$ is the appropriate neutral element. The unusual orientation of rules for inverses will ensure strong properties of the rewrite system, as explained in [6]. In addition, we have the following rewrite rules:

$$
\mathcal{R}_0 = \left\{
\begin{aligned}
\exp(h(x), y) &\to h(x \star y) & J_\bullet(h(x)) &\to h(J_+(x)) \\
\exp(\exp(x, y), z) &\to \exp(x, y \star z) & h(e_+) &\to e_\bullet \\
h(x) \bullet h(y) &\to h(x + y) & J_\bullet(h(x) \bullet y) &\to h(J_+(x)) \bullet J_\bullet(y) \\
h(x) \bullet h(y) \bullet z &\to h(x + y) \bullet z & \exp(e_\bullet, x) &\to h(e_+ \star x)
\end{aligned}
\right.
$$

The rewriting system $\mathcal{R} = \mathcal{R}_{\mathsf{AG}(\star)} \cup \mathcal{R}_{\mathsf{AG}(\bullet)} \cup \mathcal{R}_{\mathsf{AG}(+)} \cup \mathcal{R}_0$ consists of the 38 rewrite rules and the following result has been mechanically verified using CiME [8].

Lemma 1. $\mathcal{R}$ *is convergent modulo associativity and commutativity.*

The normal form (modulo AC) of t is written $t{\downarrow}$. Furthermore, not only $\mathcal{R}$ is convergent, but also:

Lemma 2. $(\mathcal{R}, \mathsf{AC})$ *is a decomposition of the equational theory* EP *which has the finite variant property.*

This property has been introduced in [6] and ensures that, for any term (or finite set of terms) t, there is a finite computable set of substitutions $\theta_1, \ldots, \theta_n$ such that, for any substitution σ, there exists an index i and a substitution σ' such that $t\sigma{\downarrow} = t\theta_i{\downarrow}\sigma'$. In other words, all possible reductions in an instance of t can be computed in advance. The lemma can be proved using a sufficient condition introduced in [6] and called *boundedness*. The interest of this property is twofold. First, due to the fact that unification is decidable for the theory AC, it ensures that unification is also decidable for EP. Secondly, such a property will be certainly useful to lift our result to solve intruder deduction constraints with variables in order to decide the security problem in presence of an active attacker.

3.2 Notion of Subterm

We assume the reader familiar with the basic vocabulary and results on term rewriting systems and term rewriting systems modulo AC. As usual, AC symbols are also considered as variadic symbols and may be used in infix notation and terms are flattened. For $\circ \in \{\star, +, \bullet\}$, we define $\mathrm{inv}_\circ(u)$ as the term $J_\circ(u){\downarrow}$. For instance, we have that $\mathrm{inv}_\bullet(h(J_+(a))) = J_\bullet(h(J_+(a))){\downarrow} = J_\bullet(h(J_+(a))){\downarrow} = h(a)$.

Definition 1. *We denote by* $top(t)$ *the root symbol of the term* t. $\mathrm{TOP}(u)$ *is defined by* $\mathrm{TOP}(J_\circ(v \circ w)) = \circ$, $\mathrm{TOP}(h(w + v)) = \bullet$, $\mathrm{TOP}(h(J_+(u + v))) = \bullet$ *and* $\mathrm{TOP}(u) = top(u)$ *otherwise.*

For instance, we have that $\mathrm{TOP}(h(a+b)) = \bullet$, $\mathrm{TOP}(h(a)) = h$, $\mathrm{TOP}(J_+(a+b)) = +$ and $\mathrm{TOP}(J_+(a)) = J_+$.

Definition 2. *Let* $\circ \in \{\star, +, \bullet\}$, *the set* $\mathrm{DS}_\circ(u)$ *is defined by*

- $\mathrm{DS}_\circ(u \circ v) = \mathrm{DS}_\circ(u) \cup \mathrm{DS}_\circ(v)$,
- $\mathrm{DS}_\circ(J_\circ(u)) = \{J_\circ(v) \mid v \in \mathrm{DS}_\circ(u)\}$,
- $\mathrm{DS}_\bullet(h(u)) = \{h(v) \mid v \in \mathrm{DS}_+(u)\}$, *and*
- $\mathrm{DS}_\circ(u) = \{u\}$ *if* $\mathrm{TOP}(u) \neq \circ$.

In particular, note that $\mathrm{DS}_\bullet(h(J_+(a + b))) = \{h(J_+(a)), \; h(J_+(b))\}$.

Definition 3 (subterms). *Let* t *be a term in normal form,* $Sub(t)$ *is the smallest set of terms such that* $t \in Sub(t)$ *and if* $u \in Sub(t)$ *then*

- *either* $\circ = \mathrm{TOP}(u) \in \{\star, \bullet, +\}$ *and* $\mathrm{DS}_\circ(u) \subseteq Sub(t)$
- *or else* $u = f(u_1, \ldots, u_n)$ *and* $u_1, \ldots, u_n \in Sub(t)$.

This notion is extended as expected to set of terms.

Example 1. Let $t_1 = J_+(a + b)$, $t_2 = h(J_+(b))$, $t_3 = J_\star(J_+(b)) \star c$ and $t_4 = h(c)$. We have that $Sub(t_1) = \{t_1, J_+(a), J_+(b), a, b\}$, $Sub(t_2) = \{t_2, J_+(b), b\}$, $Sub(t_3) = \{t_3, J_\star(J_+(b)), J_+(b), b, c\}$, and $Sub(t_4) = \{t_4, c\}$.

3.3   Technical Lemmas on Rewriting

The lemmas stated and proved below are used in the proof of Proposition 2.

Lemma 3. *Let $t, t_1, \ldots, t_n$ be terms in normal form, $n \geq 1$, $\circ \in \{\star, \bullet, +\}$, $\text{TOP}(t) \notin \{\circ, e_\circ\}$ and assume that $\text{TOP}((t \circ t_1 \circ \ldots \circ t_n)\!\downarrow) \neq \circ$ and $(t_1 \circ \ldots \circ t_n)\!\downarrow \neq e_\circ$. Then, there is an index i such that $\text{inv}_\circ(t) \in \text{DS}_\circ(t_i)$.*

Proof. The rewrite system $\mathcal{R}$ is convergent. So we can choose a strategy for reducing $t \circ t_1 \circ \ldots \circ t_n$ to its normal form. Given a term u, we order possible redexes $l\sigma \to r\sigma$ in u increasing order of priority as follows:

1. $l = J_\circ(x) \circ J_\circ(y) \circ z$ and $J_\circ(x)\sigma = t$ (or $J_\circ(y)\sigma = t$, the t in the lemma's statement)
2. $l = h(x) \bullet h(y) \bullet z$ and $h(x)\sigma = t$ (or $h(y)\sigma = t$)
3. $l = h(x) \bullet h(y) \bullet z$, and $h(x)\sigma \neq t, h(y)\sigma \neq t$
4. all other cases

We contract always a redex with a maximal priority. This means that the first two cases are applied, only when other rules instances are not a redex in u.

Then we prove the result on the length of such a reduction sequence of $t \circ t_1 \circ \ldots \circ t_n$ to its normal form.

The case where the reduction length is 0 does not occur. Now, we investigate the possible rules, which are applied for the first reduction step. There are 7 cases when $\circ \neq \bullet$ and two additional cases when $\circ = \bullet$:

Case 1: The rule is $x \circ e_\circ \to x$. Since $t, t_1, \ldots, t_n$ are in normal form, we must have $t_i = e_\circ$ for some i. We simply apply the induction hypothesis. Note that, because $(t_1 \circ \ldots \circ t_n)\!\downarrow \neq e_\circ$, n must be at least 2.

Case 2: The rule is $x \circ J_\circ(x) \to e_\circ$: $t \circ t_1 \circ \ldots \circ t_n = x\sigma \circ J_\circ(x\sigma)$. Either $t = J_\circ(x\sigma)$ and, since $\text{TOP}(t) \neq \circ$, we must have $n = 1$ and $t_1 = \text{inv}_\circ(t)$ or else there is an index i such that $t_i = J_\circ(x\sigma)$ or $t_i = J_\circ(x\sigma) \circ t'_i$. In the first case, $x\sigma = t \circ u$ and then $t_i = J_\circ(t \circ u)$. In the second case either $x\sigma = t \circ u$ and $t_i = J_\circ(t \circ u) \circ t'_i$ or $t'_i = t \circ u$ and $t_i = t \circ u \circ J_\circ(x\sigma)$.

Case 3: The rule is $J_\circ(x) \circ x \circ y \to y$. Then, as in case 2, $t = J_\circ(x\sigma)$ and, for some i, $t_i = \text{inv}_\circ(t) \circ u$ or else there is an index i such that $t_i = J_\circ(x\sigma) \circ t'_i$. In that case, either $t_i = t \circ u$ or $y\sigma = t \circ t'_1 \circ \ldots \circ t'_k$ and, for each k, t'_k is in normal form and there is an injection π from $\{1, \ldots, k\}$ in $\{1, \ldots, n\}$ such that, for every j, $t_{\pi(j)} = t'_j \circ u_j$. Moreover, $(t'_1 \circ \ldots \circ t'_k)\!\downarrow = (t_1 \circ \ldots \circ t_n)\!\downarrow \neq e_\circ$. Then, we can apply the induction hypothesis: there is an index j such that $t'_j = \text{inv}_\circ(t)$ or $t'_j = \text{inv}_\circ(t) \circ u$ or $t'_j = J_0(t \circ u) \circ v$ or $t'_j = J_0(t \circ u)$. In each case, choosing $i = \pi(j)$, we get the desired properties.

Case 4: The rule is $J_\circ(x) \circ J_\circ(y) \circ z \to J_\circ(x \circ y) \circ z$. If $t = J_\circ(x)\sigma$, then, by hypothesis on the strategy, $J_\circ(y\sigma) \circ z\sigma$ is in normal form and, moreover, $z\sigma$ cannot be written $t \circ u$ (otherwise another rule applies). Then $J_\circ(x \circ y)\sigma \circ z\sigma$ is in normal form, which contradicts $\text{TOP}((t \circ t_1 \circ \ldots \circ t_n)\!\downarrow) \neq \circ$: this case cannot occur.

Now, $J_\circ(x \circ y)\sigma$ is in normal form and $z\sigma = t \circ t'_1 \circ \ldots \circ t'_k$ where the terms $t'_1, \ldots t'_k$ are in normal form and $(J_\circ(x \circ y)\sigma \circ t'_1, \ldots \circ t'_k)\!\downarrow \neq e_\circ$. We can apply the induction hypothesis: $\mathsf{inv}_\circ(t) \in \mathrm{DS}_\circ(t'_j)$ for some j or else $\mathsf{inv}_\circ(t) \in \mathrm{DS}_\circ(J_\circ(x \circ y)\sigma)$. In the first case, as in case 3, there is some index $i = \pi(j)$ such that $t_i = t'_j \circ u$, hence $t_i = \mathsf{inv}_\circ(t) \circ v \circ u$. In the second case, there are indices i_1, i_2 such that $t_{i_1} = J_\circ(x\sigma) \circ u$ and $t_{i_2} = J_\circ(y\sigma) \circ v$ (u and v might be empty here). Hence there is a variable (say x) such that $t = J_\circ(t')$ and $x\sigma = t' \circ u$. Then $t \in \mathrm{DS}_\circ(t_{i_1})$.

Case 5: The rule is $J_\circ(x) \circ J_\circ(y) \to J_\circ(x \circ y)$. This case cannot occur since the resulting term would be in normal form (remember $J_\circ(x\sigma)$ and $J_\circ(y\sigma)$ are assumed both in normal form) and we would not have $\mathrm{TOP}((t \circ t_1 \circ \ldots \circ t_n)\!\downarrow) = \circ$.

Case 6: The rule is $J_\circ(x \circ y) \circ x \to J_\circ(y)$. In this case, t cannot be $J_\circ(x \circ y)\sigma$ since $\mathrm{TOP}(t) \neq \circ$. Hence $x\sigma = t \circ u$ and there is an index i such that $t_i = J_\circ(x \circ y)\sigma \circ v$ (with possibly empty u or v). Then $t \in \mathrm{DS}_\circ(t_i)$.

Case 7: The rule is $J_\circ(x \circ y) \circ x \circ z \to J_\circ(y) \circ z$. As in case 6, $J_\circ(x \circ y)\sigma$ cannot be t itself: either $x\sigma = t \circ u$ or else $z\sigma = t \circ u$ for some (possibly empty) u. Moreover, there is an index i such that $t_i = J_\circ(x \circ y)\sigma \circ w$ (with possibly empty w).

In the first case, $t \in \mathrm{DS}_\circ(t_i)$ and, in the second case, we apply the induction hypothesis: if $z\sigma = t'_1 \circ \ldots \circ t'_k$, either there is some index j such that $\mathsf{inv}_\circ(t) \in \mathrm{DS}_\circ(t'_j)$, in which case, as before, there is some index k such that $\mathsf{inv}_\circ(t) \in \mathrm{DS}_\circ(t_k)$ or else $\mathsf{inv}_\circ(t) \in \mathrm{DS}_\circ(J_\circ(y\sigma))$. Then $t \in \mathrm{DS}_\circ(t_i)$.

Case 8: the rule is $h(x) \bullet h(y) \to h(x+y)$: let $h(x)\sigma = t = h(u_1)$, $h(y)\sigma = h(u_2)$ and $\mathrm{top}(u_1) \neq +$. According to the strategy, $h(y)\sigma$ is in normal form. Since $h(e_+) \to e_\bullet$ and $h(u_1 + u_2)\!\downarrow \neq e_\bullet$, $h(u_1 + u_2)\!\downarrow = h((u_1 + u_2)\!\downarrow)$ and we can apply the induction hypothesis to $u_1 + u_2$ (with $\circ = +$): $\mathsf{inv}_+(u_1) \in \mathrm{DS}_+(u_2)$, which implies $h(\mathsf{inv}_+(u_1)) \in \mathrm{DS}_\bullet(h(u_2))$. But $\mathsf{inv}_\bullet(h(u_1)) = h(\mathsf{inv}_+(u_1))$ by definition. Hence $\mathsf{inv}_\bullet(t) \in \mathrm{DS}_\bullet(h(u_2))$, which is the desired result.

Case 9: the rule is $h(x) \bullet h(y) \bullet z \to h(x + y) \bullet z$. If we had $h(x)\sigma = t$ (resp. $h(y)\sigma = t$), by hypothesis on the strategy, we would have $h(y)\sigma \bullet z\sigma$ in normal form. In particular, $z\sigma$ cannot be written $h(v) \bullet w$ or $h(v)$ or $J_\bullet(h(v)) \bullet w$ or $J_\bullet(h(v))$. This implies that $(t \circ \ldots \circ t_n)\!\downarrow = h(x\sigma + y\sigma)\!\downarrow \bullet z\sigma$, contradicting $\mathrm{top}((t \circ t_1 \circ \ldots \circ t_n)\!\downarrow) \neq \circ$.

It follows that $z\sigma = t \bullet t'_1 \bullet \ldots \bullet t'_k$ (and each t'_i is some t_j). Moreover, each t'_i and t itself must be headed with h (by the assumed strategy and since the normal form is not headed with $\bullet$). Let $t_i = h(u_i)$ and $t = h(u_0)$. $(t \bullet t_1 \ldots \bullet t_n)\!\downarrow = h(v)$ and $(u_0 + \ldots + u_n)\!\downarrow = v$. Now, $(u_0 + \ldots + u_n)\!\downarrow \neq e_+$ and $\mathrm{TOP}((u_0 + \ldots + u_n)\!\downarrow) \neq +$. Hence, by induction hypothesis, $\mathsf{inv}_+(u_0) \in \mathrm{DS}_+(u_i)$ for some i. It follows that $\mathsf{inv}_\bullet(t) \in \mathrm{DS}_\bullet(t_i)$.   □

Lemma 4. *Let $\circ \in \{\star, \bullet, +\}$, $t_1, \ldots, t_n, u_1, \ldots, u_m$ be terms in normal form such that for every i, $\mathrm{TOP}(t_i) = \circ$ and $\mathrm{TOP}(u_i) \notin \{\circ, e_\circ\}$. Let $t = (t_1 \circ \ldots \circ t_n \circ u_1 \circ \ldots \circ u_m)\!\downarrow$. Then for every i, either $u_i \in \mathrm{DS}_\circ(t)$ or there is an index j such that $\mathsf{inv}_\circ(u_i) \in \mathrm{DS}_\circ(t_j)$, or else there is an index j such that $u_j = \mathsf{inv}_\circ(u_i)$.*

Proof. We use the lemma 3, with u_i in place of t and adding a term $t_{n+1} = \text{inv}_o(t)$: we conclude that, for every i, either $\text{inv}_o(u_i) \in \text{DS}_o(t_{n+1})$ or $\text{inv}_o(u_i) \in \text{DS}_o(u_j)$ or $\text{inv}_o(u_i) \in \text{DS}_o(t_j)$. In the first case, $u_i \in \text{DS}_t()$, in the second case $\text{inv}_o(u_i) = u_j$. $\square$

4 Locality

We first introduce a new inference system equivalent to $\mathcal{I}_{\mathsf{EP}}$ and then we will show that this inference system is local w.r.t. to a notion of subterms F.

Definition 4 (F-local). *An inference system $\mathcal{I}$ is F-local if for any proof of $T \vdash u$ in $\mathcal{I}$ there exists one such that all intermediate formulas are in $F(T \cup \{u\})$.*

4.1 A Local Inference System

We introduce a new inference system which can be viewed as the union of two parts denoted respectively by $\mathcal{I}_1$ and $\mathcal{I}_2$. From now on we omit the rule (Eq) and consider a variant of the deduction model which works on normal forms. This means that, after each step, the term obtained is reduced to its normal form. The part $\mathcal{I}_1$ is made up of the following 7 rules where $\mathcal{F}^- = \{+, J_+, \star, J_\star, \bullet, J_\bullet, h\}$.

$$\mathcal{I}_1 = \left\{ (\mathsf{R}_f) \ \frac{T \vdash u_1 \quad \cdots \quad T \vdash u_n}{T \vdash f(u_1, \ldots, u_n)\downarrow} \ \text{where } f \in \mathcal{F}^- \right.$$

We also distinguish the rules obtained by exponentiation, depending on the first premise of the inference rule: either applying exponentiation to u, v yields a term $\exp(u, v)$ in normal form or else $u = \exp(t_1, t_2)$ or else $u = h(t_1)$. We distinguish these three cases splitting the single inference rule into three different inference rules, which will be more convenient for further proofs. We let $\mathcal{I}_2$ be the inference system made up of the three following rules:

$$\mathcal{I}_2 = \left\{ \ \frac{h(t_1) \ t_2 \ \cdots \ t_n}{h(t_1 \star \cdots \star t_n)\downarrow} \ \mathsf{Exp}_1 \qquad \frac{\exp(t_1, t_2) \ t_3 \ \cdots \ t_n}{\exp(t_1, t_2 \star \cdots \star t_n)\downarrow} \ \mathsf{Exp}_2 \qquad \frac{t \ \ u}{\exp(t, u)} \ \mathsf{Exp}_3 \right.$$

Equivalence modulo AC is easy to decide, so we omit the equality rule for AC and just work with equivalence classes modulo AC. We have the following result.

Proposition 1. *Let T be a set of terms and u a term (in normal form). We have that $T \vdash u$ is derivable in $\mathcal{I}_{\mathsf{EP}}$ if and only if $T \vdash u$ is derivable in $\mathcal{I}_1 \cup \mathcal{I}_2$.*

Definition 5 (decomposition rule). *The application of a rule in $\mathcal{I}_2$ is a decomposition if it is an instance of Exp_1 and the resulting term is of the form $h(u)$ with $\text{TOP}(u) \neq \star$. A decomposition rule for $\mathcal{I}_1$ is a rule R_f, such that one of the following occurs:*

- *$f \in \{\star, \bullet, +\}$ and the conclusion $t = (f(t_1, \ldots, t_n))\downarrow$ is such that $\text{TOP}(t) \neq f$*
- *$f = J_o$ and the rule is applied to a term of the form $J_o(t)$*

Rules, which are not decomposition rules are compositions.

4.2 Locality Result

We show that our case study satisfies the locality properties. First we need to define a suitable function F. We consider the following one:

$$
\begin{aligned}
F(T) = \quad & \mathrm{Sub}(T) \\
& \cup \{h(t) \mid t \in \mathrm{Sub}(T), \mathrm{TOP}(t) = +\} \\
& \cup \{h(\mathrm{inv}_+(t) \mid t \in \mathrm{Sub}(t), \mathrm{TOP}(t) = +\} \\
& \cup \{\mathrm{inv}_\circ(t) \mid t \in \mathrm{Sub}(T), \mathrm{TOP}(t) = \circ, \circ \in \{\star, +\}\} \\
& \cup \{h(t) \mid \exists u \in \mathrm{Sub}(T) \text{ such that } \mathrm{TOP}(u) = \circ, t \in \mathrm{DS}_\circ(u), \circ \in \{\star, +\}\} \\
& \cup \{\mathrm{inv}_\circ(t) \mid \exists u \in \mathrm{Sub}(T) \text{ such that } \mathrm{TOP}(u) = \circ, t \in \mathrm{DS}_\circ(u), \circ \in \{\star, +, \bullet\}\} \\
& \cup \{h(\mathrm{inv}_\circ(t)) \mid \exists u \in \mathrm{Sub}(T) \text{ such that } \mathrm{TOP}(u) = \circ, t \in \mathrm{DS}_\circ(u), \circ \in \{\star, +\}\}
\end{aligned}
$$

Lemma 5. *The size of $F(T)$ (number of distinct subterms) is linear in the size of T.*

Proof. More precisely, the size of $F(T)$ is bounded by 10 times the size of T. For, it suffices to note that, all terms in $F(T)$ are always in $\mathrm{Sub}(T) \cup h(\mathrm{Sub}(T)) \cup \mathrm{inv}_\circ(\mathrm{Sub}(T)) \cup h(\mathrm{inv}_\circ(\mathrm{Sub}(T)))$ for some $\circ$.

The remainder of the paper is devoted to the proof of the following result.

Proposition 2. *The inference system $\mathcal{I}_1 \cup \mathcal{I}_2$ is F-local.*

Example 2. Here are some examples of proofs, which satisfy the requirements of the proposition:

$$
\cfrac{\cfrac{\cfrac{a}{J_+(a)}\,R_{J_+}}{h(a+b+c)\quad h(J_+(a))}\,R_h}{h(b+c)}\,R_\bullet
\qquad
\cfrac{\cfrac{a+b+c}{h(a+b+c)}\,R_h \quad h(J_+(a))}{h(b+c)}\,R_\bullet
$$

$$
\cfrac{h(b)\quad \cfrac{a\star b}{J_\star(a\star b)}\,R_{J_\star}}{h(J_\star(a))}\,\mathrm{Exp}_1
\qquad
\cfrac{\cfrac{\cfrac{a+b}{J_+(a+b)}\,R_{J_+}}{h(J_+(a+b))}\,R_h \quad h(a)}{h(J_+(b))}\,R_\bullet
$$

An an example of proof rewriting:

$$
\cfrac{\cfrac{\cfrac{a+b\quad c}{a+b+c}\,R_+}{h(a+b+c)}\,R_h \quad h(J_+(a))}{h(b+c)}\,R_\bullet
\quad\Longrightarrow\quad
\cfrac{\cfrac{a+b}{h(a+b)}\,R_h \quad h(J_+(a))\quad \cfrac{c}{h(c)}\,R_h}{h(b+c)}\,R_\bullet
$$

To prove this result, we consider normal proofs of t which are minimal in size. Then we prove the result by induction on the number of layers. Then it is a series of case study, mainly relying on Lemmas 3, 4, and technical lemmas carefully investigating the cases in which there is a decomposition. We normalize the proofs according to the rules given in Figure 2. These rules are (strongly) terminating (but not confluent). This is our notion of cut elimination.

Before we switch to the proof of this proposition in the next subsections, let us note that theorem 1 is a consequence of the proposition and the following lemma:

Lemma 6 (one-step deducibility). *Given a finite set of terms T, a term t and a function symbol f, it can be decided in polynomial time whether there are terms $t_1, \ldots, t_n \in T$ such that $f(t_1, \ldots, t_n){\downarrow} = t$.*

The proof of this lemma relies on standard techniques: if f is not an associative-commutative symbol, then n is fixed and a simple enumeration gives a polynomial algorithm. Otherwise, in all cases, except when $f = \bullet$, only the Abelian group properties of a single symbol have to be considered and the problem amounts to solve a system of linear equations over $\mathbb{Z}$, as already noticed by several authors. When $f = \bullet$, we have that $t = h(t') \bullet t''$ for some terms t' and t''. Let, for $u \in T$, $f_1(u)$, $f_2(u)$ be such that $u = h(f_1(u)) \bullet f_2(u)$, $f_1(u)$ and $f_2(u)$ being possibly empty. The one-step deducibility problem reduces to a system of two systems of linear equations over $\mathbb{Z}$: $\sum_{u \in T} z_u f_1(u) = t'$ and $\prod_{u \in T} f_2(u)^{z_u} = t''$.

Now, the algorithm works as follows. Given T and t, we compute $F(T) \cup F(t)$ (linear time) and then use a fixed point algorithm for the computation of deducible terms in $F(T) \cup F(t)$. Initially, the set D of deducible terms is set to T. Then until a fixed point is reached, add to D the terms in $F(T) \cup F(t)$ that are deducible in one step from terms in D.

This is a polynomial algorithm as one-step deducibility can be checked in polynomial time according to Lemma 6.

4.3   Preliminary Lemmas

Lemma 7. *If t is obtained by decomposition using $\mathsf{R}_f \in \mathcal{I}_1$, one of the following holds:*

- $t \in \{e_+, e_\star, e_\bullet\}$
- *The premise is $f(t)$ ($f \in \{J_+, J_\star, J_\bullet\}$)*
- $f \in \{\star, +, \bullet\}$ *and there is a premise u such that $t \in \mathrm{DS}_f(u)$.*

Proof. The rule R_f can be a decomposition only when $f \in \{J_\circ, \circ\}$ and $\circ \in \{\star, +, \bullet\}$. If $f = J_\circ$, we are in the second case of the conclusion of the lemma. Only remains to consider $f \in \{\star, +, \bullet\}$. Let then $t_1, \ldots, t_n$ be the premises of the rule and t be the conclusion. Either $t = e_f$ (then we fall into the first case of the conclusion) or else $(f(\mathrm{inv}_f(t), t_1, \ldots, t_n)){\downarrow} = e_\circ$ and we can apply Lemma 3: $\mathrm{inv}_f(\mathrm{inv}_f(t)) \in \mathrm{DS}_f(t_i)$ for some i, which is the desired result. $\qquad\square$

$$\frac{\dfrac{h(t_1)\ \ t_2\ \ \ldots\ \ t_n}{h(t_1 \star \ldots \star t_n)\!\downarrow}\ \mathsf{Exp}_1 \quad u_2\ \ldots\ u_m}{h(t_1 \star t_2 \ldots \star t_n \star u_2 \ldots \star u_m)\!\downarrow}\ \mathsf{Exp}_1 \quad\Rightarrow\quad \frac{h(t_1)\ \ t_2\ \ \ldots\ \ t_n\ \ u_2\ \ldots\ \ u_m}{h(t_1 \star t_2 \ldots \star t_n \star u_2 \ldots \star u_m)\!\downarrow}\ \mathsf{Exp}_1$$

$$\frac{\dfrac{\exp(t_1,t_2)\ \ t_3\ \ \ldots\ \ t_n}{\exp(t_1, t_2 \star \ldots \star t_n)\!\downarrow}\ \mathsf{Exp}_2 \quad u_3\ \ldots\ u_m}{\exp(t_1, t_2 \star \ldots t_n \star u_3 \star \ldots \star u_m)\!\downarrow}\ \mathsf{Exp}_2 \quad\Rightarrow\quad \frac{\exp(t_1,t_2)\ \ t_3\ \ \ldots\ \ t_n\ \ u_3\ \ldots\ \ u_m}{\exp(t_1, t_2 \star \ldots t_n \star u_3 \star \ldots \star u_m)\!\downarrow}\ \mathsf{Exp}_2$$

$$\frac{h(t_1)\ \ t_2\ \ \ldots\ \ \dfrac{u_1\ \ldots\ u_m}{(u_1 \star \ldots \star u_m)\!\downarrow}\ \mathsf{R}_\star\ \ \ldots\ t_n}{h(t_1 \star t_2 \ldots u_1 \star \ldots u_m \star \ldots \star t_n)\!\downarrow}\ \mathsf{Exp}_1 \quad\Rightarrow\quad \frac{h(t_1)\ \ t_2\ \ \ldots\ \ u_1\ \ldots\ \ u_m\ \ldots\ \ t_n}{h(t_1 \star t_2 \ldots u_1 \star \ldots u_m \star \ldots \star t_n)\!\downarrow}\ \mathsf{Exp}_1$$

$$\frac{\exp(t_1,t_2)\ \ \ldots\ \ \dfrac{u_1\ \ldots\ u_m}{(u_1 \star \ldots \star u_m)\!\downarrow}\ \mathsf{R}_\star\ \ \ldots\ t_n}{\exp(t_1, t_2 \star \ldots \star u_1 \star \ldots \star u_m \star \ldots \star t_n)\!\downarrow}\ \mathsf{Exp}_2 \quad\Rightarrow\quad \frac{\exp(t_1,t_2)\ \ \ldots\ \ u_1\ \ldots\ \ u_m\ \ldots\ \ t_n}{\exp(t_1, t_2 \star \ldots \star u_1 \star \ldots \star u_m \star \ldots \star t_n)\!\downarrow}\ \mathsf{Exp}_2$$

$$\frac{\dfrac{t_1\ \ t_2}{\exp(t_1,t_2)}\ \mathsf{Exp}_3 \quad t_3\ \ldots\ t_n}{\exp(t_1, t_2 \star \ldots \star t_n)\!\downarrow}\ \mathsf{Exp}_2 \quad\Rightarrow\quad \frac{t_1 \quad \dfrac{t_2\ \ldots\ t_n}{(t_2 \star \ldots \star t_n)\!\downarrow}\ \mathsf{R}_\star}{\exp(t_1, t_2 \star \ldots \star t_n)\!\downarrow}\ \mathsf{Exp}_3$$

$$\frac{t_1\ \ \ldots\ \ \dfrac{u_1\ \ldots\ u_m}{(u_1 \circ \ldots \circ u_m)\!\downarrow}\ \mathsf{R}_\circ\ \ \ldots\ t_n}{(t_1 \circ \ldots \circ u_1 \circ \ldots \circ u_m \circ \ldots \circ t_n)\!\downarrow}\ \mathsf{R}_\circ \quad\Rightarrow\quad \frac{t_1\ \ \ldots\ \ u_1\ \ldots\ \ u_m\ \ldots\ \ u_n}{(t_1 \circ \ldots \circ u_1 \circ \ldots \circ u_m \circ \ldots \circ t_n)\!\downarrow}\ \mathsf{R}_\circ$$

$$\frac{\dfrac{u_1\ \ldots\ u_m}{(u_1 + \ldots + u_m)\!\downarrow}\ \mathsf{R}_+}{h((u_1 + \ldots + u_m)\!\downarrow)}\ \mathsf{R}_h \quad\Rightarrow\quad \frac{\dfrac{u_1}{h(u_1)}\ \mathsf{R}_h\ \ \ldots\ \dfrac{u_m}{h(u_m)}\ \mathsf{R}_h}{(h(u_1 + \ldots + u_m))\!\downarrow}\ \mathsf{R}_\bullet$$

$$\frac{\dfrac{u_1\ \ldots\ u_m}{(u_1 \circ \ldots \circ u_m)\!\downarrow}\ \mathsf{R}_\circ}{J_\circ(u_1 \circ \ldots \circ u_m)\!\downarrow}\ \mathsf{R}_{J_\circ} \quad\Rightarrow\quad \frac{\dfrac{u_1}{J_\circ(u_1)\!\downarrow}\ \mathsf{R}_{J_\circ}\ \ldots\ \dfrac{u_m}{J_\circ(u_m)\!\downarrow}\ \mathsf{R}_{J_\circ}}{J_\circ(u_1 \circ \ldots \circ u_m)\!\downarrow}\ \mathsf{R}_\circ$$

$$\frac{\dfrac{u}{h(u)}\ \mathsf{R}_h \quad v_1\ \cdots\ v_n}{h(u \star v_1 \star \ldots \star v_n)\!\downarrow}\ \mathsf{Exp}_1 \quad\Rightarrow\quad \frac{\dfrac{u\ \ v_1\ \cdots\ v_n}{(u \star v_1 \star \ldots \star v_n)\!\downarrow}\ \mathsf{R}_\star}{h(u \star v_1 \star \ldots \star v_n)\!\downarrow}\ \mathsf{R}_h$$

Fig. 2. Proof normalization rules

Lemma 8. *If t is obtained by a decomposition rule of $\mathcal{I}_2$, then the premises can be written $h(t_1), t_2, \ldots, t_n$, $t = h(u)$ and there an index i such that $t_i = e_\star$ or $u \in \mathrm{DS}_\star(t_i)$.*

Proof. By definition, only Exp_1 can be a decomposition: the premises are $h(t_1)$, $t_2, \ldots, t_n$ and the conclusion is $h(u)$ with $u = t_1 \star \ldots \star t_n\!\downarrow$. Now, if $\mathrm{TOP}(u) \neq \star$, by definition, the rule $\mathsf{R}_\star$ with premises $t_1, \ldots, t_n$ and conclusion u is a decomposition. By Lemma 7, $u = e_\star$ or there is an index i such that $u \in \mathrm{DS}_\star(t_i)$. $\square$

Lemma 9. *For any set of terms in normal form, $F(F(T)) = F(T)$.*

Proof. $F(T) \subseteq F(F(T))$ by definition. For the converse inclusion, first terms in $\mathrm{Sub}(F(T))$ which are not in $\mathrm{Sub}(T)$ are always in $F(T)$. Now, we investigate each other case:

- If $t = h(u)$ with $u \in \mathrm{Sub}(F(T))$ and $\mathrm{TOP}(u) = +$. Then it follows that $u \in \mathrm{Sub}(T)$ or $u = \mathrm{inv}_+(v)$ with $v \in \mathrm{Sub}(T)$, hence $t \in F(T)$
- If $t = h(\mathrm{inv}_+(u))$ with $u \in \mathrm{Sub}(F(T))$ and $\mathrm{TOP}(u) = +$, it is the same as above.
- If $t = \mathrm{inv}_\circ(u)$ with $u \in \mathrm{Sub}(F(T))$ and $\mathrm{TOP}(u) = \circ \in \{\star, +\}$, then either $u \in \mathrm{Sub}(T)$ or $\mathrm{inv}_\circ(u) \in \mathrm{Sub}(T)$. In both cases $t = \mathrm{inv}_\circ(u) \in F(T)$.
- If $t = h(u)$ with $u \in \mathrm{DS}_\circ(v)$, $\mathrm{TOP}(u) = \circ$ and $v \in \mathrm{Sub}(F(T))$ and $\circ \in \{\star, +\}$ then either v or $\mathrm{inv}_\circ(v)$ is in $\mathrm{Sub}(T)$. In the first case we get $t \in F(T)$. In the latter case $\mathrm{inv}_\circ(u) \in \mathrm{DS}_\circ(\mathrm{inv}_\circ(v))$, hence $t = h(\mathrm{inv}_\circ(\mathrm{inv}_\circ(u))) \in F(T)$.
- If $t = \mathrm{inv}_\circ(u)$, $v \in \mathrm{Sub}(F(T))$, $\mathrm{TOP}(v) = \circ \in \{\star, +, \bullet\}$ and $u \in \mathrm{DS}_\circ(v)$, again either $v \in \mathrm{Sub}(T)$ or $\mathrm{inv}_\circ(v) \in \mathrm{Sub}(T)$. In the first case we conclude directly $t \in F(T)$. In the latter case, $\mathrm{inv}_\circ(u) \in \mathrm{DS}_\circ(\mathrm{inv}_\circ(v))$, hence $t \in \mathrm{Sub}(T)$
- The last case is similar to previous ones. $\qquad\square$

4.4   Proof of our Locality Result

We are now able to prove our locality result.

Proposition 2. *The inference system* $\mathcal{I}_1 \cup \mathcal{I}_2$ *is F-local.*

Proof. We consider a minimal (in terms of size) normal proof of t from the set of hypotheses H. We prove by induction on the proof size that, if the last rule is a composition, then all terms in the proof belong to $F(H) \cup F(t)$ and, if the last rule is a decomposition, then all terms in the proof belong to $F(H)$. In the base case, the proof consists of an axiom only and the result follows. Otherwise, we distinguish cases depending on the last rule used in the proof.

The last rule is R_h. If $\mathrm{TOP}(t) \neq \bullet$, then we simply have to apply the induction hypothesis: $t = h(u)$ and all terms in the proof of u are in $F(H) \cup F(u)$, hence in $F(H) \cup F(t)$.

Now, if $t = h(u)$, then, by proof normalization, u cannot be obtained by R_+. It follows that it must be obtained by decomposition (or possibly R_{J_+}). In any case, $u \in F(H)$ by induction hypothesis and, since $\mathrm{TOP}(u) = +$, $u \in \mathrm{Sub}(H) \cup J_+(\mathrm{Sub}(H))$. It follows that $t, u \in F(H)$.

If the last rule is a composition $\mathsf{R}_\circ$ with $\circ \in \{+, \star, \bullet\}$

$$\frac{\dfrac{\Pi_1}{u_1}\,\mathsf{R}_{f_1} \quad \cdots \quad \dfrac{\Pi_n}{u_n}\,\mathsf{R}_{f_n}}{t}\,\mathsf{R}_\circ$$

Consider the set S of indices i such that $\mathrm{TOP}(u_i) = \circ$ (we may rule out the cases where $u_i = e_\circ$, which correspond to non-minimal proofs). By lemma 4, for every $i \notin S$, either $u_i \in DS_\circ(t)$ or there is an index j such that $inv_\circ(u_i) \in DS_\circ(u_j)$. In the first case $u_i \in Sub(t)$. In the second case, we claim that if $\circ \in \{\star, +\}$, then u_j must be obtained by decomposition: $f_j \notin \{\circ, J_\circ\}$ by proof normalization and therefore $TOP(u_j) = \circ$ implies it is obtained by decomposition (this does not hold when $\circ = \bullet$). In case $\circ = \bullet$, either u_j is obtained by decomposition, or $u_j = h(v_j)$ is obtained by R_h and, by proof normalization and since $TOP(u_j) = \bullet$, v_j must be obtained by decomposition and $TOP(v_j) = +$.

By induction hypothesis, $u_j \in F(H)$ or $u_j = h(v_j)$ and $v_j \in F(H)$, $TOP(v_j) = +$, in which case, again $u_j \in F(H)$. And $inv_\circ(u_i) \in Sub(u_j)$, hence $u_i \in F(H)$.

To sum up: for every i, either $TOP(u_i) \neq \circ$ and $u_i \in Sub(t) \cup F(H)$ or else $TOP(u_i) = \circ$ and $u_i \in F(H)$. By the induction hypothesis, for every i, all terms in the proof of u_i belong to $F(H)$ or to $F(u_i)$. Hence, by lemma 9, all terms in the proof of t belong to $F(t) \cup F(H)$.

The last rule is $R_{J_\circ}$. Let $t = J_\circ(u)\!\downarrow$. By proof normalization, u is not obtained by $R_\circ$ and by minimality, it cannot be obtained by $R_{J_\circ}$. Then, if $TOP(u) \in \{\circ, J_\circ\}$, u must be obtained by decomposition or (R_h and $\circ = \bullet$). In both cases $u \in F(H)$ (either the induction hypothesis or the first case above).

Now, if $TOP(u) \notin \{\circ, J_\circ\}$, $t = J_\circ(u)$ and $u \in Sub(t)$. We conclude by applying the induction hypothesis.

The last rule is a decomposition $R_\circ$, $\circ \in \{\star, \bullet, +\}$. Let $t = t_1 \circ \ldots \circ t_n\!\downarrow$. We discard the cases in which $t_i = e_\circ$ for some i (there is a simpler proof). Then the rule being a decomposition, by lemma 7, $t \in Sub(t_i)$ for some i.

If $t_1, \ldots, t_n \in F(H)$, then by induction hypothesis, we get a proof in which all terms are in $F(H)$. Otherwise, let us assume that some t_j is not in $F(H)$, hence, by induction hypothesis, t_j is obtained by composition.

By contradiction, assume $TOP(t_j) = \circ$. Then, because it is obtained by composition and because of proof normalization rules, either t_j is obtained by $R_{J_\circ}$ or $\circ = \bullet$ and t_j is obtained by R_h. In the first case, $t_j = J_\circ(u_j)\!\downarrow$ and, by proof normalization, u_j is not obtained by $R_\circ$, while $TOP(u_j) = \circ$. This implies that u_j is obtained by decomposition, and therefore, by induction hypothesis, $u_j \in F(H)$, which in turn contradicts $t_j \notin F(H)$. In the second case, $t_j = h(u_j)$ and $TOP(u_j) = +$. By proof normalization, u_j cannot be obtained by R_+. It follows that u_j is obtained by decomposition (or else by R_{J_+}). Again, this will yield a contradiction with $t_j \notin F(H)$. Similarly, we rule out $TOP(t_j) = J_\circ$.

Now, $TOP(t_j) \notin \{\circ, J_\circ\}$ and, by lemma 3, either $t_j = e_\circ$ (in which case there is a simpler proof) or $t_j = t$ (in which case there is a simpler proof) or else there is an index $k \neq j$ such that $inv_\circ(t_j) \in DS_\circ(t_k)$. Moreover, we cannot have $t_k = inv_\circ(t_j)$: there would be a simpler proof, simply discarding t_j and t_k from the proof of t. Therefore $TOP(t_k) = \circ$.

Now, we can reason as for t_j: by proof normalization, t_k must have been obtained by decomposition and therefore, by induction hypothesis,

$t_k \in F(H)$. Then $t_j \in F(H)$ (since $\text{inv}_\circ(t_j) \circ u \in F(H)$ for some u). This is again a contradiction.

It follows that all t_i's must be in $F(H)$.

The last rule is a decomposition Exp_1

$$\frac{h(t_1) \; t_2 \; \ldots \; t_n}{h(t_1 \star \ldots \star t_n)\downarrow}$$

and $t = h(u) = h(t_1 \star \ldots \star t_n)\downarrow$ and moreover, $\text{TOP}(u) \neq \star$.

By proof normalization, $h(t_1)$ can only be obtained by $\mathsf{R}_\bullet$, or a decomposition rule distinct from E_1. In all cases, either $h(t_1) \in F(H)$ or else $\text{TOP}(t_1) = +$.

Similarly, none of the t_i's $(i \geq 2)$ can be obtained by $\mathsf{R}_\star$. Let $u_i = t_i$ if t_i is not obtained by $\mathsf{R}_{J_\star}$ and $u_i = \text{inv}_\star(t_i)$ otherwise. Assume by contradiction that, for some i, $u_i \notin F(H)$. Then, in particular, by induction hypothesis, u_i is obtained by composition. By proof normalization, it cannot be by a rule $\mathsf{R}_\star, \mathsf{R}_{J_\star}$, hence $\text{TOP}(u_i) \neq \star$ and thus $\text{TOP}(t_i) \neq \star$. But then, by lemma 4, either $t_i \in \text{DS}_\star(u)$ or else $\text{inv}_\star(t_i) \in \text{DS}_\star(t_j)$ for some j. We cannot have $t_i = \text{inv}_\star(t_j)$: there would be a simpler proof. Therefore, if $\text{inv}_\star(t_i) \in \text{DS}_\star(t_j)$, we must have $\text{TOP}(t_j) = \star$, hence the corresponding u_j cannot be obtained by composition. It follows that, for every i, either $u_i \in F(H)$ or else $\text{inv}_\star(t_i) \in \text{DS}_\star(t_j)$ and $u_j \in F(H)$. In the latter case, either $u_j = t_j$ and then $\text{inv}_\star(t_i) \in \text{Sub}(t_j)$ implies $t_i \in F(H)$. or else $u_j = \text{inv}_\star(t_j)$ and $t_i \in \text{DS}_\star(u_j) \subseteq F(H)$.

In all cases, for every i, $t_i \in F(H)$.

By lemma 8, there is an index i such that $u \in \text{DS}_\star(t_i)$. Now, $t \neq t_i$ and $t \neq h(t_i)$ (otherwise there is a simpler proof). Hence $\text{TOP}(t_i) = \star$. It follows that $t_i \in \text{Sub}(H) \cup J_\star(\text{Sub}(H))$. Then $u \in \text{Sub}(H) \cup J_\star(\text{Sub}(H))$ and there exists a v such that $u \star v \in \text{Sub}(H)$: $t = h(u) \in F(H)$.

The last rule is a composition Exp_1. We use the same notations as in the previous case. By proof normalization, for every i, $t_i \in F(H)$ or else $\text{TOP}(t_i) \neq \star$. We apply again lemma 4: if $t_i \notin F(H)$, then either $\text{inv}_\star(t_i) \in \text{DS}_\star(t_j)$ for some $j \neq i$ or else $t_j \in \text{DS}_\star(u)$. In the first case, we will have again $t_i \in F(H)$ since $t_j \neq \text{inv}_\star(t_i)$ by minimality and therefore $t_j \in F(H)$. In the end, for every $i > 1$, either $t_i \in F(H)$ or $t_i \in F(t)$.

For $h(t_1)$, the reasoning is the same as in the previous case: either $\text{TOP}(t_1) \neq \star$ or $h(t_1)$ is obtained by decomposition.

The last rule is Exp_2

$$\frac{\exp(t_1, t_2) \; t_3 \; \ldots \; t_n}{\exp(t_1, t_2 \star \ldots \star t_n)\downarrow}$$

We let $u = t_2 \star \ldots \star t_n\downarrow$

In this case, $t_2, t_3, \ldots, t_n$ play exactly the same roles as $t_1, \ldots$ in the Exp_1 case. It is actually even simpler: $\exp(t_1, t_2)$ cannot be obtained by a composition (by proof normalization), hence $\exp(t_1, t_2) \in \text{Sub}(H)$. Concerning $t_3, \ldots, t_n$, for each index i, either $t_i \in F(H)$ or else $t_i \in \text{DS}_\star(u)$. So, each of the premises is either in $F(H)$ or in $F(t)$ and it suffices to apply the induction hypothesis (together with lemme 9).

The last rule is Exp_3. In this case, the last rule is a composition rule and the two premises are in $\mathrm{Sub}(t)$. It suffices to apply the induction hypothesis. $\square$

5   Conclusion and Future Works

This paper is only one of the steps on the way of solving the case study. We only showed that, for a passive intruder, the security problem can be solved in PTIME.

The next step (on which we are currently working) is to consider an active intruder. This means solving deducibility constraints modulo the equational theory of the electronic purse.

In this context, we will use properties of the rewrite system, for instance the finite variant property. That is why the rewrite rules are oriented in an unusual way, which introduces some technical complications.

Acknowledgments

We thank an anonymous referee for his comments and we thank Jean-Pierre Jouannaud for introducing us to this area of research.

References

1. Arnaud, M., Cortier, V., Delaune, S.: Combining algorithms for deciding knowledge in security protocols. Research Report 6118, INRIA, 28 pages (February 2007)
2. Chevalier, Y., Kuester, R., Rusinowitch, M., Turuani, M.: An NP decision procedure for protocol insecurity with xor. In: Kolaitis [14]
3. Chevalier, Y., Küsters, R., Rusinowitch, M., Turuani, M.: Deciding the security of protocols with Diffie-Hellman exponentiation and products in exponents. In: Radhakrishnan, J., Pandya, P. (eds.) Proc. FST/TCS 2003, LNCS, vol. 2914, Springer, Heidelberg (2003)
4. Chevalier, Y., Rusinowitch, M.: Combining intruder theories. In: Caires, L., Italiano, G.F., Monteiro, L., Palamidessi, C., Yung, M. (eds.) ICALP 2005. LNCS, vol. 3580, pp. 639–651. Springer, Heidelberg (2005)
5. Chevalier, Y., Rusinowitch, M.: Hierarchical combination of intruder theories. In: Pfenning, F. (ed.) RTA 2006. LNCS, vol. 4098, pp. 108–122. Springer, Heidelberg (2006)
6. Comon-Lundh, H., Delaune, S.: The finite variant property: How to get rid of some algebraic properties. In: Giesl, J. (ed.) RTA 2005. LNCS, vol. 3467, pp. 294–307. Springer, Heidelberg (2005)
7. Comon-Lundh, H., Shmatikov, V.: Intruder deductions, constraint solving and insecurity decision in preence of exclusive or. In: Kolaitis [14]
8. Contejean, E., Marché, C.: CiME: Completion modulo E. In: Rewriting Techniques and Applications. LNCS, vol. 1103, pp. 416–419. Springer, Heidelberg (1996)

9. Cortier, V., Delaune, S., Lafourcade, P.: A survey of algebraic properties used in cryptographic protocols. Journal of Computer Security 14(1), 1–43 (2006)
10. Delaune, S., Lafourcade, P., Lugiez, D., Treinen, R.: Symbolic protocol analysis in presence of a homomorphism operator and exclusive or. In: Buglesi, M., Preneel, B., Sassone, V., Wegener, I. (eds.) ICALP 2006. LNCS, vol. 4052, pp. 132–143. Springer, Heidelberg (2006)
11. Dershowitz, N., Jouannaud, J.-P.: Rewrite systems. In: van Leeuwen, J. (ed.): Handbook of Theoretical Computer Science, vol. B, pp. 243–309. North Holland (1990)
12. Dolev, D., Yao, A.: On the security of public key protocols. In: Proc. IEEE Symp. on Foundations of Computer Science, pp. 350–357 (1981)
13. Kapur, D., Narendran, P., Wang, L.: Analyzing protocols that use modular exponentiation: Semantic unification techniques. In: Nieuwenhuis, R. (ed.) RTA 2003. LNCS, vol. 2706, Springer, Heidelberg (2003)
14. Kolaitis, P. (ed.): 18th Annual IEEE Symposium on Logic in Computer Science, Ottawa, Canada, IEEE Computer Society, Washington (June 2003)
15. Millen, J., Shmatikov, V.: Symbolic protocol analysis with products and diffie-hellman exponentiation. Invited submission to Journal of Computer Security (selected papers of CSFW-16) (2004)
16. Rusinowitch, M., Turuani, M.: Protocol insecurity with finite number of sessions is NP-complete. In: Proc.14th IEEE Computer Security Foundations Workshop, Cape Breton, Nova Scotia (June 2001)
17. Shmatikov, V.: Decidable analysis of cryptographic protocols with products and modular exponentiation. In: Schmidt, D. (ed.) ESOP 2004. LNCS, vol. 2986, pp. 355–369. Springer, Heidelberg (2004)
18. Security protocols open repository http://www.lsv.ens-cachan.fr/spore/

Applying a Theorem Prover to the Verification of Optimistic Replication Algorithms

Abdessamad Imine[1] and Michaël Rusinowitch[2]

[1] Université Henri Poincaré & LORIA[*]
[2] INRIA & LORIA
{imine,rusi}@loria.fr

Abstract. The Operational Transformation (OT) approach is a technique for supporting optimistic replication in collaborative and mobile systems. It allows the users to concurrently update the shared data and exchange their updates in any order since the convergence of all replicas, *i.e.* the fact that all users view the same data, is ensured in all cases. However, designing algorithms for achieving convergence with the OT approach is a critical and challenging issue. In this paper, we address this issue for the important case where the shared data has a linear structure such as lists, texts, ordered XML trees, etc. We analyze the problem and we propose a generic solution with its formal analysis. We also show in this work how to support the formal design of an OT algorithm with a rewrite-based theorem prover. This theorem prover enables us to envisage the large number of cases required for the correctness proof of the algorithm. Since the manual proofs of all previously published algorithms were wrong, this shows the decisive advantage of using an automatic prover in this context.

1 Introduction

Users involved in collaborative and mobile environments generally work on replicas of shared data. During disconnection periods, they can concurrently execute updates on replicas. This leads to potentially divergent replicas (*i.e.* different states). One of the main issues in such environments is to maintain *consistency* (or convergence) among replicas after reconnection. Originating from real-time groupware research [7], the *Operational Transformation* (OT) approach provides an interesting solution [8,17] to this problem. Using this approach, after reconnection, a user A might get an operation op previously executed during disconnection by some other user B on a replica of the shared data. Rather than executing op "as is" on his replica, User A may have to execute a variant of op, say op' – called a *transformation* of op – that intuitively intends to achieve the same effect as op. When the transformed operations are executed, they create the illusion that all operations have been executed in the intended execution context and in the intended order.

---

[*] UMR 7503 CNRS-INPL-INRIA-Nancy2-UHP. Campus Scientifique, BP 239, 54506 Vandoeuvre-ls-Nancy Cedex, France.

H. Comon-Lundh et al. (Eds.): Jouannaud Festschrift, LNCS 4600, pp. 213–234, 2007.

Compared to other replication systems [20], the advantages of the OT approach are: (i) *it enables an unconstrained concurrency, i.e.* it does not require any global order on concurrent operations unlike traditional consistency criteria such as linearizability [9]; (ii) *it transforms operations to run in any order even when they do not naturally commute*; (iii) *it produces a convergence state that precisely preserves the intentions of all the operations executed during disconnection periods.* Many collaborative applications are based on the OT approach such as Joint Emacs [18] a groupware based on text editor Emacs, CoWord [26] (a collaborative word processor) and CoPowerPoint [23] (a real-time collaborative multimedia slides creation and presentation system).

The OT approach consists of application-dependent transformation algorithms. Thus, for every possible pair of concurrent operations, the application programmer has to specify how to merge these operations regardless of reception order. According to Ressel et al. [18], an OT algorithm needs to fulfill two conditions (which will be detailed in Section 2) in order to ensure convergence. Finding such an OT algorithm and proving that it satisfies the convergence conditions is considered as a task, because this proof is often unmanageably complicated [24] due to the large number of cases to envisage. To overcome this problem we have used the SPIKE theorem prover [4,21] for automating the verification process. Since the OT algorithms are based on editing operations, that are easily expressed with conditional rewrite rules, we found that the SPIKE theorem prover is well-suited for this verification task. Indeed it has permitted us to detect bugs in many well-known OT algorithms from the literature [11,12]. Moreover, the SPIKE prover has already been intensively applied to the design and debugging of a file synchronizer [17] distributed with the industrial collaborative development environment, LibreSource Community[1], proposed by ARTENUM Company.

However, although in theory [18], the OT approach is able to achieve convergence in the presence of *arbitrary transformation orders*, some types of collaborative objects still represent a serious challenge for the application of the OT approach. Indeed, the convergence property has never been achieved properly when the collaborative object can be given a linear structure (such as a list, a text or an ordered XML tree): all proposed OT algorithms [7,18,25,22,12,15] for these datatypes fail to meet the convergence property. In this paper, we analyse thoroughly the source of these failures and we propose a new OT algorithm for achieving the convergence. Unlike previous works we have been able to give a formal verification thanks to a theorem prover. Furthermore, our OT algorithm is generic since it can be applied to any data with a linear structure.

This paper is organized as follows. We present the operational transformation model in Section 2. The ingredients of our formalization for the linear collaborative object into a theorem prover language are given in Section 3. In this section, we analyze convergence problems that still remain and sketches an abstract solution. Section 4 presents the ingredients of our solution giving a new OT algorithm for the linear collaborative object. Section 5 gives the formal analysis of this algorithm. Section 6 discusses related work, and concludes.

---

[1] http://dev.libresource.org

2   Operational Transformation Approach

2.1   The Model

OT is an optimistic replication technique which allows many users (or sites) to concurrently update the shared data and next to synchronize their divergent replicas in order to obtain the same data. The updates of each site are executed on the local replica immediately without being blocked or delayed, and then are propagated to other sites to be executed again. Accordingly, every update is processed in four steps: (i) *generation* on one site; (ii) *broadcast* to other sites; (iii) *reception* on one site; (iv) *execution* on one site.

The shared object: We deal with a shared object that admits a linear structure. To represent this object we use the *list* abstract data type. A *list* is a finite sequence of elements from a data type $\mathcal{E}$. This data type is only a template and can be instantiated by many other types. For instance, an element may be regarded as a character, a paragraph, a page, a slide, an XML node, etc. Let $\mathcal{L}$ be the set of lists.

The primitive operations: It is assumed that a list state can only be modified by the following primitive operations: (i) $Ins(p, e)$ which inserts the element e at position p; (ii) $Del(p)$ which deletes the element at position p. We assume that positions are given by natural numbers. The set of operations is defined as follows: $\mathcal{O} = \{Ins(p, e) | e \in \mathcal{E} \text{ and } p \in \mathbb{N}\} \cup \{Del(p) | p \in \mathbb{N}\}$. Since the shared object is replicated, each site will own a local state l that is altered only by local operations. The initial state, denoted by l_0, is the same for all sites. The function $Do : \mathcal{O} \times \mathcal{L} \to \mathcal{L}$, computes the state $Do(o, l)$ resulting from applying operation o to state l. We say that o is *generated* on state l. We denote by $[o_1; o_2; \ldots; o_n]$ an operation sequence. Applying an operation sequence to a list l is recursively defined as follows: (i) $Do([], l) = l$, where $[]$ is the empty sequence and; (ii) $Do([o_1; o_2; \ldots; o_n], l) = Do(o_n, Do(\ldots, Do(o_2, Do(o_1, l))))$. Two operation sequences seq_1 and seq_2 are *equivalent*, denoted by $seq_1 \equiv seq_2$, iff $Do(seq_1, l) = Do(seq_2, l)$ for all lists l.

Definition 1. *Let an operation o_1 be generated at site i and an operation o_2 be generated at site j. We say that o_2 causally depends on o_1, denoted $o_1 \to o_2$, iff: (i) $i = j$ and o_1 was generated before o_2; or, (ii) $i \neq j$ and the execution of o_1 at site j has happened before the generation of o_2.*

Definition 2. *Two operations o_1 and o_2 are said to be* concurrent, *denoted by $o_1 \parallel o_2$, iff neither $o_1 \to o_2$ nor $o_2 \to o_1$.*

We assume that concurrency between operations is detected by one of the many known techniques [20]. Our analysis is independant from the chosen one.

In the following, we define the conflict relation between two insert operations:

Definition 3. *(Conflict Relation) Two insert operations $o_1 = Ins(p_1, e_1)$ and $o_2 = Ins(p_2, e_2)$, generated on different sites, conflict with each other iff: (i) $o_1 \parallel o_2$; (ii) o_1 and o_2 are generated on the same list state; and, (iii) $p_1 = p_2$, i.e. they have the same insertion position.*

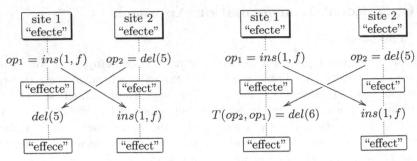

Fig. 1. Incorrect integration   **Fig. 2.** Integration with transformation

2.2 Transformation Principle

A crucial issue when designing collaborative objects with a replicated architecture and arbitrary messages communication between sites is the *consistency maintenance* (or *convergence*) of all replicas. To illustrate this problem, consider the following example:

Example 1. Consider the following group text editor scenario (see Figure 1): there are two users (on two sites) working on a shared document represented by a sequence of characters. These characters are addressed from 0 to the end of the document. Initially, both copies hold the string " *efecte*". User 1 executes operation $op_1 = Ins(1, f)$ to insert the character f at position 1. Concurrently, user 2 performs $op_2 = Del(5)$ to delete the character e at position 5. When op_1 is received and executed on site 2, it produces the expected string "*effect*". But, when op_2 is received on site 1, it does not take into account that op_1 has been executed before it and it produces the string "*effece*". The result at site 1 is different from the result of site 2 and it apparently violates the intention of op_2 since the last character e, which was intended to be deleted, is still present in the final string. Consequently, we obtain a *divergence* between sites 1 and 2. It should be pointed out that even if a serialization protocol [7] was used to require that all sites execute op_1 and op_2 in the same order (*i.e.* a global order on concurrent operations) to obtain an identical result *effece*, this identical result is still inconsistent with the original intention of op_2.

To maintain convergence, the OT approach has been proposed by [7]. When User X gets an operation op that was previously executed by User Y on his replica of the shared object User X does not necessarily integrate op by executing it "as is" on his replica. He will rather execute a variant of op, denoted by op' (called a *transformation* of op) that *intuitively intends to achieve the same effect as op*. This approach is based on a transformation function T that apply to couples of concurrent operations defined on the same state.

Example 2. In Figure 2, we illustrate the effect of T on the previous example. When op_2 is received on site 1, op_2 needs to be transformed according to op_1

as follows: $T((Del(5), Ins(1, f)) = Del(6)$. The deletion position of op_2 is incremented because op_1 has inserted a character at position 1, which is before the character deleted by op_2. Next, op_2' is executed on site 1. In the same way, when op_1 is received on site 2, it is transformed as follows: $T(Ins(1, f), Del(5)) = Ins(1, f)$; op_1 remains the same because f is inserted before the deletion position of op_2.

In the OT approach, every site is equiped by two main components [7,18]: the *integration component* and the *transformation component*. The integration component is responsible for receiving, broadcasting and executing operations. It is rather *independent* of the type of the collaborative objects. Several integration algorithms have been proposed in the groupware research area, such as dOPT [7], adOPTed [18], SOCT2,4 [22,27] and GOTO [24]. The transformation component is a set of OT algorithms which is responsible for merging two concurrent operations defined on the same state. Every OT algorithm is *specific* to the semantics of a collaborative object. Every site generates operations sequentially and stores these operations in a stack also called a *history*. When a site receives a remote operation op, the integration component executes the following steps:

1. from the local history it determines the sequence *seq* of operations that are concurrent to op;
2. it calls the transformation component in order to get operation op' that is the transformation of op according to *seq*;
3. it executes op' on the current state;
4. it adds op' to the local history.

In this paper, we only deal with the design of OT algorithms for linear collaborative objects such as lists, texts or ordered XML trees.

2.3   Transformation Algorithm

We present now a well known transformation algorithm designed by Ellis and Gibbs [7] who have introduced the OT approach.

This algorithm allows to synchronize a collaborative text object, shared by two or more users. There are two editing operations: $Ins(p, c, pr)$ to insert a character c at position p and $Del(p, pr)$ to delete a character at position p. Operations Ins and Del are extended with another parameter pr^2. This one represents a priority scheme that is used to solve a conflict occurring when two concurrent insert operations were originally intended to insert different characters at the same position. Note that concurrent editing operations have always different priorities. In Figure 3, we give the four transformation cases for Ins and Del proposed by Ellis and Gibbs. There are two interesting situations in the first case (Ins and Ins). The first situation is when the arguments of the two insert

---

[2] This priority is the site identifier where operations have been generated. Two operations generated from different sites have always different priorities.

$T(Ins(p_1, c_1, pr_1), Ins(p_2, c_2, pr_2)) =$
if $p_1 < p_2$ **then return** $Ins(p_1, c_1, pr_1)$
elseif $p_1 > p_2$ **then return** $Ins(p_1 + 1, c_1, pr_1)$
    elseif $c_1 == c_2$ **then return** Nop()
        elseif $pr_1 > pr_2$ **then return** $Ins(p_1 + 1, c_1, pr_1)$
            else return $Ins(p_1, c_1, pr_1)$
endif;

$T(Ins(p_1, c_1, pr_1), Del(p_2, pr_2)) =$
if $p1 < p2$ **then return** $Ins(p_1, c_1, pr_1)$
else return $Ins(p_1 - 1, c_1, pr_1)$
endif;

$T(Del(p_1, pr_1), Ins(p_2, c_2, pr_2)) =$
if $p_1 < p_2$ **then return** $Del(p_1, pr_1)$
else return $Del(p_1 + 1, pr_1)$
endif;

$T(Del(p_1, pr_1), Del(p_2, pr_2)) =$
if $p_1 < p_2$ **then return** $Del(p_1, pr_1)$
elseif $p_1 > p_2$ **then return** $Del(p_1 - 1, pr_1)$
    else return Nop()
endif;

Fig. 3. Transformation function defined by Ellis and Gibbs [7]

operations are equal (*i.e.* $p_1 = p_2$ and $c_1 = c_2$). In this case the function T returns the idle operation Nop that has a null effect on a text state [3]. The second interesting situation is when only the insertion positions are equal (*i.e.* $p_1 = p_2$ but $c_1 \neq c_2$). Such conflicts are resolved by using the priority order associated with each insert operation. The insertion position will be shifted to the right and will be $(p_1 + 1)$ when Ins has a higher priority. The remaining cases for T are quite simple.

2.4   Partial Concurrency Problem

Definition 4. *Let seq be a sequence of operations. Transforming any editing operation o according to seq is denoted by* $T^*(o, seq)$ *and is recursively defined as follows:*

$$T^*(o, []) = o \text{ where } [] \text{ is the empty sequence;}$$
$$T^*(o, [o_1; o_2; \ldots; o_n]) = T^*(T(o, o_1), [o_2; \ldots; o_n])$$

We say that o has been concurrently generated according to all operations of seq.

---

[3] The definition of T is completed by: $T(Nop, op) = Nop$ and $T(op, Nop) = op$ for every operation op.

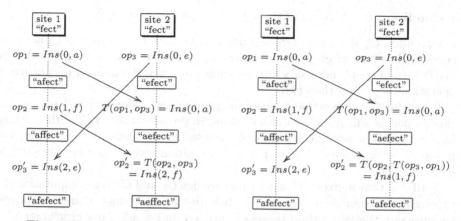

Fig. 4. Wrong application of T **Fig. 5.** Correct application of T

Definition 5. *Two concurrent operations o_1 and o_2 are said to be* partially concurrent *iff o_1 is generated on list state l_1 at site 1 and o_2 is generated on list state l_2 at site 2 with $l_1 \neq l_2$.*

In case of partial concurrency situation the transformation function T may lead to data divergence. The following example illustrates this situation.

Example 3. Consider two users trying to correct the word *"fect"* as in Figure 4. User 1 generates two operations op_1 and op_2. User 2 concurrently generates operation op_3. We have $op_1 \rightarrow op_2$ and $op_1 \parallel op_3$, but op_2 and op_3 are partially concurrent as they are generated on different text states. At site 1, op_3 has to be transformed against the sequence $[op_1; op_2]$, *i.e.* $op_3' = T^*(op_3, [op_1; op_2]) = Ins(2, e)$. The execution of op_3' gives the word *"afefect"*. At site 2, transforming op_1 against op_3 gives $op_1' = op_1 = Ins(0, a)$ and transforming op_2 against op_3 results in $op_2' = Ins(2, f)$ whose the execution leads to the word *"aeffect"* which is different from what is obtained at site 1. This divergence situation is due to a wrong application of T to the operations op_2 and op_3 at site 2. Indeed, the function T requires that both operations are concurrent and defined on the same state. However, op_3 is generated on *"fect"* while op_2 is generated on *"afect"*.

In order to solve this partial concurrency problem, op_2 should not be directly transformed with respect to op_3 because op_2 causally depends on op_1 (see Figure 5). Instead op_3 must be transformed against op_1 and next op_2 may be transformed against the result.

2.5   Convergence Conditions

Using an OT algorithm requires us to verify two conditions [18]. For all o, o_1 and o_2 pairwise concurrent operations:

- **Condition C_1:** $[o_1 ; T(o_2, o_1)] \equiv [o_2 ; T(o_1, o_2)]$.

- **Condition** C_2: $T^*(o, [o_1 ; T(o_2, o_1)]) = T^*(o, [o_2 ; T(o_1, o_2)])$.

Condition C_1 defines a *state identity* and ensures that if o_1 and o_2 are concurrent, the effect of executing o_1 before o_2 is the same as executing o_2 before o_1. This condition is necessary but not sufficient when the number of concurrent operations is greater than two.

Condition C_2 ensures that transforming o along equivalent and different operation sequences will give the same operation. In previous work [18,16], the authors have proved that conditions C_1 and C_2 are sufficient to ensure the convergence property for *any number* of concurrent operations which can be executed in *arbitrary order*.

Verifying that a given OT algorithm satisfies C_1 and C_2 is a computationally expensive problem even for a simple text document. Using a theorem prover to automate the verification process is needed and would be a crucial step for building correct collaborative objects based on OT approach [12,13].

Using a theorem-proving approach [12,13], we have detected that the function T of Figure 3 contains some subtle bugs that lead to divergence situations. These situations are detailed in the following section.

3   Modeling and Verifying the Linear Collaborative Object

3.1   Formal Specification

We simply represent a linear collaborative object with algebraic specifications. So we define the `List` sort which admits two constructors: (i) `nil` (*i.e.*, an empty list); (ii) `cons(l,e)` (*i.e.*, a list composed by an element e added to the end of the list l). The `List` sort is parameterized by the element sort. This sort may be instanciated in various ways: character, paragraph, page, XML node.

We consider that all "operations" of the linear collaborative object are of sort `Opn` which admit three constructors:

- `Ins(p,e,pr)` inserts element e at position p,
- `Del(p)` deletes the element at position p,
- `Nop` is the idle operation.

We assume that the sort of the operation priority is natural numbers. In order to define the effect of operations on lists, we define a function `Do : List Opn -> List` by a set of conditional rewrite rules. For example, the change caused by the operation $Del(p)$ is recursively defined as follows, where `s` is the successor on natural numbers and `Length(l)` returns the length of the list `l`:

```
Do(nil, Del(p)) = nil;
s(p) = Length(l) => Do(cons(l,e),Del(p)) = l;
(s(p) > Length(l))=true => Do(cons(l,e),Del(p)) = cons(l,e);
(s(p) < Length(l))=true => Do(cons(l,e),Del(p)) =
cons(Do(l,Del(p)),e)
```

An OT algorithm is defined by a function on two arguments with profile T : Opn Opn -> Opn. For example, the following transformation:

$$T(Del(p_1), Ins(p_2, c_2, pr_2)) = \textbf{if } p_1 > p_2 \textbf{ then return } Del(p_1 + 1) \textbf{ else return } Del(p_1)$$

is defined by two conditional rules:

```
(p1 > p2) = true  => T(Del(p1),Ins(p2,e2,pr2)) = Del(p1+1)
(p1 > p2) = false => T(Del(p1),Ins(p2,e2,pr2)) = Del(p1)
```

In all applications we have encountered we have been able to express the transformation functions by conditional rewrite rules in a straightforward and almost mechanical way.

3.2 Specification of Conditions C_1 and C_2

We now express the copy convergence conditions as conjectures to be proved in our algebraic setting. Convergence conditions C_1 and C_2 are formulated as follows.

Let Pr : Opn -> Nat be a function that gives for every operation its priority.

Definition 6. (Condition C_1)

```
              Pr(op1) <> Pr(op2) =>
Do(Do(1, op1), T(op2,op1)) = Do(Do(1,op2),T(op1,op2))
```

The precondition Pr(op1) <> Pr(op2) expresses simply that operations op1 and op2 are concurrent.

Definition 7. (Condition C_2)

```
Pr(op) <> Pr(op1), Pr(op) <> Pr(op2), Pr(op1) <> Pr(op2) =>
    T(T(op,op1),T(op2,op1)) = T(T(op, op2),T(op1,op2))
```

3.3 The Theorem Prover: Spike

To automatically check the copy convergence conditions C_1 and C_2 we rely on SPIKE [4,21], a rewrite-based induction theorem prover. SPIKE was employed for the following reasons: (i) its high automation degree; (ii) its ability to perform case analysis (to deal with multiple methods and many transformation cases); (iii) its ability to find counter-examples; (iv) its built-in *decision procedures* [1] that allow to automatically eliminate arithmetic tautologies. This theorem prover has been successfully applied to complex case-studies [19,2]. The test set mechanisms that are employed to detect counter-examples in early stages of a proof attempt has been inspired by the *inductionless induction* paradigm (see e.g. [14]). In order to motivate our use of SPIKE , we begin with a short description of its proof engine.

Principles. SPIKE 's proof method is an extension of Cover Set Induction with different reasoning techniques, most of them based on conditional rewriting [6], case analysis and subsumption. The method combines the advantages of explicit induction (e.g. less failure) and of proofs by consistency [4,21] (ability to detect counter-examples).

In a nutshell, the method is parameterized by a set of axioms Ax, and proceeds by modifying incrementally two sets of clauses, (E, H), where E contains the conjectures to be checked and H contains clauses, previously in E, that have been reduced. The method is modelled by means of the relation $(E, H) \xrightarrow[Ax]{Spike} (E', H')$ which is described below. We say that a formula ϕ is an inductive theorem w.r.t. Ax if there exists a finite derivation of the form $(\{\phi\}, \emptyset) \xrightarrow[Ax]{Spike} \cdots \xrightarrow[Ax]{Spike} (\emptyset, H)$; we call this derivation a proof of ϕ.

Proof system. Given a set of conditional rules R derived from the orientation of Ax, SPIKE computes covering substitutions which is a family of substitutions covering all possible cases for induction variables. These substitutions are applied to conjectures *generating* special instances which are then *simplified* by rules, lemmas and induction hypotheses. This instantiation/simplification operation creates new subgoals that are processed in the same way in the following steps. Concretely, the relation $(E \cup \{C\}, H) \xrightarrow[Ax]{Spike} (E', H')$, that transforms the current conjecture C, is defined by two rules: GENERATE and SIMPLIFY. The GENERATE inference rule computes appropriate covering substitutions which are then applied to C. These so-built instances are then simplified by rules and lemmas and appropriate instances of E and H. The set of induction hypotheses available for the simplification of the cover-set instance $C\sigma$ are ad-hoc instances of the current set of E, $\{C\}$ and H, strictly smaller (w.r.t. a decreasing order over clauses $\prec_c$) than $C\sigma$. The SIMPLIFY inference rule transforms a conjecture into a (potentially empty) set of new and simpler conjectures.

Strategies. SPIKE offers the user some limited, but useful, mechanisms to interact with the proof engine. For each conjecture, the user can i) introduce intermediate lemmas that are first proven automatically and then used to establish the conjecture; ii) define a particular proof strategy that gives the order of execution for inference rules; iii) influence the inner mechanisms of some inference rules; for example the user can specify the order in which reducible terms are rewritten or the way the induction variables are chosen. These interaction mechanisms are crucial to guarantee that proof runs finish with success—when an empty set of conjectures is obtained. Of course, not all proof runs are successful; they may also diverge, or finish with failure; in the latter case the prover provides (under certain conditions) a counterexample to the initial conjectures.

Soundness. SPIKE 's inference engine is sound that is every conjecture that is successfully processed is valid in the initial model of the given specification; Moreover it is refutationally sound, i.e. the detection of a counterexample implies the existence of a counterexample in the initial conjectures [3].

3.4 Convergence Problems

We present the divergence situations discovered when checking the convergence conditions C_1 and C_2 for the function T of Figure 3 by SPIKE .

Checking Proofs. In the following we describe how SPIKE checks the conjecture C_1:

$$Pr(op1) <> Pr(op2) =>$$
$$Do(Do(1, op1), T(op2,op1)) = Do(Do(1,op2),T(op1,op2))$$

Firstly, a **Generate** rule is applied and 18 instances are produced after the variables 1, op1 and op2 are replaced respectively with the elements of the test set covering all cases of sort List, i.e. {nil, cons(1,e)}, and sort Opn, i.e. {Ins(p1,e1, pr1), Del(p2), Nop}. In order to store the initial conjecture, we need to simplify by rewriting or eliminate these instances.

Consider the instance where 1, op1 and op2 are substituted respectively by nil, Ins(p1,e1, pr1) and Del(p2). We obtain the following conjecture:

$$Do(Do(nil, Ins(p1,e1, pr1)), T(Del(p2),Ins(p1,e1, pr1))) =$$
$$Do(Do(nil,Del(p2)),T(Ins(p1,e1, pr1),Del(p2)))$$

A case rewriting is applied to reduce this conjecture with conditional rewrite rules corresponding to the functions T and Do without attempting to check their preconditions. Consider the case where the positions p1 and p2 are equal and p1-1 is equal to zero. We obtain the following conjecture:

$$Do(Do(nil, Ins(p1,e1, pr1)), Del(p1 + 1)) = Do(Do(nil,Del(p1)),$$
$$Ins(p1 - 1,e1, pr1))$$

By rewriting we get the following inconsistency: nil = cons(nil,e1). This means that the conjecture C_1 is false.

From this inconsistency, we have derived a scenario violating the condition C_1 that is depicted in Figure 6 (for clarity we have omitted the priority parameter). There are two users: (i) $user_1$ inserts x in position 1 (op_1) while $user_2$ concurrently deletes the character at the same position (op_2). (ii) When op_2 is received by site 1, op_2 must be transformed according to op_1. So T(Del(1),Ins(1,x)) is called and Del(2) is returned. (iii) In the same way, op_1 is received on site 2 and must be transformed according to op_2. T(Ins(1,x),Del(1)) is called and returns Ins(0,x). Condition C_1 is violated. Accordingly, the final results on both sites are different.

The error comes from the definition of T(Ins(p1,c1,pr1), Del(p2,pr2)) (see Figure 3). The condition p1 < p2   should be rewritten p1 <= p2. This modification is sufficient to satisfy the condition C_1.

After the above modification in order to satisfy the condition C_1, we describe now how SPIKE deals with the checking of conjecture C_2:

$$Pr(op) <> Pr(op1), Pr(op) <> Pr(op2), Pr(op1) <> Pr(op2) =>$$
$$T(T(op,op1),T(op2,op1)) = T(T(op, op2),T(op1,op2))$$

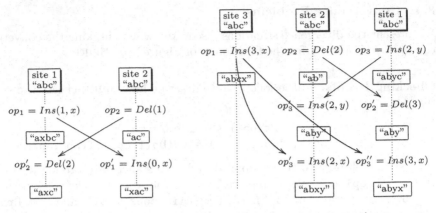

Fig. 6. Scenario violating C_1 **Fig. 7.** Scenario violating C_2

SPIKE generates 27 instances by substituting in all possible ways the variables op, op1 and op2 that are instantiated by the elements of the test set {Ins(p1,e1,pr1), Del(p2), Nop}. Consider the instance where op = Ins(p,e,pr), op1 = Ins(p1,e1,pr1) and op2 = Del(p2) and the case where p1 = p - 1 and p2 = p. After rewriting, we get the following conjecture :

```
T(Ins(p+1,e,pr),Del(p+1)) = T(Ins(p-1,e,pr),Ins(p-1,e1,pr1))
```

Two inconsistencies are produced from this conjecture: (i) Ins(p,e) = Nop if e = e1; (ii) Ins(p,e) = Ins(p-1, e) if e <> e1 and pr <= pr1.

Both inconsistencies lead to violation of the condition C_2. Figure 7 presents a scenario for C_2 violation. In this scenario $seq = [op_2; op_3']$ and $seq' = [op_3; op_2']$ are two equivalent sequences. Using the function T of Figure 3 we must have $T(op_1, seq) = T(op_1, seq')$:

$$T^*(op_1, seq) = op_1' = T(T(op_1, op_2), op_3') = Ins(2, x)$$
$$T^*(op_1, seq') = op_1'' = T(T(op_1, op_3), op_2') = Ins(3, x)$$

As we can see, $op_1' \neq op_1''$, C_2 is violated; and therefore the convergence is not achieved. The scenario illustrated in Figure 7 is called C_2 *puzzle*.

Analyzing the Convergence Problem. To better understand the source of this problem, we consider the C_2 puzzle (see Figure 7). There are three concurrent operations $op_1 = Ins(3, x)$, $op_2 = Del(2)$ and $op_3 = Ins(2, y)$ where the insertion positions initially have the following relation: $Pos(op_1) > Pos(op_3)$ with $Pos(Ins(p, c, pr)) = p$.

According to Definition 3, op_1 and op_3 are not in conflict. In this scenario we have two equivalent operation sequences $S_1 = [op_2; op_3']$ and $S_2 = [op_3; op_2']$ where $op_3' = T(op_3, op_2)$ and $op_2' = T(op_2, op_3)$. The above relation between op_1 and op_3 is not preserved when transforming op_1 along sequence S_1 since $Pos(T(op_1, op_2)) = Pos(op_3')$.

The transformation process may lead to two concurrent insert operations (with different initial insertion positions) to get into a *false conflict situation* (the same insertion position). Unfortunately, the initial relation between the positions of these operations is lost during their transformations with other operations. However we need to know how the insert operations were generated in order to avoid the divergence problem.

In the following, we propose a new approach to solve this divergence problem. Intuitively, we notice that storing previous insertion positions for every transformation step is sufficient to recover the original position relation between two concurrent insert operations.

4 Our Solution

In this section, we present our approach to achieving convergence for linear collaborative objects. Firstly, we will introduce the key concept of position word for keeping track of insertion positions. Next, we will give our new OT function and how this function resolves the divergence problem. Finally, we will give the formal analysis of this algorithm.

4.1 Position Words

For any set of symbols Σ called an *alphabet*, Σ^* denotes the set of *words* over Σ. The empty word is denoted by ϵ. For $\omega \in \Sigma^*$, then $|\omega|$ denotes the *length* of ω. If $\omega = uv$, for some $u, v \in \Sigma^*$, then u is a *prefix* of ω and v is a *suffix* of ω.

For every $\omega \in \Sigma^*$, such that $|\omega| > 0$, we denote $Base(\omega)$ (resp. $Top(\omega)$) the *last* (resp. *first*) symbol of ω. Thus, $Top(abcde) = a$ and $Base(abcde) = e$. We assume that Σ is totally ordered and denote the strict part of this order by $>$. If $\omega_1, \omega_2 \in \Sigma^*$, then $\omega_1 \preceq \omega_2$ is the *lexicographic ordering* of Σ^* if: (i) ω_1 is a prefix of ω_2, or (ii) $\omega_1 = \rho u$ and $\omega_2 = \rho v$, where $\rho \in \Sigma^*$ is the longest prefix common to ω_1 and ω_2, and $Top(u)$ precedes $Top(v)$ in the alphabetic order.

Definition 8. *(p-word)* *We consider the natural numbers* $\mathbb{N}$ *as an alphabet. We define the set of p_words* $\mathcal{P} \subset \mathbb{N}^*$ *as follows: (i)* $\epsilon \in \mathcal{P}$*; (ii) if* $n \in \mathbb{N}$ *then* $n \in \mathcal{P}$*; (iii) if* ω *is a nonempty p-word and* $n \in \mathbb{N}$ *then* $n\omega \in \mathcal{P}$ *iff* $n - Top(\omega) \in \{0, 1, -1\}$.

We observe immediately that we can concatenate two p-words to get another one if the end of the first and the origin of the second one differs of at most 1:

Theorem 1. *Let* ω_1 *and* ω_2 *be two nonempty p-words. The concatenation of* ω_1 *and* ω_2*, written* $\omega_1 \cdot \omega_2$ *or simply* $\omega_1\omega_2$*, is a p-word iff either* $Base(\omega_1) = Top(\omega_2)$ *or* $Base(\omega_1) = Top(\omega_2) \pm 1$.

For example, $\omega_1 = 00$, $\omega_2 = 1232$ and $\omega_1\omega_2 = 001232$ are p-words but $\omega_3 = 3476$ is not.

Definition 9. *The equivalence relation on the set of p_words* $\mathcal{P}$ *is defined by:* $\omega_1 \equiv_{\mathcal{P}} \omega_2$ *iff* $Top(\omega_1) = Top(\omega_2)$ *and* $Base(\omega_1) = Base(\omega_2)$, *where* $\omega_1, \omega_2 \in \mathcal{P}$.

We can also show that this relation is a congruence using Definitions 8 and 9:

Proposition 1. *The equivalence relation* $\equiv_{\mathcal{P}}$ *is a* right congruence, *that is, for all* $\rho \in \mathcal{P}$: *if* $\omega_1 \equiv_{\mathcal{P}} \omega_2$ *then* $\omega_1 \rho \equiv_{\mathcal{P}} \omega_2 \rho$

4.2   OT Algorithm

In order to preserve the order relation between two insert operations, we propose to store all different positions occupied by an element during the transformation process. It means that instead of the single position we maintain a stack of positions called a *p-word*. Each time an operation is transformed we push the last position before transformation in the *p*-word. The size of the stack is proportional to the number of concurrent operations. In Figure 8 we give the details of our new OT function. When two insertion operations insert two different elements at the same position (they are in conflict), a choice has to be done: which element must be inserted before the other? The solution that is generally adopted consists in associating a priority to each insert operation (*i.e.*, the site identifier). In our OT function, when a conflict occurs, the character of an insertion operation whose site identifier pr is the highest is inserted before the other.

If two *p*-words are identical it means that the two associated insert operations are equal. Otherwise the *p*-word allows to track the order relation between the two operations. We shall therefore redefine the insert operation as $Ins(p, e, w, pr)$ where p is the insertion position, e the element to be added, w a *p*-word and pr is the site identifier. When an operation is generated, the *p*-word is empty, *i.e.* $Ins(3, x, \epsilon, pr)$. When an operation is transformed and the insertion position is changed, the original position is pushed to the *p*-word. For example, $T(Ins(3, x, \epsilon, pr), Del(1)) = Ins(2, x, [3], pr)$ and $T(Ins(2, e, [3], pr), Ins(1, e', \epsilon, pr')) = Ins(3, e, [2 \cdot 3], pr)$.

We define a function PW which enables to construct *p*-words from editing operations. It takes an operation as argument and returns its *p*-word:

$$PW(Ins(p, c, w, pr)) = \begin{cases} p & \text{if } w = \epsilon \\ pw & \text{if } w \neq \epsilon \text{ and} \\ & (p = Top(w) \\ & \text{or } p = Top(w) \pm 1) \\ \epsilon & \text{otherwise} \end{cases}$$

$$PW(Del(p)) = p$$

We define the strict part of a total order on the insert operations as follows:

Definition 10. *Given two insert operations* $o_1 = Ins(p_1, e_1, w_1, pr_1)$ *and* $o_2 = Ins(p_2, e_2, w_2, pr_2)$ *we define* $o_1 \sqsubset o_2$ *iff one of the following conditions holds:* (i) $PW(o_1) \prec PW(o_2)$; (ii) $PW(o_1) = PW(o_2)$ *and* $pr_1 < pr_2$.

$T(Ins(p_1, c_1, w_1, pr_1), Ins(p_2, c_2, w_2, pr_2)) =$
let $\alpha_1 = PW(Ins(p_1, c_1, w_1, pr_1))$ **and** $\alpha_2 = PW(Ins(p_2, c_2, w_2, pr_2))$
if $(\alpha_1 \prec \alpha_2$ **or** $(\alpha_1 = \alpha_2$ **and** $pr_1 < pr_2))$
then return $Ins(p_1, c_1, w_1, pr_1)$
elseif $(\alpha_1 \succ \alpha_2$ **or** $(\alpha_1 = \alpha_2$ **and** $pr_1 > pr_2))$
   then return $Ins(p_1 + 1, c_1, p_1 w_1, pr_1)$
endif;

$T(Ins(p_1, c_1, w_1, pr_1), Del(p_2)) =$
if $p_1 > p_2$ **then return** $Ins(p_1 - 1, c_1, p_1 w_1, pr_1)$
elseif $p_1 < p_2$ **then return** $Ins(p_1, c_1, w_1, pr_1)$
   else return $Ins(p_1, c_1, p_1 w_1, pr_1)$
endif;

$T(Del(p_1), Del(p_2)) =$
if $p_1 < p_2$ **then return** $Del(p_1)$
elseif $p_1 > p_2$ **then return** $Del(p_1 - 1)$
   else return Nop
endif;

$T(Del(p_1), Ins(p_2, c_2, w_2, pr_2)) =$
if $p_1 < p_2$ **then return** $Del(p_1)$
else return $Del(p_1 + 1)$
endif;

Fig. 8. New OT function

For convenience of notation we also use $o_2 \sqsupseteq o_1$ to state that $o_1 \sqsubseteq o_2$.

Figure 9 shows how the p-words solve the C_2 puzzle depicted in Figure ??.b. When op_1 is transformed according to ops_3, $3 > 2$, so op_1 is inserted after op_3. This order relation must be preserved when $op'_1 = T(Ins(3, x, \epsilon, 1), Del(2)) = Ins(2, x, [3], 1)$ will be transformed according to op'_3. To preserve the relation detected between op_1 and op_3, we must observe $PW(op'_1) \succ PW(op'_3)$. As $[2; 3] \succ [2; 2]$ is true, the order relation is preserved.

However, there is still a problem. This solution leads to the convergence (*i.e.* the same states), but C_2 is not satisfied. Indeed, we can verify in Figure 9 that:

$$T^*(op_1, [op_2; op'_3]) \neq T^*(op_1, [op_3; op'_2])$$

When two identical insertions operations are transformed according to two equivalent operation sequences, their p-words may get different. If they are different, they can be considered as equivalent if the top and the base of their p-words are equal. From the equivalence of p-words, we define the equivalence of two editing operations.

Definition 11. *Given two editing operations op_1 and op_2, we say that op_1 and op_2 are equivalent and we denote it also by $op_1 \equiv_P op_2$ iff one of the following conditions holds:*

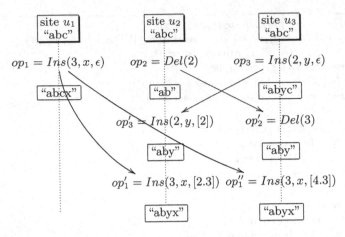

Fig. 9. Correct execution of C_2 puzzle

1. $op_1 = Ins(p_1, e_1, w_1, pr_1)$, $op_2 = Ins(p_2, e_2, w_2, pr_2)$, $e_1 = e_2$, $pr_1 = pr_2$, and $PW(op_1) \equiv_\mathcal{P} PW(op_2)$;
2. $op_1 = Del(p_1)$, $op_2 = Del(p_2)$ and $p_1 = p_2$.

With the above operation equivalence we can propose a weak form of the condition C_2 that is sufficient to ensure the state convergence in these situations. This condition is called C_2'.

Definition 12. (Condition C_2') *We say T satisfies C_2' iff T satisfies C_1 and for every concurrent editing operations op, op_1 and op_2* [4]:

$$T^*(op, [op_1 \,; T(op_2, op_1)]) \equiv_\mathcal{P} T^*(op, [op_2 \,; T(op_1, op_2)])$$

5   Verifying C_1 and C_2'

In the following, we show that C_1 is satisfied in our setting using the fact that the original relation between two concurrent insert operations is preserved by transformation. Then we show that C_2' is satisfied. The most of proofs have been automatically checked by the theorem prover SPIKE [4].

5.1   Conservation of p-Words

In the following, we show that our OT function does not lose any information about position words.

Lemma 1. *Given an insert operation $op_1 = Ins(p_1, e_1, w_1, pr_1)$. For every editing operation $op \in \mathcal{O}$ such that $op \parallel op_1$, $PW(op_1)$ is a suffix of $PW(T(op_1, op))$.*

---

[4] Operations op, op_1 and op_2 have different priorities.

The following theorem states that the extension of our OT function to sequences, *i.e.* T^*, does not lose any information about position words.

Theorem 2. *Given an insert operation* $op_1 = Ins(p_1, c_1, w_1, pr_1)$. *For every operation sequence seq,* $PW(op_1)$ *is a suffix of* $PW(T^*(op_1, seq))$.

Proof. By induction on the length of *seq*.

We can use the position relations between insert operations as an *invariant* which must be preserved when these operations are transformed and executed in all remote sites.

Lemma 2. *For all concurrent insert operations* op_1 *and* op_2 *and for all editing operations* $op \in \mathcal{O}$ *such that* $op \parallel op_1$ *and* $op \parallel op_2$:

$$op_1 \sqsubset op_2 \text{ implies } T(op_1, op) \sqsubset T(op_2, op)$$

Proof. We have to consider two cases: $op = Ins(p, c, w, pr)$ and $op = Del(p)$.

The following theorem shows that the extension of our OT function to sequence, *i.e.* T^*, preserves also the invariance property.

Theorem 3. *For all concurrent insert operations* op_1 *and* op_2 *all sequences of operations seq:*

$$PW(op_1) \sqsubset PW(op_2) \text{ implies } PW(T^*(op_1, seq)) \sqsubset PW(T^*(op_2, seq)).$$

Proof. By induction on the length of *seq*.

5.2 Convergence Properties

Recall that the condition C_2' means that transforming an operation along two equivalent operation sequences will generate only equivalent operations (as opposed to C_2). In the following, we sketch the proof that C_1 and C_2' are verified by our transformations. The complete proofs of Theorems 4 and 5 below have been automatically checked by the theorem prover SPIKE.

The following theorem shows that our OT function satisfies C_1.

Theorem 4. *For all editing operations* $op_1, op_2 \in \mathcal{O}$ *and for all list states* l *we have:*

$$Do([op_1; T(op_2, op_1)], l) = Do([op_2; T(op_1, op_2)], l)$$

Proof. Consider the following case: $op_1 = Ins(p_1, e_1, w_1, pr_1)$, $op_2 = Ins(p_2, e_2, w_2, pr_2)$ and $PW(op_1) \prec PW(op_2)$. According to this order, e_1 is inserted before e_2. If op_1 has been executed then when op_2 arrives it is shifted ($op_2' = T(op_2, op_1) = Ins(p_2 + 1, c_1, p_2 w_2, pr_2)$) and op_2' inserts e_2 to the right of e_1. Now, if op_1 arrives after the execution of op_2, then op_1 is not shifted, *i.e.* $op_1' = T(op_1, op_2) = op_1$. The element e_1 is inserted as it is to the left of e_2. Thus executing $[op_1, op_2']$ and $[op_2, op_1']$ on the same object state gives also the same object state.

Theorem 5 shows that our OT function also satisfies C_2'. This theorem means that if T satisfies condition C_1 then when transforming op_1 against two equivalent sequences $[op_2; T(op_3, op_2)]$ and $[op_3; T(op_2, op_3)]$ we will obtain two equivalent operations according to Definition 11.

Theorem 5. *If the function T satisfies C_1 then for all $op, op_1, op_2 \in \mathcal{O}$ we have:*

$$T^*(op, [op_1; T(op_2, op_1)]) \equiv_\mathcal{P} T^*(op, [op_2; T(op_1, op_2)]).$$

Proof. Consider the case where $op = Ins(p, e, w, pr)$, $op_1 = Ins(p_1, e_1, w_1, pr_1)$, $op_2 = Del(p_2)$, $p_1 = p_2$, and $p > p_2 + 1$. Using our OT function (see Figure 8), we have $op_1' = T(op_1, op_2) = Ins(p_1, e_1, p_1 w_1, pr_1)$ and $op_2' = T(op_2, op_1) = Del(p_2+1)$. When transforming op against the sequence $[Ins(p_1, e_1, w_2); Del(p_2+1)]$ we get $op' = Ins(p, e, (p+1)pw, pr)$ and when transforming op against $[Del(p_2); Ins(p_1, e_1, p_1 w_1)]$ we obtain $op'' = Ins(p, c, (p-1)pw, pr)$. Operations op' and op'' have the same insertion position and the same element. It remains to show that $PW(op') \equiv_\mathcal{P} PW(op'')$. As $p(p-1)p \equiv_\mathcal{P} p(p+1)p$ and the equivalence relation $\equiv_\mathcal{P}$ is a right congruence by Proposition 1 then op' and op'' are equivalent.

It is easy to prove that C_2' is sufficient for n concurrent operations defined on the same state with $n > 3$.

5.3 C_2' is Not Sufficient

In the previous section we have showed that C_2' solves the divergence problems when the operations are concurrent and defined on the same state. However there exists some situations where C_2' is not sufficient when we consider a causality dependency between operations.

Figure 10 presents a scenario for such a situation: $o_1 = Ins(2, x, \epsilon)$ is generated at site 1 and $o_2 = Ins(2, y, \epsilon)$ is generated at site 2 and it causally depends on $o_3 = Del(2)$. When o_1 arrives at site 2 it is first transformed against o_3 and this results in $o_1' = T(o_1, o_3) = Ins(2, x, [2])$. Note that at site 2 we have $o_2 \sqsubset o_1'$ and so the insertion position of o_1' will be incremented after being transformed against o_2, i.e. $T(o_1', o_2) = Ins(3, y, [2.2])$. As o_2 is partially concurrent to o_4, its execution at site 3 requires a correct transformation (see Section 2.4). This transformation results in $o_2' = T(o_2, T(o_4, o_3)) = Ins(2, y, [2])$. Arriving at site 3, o_1 is first transformed against the sequence $[o_4; o_3']$ and $o"_1 = T(o_1, [o_4; o_3']) = Ins(2, y, [2])$ is returned. In this case, it is clear that $o"_1 \sqsubset o_2'$ (as $pr_1 < pr_2$ with $pr_1 = 1$ and $pr_2 = 2$) and so the insertion position of $o"_1$ will remain unchanged after being transformed against o_2'. This relation is different from what we have discovered at site 2. Consequently, this variation of relation between o_1 and o_2 at different sites inevitably leads to the divergence situation as illustrated in Figure 10.

In Table 1 we enumerate all cases given by SPIKE that lead to violation of C_2'.

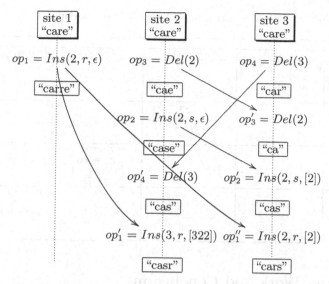

Fig. 10. Divergence in the presence of causal precedence

Discussion. The C_2 *puzzle* (see Figure 7) shows that the previous OT solutions are unable to ensure convergence even for three concurrent operations defined on the same state. To overcome this problem, we have proposed a weakened form for Condition C_2 in order to synchronize linear collaborative objects by our new OT algorithm. Using the SPIKE theorem prover allows us to cover automatically a large number of situations when checking this algorithm, *w.r.t.* the convergence properties. We come to the conclusion that:

1. the condition C'_2 is sufficient when using n concurrent editing operations defined on the same state $(n \geq 2)$, and,
2. however there are cases involving partial concurrent insert operations where C'_2 is not sufficient for achieving this convergence property.

Consequently, we cannot plug our OT algorithm in standard integration algorithms such as adOPTed [18] and SOCT2 [22]. On one hand, these algorithms are based on C_2 that is a stronger condition than C'_2, and on the other hand, they use a concurrency detection technique that imposes a particular causality dependency of editing operations even though the collaborative object semantics do not require such a dependency [5].

Note that most of the problematic scenarios given by Table 1 result from the causal dependency $o_3 \rightarrow o_2$ where $o_3 = Del(p_3)$ and $o_2 = Ins(p_2, e_2, w_2, pr_2)$. However it is an artificial dependency since an insert should not depend from a delete operation: an editing operation can only depend on insert operations. As a matter of fact we can show that C'_2 is sufficient for ensuring the convergence property, if we can avoid the situations listed in Table 1. We have designed in [10] an *integration algorithm* for this purpose. It works by maintaining histories in a canonical form.

Table 1. Situations where C_2' is not satisfied

		o_3		
	$Del(p_3)$	$Del(p_3)$	$Del(p_3)$	$Ins(p_3,e_3,w_3,pr_3)$
$Del(p_4)$	$p_1=p_2,\ w_1=w_2,$ $p_2=p_3$ $p_4=p_3+1,$ $\natural=\sqsubset$			
$Del(p_4)$		$p_1=p_2,\ w_1=w_2,$ $pr_1<pr_2,\ p_4=p_2,$ $p_3=p_4+1,$ $\natural=\sqsubset$		
o_4 $Del(p_4)$			$p_1=p_2,\ w_1=w_2,$ $p_1=p_4,$ $p_4=p_3+1,$ $\natural=\sqsupset$	
$Del(p_4)$				$p_1=p_2,\ p_2=p_3,$ $p_3=p_4,\ w_1=w_2,$ $w_2=w_3,\ pr_1<pr_3,$ $pr_1<pr_2,$ $\natural=\sqsupset$

6   Related Work and Conclusion

Several techniques have been proposed to address C_2 puzzle. These can be categorized as follows:

The first approach tries to avoid the C_2 puzzle scenario. This is achieved by constraining the communication among replicas in order to restrict the space of possible execution order. For example, the SOCT4 algorithm [27] uses a sequencer, associated with a deferred broadcast and a sequential reception, to enforce a continuous global order on updates. This global order can also be obtained by using an undo/do/redo scheme like in GOTO [24].

The second approach tries to resolve the C_2 puzzle. In this case, concurrent operations can be executed in any order, but transformation functions require to satisfy the C_2 condition. This approach has been developed in adOPTed [18], SOCT2 [22], and GOT [25]. Unfortunately, we have proved in [12] that all previously proposed transformation functions fail to satisfy this condition.

In this paper we have pointed out correctness problems of the existing OT algorithms used to synchronize linear collaborative objects (such as document text or XML files) and we have proposed a solution based on a weak form of Condition C_2. Using our theorem-proving approach [12,13] we have provided a formal analysis of our OT algorithm. Furthermore, our solution is generic since it can be applied to any linear data-structure.

As this weak form still cannot ensure the convergence state in some cases, we cannot plug our OT algorithm in standard integration algorithms based on the condition C_2, such as adOPTed [18] and SOCT2 [22]. So, we have designed a new integration algorithm based only on conditions C_1 and C_2'. The details of this algorithm are given in [10].

Acknowledgment. The second author is extremely grateful to Jean-Pierre Jouannaud for his constant support and encouragement.

References

1. Armando, A., Rusinowitch, M., Stratulat, S.: Incorporating decision procedures in implicit induction. Journal of Symbolic Computation 34(4), 241–258 (2001)
2. Barthe, G., Stratulat, S.: Validation of the javacard platform with implicit induction techniques. In: Nieuwenhuis, R. (ed.) RTA 2003. LNCS, vol. 2706, pp. 337–351. Springer, Heidelberg (2003)
3. Bouhoula, A.: Using induction and rewriting to verify and complete parameterized specifications. Theor. Comput. Sci. 170(1-2), 245–276 (1996)
4. Bouhoula, A., Kounalis, E., Rusinowitch, M.: Automated Mathematical Induction. Journal of Logic and Computation 5(5), 631–668 (1995)
5. Cheriton, D.R., Skeen, D.: Understanding the limitations of causally and totally ordered communication. In: SOSP, pp. 44–57 (1993)
6. Dershowitz, N., Jouannaud, J.-P.: Rewrite systems. In: Handbook of Theoretical Computer Science, vol. B: Formal Models and Sematics (B), pp. 243–320 (1990)
7. Ellis, C.A., Gibbs, S.J.: Concurrency Control in Groupware Systems. In: SIGMOD Conference, vol. 18, pp. 399–407 (1989)
8. Guerraoui, R., Hari, C.: On the consistency problem in mobile distributed computing. In: Proceedings of the second ACM international workshop on Principles of mobile computing, pp. 51–57. ACM Press, New York (2002)
9. Herlihy, M.P., Wing, J.M.: Linearizability: a correctness condition for concurrent objects. ACM Trans. Program. Lang. Syst. 12(3), 463–492 (1990)
10. Imine, A.: Conception Formelle d' Algorithmes de Réplication Optimiste. Vers I' Edition Collaborative dans les Réseaux Pair-á-Pair. Thèse de doctorat, Université Henri Poincaré, Nancy (December 2006)
11. Imine, A., Molli, P., Oster, G., Rusinowitch, M.: Development of Transformation Functions Assisted by a Theorem Prover. In: Fourth International Workshop on Collaborative Editing (ACM CSCW'02), Collaborative Computing in IEEE Distributed Systems Online (November 2002)
12. Imine, A., Molli, P., Oster, G., Rusinowitch, M.: Proving Correctness of Transformation Functions in Real-Time Groupware. In: 8th European Conference of Computer-supported Cooperative Work, Helsinki, Finland, 14.-18. September 2003. Kluwer Academic publishers, Dordrecht (2003)
13. Imine, A., Molli, P., Oster, G., Rusinowitch, M.: Deductive verification of distributed groupware systems. In: Rattray, C., Maharaj, S., Shankland, C. (eds.) AMAST 2004. LNCS, vol. 3116, pp. 226–240. Springer, Heidelberg (2004)
14. Jouannaud, J.-P., Kounalis, E.: Automatic proofs by induction in theories without constructors. Inf. Comput. 82(1), 1–33 (1989)
15. Li, D., Li, R.: Ensuring Content Intention Consistency in Real-Time Group (ed.) In: The 24th International Conference on Distributed Computing Systems (ICDCS 2004), Tokyo, Japan, March 2004, IEEE Computer Society, Washington (2004)
16. Lushman, B., Cormack, G.V.: Proof of correctness of ressel's adopted algorithm. Information Processing Letters 86(3), 303–310 (2003)
17. Molli, P., Oster, G., Skaf-Molli, H., Imine, A.: Using the transformational approach to build a safe and generic data synchronizer. In: Proceedings of the 2003 international ACM SIGGROUP conference on Supporting group work, pp. 212–220. ACM Press, New York (2003)
18. Ressel, M., Nitsche-Ruhland, D., Gunzenhauser, R.: An Integrating, Transformation-Oriented Approach to Concurrency Control and Undo in Group Editors. In: Proceedings of the ACM Conference on Computer Supported Cooperative Work (CSCW'96), Boston, Massachusetts, USA, pp. 288–297 (November 1996)

19. Rusinowitch, M., Stratulat, S., Klay, F.: Mechanical Verification of an Ideal ABR Conformance Algorithm. Journal of Automated Reasoning 30(2), 153–177 (2003)
20. Saito, Y., Shapiro, M.: Optimistic replication. ACM Comput. Surv. 37(1), 42–81 (2005)
21. Stratulat, S.: A general framework to build contextual cover set induction provers. Journal of Symbolic Computation 32(4), 403–445 (2001)
22. Suleiman, M., Cart, M., Ferrié, J.: Concurrent Operations in a Distributed and Mobile Collaborative Environment. In: Proceedings of the Fourteenth International Conference on Data Engineering, Orlando, Florida, USA, February 23-27, 1998, pp. 36–45. IEEE Computer Society Press, Washington (1998)
23. Sun, C.: The copowerpoint project http://reduce.qpsf.edu.au/copowerpoint/ (2004)
24. Sun, C., Ellis, C.: Operational transformation in real-time group editors: issues, algorithms, and achievements. In: Proceedings of the 1998 ACM conference on Computer supported cooperative work, pp. 59–68. ACM Press, New York (1998)
25. Sun, C., Jia, X., Zhang, Y., Yang, Y., Chen, D.: Achieving convergence, causality-preservation and intention-preservation in real-time cooperative editing systems. ACM Transactions on Computer-Human Interaction (TOCHI) 5(1), 63–108 (March 1998)
26. Sun, D., Xia, S., Sun, C., Chen, D.: Operational transformation for collaborative word processing. In: CSCW '04: Proceedings of the 2004 ACM conference on Computer supported cooperative work, New York, NY, USA, 2004, pp. 437–446. ACM Press, New York (2004)
27. Vidot, N., Cart, M., Ferri é, J., Suleiman, M.: Copies convergence in a distributed real-time collaborative environment. In: Proceedings of the ACM Conference on Computer Supported Cooperative Work (CSCW'00), Philadelphia, Pennsylvania, USA (December 2000)

Towards Modular Algebraic Specifications for Pointer Programs: A Case Study

Claude Marché[1,2]

[1] INRIA Futurs, ProVal, Parc Orsay Université, F-91893
[2] Lab. de Recherche en Informatique, Univ Paris-Sud, CNRS, Orsay, F-91405

Abstract. We present on an example the framework currently under development in the WHY/KRAKATOA/CADUCEUS platform for proving that a JAVA or a C program is a correct implementation of some model defined by algebraic specifications, in a modular setting.

1 Introduction

Deductive verification of properties of programs is a difficult task that has been addressed for a long time. The first significant step is due to Floyd in 1967 [1] and Hoare in 1969 [2], introducing the Floyd-Hoare logic, whose principle is to pose *pre-conditions* and *post-conditions* on programs. These are logical assertions on program variables, which serve as a specification: verification amounts to proving that in any state satisfying the pre-condition, execution of the program leads to a state that satisfies the post-condition. Floyd-Hoare logic rules, or *weakest precondition calculus* proposed by Dijkstra in 1975 [3], provide a means to reduce this problem to checking the validity of first-order formulas. By these means, computer assisted program verification relies on computer-assisted theorem proving or *automated deduction*.

Computer-assisted theorem proving is also a difficult task with a long history. A landmark approach is the *resolution* principle proposed by Robinson in 1965. Later *paramodulation* and *completion* where proposed to reason with the equality predicate. This leaded to the development of powerful computer tools for automated proving in first-order logic with equality (see the CASC competition http://www.cs.miami.edu/~tptp/CASC/). Another disruptive advance was the *congruence closure* [4] and the combination of decision procedures for specific theories [5] leading to powerful tools for automated proving in first-order logic with equality and built-in theories, in particular linear arithmetic (tools of the SMT category [6]).

But computer-assisted theorem proving was not only aimed at providing fully automatic decision procedures. Starting with the AUTOMATH system in 1968, a large set of techniques and tools have been proposed to assist a user to *build* some proof. In 1969, the LCF SYSTEM introduced the key notion of tactics. In 1971 appeared the NQTHM prover by Boyer and Moore, whose descendant is now ACL2. The latter has been especially successful for verifying circuits. Other proof assistants like COQ, ISABELLE or PVS propose ways to build certified proofs, of mathematical theorems or of programs. However, they support mainly programs that belong to the pure functional family, not programming languages like JAVA or C which manipulate mutable data structures, which we refer to as *pointer programs*.

H. Comon-Lundh et al. (Eds.): Jouannaud Festschrift, LNCS 4600, pp. 235–258, 2007.
© Springer-Verlag Berlin Heidelberg 2007

A different class of systems are tools for formal specification and prototyping. An early system of this kind is OBJ, which aims at proposing a formal specification language mainly based on first-order logic with equality. Descendants of OBJ include the CAFEOBJ, MAUDE, and LARCH systems. Unlike a proof assistant, such a system is more focused on engineering purposes, and proposes in particular a *modular* setting to build specifications incrementally. Verification is mainly based on calling an automated theorem prover. The B system is also of this kind, where an effort has been made to integrate mutability features via the so-called *B-machines*, and the technique of *refinement*, which allows one to develop a prototype incrementally, from an abstract view to more and more detailed and concrete realizations.

The fast growth of the role of software in daily life leads to a growing interest in methods which offer security verifications during the software development. However, the techniques that emerged in industry were not of the kind of deductive verification described above: these are *approximate* methods like *abstract interpretation* and *model checking*, which do not guarantee that a software is completely free of bugs, but have shown themselves very efficient in finding bugs. A renewal of interest in Floyd-Hoare style techniques came from the principle of *design by contract* for object-oriented languages, which is based on posing pre-conditions, post-conditions but also *invariants* on objects. This principle was used in the EIFFEL system, where assertions were checked at run-time, but also statically by so-called *extended static checkers* like ESC-MODULA and ESC-JAVA. Several other static checkers were proposed for JAVA: LOOP, KEY, JACK, JIVE, etc. Similarly for C#, the SPEC# tool has been developed.

The WHY/KRAKATOA/CADUCEUS platform [7] proposes tools to perform static verification of this kind, for JAVA source code (KRAKATOA) but also for C code (CADUCEUS). But an originality of this platform is that a translation is performed to the WHY language which is closer to the family of functional languages for which proof assistants like COQ are powerful. Yet, there is still ongoing research around this approach to integrate aspects of modular specification and refinement. In this paper we illustrate these aspects on an example: priority queues, implemented by a heap data structure. Notice that we are going to use platform features that are still under development, and are not yet available in the distributed version. The main purpose is to illustrate how it is possible to relate a pointer program, manipulating mutable data structures, like a JAVA program, to a purely algebraic specification. Another purpose is to illustrate the scientific issues that are still to be addressed.

This paper is organized as follows: in Section 2 we first summarize the platform features we need, Section 3 presents the case study step by step, and in Section 4 we discuss the approach and perspectives.

2   Preliminaries

2.1   The WHY/KRAKATOA/CADUCEUS Platform

The WHY/KRAKATOA/CADUCEUS platform [7] is a set of tools for deductive verification of JAVA and C source code. In both cases, the requirements are specified as *annotations* in the source, in a special style of comments. For JAVA, these specifications are given in JML (the *Java Modeling Language* [8]) and are interpreted by the

KRAKATOA tool. For C, we designed our own specification language, largely inspired from JML. Those are interpreted by the CADUCEUS tool. The tools are available as open source software at `http://why.lri.fr/`.

The general approach is to generate *Verification Conditions* (also called *proof obligations*): logical formulas whose validity implies the soundness of the code with respect to the given specification. This includes both verification conditions to guarantee the absence of run-time errors: null pointer dereferencing, out-of-bounds array access, etc.; and verification of user-defined assertions. The verification conditions can be discharged using one or several theorem provers.

The main originality of this platform is that a large part is common to C and JAVA. In particular there is a unique, stand-alone, verification condition generator called WHY, which is able to output verification conditions in the native syntax of many provers, either automatic or interactive ones. The overall architecture is presented in Figure 1.

In the case study we consider in the following, we use JAVA, but most things applies to C too (and potentially similar language like C++ or C# if they are supported in the future).

2.2 The WHY Intermediate Language

A main specificity of our approach is to use WHY as an intermediate language. As a programming language, it is a quite simple language with basic constructs like `if` and `while`. Its imperative features are limited to providing mutable variables: there are no complex, in-place modifiable, data types like arrays or structures. Indeed, the type of such a mutable variable is necessarily some logical sort, that is a type defined in the specification part of the language. This specification part is a standard first-order language where one may introduce logical sorts, functions, predicates and axioms, very much like in an algebraic specification language like OBJ. The type of a mutable

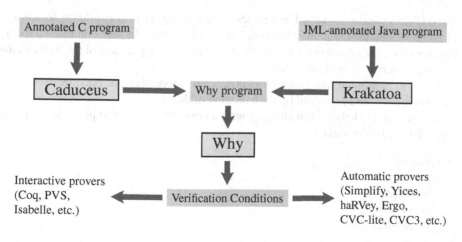

Fig. 1. Platform Architecture

variable is then either a built-in type (booleans, mathematical integers and reals) or an introduced abstract datatype.

This algebraic specification feature is indeed internally used to describe the semantics of execution of JAVA or C programs, with an appropriate modeling of memory [9,10]. This modeling of the memory heap is defined by introducing abstract data types together with operations and an appropriate first-order axiomatization. Our heap memory models for C and Java both follow the principle of the Burstall-Bornat 'component-as-array' model [11]. Each Java object field (resp. C structure field) becomes a *Why mutable variable* containing a purely applicative map. This map is equipped with an access function acc so that $acc(f, p)$ denotes the field of the structure pointed-to by p; and an update function upd so that $upd(f, p, v)$ denotes a new map f' identical to f except at position p where it has value v. These two functions satisfy the so-called *theory of arrays*:

$$acc(upd(f, p, v), p) = p$$
$$p \neq p' \rightarrow acc(upd(f, p, v), p') = acc(f, p')$$

In Java, arrays of integers are also interpreted using a mutable variable $intA$, and an access function $array\_acc$ such that $t[i]$ is represented by $array\_acc(intA, t, i)$. Arrays of booleans and objects are interpreted similarly using variables $boolA$ and $objA$ [12]. In C, pointer arithmetic is also modelled by such logical functions [10].

2.3 Basics of the Specification Language

A *contract* of a method has the general form

```
normal_behavior
    requires P
    assigns locs
    ensures Q
```

P and Q are logical assertions, P is a *pre-condition* and Q is a *post-condition*, locs is a set of memory locations, that may be modified by the method. In post-conditions, special construct \old(e) denotes the value of expression e in the pre-state of the method, and \result denotes the return value.

It is also possible to introduce *class invariants*: properties that must be established by constructors, and preserved by each method of the class.

If a method is likely to stop abruptly with an exception, it is also possible to specify this behavior by the variant:

```
behavior
    requires P
    assigns locs
    ensures Q
    signals (E) Q'
```

where E is the name of the exception.

The assertions are written in first-order logic with a JAVA-like syntax. This means that conjunction and disjunction are denoted as && and | |, and equality as ==. Other constructs are added, e.g. ==> for implication and $(\backslash$ forall $type\ x; P)$ for universal quantification.

Side-effect free JAVA expressions are also allowed in annotations, like array access t[i] and field access o.f.

2.4 Algebraic Specifications

New abstract logical sorts s can be introduced by

logic type s

Logical function and predicate symbols are introduced by their profile, using a JAVA-like syntax putting the type before the parameter name:

logic <result type> $f(type_1\ x_1, \ldots, type_n\ x_n)$
predicate $P(type_1\ x_1, \ldots, type_n\ x_n)$

A logical theory is presented by axioms of the form

axiom name : P

where P is any closed formula.

2.5 Model Fields

An advanced feature we are going to use is the notion of *model field*. In JML, these are almost like other JAVA fields, except that they are visible only in specifications. Their types must be a *model class* which are specific JAVA classes whose instances must be *persistent*, that is cannot be modified in-place. In JML they are used mainly for the runtime assertion checker: using JAVA objects for models is clearly suitable in that case, since specifications are then executables. Making them side-effect free is of course mandatory to avoid interference between specification are execution of JAVA code. However, although these model fields provide a natural means of abstraction and modular reasoning [13], their exact semantics is not well fixed [14]. The relations with refinement like in B is not well understood either [15].

Using JAVA objects as models raises more issues in the context of static verification: JAVA code of model classes and methods must be interpreted in some way into logical specifications, which raises issues related in particular to undefinedness of values, detection of absence of side-effects, etc. [16]. To avoid these issues, in KRAKATOA we decided that model fields should not be JAVA objects but algebraic data types defined in the specification language. This is an unique feature of our platform, which forms a bridge between the JAVA side and the algebraic specification side.

In practice a model field is declared like any other field, with the modifier model. Unlike other fields, model fields may also occur in JAVA interfaces.

3   The Case Study: Priority Queues

We present now our case study step by step, following what should be a standard software engineering process starting from the abstract interface and progressively obtain an implementation. Our method is similar to the refinement process in B.

Our aim in this case study is to develop a library providing *priority queues*. These are collections of data where to each datum is associated an integer called its *priority*. There are two main operations we want to perform on such a queue: adding a new datum to the collection, and extracting from the queue the datum with the highest priority. To keep things simpler, since the data contents are meaningless, we consider here that the data are reduced to their priority, so that priority queues are indeed collections of integers.

3.1   Step 1: Abstract Queue Interface

The main first step is to describe an interface for the priority queue library. We proceed in four sub-steps: first, a JAVA interface is introduced, giving just the profiles of methods we need. Then, to provide a formal specification for these methods, we introduce a signature (sorts, function and predicate symbols) for a logical datatype of *bags* to be used as a model in our third sub-step where we add annotations to the JAVA source of our interface. Finally, we provide an axiomatization of our logical datatype of bags, and discuss several issues.

Abstract Queues as a JAVA Interface. Since we aim at producing JAVA code at the end, it is natural to use the native interface mechanism of JAVA, so that we can first describe our interface as in Figure 2.

The method profiles given exactly reflect the two main operations one needs for a queue: insertion and extraction of the maximum. Additionally, it is of course useful to have some way to create an empty queue. It would be natural to introduce a constructor,

---

```
interface AbstractQueue {

    // returns a new empty queue
    static AbstractQueue create();

    // insert n into queue this
    void insert(int n);

    // extracts the maximal element of queue this
    // throws an exception if queue is empty
    int pop() throws EmptyQueueException;
}
```

Fig. 2. Queue interface

but JAVA do not allow constructors in interfaces so for that technical reason we introduce the static method `create` instead.

We also provide the information that the `pop` method may not proceed properly if the queue is empty, by adding a `throws` clause.

Profiles and `throws` is the only specification information we can put at the level of JAVA, so now we go further by adding annotations.

Algebraic Specification of Bags. We want to formally specify this interface using the specification language of KRAKATOA, in particular its model feature introduced in Section 2.5. Since the informal specification above is talking about a collection of data, we first introduce such a datatype in the logic side. Notice that in our collections we allow several occurences of the same integer: in practice in a priority queue, it is possible to have several data with the same priority level. So the natural logical datatype to consider is the type of *multisets* or *bags*. It is a quite standard algebraic datatype, the signature we consider is given in Figure 3 (in KRAKATOA syntax).

```
// bag is a sort name for multisets of integers
//@ logic type bag;

// empty bag
//@ logic bag empty_bag();

// singleton {n}
//@ logic bag singleton(int n);

// union of b1 and b2
//@ logic bag union(bag b1, bag b2);

// shortcut: adding an element to a bag
//@ logic bag add_bag(bag b, int n) { union(b, singleton(n)) }

// nb of occurences of element n in bag b
//@ logic int occ(int n, bag b);

// m is a maximal element of b
/*@ predicate is_max_bag(bag b, int m) {
  @    occ(m,b) >= 1 &&
  @    (\forall int x ; occ(x,b) >= 1 ==> x <= m) }
  @*/

// the maximum of bag b (any value if b empty)
//@ logic int bag_max(bag b);
```

Fig. 3. Signature for bag logical datatype

This is only a signature for the considered algebraic datatype, and we need to provide an axiomatization of it. We will do it below, but it is not necessary to do it before giving the formal specification of our abstract interface. Notice that in our specification language we consider only total functions, so bag_max is defined even for the empty_bag: we will have to be careful about this situation (similarly to the handling of division by zero).

Formal Specification of Queue Interface. We can now specify our priority queue interface. First, we add a model field to it, of sort bag.

```
//@ model bag elements;
```

Such a field will of course remain abstract, that is it will not be implemented. It is however some *mutable* abstract data, that is eventually modified by methods of that interface. As such, it serves as an abstract state of the future implemented class. It is also very similar to a state variable in some abstract B machine.

The specification of the creation method is then as follows.

```
/*@ normal_behavior
  @    assigns \nothing;
  @    ensures \fresh(\result) &&
  @               \result.elements == empty_bag();
  @*/
static AbstractQueue create();
```

The post-condition (ensures clause) tells first that the result queue is freshly allocated, and second it tells it has no elements yet, by saying that its abstract state is an empty bag. The assigns clause additionally specifies that no change are made on already allocated objects.

The insertion is then specified as follows, again in term of the model field.

```
/*@ normal_behavior
  @    assigns elements;
  @    ensures elements == add_bag(\old(elements),n);
  @*/
void insert(int n);
```

First, the assigns clause says that the abstract state is changed (and nothing else), and second the ensures clause gives a relation between its old and its new value: the given element has been added.

Finally the extraction is specified as follows.

```
/*@ behavior
  @    assigns elements;
  @    ensures \result == bag_max(\old(elements)) &&
  @        \old(elements) == add_bag(elements,\result);
  @    signals (EmptyQueueException)
  @        \old(elements) == elements &&
```

```
@          elements == empty_bag();
@*/
int pop();
```

The ensures clause provides a post-condition when terminating normally: the maximal element is returned, and this element is removed from the abstract model. The signals clause provides a post-condition when terminating abruptly by the exception: the model is not changed, and even more precisely, it was empty.

This complete our first step of building a formally specified interface for queues. The informal specification has been turned into a formal one in a quite straghtforward way, thanks to the introduction of the multiset model field.

Axiomatization of Bags. At this step of giving an abstract specification of priority queues, we do not need any concrete representation of bags, so we just propose a set of first-order axioms to present some properties we expect from bags operations above. The corresponding axiomatization, which forms an algebraic specification of bags, is given Figure 4.

Remark that since we just pose axioms, the axiomatization is not guaranteed to be consistent. To establish the consistency, one possibility offered by the platform is to generate a template for interactive theorem provers, e.g. COQ. In that case, one can fill the template manually by providing concrete definitions and then prove that axioms are indeed valid formulas. In other words, this is a way to *realize* the axiomatization, that is providing a model, and this implies consistency.

However, in that particular case this is far from trivial to make such a realization. A quite elegant way to realize bags in COQ could be as functions from $\mathbb{Z}$ to $\mathbb{N}$. However, in that case the axiom of extensionality of bag equality would not be provable, and should be admitted, as known to be consistent (http://pauillac.inria.fr/coq/V8.1/faq.html#htoc37). Moreover, the bag_max function would be realizable only on finite sets so more work would be required.

Another possible solution would be to introduce a concrete inductive datatype whose constructors would the empty bag, the singleton and the union. But in that case equality of bags should not be interpreted as COQ equality (because it would be inconsistent), but as a new predicate for bags, whose definition would exactly be the extensionality axiom. To make this usuable in COQ, it should indeed produce a new *setoid*, to allow declaration of morphism and reasoning by equality replacement. In the current state of the platform, this possibility is not implemented but it could possible in the future.

Another possibility not available in the platform but could also be in the future, is to provide a template in some algebraic specification environment. In particular, in the Maude system it is possible to introduce a function symbols with respect some built-in theory such associativity, commutativity, identity. This would be very handy for union of multisets. Other functions and predicates could be defined by rewrite rules. However, again the extensionality axioms would not hold, so again the equality of bags should declared as a new predicate.

Another solution could be to find a concrete representation of bags as an inductive datatype with free constructors. This may possible, e.g. using Patricia trees [17], but quite tricky.

```
// union is associative, commutative, with identity empty_bag
/*@ axiom union_assoc: (\forall bag b1,b2,b3;
  @      union(union(b1,b2),b3) == union(b1,union(b2,b3)));
  @*/
/*@ axiom union_comm: (\forall bag b1,b2;
  @      union(b1,b2) == union(b2,b1));
  @*/
/*@ axiom union_empty_id_left: (\forall bag b;
  @      union(empty_bag(),b) == b);
  @*/
/*@ axiom union_empty_id_right: (\forall bag b;
  @      union(b,empty_bag()) == b);
  @*/

// occ non−negative
/*@ axiom occ_non_negative:
  @      (\forall int n; (\forall bag b; occ(n,b) >=0 ));
  @*/

// occ characterization over empty_bag, singleton and union
/*@ axiom occ_empty:
  @      (\forall int n; occ(n,empty_bag()) == 0);
  @*/
/*@ axiom occ_singleton_eq:
  @      (\forall int n; occ(n,singleton(n)) == 1);
  @*/
/*@ axiom occ_singleton_neq:
  @      (\forall int n,m ; n != m ==> occ(n,singleton(m)) == 0);
  @*/
/*@ axiom occ_union:
  @      (\forall int n; (\forall bag b1,b2;
  @      occ(n,union(b1,b2)) == occ(n,b1)+occ(n,b2))) ;
  @*/

// extensionality of bag equality
/*@ axiom bag_ext: (\forall bag b1,b2;
  @      (\forall int n; occ(n,b1) == occ(n,b2)) ==> b1 == b2);
  @*/

// bag_max characterization
/*@ axiom bag_max_def: (\forall bag b; b != empty_bag() ==>
  @      is_max_bag(b,bag_max(b)));
  @*/
/*@ axiom bag_max_elim: (\forall bag b; (\forall int n;
  @      is_max_bag(b,n) ==> n == bag_max(b)));
  @*/
```

Fig. 4. Algebraic specification of bags

To conclude this discussion, using algebraic specifications is a natural and useful technique to provide abstract models and formal specification of programs, but even for a simple and standard type like bags, there is still a poor support.

Notice finally that there is a quick test for inconsistency: try to derive false, using any automated theorem prover. This is of course incomplete. For the rest of this paper, we just ignore these issues, and just assume the axiomatization given above is consistent.

3.2   Step 2: Refinement into Logical Heaps

In this second step, we now take some decisions about the implementation we have in mind. A classical representation of a priority queue is a *heap*, that is a binary tree having the *heap* property: the value at any node is greater or equal to any values appearing in the subtree below. In particular, the root necessarily contains the maximal element in the tree.

We have here three substeps: first we consider an algebraic specification of binary trees and heaps. Second, we discuss the notion of refinement in general, and the necessary proof obligations involved. Third, we refine our interface for queue and proceed with the verification of the refinement obligations.

Algebraic Specifications of Binary Trees and Heaps. The declarations for the new logic type btree for binary trees are given in Figure 5. As for bags, we introduce only the functions symbols we need to specify the refined interface. We need also to relate the heap representation with the bag representation: the collection of elements is the multiset of integers which occurs in the tree. We express this by the additional logical function tree_contents. We now have the necessary logical constructions to propose a refinement of our JAVA interface.

```
// btree is a sort name for binary trees, with integer values on nodes
//@ logic type btree;

// the empty tree
//@ logic btree empty_tree();

// the value at the root, unspecified if t empty
//@ logic int tree_root(btree t);

// predicate specifying t has the heap property
//@ predicate is_heap(btree t);

// returns the contents of t, as a multiset
//@ logic bag tree_contents(btree t);
```

Fig. 5. First-order signature for binary trees

```
interface AbstractHeap extends AbstractQueue {

    //@ model btree tree;
    /*@ invariant is_heap(tree) &&
      @       tree_contents(tree) == elements;
      @*/
}
```

It starts by providing a new model field of type binary tree, and an invariant which specifies both that the tree model is a heap, and the relation with the more abstract bag model: the bag model is always the contents of the tree.

Notice that we do not specify anything about the shape of the binary tree. For efficiency reason, it should be balanced, but this is not required for correction. In particular, this means that the heap model field is not unique: the specification is not deterministic.

The refined specification for the create method is the following, specifying that the tree model of the result is the empty tree.

```
/*@ normal_behavior
  @    assigns \nothing;
  @    ensures \fresh(\result) &&
  @               \result.tree == empty_tree();
  @*/
AbstractQueue create();
```

The refined specification for the insert method is the following.

```
/*@ normal_behavior
  @    assigns tree;
  @    ensures is_heap(tree) &&
  @       tree_contents(tree) ==
  @           add_bag(tree_contents(\old(tree)),n);
  @*/
void insert(int n);
```

It specifies only that the tree model is modified, its new value is still a heap, and that the contents of the tree satisfies the same property as the bag model itself. This may sounds strange that we repeat two properties: we say that the result is a heap, whereas we already said it was an invariant, and we say that the contents of the tree satisfies the same property as the bag model, whereas we said in the invariant that the bag model is the contents of the tree model. The crucial point here is the semantics of the refinement: what we specify is a refined interface, and we will have to *prove* that the invariant is preserved, we do not assumed it. This is detailed in next section below.

Finally, the refined specification of method pop is as follows.

```
/*@ behavior
  @    assigns tree;
  @    ensures \result == tree_root(\old(tree)) &&
  @       is_heap(tree) &&
  @       \old(tree) != empty_tree() &&
  @       tree_contents(\old(tree)) ==
  @             add_bag(tree_contents(tree),\result);
  @    signals (EmptyQueueException)
  @        \old(tree) == tree && tree == empty_tree();
  @*/
int pop() throws EmptyQueueException;
```

Again, we repeat that the result tree model is a heap, and that the contents satisfies the same property as the bag model. But we indeed add a bit of information: the returned value is the root of the tree model. This will require a non-trivial proof of refinement.

Verification Conditions for Refinement in General. At this step, we want to check that any implementation of interface `AbstractHeap` will be also a correct implementation of `AbstractQueue`.

Generally speaking, let us assume we specify an abstract interface with

- a model field a
- a method m with an argument x and
- a precondition $Pre_{abs}(x, a)$;
- a postcondition $Post_{abs}(x, a, a', r)$, where a' denotes the new value of a, and r the returned value.

Let us assume we refine this interface with

- a model field b;
- an invariant $I(a, b)$ relating abstract and refined model fields;
- a refined precondition for m $Pre_{ref}(x, b)$
- a refined postcondition $Post_{ref}(x, b, b', r)$

The situation is illustrated by the follwing diagram of

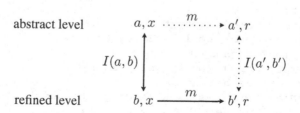

Validity of the refinement means that whenever a refined step occurs (lower plain arrow) from a state which has abstract model a (left plain double arrow), there exists an abstract transition (upper dotted arrow) for which representation invariant is preserved (right dotted double arrow). This corresponds to the formula

$$\forall a, b, x, I(a, b) \wedge Pre_{abs}(x, a) \rightarrow$$
$$Pre_{ref}(x, b) \wedge$$
$$\forall b', r, Post_{ref}(x, b, b', r) \rightarrow$$
$$\exists a', I(a', b') \wedge Post_{abs}(x, a, a', r)$$

COQ Specifications of Trees, and Proof of Refinement. To prove the verification conditions for refinement, we need to provide a theory for the signature of binary trees given above. Because of the recursive nature of binary trees, it is not handy to give just a first-order axiomatization as we did for bags. In the WHY/KRAKATOA/CADUCEUS platform, a way to achieve this is to provide an incomplete axiomatization, and delay some parts to a back-end prover that supports inductive definitions. For this case study, we decide to use COQ. The logical definitions of binary trees and the heap property are then given in COQ syntax in Figure 6. Notice that on the COQ side, the JAVA type int for 32-bit integers is simply modelled by mathematical integers in $\mathbb{Z}$: the

```
(* inductive definition of binary trees of integers *)
Inductive btree : Set :=
| Empty_tree : btree
| Node : ∀ (left:btree) (root:Z) (right: btree), btree.

(* extract the value at root.
   If tree empty, just return a arbitrary value *)
Definition tree_root (b:btree) : Z :=
 match b with
  | Empty_tree ⇒ 0
  | Node _ r _ ⇒ r
 end.

(* recursive definition of the heap property *)
Fixpoint is_heap(t : btree) : Prop :=
  match t with
   | Empty_tree ⇒ True
   | Node Empty_tree _ Empty_tree ⇒ True
   | Node (Node _ n1 _ as l) n Empty_tree ⇒
       n ≥ n1 ∧ is_heap l
   | Node Empty_tree n (Node _ n2 _ as r) ⇒
       n ≥ n2 ∧ is_heap r
   | Node (Node _ n1 _ as l) n (Node _ n2 _ as r) ⇒
       n ≥ n1 ∧ is_heap l ∧ n ≥ n2 ∧ is_heap r
  end.
```

Fig. 6. COQ realization of binary trees signature

```
(* recursive definition of the multiset of elements in a tree *)
Fixpoint tree_contents(t : btree) : bag :=
  match t with
  | Empty_tree ⇒ empty_bag
  | Node l n r ⇒
      add_bag (union (tree_contents l) (tree_contents r)) n
  end.
```

Fig. 7. COQ realization of `tree_contents`

---

absence of overflow is controlled at the WHY level by generating appropriate proof obligations.

We also we to give a definition of `tree_contents`. For that purpose we rely on an existing definition of bags which is indeed the COQ definition automatically generated by WHY from the axiomatization of bags given in Figure 4. This is given on figure 7.

Generally speaking, this technique of delaying definitions to the back-end prover means that the semantics of the specifications is not anymore the set of all first-order models of the given algebraic specifications (the so-called *loose* semantics), but only the subset of those which satisfy the additional inductive definitions, in particular only the models *generated by constructors* of inductive data types are considered (the *initial* semantics).

We can now proceed with verifying the proof obligations for refinement. As we noticed, the refined specifications for `create` and `insert` are just made but repeating the properties with expect, from the invariant and the specifications of abstract queue methods we need to satisfy, and consequently proving refinement conditions for `create` and `insert` is straightforward. For `pop` it is not: we have to prove that the root value of the tree is indeed the maximal element of the multiset of its value. This can be proved in COQ using a few auxiliary lemmas given in Figure 8.

To obtain a decent level of automation, we indeed use a new feature available in COQ version 8.1, which is the ability to call automatic provers within the process of proving a goal in COQ, under the form of a tactic that tries to proof the current sub-goal using the first-order hypothesis of the context. For the lemmas of Figure 8, we indeed used the tactics `simplify` or `ergo` that call the external automated provers Simplify and ERGO respectively. This greatly helps the proofs in particular on subgoals related to bags, that needs to be proved by applying the axioms of the first-order axiomatization of bags. But caution is required: when calling these tactics, the answer of the back-end prover is trusted by COQ. To recover the standard skeptical approach of COQ, the prover should not only answer yes, but also provide a proof trace that could be double-checked. This is one of the ongoing work around the ERGO prover.

A general remaining issue is how to combine automatic provers and interactive ones. One point we consider for the future is to allow inductive definitions directly at the source level, with incomplete first-order encodings (that is only the "theory of constructors") when automated provers are in use.

General speaking, we should provide librairies of general purpose logical data structures, such as binary trees or bags.

```
Lemma is_heap_left: ∀ (t1 t2:btree) (r:ℤ),
  is_heap (Node t1 r t2) → is_heap t1.

Lemma is_heap_right: ∀ (t1 t2:btree) (r:ℤ),
  is_heap (Node t1 r t2) → is_heap t2.

Fixpoint forall_tree (P:ℤ→Prop) (b:btree)
                      { struct b } : Prop :=
  match b with
  | Empty_tree ⇒ True
  | Node t1 r t2 ⇒
      P r ∧ forall_tree P t1 ∧ forall_tree P t2
  end.

Definition ge_tree (x:ℤ) (b:btree) :=
  forall_tree (fun y ⇒ x ≥ y) b.

Lemma ge_tree_heap: ∀ (t t1 t2:btree) (r x:ℤ),
  t = Node t1 r t2 → is_heap t → x ≥ r → ge_tree x t.

Lemma forall_tree_contents :
  ∀ (P:ℤ → Prop) (t:btree) (x:ℤ),
    forall_tree P t → occ x (tree_contents t) ≥ 1 → P x.

Lemma pop_refinement_po:
  ∀ a:bag, ∀ b:btree,
    is_heap b ∧ a = tree_contents b →
    ∀ b':btree, ∀ r:ℤ,
      r = tree_root b ∧ is_heap b' ∧ b ≠ empty_tree ∧
      tree_contents b = add_bag (tree_contents b') r →
      ∃ a':bag,
        is_heap b' ∧ a' = tree_contents b' ∧ r = bag_max a ∧
        a = add_bag a' r.
```

Fig. 8. COQ proof of refinement obligations for pop

3.3   Step 3: Providing a JAVA implementation

The third step of our case study is now to provide a JAVA implementation of the refined interface for queues. Following classical data structure and algorithms for queues [18], we propose an efficient implementation based on storing a binary tree into an array, where the root is stored at index 0 and the two children of the node at index i are stored at index $2i+1$ and $2i+2$. This is indeed a compact representation of *complete* trees: every level is full except the last level which is filled from the left.

The key step is then to formally specify this representation, relating the JAVA encoding and the logical type of heaps. The class implementation, without methods

```
/* returns the binary tree stored in t
 * between indexes root and [bound—1] included
 */
/*@ logic btree tree_of_array(int t[],int root, int bound)
  @    reads t[*];
  @*/


class Queue implements AbstractHeap {

    int size;
    int t[];

    /*@ private invariant
      @    t != null && 0 <= size && size <= t.length ;
      @*/

    //@ invariant tree == tree_of_array(t,0,size);
}
```

Fig. 9. class implementing queues and its invariants (without the methods)

---

yet, is given on Figure 9. The `tree_of_array` function is a *hybrid* logical function, which mixes both JAVA data types and logical types. It is declared as any other logical function, its intended meaning is to return the binary tree stored in the array *t* between the indexes *root* (included) and *bound* (excluded). As for other binary tree functions, we decide to delay its definition to the back-end prover side.

The essential issue here is how such a hybrid predicate can relate the JAVA side and the logical side. This is here that we use that fact that in our platform, JAVA execution itself is modelled into the logical language which serve as user models, as described in Section 2.2. Such an hybrid predicate, translated into the intermediate logical setting of WHY, takes extra arguments corresponding to variables representing the JAVA memory. Indeed, this is the purpose of the `reads` clause in the declaration of `tree_of_array` above: by putting `t[*]` in this clause, we declare that the later definition of `tree_of_array` will access the JAVA memory part corresponding to `t[0],t[1],...,t[t.length-1]`. On the logical side, this memory will appear as the extra variable named `intA` (see Section 2.2) of type `int memarray` (standing for "a memory region for arrays of integers") and the JAVA array access `t[i]` is represented in the logical side as `array_acc(intA,t,i)`. This "glue" between the JAVA side and the logical side is of course the tricky part of the development process, that the user has to learn, but we argue that this JAVA memory model is quite concise so that it should not be a blocking step.

We continue to use COQ as the back-end prover, and `tree_of_array` can be defined as a general recursive function [19] as shown in Figure 10 (for readability, we simplified the real COQ syntax).

```
Function tree_of_array (intA:memarray ℤ) (t:value)
   (root:ℤ) (bound:ℤ) :=
 if (0 ≤ root < bound) then
     Node (tree_of_array intA t (2*root+1) bound)
         (array_acc intA t root)
         (tree_of_array intA t (2*root+2) bound)
 else Empty_tree.
```

Fig. 10. COQ definition of `tree_of_array` hybrid function

We now give implementations of the methods needed for the class `Queue` to be an implementation of `AbstractQueue`. For implementing `create`, we additionally provide a JAVA constructor, which has to build a new `Queue` satisfying the invariants. Code is given in Figure 11. KRAKATOA/WHY generates 9 verification conditions for the constructor and 8 for the `create` function. Most of them comes from the safety of JAVA executions: no null pointer dereferencing, no array access out-of-bounds, validity of sub-typing, validity of assigns clauses. There is of course also the proof that the implementation of `create` satisfies the post-condition given in the `AbstractHeap` interface: but since the original value of `size` is 0, it is straightforward to show that the tree model is initially empty. Indeed, all the 17 proof obligations are automatically discharged by SIMPLIFY and ERGO.

For the `insert` method, we follow the classical algorithm, which tries to add the new element in the first free cell. Since this insertion may destroy the heap property, we need to move this new element up, until we reach a greater parent. This is illustrated in Figure 12.

Prior to this, we need to be sure that there is enough space in the array, otherwise enlarge it. For that purpose an auxiliary static method `copy` is called to copy a portion of an array to another one. This results in the code given in Figure 13. Notice that we

```
/*@ normal_behavior
  @    assigns \nothing;
  @    ensures size == 0 && t != null;
  @*/
Queue() {
      size = 0;
      t = new int[7];
}

static Queue create() {
     return new Queue();
}
```

Fig. 11. JAVA code of `create` method

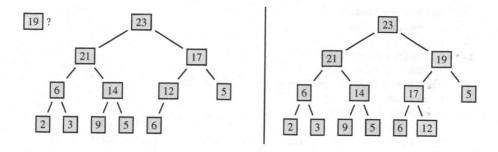

Fig. 12. Insert new element 19 in a heap

use for the first `if` statement a local annotation, to give a specification to this particular statement. It states that after the statement the array `t` may have been modified, it still contains the elements of the heap, and is necessarily large enough to store a new element. This local annotation acts like a lemma for the weakest precondition calculus, avoiding to go into branches of the `if`, which would duplicate assertions.

For this method, 83 verification conditions are generated. 74 of them, related to JAVA execution safety are automatically discharged by automatic provers. The remaining obligations are the ones related to the functional behavior, e.g. showing that the result tree model is still a heap. For those, it is mandatory to use COQ again, since their validity must be proved using induction on trees. This part requires quite a significant work, involving the proof of several auxiliary lemmas related on the `tree_of_array` hybrid function. For example, to prove that after the enlargement of the array, the new array still contains the tree of the old array, it must be proved that for any two memory states $intA_1$ and $intA_2$ for int arrays, and for any t_1, t_2, i, j, the trees (`tree_of_array` $intA_1$ t_1 i j) and (`tree_of_array` $intA_2$ t_2 i j) are equal whenever (`array_acc` $intA_1$ t_1 k) = (`array_acc` $intA_2$ t_2 k) for each k such that $i \leq k < j$. This is clearly a part of the development which requires a significant expertise both in COQ and in the JAVA memory model.

Finally, for the method `pop()`, we just need to return the root of the tree, and the last element of the array must be reinserted in the tree. The corresponding modification of the tree is illustrated in Figure 14, and the code of that method is given in Figure 15.

For `pop`, 142 verification conditions are generated by KRAKATOA/WHY, and 106 of them are discharged automatically.

Discussion and Open Issues. The verification conditions generated for JAVA implementations of methods above, regarding the functional behaviors, are similar to refinement obligations of Section 3.2. The difference is that the refined level is now not a transition of some abstract machine but a true JAVA method body. But in such a setting, involving in particular mutable data structures, there is no theoretical study showing that the proof obligations proposed are sound, i.e. that they guarantee that the

```
/*@ normal_behavior
  @   assigns size,t,t[*];
  @*/
public void insert(int n) {
    // enlarge array t if needed
    // the following is a local specification on the if statement
    /*@ assigns t;
        ensures
            (\forall int j; 0 <= j && j < size; t[j]==\old(t[j]))
            && t != null && size < t.length && t instanceof int[];
    */
    if (size == t.length) {
        int oldt[] = t;
        t = new int[2*size+1];
        copy(oldt,t,0,size-1,0);
    }
    int i = size;
    /*@ loop_invariant
      @   0 <= i && i <= size &&
      @   (i == size ==>
      @       is_heap(tree_of_array(t,0,size)) &&
      @       tree_contents(tree_of_array(t,0,size)) = elements) &&
      @   (i < size ==>
      @       is_heap(tree_of_array(t,0,size+1)) &&
      @       tree_contents(tree_of_array(t,0,size+1)) =
      @           add_bag(elements,t[i]));
      @ decreases i;
      @*/
    while (i > 0) {
        int parent = (i-1)/2;
        int x = t[parent];
        if (x >= n) break;
        t[i] = x;
        i = parent;
    }
    t[i] = n;
    size++;
}
```

Fig. 13. JAVA code of insert method

---

implementation respects the interface. This opens challenging issues regarding object creation and initialisation, regarding whether class invariants could temporarily violated inside methods bodies [16]. We discuss more about these issues in the next subsection.

3.4   Using Abstract Queues as a Library

One important aspect we aim at by proposing our modular algebraic specification approach is to allow the use of certified libraries.

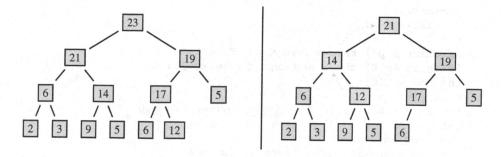

Fig. 14. Removing root 23, and reinserting last element 12 in a heap

Let us consider a toy example of use of our interface for queues as follows.

```
/*@ normal_behavior
  @    requires q != null && q.elements == empty_bag();
  @    ensures \result == 5;
  @*/
public static int test(AbstractQueue q) {
    q.insert(1);
    q.insert(3);
    q.insert(5);
    q.insert(4);
    return q.pop();
}
```

When proving the obligation that the result is 5, we do not see any implementation details of queues, we only see the abstract specification for queues, hence essentially it amounts to prove that 5 is the maximal element of the bag $\{1, 3, 5, 4\}$.

This is a very important and useful aspect of our modular development of the queue library: only the abstract interface is visible to the user. It is useful to hide implementation details, and it still allows us to reason on queues, by just reasoning on the multiset model of them.

The problem is that no meta-theory exist showing that such a modular approach is safe in the setting of JAVA where object states are mutable. In presence of mutable data structures, ensuring that a class invariant is preserved may be extremely tricky, leading to the ongoing research on *ownership* systems[20]. Ensuring that the internal data structure, like the internal array in our example, remains consistent during execution, requires to checks whether no outside object may modify internal data directly, without using provided methods. JAVA visibility scopes are clearly insufficient for that purpose: for example, if a method just returns one of the field, such as array t in our example, then direct modification of this field is possible. This is again related to ownership, but also to property of *separation*: one may want to prove that the heap memory involved in the internal representation of an object is always separated form other parts of heap memory. This is the purpose of all the current work around *separation logic* [21], and

```
/*@ behavior
  @    assigns size,t[*];
  @*/
public int pop() throws EmptyQueueException {
    if (size == 0) throw new EmptyQueueException();
    int max = t[0];
    size--;
    int last = t[size]; // last element, to reinsert in the heap
    int i = 0;
    /*@ loop_invariant
      @  is_heap(tree_of_array(t,0,size)) &&
      @  (i == 0 ==> elements ==
      @    add_bag(tree_contents(tree_of_array(t,0,size)),last))
      @  &&
      @  (i > 0 ==> add_bag(elements,t[i]) ==
      @    add_bag(add_bag(tree_contents(tree_of_array(t,0,size)),
      @                       max),last));
      @ decreases size-i;
      @*/
    while (i < size) {
        int left = 2*i+1; // the left child
        int right = 2*i+2; // the right child
        if (left >= size) /* there is no child */ break;
        int larger = left; // will refer to the larger child
        if (right < size && t[left] < t[right]) larger = right;
        if (last >= t[larger]) break;
        // move larger child in place of its parent
        t[i] = t[larger];
        // continue with the larger child
        i = larger;
    }
    t[i] = last;
    return max;
}
```

Fig. 15. JAVA code of pop method

---

static analysis of regions [22]. We propose a preliminary work [23] on the use of region analysis in the context of deductive verification based on weakest precondition calculus as in our platform, but there is clearly important challenges that remains open.

4   Conclusions and Perspectives

We presented an example of a development of a certified general-purpose library component for an imperative programming language (JAVA), with a high-level modeling of its behavior using algebraic specifications, which can be seen as the public view of this component.

Among the large amount of work on this subject, our originality relies on the interpretation of the source code into the intermediate specification and programming language WHY, in which we both specify the semantics of JAVA or C execution, and the user-specified models. This allows us to model a JAVA program not by model classes like in JML, but by algebraic data types from an algebraic specification. The wide range of back-end provers allows the user to use either a standard first-order axiomatization which is understood by all provers, or more advanced logical features of a specific back-end prover, such as inductive data types and recursive functions. Accordingly, proof obligations can be discharged by standard first-order reasoning but also using induction. We hope these key features will allow to go beyond in the future, especially for the construction of certified librairies, which in turn will allow reutilization.

Development of certified librairies has been considered a main direction of research by the working group on the "grand challenge 6" (http://www.fmnet.info/gc6/, http://vstte.ethz.ch/content.html) on dependable software. Indeed, reutilization is key: this is a main feature to achieve to improve the impact of heavy formal methods in software development.

The future works include first the integration of refinement into the intermediate language WHY, which in particular requires extending the language by adding a notion of encapsulated components. Similarly, we want to support a system of interfaces and model fields in the C front-end of our platform, but C language lacks constructs for components. In the future, we also plan to add a C++ front-end, which will combining issues from JAVA and C.

In we have seen in Section 3.4, the main theoretical challenge is to support invariants and refinement in a setting allowing mutable data structures. This issue is connected to currently active research topics, regarding separation, ownership systems, region-based memory analysis.

Acknowledgments. The current work on refinement techniques for JAVA programs is joint with Jean-Christophe Filliâtre, Christine Paulin, Nicolas Rousset, and Wendi Urribarí.

References

1. Floyd, R.W.: Assigning meanings to programs. In: Schwartz, J.T. (ed.) Mathematical Aspects of Computer Science. In: Proceedings of Symposia in Applied Mathematics, Providence, Rhode Island, American Mathematical Society, vol. 19, pp. 19–32 (1967)
2. Hoare, C.A.R.: An axiomatic basis for computer programming. Communications of the ACM 12(10), 576–580, 583 (1969)
3. Dijkstra, E.W.: A discipline of programming. In: Series in Automatic Computation, Prentice Hall Int, Englewood Cliffs (1976)
4. Downey, P.J., Sethi, R., Tarjan, R.E.: Variations on the common subexpressions problem. Journal of the ACM 27(4) 771–785 (1980)
5. Nelson, G., Oppen, D.C.: Fast decision procedures based on congruence closure. Journal of the ACM 27, 356–364 (1980)
6. Ranise, S., Tinelli, C.:The smt-lib format: An initial proposal. In: Proceedings of PDPAR'03 (2003)

7. Filliâtre, J.C., Marché, C.: The Why/Krakatoa/Caduceus platform for deductive program verification. In: Damm, W., Hermanns, H. (eds.) CAV 2007, LNCS, vol. 4590. Springer, Heidelberg (2007)

8. Burdy, L., Cheon, Y., Cok, D., Ernst, M., Kiniry, J., Leavens, G.T., Leino, K.R.M., Poll, E.: An overview of JML tools and applications. International Journal on Software Tools for Technology Transfer (2004)

9. Marché, C., Paulin-Mohring, C.: Reasoning about Java programs with aliasing and frame conditions. In: Hurd, J., Melham, T. (eds.) TPHOLs 2005. LNCS, vol. 3603, Springer, Heidelberg (2005)

10. Filliâtre, J.C., Marché, C.: Multi-prover verification of C programs. In: Davies, J., Schulte, W., Barnett, M. (eds.) ICFEM 2004. LNCS, vol. 3308, pp. 15–29. Springer, Heidelberg (2004)

11. Bornat, R.: Proving pointer programs in Hoare logic. In: Mathematics of Program Construction, pp. 102–126 (2000)

12. Marché, C., Paulin-Mohring, C., Urbain, X.: The Krakatoa tool for certification of Java/JavaCard programs annotated in JML. Journal of Logic and Algebraic Programming 58, 89–106 (2004), http://krakatoa.lri.fr

13. Cheon, Y., Leavens, G., Sitaraman, M., Edwards, S.: Model variables: cleanly supporting abstraction in design by contract. Softw. Pract. Exper. 35(6), 583–599 (2005)

14. Breunesse, C.B., Poll, E.: Verifying jml specifications with model fields. In: Formal Techniques for Java-like Programs (FTFJP'03) (2003)

15. Boulmé, S., Potet, M.L.: Interpreting invariant composition in the B method using the Spec# ownership relation: a way to explain and relax Brestrictions. In: Julliand, J., Kouchnarenko, O. (eds.) B 2007. LNCS, vol. 4355, Springer, Heidelberg (2006)

16. Leavens, G.T., Leino, K.R.M., Müller, P.: Specification and verification challenges for sequential object-oriented programs. Formal Aspects of Computing (to appear 2007)

17. Okasaki, C., Gill, A.: Fast mergeable integer maps. In: Workshop on ML, pp. 77–86 (1998)

18. Sedgewick, R.: Algorithms in Java, Parts 1-4, 3rd edn. Addison-Wesley, London, UK (2003)

19. Barthe, G., Courtieu, P.: Efficient Reasoning about Executable Specifications in Coq. In: Carreño, V.A., Muñoz, C.A., Tahar, S. (eds.) TPHOLs 2002. LNCS, vol. 2410, pp. 31–46. Springer, Heidelberg (2002)

20. Barnett, M., DeLine, R., Fähndrich, M., Leino, K.R.M., Schulte, W.: Verification of object-oriented programs with invariants. Journal of Object Technology 3(6), 27–56 (2004)

21. Reynolds, J.C.: Separation logic: a logic for shared mutable data structures. In: 17h Annual IEEE Symposium on Logic in Computer Science. IEEE Computer Society Press, Los Alamitos (2002)

22. Tofte, M., Talpin, J.P.: Region-based memory management. In: Information and Computation, 132th edn. pp. 109–176. Academic Press, San Diego (1997)

23. Hubert, T., Marché, C.: Separation analysis for deductive verification. In: Heap Analysis and Verification (HAV'07), Braga, Portugal (2007)
http://www.lri.fr/~marche/hubert07hav.pdf

Modeling Permutations in Coq for Coccinelle

Evelyne Contejean

Laboratoire de Recherche en Informatique, CNRS, Univ Paris-Sud, Orsay F-91405
INRIA Futurs, ProVal, Parc Orsay Université, F-91893
contejea@lri.fr

Abstract. In this paper we present the part of the Coccinelle library which deals with list permutations. Indeed permutations naturally arise when formally modeling rewriting in Coq, for instance RPO with multiset status and equality modulo AC. Moreover the needed permutations are up to an equivalence relation, and may be used to inductively define the same relation (equivalence modulo RPO). This is why we introduce the notion of permutation w. r. t. an arbitrary relation. The advantages of our approach are a very simple inductive definition (with only 2 constructors), the adequacy with the mathematical definition, the ability to define a relation using recursively permutations up to this very relation, and a fine grained modularity (if R enjoys a property, so does `permut R`).

1 Introduction

In the domain of term rewriting [7], permutations naturally arise with equality modulo AC and RPO with multiset status.

It is considered as well-known folklore [8,3] that when a function symbol + is associative and commutative:

$$(x + y) + z = x + (y + z) \qquad (A)$$
$$x + y \;\; = \;\; y + x \qquad (C)$$

two terms flatten w. r. t. + are equal modulo if and only their direct subterms are AC-equal up to a permutation:

$$a_1 + a_2 + \ldots a_n =_{AC} b_1 + \ldots b_m$$

iff $n = m$ and there exists a permutation π over $\{1, \ldots, n\}$ such that $\forall i$, $a_i =_{AC} b_{\pi(i)}$.

Concerning RPO [6], permutations are only needed when some symbols have a multiset status. Usually RPO is primarily defined by inference rules for $\leq_{RPO}$, and $\equiv_{RPO}$ and $<_{RPO}$ are then derived ($\equiv_{RPO} = \leq_{RPO} \cap \geq_{RPO}$ and $<_{RPO} = \leq_{RPO} \setminus \geq_{RPO}$.

In our formal modeling, we have chosen to define first $\equiv_{RPO}$ by a Coq Inductive, and then $<_{RPO}$ by another Inductive using $\equiv_{RPO}$.

This second definition in particular contains the following case:
$f(s_1, s_2, \ldots, s_p) <_{RPO} f(t_1, t_2, \ldots, t_q)$ if f has a multiset status and there exists $n \leq p, q$, a permutation π over $\{i_1, \ldots, i_n\}$ such that:

H. Comon-Lundh et al. (Eds.): Jouannaud Festschrift, LNCS 4600, pp. 259–269, 2007.

1. $s_{i_j} \equiv_{RPO} t_{\pi(i_j)}$,
2. $\{t_1, \ldots, t_q\} \setminus \{t_{\pi(i_1)}, \ldots, t_{\pi(i_n)}\} \neq \emptyset$,
3. $\forall i, i \notin \{i_1, \ldots, i_n\} \implies \exists t_j \in \{t_1, \ldots, t_q\} \setminus \{t_{\pi(i_1)}, \ldots, t_{\pi(i_n)}\}, s_i <_{RPO} t_j$.

With this definition, the RPO is able to compare more terms than an ordering where the equivalence is defined to be the syntactic equality, as done in the works of Adam Koprowski [11] or of Coupet-Grimal and Delobel [5].

For example, assuming that a, b, c and d are constants, f and g are binary function symbols, f with lexicographic status and g with multiset status, and the precedence is $c < d$, our version yields $f(g(a,b),c) <_{RPO} f(g(b,a),d)$, whereas the weakest version cannot compare these terms since $g(a,b)$ and $g(b,a)$ are equivalent, but not syntactically equal.

1.1 The COCCINELLE Library

COCCINELLE [4] is a public COQ [12] library which is intended to be a modeling of rewriting as well as a (partial) mirror of the CIME tool. To start with, COC-CINELLE contains a modeling of the mathematical notions needed for rewriting, such as term algebras, generic rewriting, generic and AC equational theories and RPO with status. It contains also properties of these structures, for example that RPO is well-founded whenever the underlying precedence is so. This is enough for "interpreting traces", for instance traces of equality modulo or termination traces.

Due to the mirror purpose, some of the types of COCCINELLE (terms, etc.) are translated from CIME (in OCAML) to COQ, as well as some functions (AC matching). Translating functions and proving their full correctness obviously provides a certification of the underlying algorithm. Moreover, some proofs may require that *all* objects satisfying a certain property have been built: for instance in order to prove local confluence of a TRS, one need to get all critical pairs, hence a unification algorithm which is complete[1]. This kind of completeness proof has no counterpart in CIME.

If we want to model equality modulo AC and RPO in COCCINELLE, we first need permutations. Due to the term definition in COCCINELLE, these are not mathematical permutations of $\mathscr{S}_n$, that is one-to-one functions over the finite set $\{1, \ldots, n\}$, but a binary predicate permut over lists, such that

$$\text{permut}(l_1, l_2) \iff \begin{cases} \text{length}(l_1) = \text{length}(l_2) \wedge \\ \exists \pi \in \mathscr{S}_{\text{length}(l_1)} \wedge \forall i \leq \text{length}(l_1), l_1[i] = l_2[\pi(i)] \end{cases}$$

2 First Attempt and Related Works

2.1 A First Solution Based on Counting Elements

A first very naïve solution is based on counting the number of occurrences for each element present in both lists. The lists are permutations of each other

---

[1] Local confluence is not part of COCCINELLE yet.

whenever every element occurs the same number of times in both of them. In order to define this notion of permutation, one has first to define the counting function. This is done by `list_to_multiset`, since in Coq, a multiset is simply a function from a given set to the natural numbers. The tricky point is that in order to properly count the number of occurrences of a given element, one has to know whether two elements are identical or not; this means that the equality over the elements of the lists has to be *decidable*. This property appears in the definition below as `eq_elt_dec`.

Fixpoint list_to_multiset (l : list elt) {struct l} : multiset elt :=
  match l **with**
  | nil => EmptyBag elt
  | h :: tl => munion (SingletonBag _ eq_elt_dec h) (list_to_multiset tl)
  end.

Definition list_permut (l1 l2 : list elt) : **Prop** :=
  meq (list_to_multiset l1) (list_to_multiset l2).

This definition has two main drawbacks. First, as said above, it requires that the equality is decidable. Second, the equality is the Leibniz equality, and not an arbitrary equivalence relation. This leads to a quite ugly definition of RPO. For example the inductive definition of equivalence modulo RPO of two terms has the following form:

Inductive equiv : term −> term −> **Prop** :=
  | Eq : ∀ t, equiv t t
  | Eq_lex : ∀ f l1 l2, status f = Lex −> equiv_list_lex l1 l2 −>
    equiv (Term f l1) (Term f l2)
  | Eq_mul : ∀ f ll l1 l2, status f = Mul −>
    (∀ t1 t2, In (t1,t2) ll −> equiv t1 t2) −>
    permut l1 (map fst) ll) −> permut l2 (map snd ll) −>
    equiv (Term f l1) (Term f l2)

with equiv_list_lex : list term −> list term −> **Prop** :=
  | Eq_list_nil : equiv_list_lex nil nil
  | Eq_list_cons : ∀ t1 t2 l1 l2, equiv t1 t2 −> equiv_list_lex l1 l2 −>
    equiv_list_lex (t1 :: l1) (t2 :: l2).

When the common top symbol of two terms has a multiset status, one has to introduce a list of pairs of equivalent subterms l1, and then use the notion of permutation over the first (resp. the second) projection of the list. This intermediate list l1 can be avoided in the lex case, but not in the multiset case, since the definition of permutation does not support another relation than equality.

This leads to investigate other solutions.

2.2   A Second Solution also Based on Counting Elements

The second solution (inspired by ours) is in the CoQ standard library (Sorting/Permutation.v). This is the one which is used in CoLoR [1] a CoQ library for rewriting mainly focused on termination.

The only difference with the first definition is that the equality is replaced by an arbitrary relation.

Variable A : Set.
Variable eqA : relation A.
Hypothesis eqA_dec : $\forall$x y, {eqA x y} + { eqA x y}.
Let emptyBag := EmptyBag A.
Let singletonBag := SingletonBag _ eqA_dec.

Fixpoint list_contents (l: list A) : multiset A :=
  match l **with**
    | nil => emptyBag
    | a :: l => munion (singletonBag a) (list_contents l)
  end.

Definition permutation (l m: list A) :=
  meq (list_contents l) (list_contents m).

But this definition still requires a decidable relation. This forbids to use it for a nicer definition of RPO: one cannot provide a proof of decidability of a relation before having defined this very relation. Moreover, if the relation **eqA** is not an equivalence relation, this definition of permutation may not be the wanted one: indeed by construction **permutation** is an equivalence and **permutation**(a_1 :: **nil**)(a_2 :: **nil**) is by definition equivalent to $\forall a$, **eqA** a_1 a $\Longleftrightarrow$ **eqA** a_2 a, which is not the same as **eqA** a_1 a_2.

2.3   A Third Solution Based on Moving Elements

Another kind of definition is provided by the CoQ standard library in List/List.v. It is no longer based on counting elements, but on moving them. This allows to get rid of the decidability of the underlying relation. However in the CoQ standard library, this relation is still the Leibniz equality.

Inductive Permutation : list A $->$ list A $->$ **Prop** :=
  | perm_nil: Permutation nil nil
  | perm_skip: $\forall$ (x:A) (l l ': list A), Permutation l l' $->$
                              Permutation (x :: l) (x :: l')
  | perm_swap: $\forall$ (x y:A) (l: list A), Permutation (y :: x :: l) (x :: y :: l)
  | perm_trans:
      $\forall$ (l l' l '': list A), Permutation l l' $->$ Permutation l' l'' $->$
                    Permutation l l ''.

3   A Fourth (and Hopefully Last) Solution

In this work, we propose a definition in the same spirit of the one which consists in moving the elements. It is parameterized by an arbitrary relation R, for which absolutely no property is required.

Inductive permut (A : **Set**) (R : relation A) : (list A –> list A –> **Prop**) :=
| Pnil : permut R nil nil
| Pcons : ∀ a b l l1 l2, R a b –> permut R l (l1 ++ l2) –>
                     permut R (a :: l) (l1 ++ b :: l2).

This definition allows a nice definition of RPO. Indeed, now it is possible to use inside a recursive call for defining a relation, permutation up to the same relation.

Inductive equiv : term –> term –> **Prop** :=
| Eq : ∀ t, equiv t t
| Eq_lex : ∀ f l1 l2, status f = Lex –> equiv_list_lex l1 l2 –>
  equiv (Term f l1) (Term f l2)
| Eq_mul : ∀f l1 l2,   status f = Mul –> permut equiv l1 l2 –>
  equiv (Term f l1) (Term f l2)

with equiv_list_lex : list term –> list term –> **Prop** :=
| Eq_list_nil : equiv_list_lex nil nil
| Eq_list_cons : ∀t1 t2 l1 l2, equiv t1 t2 –> equiv_list_lex l1 l2 –>
  equiv_list_lex (t1 :: l1) (t2 :: l2).

Inductive rpo : term –> term –> **Prop** :=
| Subterm : ∀f l t s, In s l –> rpo_eq t s –> rpo t (Term f l)
| Top_gt :
    ∀ f g l l', prec g f –> (∀ s', In s' l' –> rpo s' (Term f l)) –>
  rpo (Term g l') (Term f l)
| Top_eq_lex :
    ∀ f l l', status f = Lex –> rpo_lex l' l –>
    (∀ s', In s' l' –> rpo s' (Term f l)) –> rpo (Term f l') (Term f l)
| Top_eq_mul :
    ∀ f l l', status f = Mul –> rpo_mul l' l –> rpo (Term f l') (Term f l)

with rpo_eq : term –> term –> **Prop** :=
| Equiv : ∀ t t ', equiv t t' –> rpo_eq t t'
| Lt : ∀ s t, rpo s t –> rpo_eq s t

with rpo_lex : list term –> list term –> **Prop** :=
| List_gt : ∀ s t l l', rpo s t –> length l = length l' –> rpo_lex (s :: l) (t :: l'')
| List_eq : ∀ s s' l l ', equiv s s' –> rpo_lex l l' –> rpo_lex (s :: l) (s' :: l')

with rpo_mul : list term –> list term –> **Prop** :=

| List_mul : ∀ a lg ls lc l l',
  permut equiv l' (ls ++ lc) –> permut equiv l (a :: lg ++ lc) –>
  (∀ b, In b ls –> ∃a', In a' (a :: lg) /\ rpo b a') –>
  rpo_mul l' l.

3.1   Adequacy with the Mathematical Definition

The last definition of **permut** exactly corresponds to mathematical permutation up to the underlying definition R, as formally proved in **Lemma** adequacy, where a mathematical permutation is defined as usual, except that it is extended by the identity function outside of its range, in order to avoid partial functions in CoQ.

Definition math_permut (n : nat) (f : nat –> nat) :=
  (∀ i, n <= i –> f i = i) /\
  (∀ i, i < n –> f i < n) /\
  (∀ i j, i < n –> j < n –> f i = f j –> i = j).

Lemma adequacy :
  ∀ (A : **Set**) (R : relation A) (l1 l2 : list A),
  permut R l1 l2 <–>
  (length l1 = length l2 /\
  ∃ pi, (math_permut (length l1) pi) /\
        ∀ i, i < length l1 –>
        match (nth_error l1 i), (nth_error l2 (pi i)) **with**
        | (Some ai), (Some b_pi_i) => R ai b_pi_i
        | _, _ => False
        end).

where **nth_error** l i returns **Some** ai whenever ai is the ith element in l and **None** when the list is not long enough. The proof of the above lemma is by induction on the length of the lists and amounts to express the relation between the function **pi** permutating the indexes of the list l2 and the corresponding function **pi'** for l2' + +l2'' where

l1 = a1 :: l1' /\ l2 = l2' ++ a2 :: l2'' /\ R a1 a2 /\ permut R l1 l2 /\ permut R l1' (l2' ++ l2'')

The relations between **pi** and **pi'** are the following:

pi = (**fun** (i : nat) =>
          match i **with**
          | 0 => length l2'
          | S i =>
              if le_lt_dec (length l2') (pi' i)
              then S (pi' i)
              else pi' i
          end)

pi' = (**fun** i =>
             if le_lt_dec (length l1) i
             then i
             else
               if le_lt_dec (pi (S i)) (pi 0)
               then pi (S i)
               else (pi (S i)) −1)

where `le_lt_dec` is a constructive test for $\leq$.

3.2   Additional Properties

Our definition of lists permutation enjoys some quite natural properties:

Lemma permut_nil :
 $\forall$ (A : **Set**) (R : relation A) l, permut R l nil −> l = nil.

Lemma list_permut_length_1:
 $\forall$A : **Set**) (R : relation A) a b, permut R (a :: nil) (b :: nil) <−> R a b.

Lemma permut_impl :
 $\forall$ (A : **Set**) (R R' : relation A) l1 l2,
 ($\forall$ a b, R a b −> R' a b) −> permut R l1 l2 −> permut R' l1 l2.

By definition of the inductive, when two lists are permutations of each other, one can add the first element of a pair related by R at the head of the first list and insert the second element anywhere in the second list, and get two lists which are still permutations of each other. The following lemma shows that one can insert the first element anywhere in the first list, and still get the same result:

Lemma permut_strong :
 $\forall$ (A : **Set**) (R : relation A) a1 a2 l1 k1 l2 k2,
 R a1 a2 −> permut R (l1 ++ k1) (l2 ++ k2) −>
 permut R (l1 ++ a1 :: k1) (l2 ++ a2 :: k2).

The next lemmas show that every element of the second list has a counterpart w. r. t. R in the first list:

Lemma permut_inv :
 $\forall$ (A : **Set**) (R : relation A) b l1 l2,
 permut R l1 (b :: l2) −> $\exists$a, $\exists$ l1', $\exists$ l1'',
 (R a b $\wedge$ l1 = l1' ++ a :: l1'' $\wedge$ permut R (l1' ++ l1'') l2).

Lemma permut_inv_strong :
 $\forall$ (A : **Set**) (R : relation A) b l1 l2' l2'',
 permut R l1 (l2' ++ b :: l2'') −> $\exists$a, $\exists$ l1', $\exists$ l1'',
 (R a b $\wedge$ l1 = l1' ++ a :: l1'' $\wedge$ permut R (l1' ++ l1'') (l2' ++ l2'')).

It is of course possible to move the elements block by block, and not one by one:

Lemma permut_block :
  ∀ (A : **Set**) (R : relation A) l1 l1' l2 l2',
  permut R l1 l2 −> permut R l1' l2' −> permut R (l1 ++ l1') (l2' ++ l2).

The next lemma makes explicit the condition under which one can remove a pair of related elements in permutated lists:

Lemma permut_cons_inside :
  ∀ (A : **Set**) (R : relation A) a b l1 l2' l2 ",
  (∀ a1 b1 a2 b2, In a1 (a :: l1) −> In b1 (l2' ++ b :: l2 ") −>
              In a2 (a :: l1) −> In b2 (l2' ++ b :: l2 ") −>
              R a1 b1 −> R a2 b1 −> R a2 b2 −> R a1 b2) −>
  R a b −> permut R (a :: l1) (l2' ++ b :: l2 ") −> permut R l1 (l2' ++ l2").

This condition means that R is obtained from f, a function from elements to sets of elements in the following way:

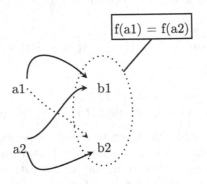

$$\forall ab, aRb \Longleftrightarrow b \in f(a)$$

3.3 Morphism Properties

The definition of **permut** is compatible with **length**, **list_size** and **map**.

Lemma list_permut_length :
  ∀ (A : **Set**) (R : relation A) l1 l2 , list_permut R l1 l2 −> length l1 = length l2.

Lemma list_permut_size :
  ∀ (A : **Set**) (R : relation A) (size : A −> nat) l1 l2,
  (∀ a a', In a l −> In a' l −> R a a' −> size a = size a') −>
  permut R l1 l2 −> list_size size l1 = list_size size l2.

Lemma list_permut_map :
  ∀ (A B : **Set**) (RA : relation A) (RB : relation B) (f : A −> B) l1 l2,
  (∀ a a', In a l1 −> In a' l2 −> RA a a' −> RB (f a) (f a')) −>
  permut RA l1 l2 −> permut RB (map f l1) (map f l2).

The next properties do not hold in general. The first one, compatibility with insertion *and* removal obviously needs the property that R is derived from a function from elements to sets of elements (*cf.* **Lemma** permut_cons_inside).

Lemma permut_add_inside :
  ∀ (A : **Set**) (R : relation A) e1 e2 l1 l2 l3 l4,
  (∀ a1 b1 a2 b2, In a1 (l1 ++ e1 :: l2) −> In b1 (l3 ++ e2 :: l4) −>
            In a2 (l1 ++ e1 :: l2) −> In b2 (l3 ++ e2 :: l4) −>
                R a1 b1 −> R a2 b1 −> R a2 b2 −> R a1 b2) −>
  R e1 e2 −> (permut R (l1 ++ l2) (l3 ++ l4) <−>
            permut R (l1 ++ e1 :: l2) (l3 ++ e2 :: l4)).

The compatibility of adding/removing a whole list holds when R is reflexive and enjoys the property of being derived from a function from elements to sets of elements. This implies that R is an equivalence relation.

Lemma permut_app1 :
  ∀ (A : **Set**) (R : relation A), (equivalence R) −>
  ∀ l l1 l2, permut R l1 l2 <−> permut R (l ++ l1) (l ++ l2).

Lemma permut_app2 :
  ∀ (A : **Set**) (R : relation A), (equivalence R) −>
  ∀ l l1 l2, permut R l1 l2 <−> permut R (l1 ++ l) (l2 ++ l).

This last lemma is very useful for proving that the equational theory *AC* is syntactic [10,9,2], and also holds when R is an equivalence relation:

Axiom ac_syntactic :
  ∀ (A : **Set**) (R : relation A) , (equivalence R) −>
  ∀ (l1 l2 l3 l4 : list A), permut R (l2 ++ l1) (l4 ++ l3) −>
  (∃ u1, ∃ u2, ∃ u3, ∃ u4, permut R l1 (u1 ++ u2) ∧
                permut R l2 (u3 ++ u4) ∧
                permut R l3 (u1 ++ u3) ∧
                permut R l4 (u2 ++ u4)).

3.4   Modular Inheritance

The last definition of **permut** also gives some nice fine grained inheritance properties, such as for example reflexivity, symmetry, transitivity and decidability.

Lemma permut_refl :
  ∀ (A : **Set**) (R : relation A) l,
  (∀ a, In a l −> R a a) −> permut R l l.

Lemma permut_sym :
  ∀ (A : **Set**) (R : relation A) l1 l2,
  (∀ a b, In a l1 −> In b l2 −> R a b −> R b a) −>
  permut R l1 l2 −> permut R l2 l1.

Lemma permut_trans :
  ∀ (A : **Set**) (R : relation A) l1 l2 l3,
  (∀ a b c, In a l1 −> In b l2 −> In c l3 −> R a b −> R b c −> R a c) −>
  permut R l1 l2 −> permut R l2 l3 −> permut R l1 l3.

Lemma permut_dec :
  ∀ (A : **Set**) (R : relation A),
  ∀ l1 l2, (∀ a1 a2, In a1 l1 −> In a2 l2 −> {R a1 a2}+{∼ R a1 a2}) −>
  {permut R l1 l2}+{∼ permut R l1 l2}.

Concerning the decidability property, the complexity of the underlying algorithm (which can be obtained by extraction) is very bad: it is a factorial, since in general, the only way to check that two lists are permutations of each other is to actually build all permutations of one list (w. r. t. to Leibniz equality), and then check that every pair of elements at the same rank in the first and in the second permuted list are related by R. However, when the relation R enjoys the property of being a function over sets, there is another algorithm which is quadratic: it consist of searching the second list for an element related to the head of the first list: whenever there is no such element, both lists are not permutation of each other, otherwise, it remains to check that the tail of the first list, and the list obtained by removing the related element in the second list are permutation of each other. Due to the additional property over R, **Lemma** permut_cons_inside applies and no backtracking is needed.

4   Conclusion

We have proposed a modeling of list permutation which has some nice properties. It is based on the idea of moving elements and is parameterized by an arbitrary relation for which no properties are required. This allows in particular to define some relations on terms which use a permutation up to a recursive call of this relation on a list of subterms, such as for instance $\equiv_{RPO}$, $<_{RPO}$ and $=_{AC}$. The decidablity of the underlying relation is not needed and the inheritance properties are modular. Moreover, the very simple inductive definition (only two constructors) is in adequacy with the mathematical definition.

References

1. Blanqui, F., Coupet-Grimal, S., Delobel, W., Hinderer, S., Koprowski, A.: CoLoR, a Coq Library on Rewriting and termination. In: Extended Abstracts of the 8th International Workshop on Termination, WST'06 (2006). http://color.loria.fr/
2. Boudet, A., Contejean, E.: "Syntactic" AC-unification. In: Jouannaud, J.-P. (ed.) CCL 1994. LNCS, vol. 845, pp. 136–151. Springer, Heidelberg (1994)
3. Contejean, E.: A certified AC matching algorithm. In: van Oostrom, V. (ed.) RTA 2004. LNCS, vol. 3091, pp. 70–84. Springer, Heidelberg (2004)
4. Contejean, E. Coccinelle, (2005)
   http://www.lri.fr/~{}contejea/Coccinelle/coccinelle.html

5. Coupet-Grimal, S., Delobel, W.: Une preuve effective de la bonne fondation de l'ordre récursif multi-ensemble sur les chemins. In: Dix-septièmes Journées Francophones des Langages Applicatifs. INRIA, INRIA, (January 2006)
6. Dershowitz, N.: Orderings for term rewriting systems. Theoretical Computer Science 17(3), 279–301 (March 1982)
7. Dershowitz, N., Jouannaud, J.-P.: Rewrite systems. In: van Leeuwen, J., (ed.) Handbook of Theoretical Computer Science, vol. B, pp. 243–320. North-Holland (1990)
8. Hullot, J.-M.: Associative commutative pattern matching. In: Proc. 6th IJCAI Tokyo, vol. I, pp. 406–412 (August 1979)
9. Jouannaud, J.-P.: Syntactic theories. In: Rovan, B. (ed.) Mathematical Foundations of Computer Science, LNCS, vol. 452, Springer, Heidelberg (1990)
10. Kirchner, C., Klay, F.: Syntactic theories and unification. In: Proc. 5th IEEE Symp. Logic in Computer Science, Philadelphia (June 1990)
11. Koprowski, A.: Certified Higher-Order Recursive Path Ordering. In: Pfenning, F. (ed.) RTA 2006. LNCS, vol. 4098, pp. 227–241. Springer, Heidelberg (2006)
12. The Coq Development Team. The Coq Proof Assistant Reference Manual – Version V8.1 (July 2006) http://coq.inria.fr

PhD Descendance Index

Author Index

Lecture Notes in Computer Science

For information about Vols. 1–4453

please contact your bookseller or Springer

Vol. 4504: J. Huang, R. Kowalczyk, Z. Maamar, D. Martin, I. Müller, S. Stoutenburg, K.P. Sycara (Eds.), Service-Oriented Computing: Agents, Semantics, and Engineering. X, 175 pages. 2007.

Vol. 4501: J. Marques-Silva, K.A. Sakallah (Eds.), Theory and Applications of Satisfiability Testing – SAT 2007. XI, 384 pages. 2007.

Vol. 4500: N. Streitz, A. Kameas, I. Mavrommati (Eds.), The Disappearing Computer. XVIII, 304 pages. 2007.

Vol. 4499: Y.Q. Shi (Ed.), Transactions on Data Hiding and Multimedia Security II. IX, 117 pages. 2007.

Vol. 4497: S.B. Cooper, B. Löwe, A. Sorbi (Eds.), Computation and Logic in the Real World. XVIII, 826 pages. 2007.

Vol. 4496: N.T. Nguyen, A. Grzech, R.J. Howlett, L.C. Jain (Eds.), Agent and Multi-Agent Systems: Technologies and Applications. XXI, 1046 pages. 2007. (Sublibrary LNAI).

Vol. 4495: J. Krogstie, A. Opdahl, G. Sindre (Eds.), Advanced Information Systems Engineering. XVI, 606 pages. 2007.

Vol. 4494: H. Jin, O.F. Rana, Y. Pan, V.K. Prasanna (Eds.), Algorithms and Architectures for Parallel Processing. XIV, 508 pages. 2007.

Vol. 4493: D. Liu, S. Fei, Z. Hou, H. Zhang, C. Sun (Eds.), Advances in Neural Networks – ISNN 2007, Part III. XXVI, 1215 pages. 2007.

Vol. 4492: D. Liu, S. Fei, Z. Hou, H. Zhang, C. Sun (Eds.), Advances in Neural Networks – ISNN 2007, Part II. XXVII, 1321 pages. 2007.

Vol. 4491: D. Liu, S. Fei, Z.-G. Hou, H. Zhang, C. Sun (Eds.), Advances in Neural Networks – ISNN 2007, Part I. LIV, 1365 pages. 2007.

Vol. 4490: Y. Shi, G.D. van Albada, J. Dongarra, P.M.A. Sloot (Eds.), Computational Science – ICCS 2007, Part IV. XXXVII, 1211 pages. 2007.

Vol. 4489: Y. Shi, G.D. van Albada, J. Dongarra, P.M.A. Sloot (Eds.), Computational Science – ICCS 2007, Part III. XXXVII, 1257 pages. 2007.

Vol. 4488: Y. Shi, G.D. van Albada, J. Dongarra, P.M.A. Sloot (Eds.), Computational Science – ICCS 2007, Part II. XXXV, 1251 pages. 2007.

Vol. 4487: Y. Shi, G.D. van Albada, J. Dongarra, P.M.A. Sloot (Eds.), Computational Science – ICCS 2007, Part I. LXXXI, 1275 pages. 2007.

Vol. 4486: M. Bernardo, J. Hillston (Eds.), Formal Methods for Performance Evaluation. VII, 469 pages. 2007.

Vol. 4485: F. Sgallari, A. Murli, N. Paragios (Eds.), Scale Space and Variational Methods in Computer Vision. XV, 931 pages. 2007.

Vol. 4484: J.-Y. Cai, S.B. Cooper, H. Zhu (Eds.), Theory and Applications of Models of Computation. XIII, 772 pages. 2007.

Vol. 4483: C. Baral, G. Brewka, J. Schlipf (Eds.), Logic Programming and Nonmonotonic Reasoning. IX, 327 pages. 2007. (Sublibrary LNAI).

Vol. 4482: A. An, J. Stefanowski, S. Ramanna, C.J. Butz, W. Pedrycz, G. Wang (Eds.), Rough Sets, Fuzzy Sets, Data Mining and Granular Computing. XIV, 585 pages. 2007. (Sublibrary LNAI).

Vol. 4481: J. Yao, P. Lingras, W.-Z. Wu, M. Szczuka, N.J. Cercone, D. Ślęzak (Eds.), Rough Sets and Knowledge Technology. XIV, 576 pages. 2007. (Sublibrary LNAI).

Vol. 4480: A. LaMarca, M. Langheinrich, K.N. Truong (Eds.), Pervasive Computing. XIII, 369 pages. 2007.

Vol. 4479: I.F. Akyildiz, R. Sivakumar, E. Ekici, J.C.d. Oliveira, J. McNair (Eds.), NETWORKING 2007. Ad Hoc and Sensor Networks, Wireless Networks, Next Generation Internet. XXVII, 1252 pages. 2007.

Vol. 4478: J. Martí, J.M. Benedí, A.M. Mendonça, J. Serrat (Eds.), Pattern Recognition and Image Analysis, Part II. XXVII, 657 pages. 2007.

Vol. 4477: J. Martí, J.M. Benedí, A.M. Mendonça, J. Serrat (Eds.), Pattern Recognition and Image Analysis, Part I. XXVII, 625 pages. 2007.

Vol. 4476: V. Gorodetsky, C. Zhang, V.A. Skormin, L. Cao (Eds.), Autonomous Intelligent Systems: Multi-Agents and Data Mining. XIII, 323 pages. 2007. (Sublibrary LNAI).

Vol. 4475: P. Crescenzi, G. Prencipe, G. Pucci (Eds.), Fun with Algorithms. X, 273 pages. 2007.

Vol. 4474: G. Prencipe, S. Zaks (Eds.), Structural Information and Communication Complexity. XI, 342 pages. 2007.

Vol. 4472: M. Haindl, J. Kittler, F. Roli (Eds.), Multiple Classifier Systems. XI, 524 pages. 2007.

Vol. 4471: P. Cesar, K. Chorianopoulos, J.F. Jensen (Eds.), Interactive TV: a Shared Experience. XIII, 236 pages. 2007.

Vol. 4470: Q. Wang, D. Pfahl, D.M. Raffo (Eds.), Software Process Dynamics and Agility. XI, 346 pages. 2007.

Vol. 4469: K.-C. Hui, Z. Pan, R.C.-k. Chung, C.C.L. Wang, X. Jin, S. Göbel, E.C.-L. Li (Eds.), Technologies for E-Learning and Digital Entertainment. XVIII, 974 pages. 2007.

Vol. 4468: M.M. Bonsangue, E.B. Johnsen (Eds.), Formal Methods for Open Object-Based Distributed Systems. X, 317 pages. 2007.

Vol. 4467: A.L. Murphy, J. Vitek (Eds.), Coordination Models and Languages. X, 325 pages. 2007.

Vol. 4466: F.B. Sachse, G. Seemann (Eds.), Functional Imaging and Modeling of the Heart. XV, 486 pages. 2007.

Vol. 4465: T. Chahed, B. Tuffin (Eds.), Network Control and Optimization. XIII, 305 pages. 2007.

Vol. 4464: E. Dawson, D.S. Wong (Eds.), Information Security Practice and Experience. XIII, 361 pages. 2007.

Vol. 4463: I. Măndoiu, A. Zelikovsky (Eds.), Bioinformatics Research and Applications. XV, 653 pages. 2007. (Sublibrary LNBI).

Vol. 4462: D. Sauveron, K. Markantonakis, A. Bilas, J.-J. Quisquater (Eds.), Information Security Theory and Practices. XII, 255 pages. 2007.

Vol. 4459: C. Cérin, K.-C. Li (Eds.), Advances in Grid and Pervasive Computing. XVI, 759 pages. 2007.